FILM AS EMBODIED ART

Bodily Meaning in the Cinema of Stanley Kubrick

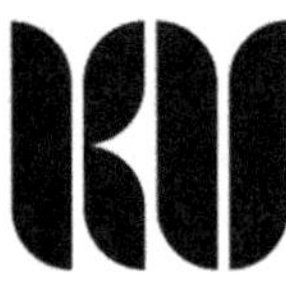

An electronic version of this book is freely available, thanks to the support of libraries working with Knowledge Unlatched. KU is a collaborative initiative designed to make high quality books Open Access for the public good. The Open Access ISBN for this book is 978-1-64469-113-7. More information about the initiative and links to the Open Access version can be found at www.knowledgeunlatched.org.

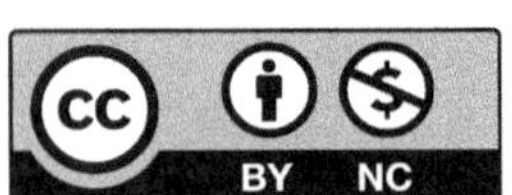

FILM AS

EMBODIED ART

Bodily Meaning in the Cinema of Stanley Kubrick

Maarten Coëgnarts

Library of Congress Cataloging-in-Publication Data

Names: Coëgnarts, Maarten, author.
Title: Film as embodied art : bodily meaning in the cinema of Stanley Kubrick / Maarten Coëgnarts.
Description: Boston : [Academic Studies Press], [2019] | Includes bibliographical references, filmography, discography, and index.
Identifiers: LCCN 2019022645 | ISBN 9781618118363 (hardback) | ISBN 9781644691120 (paperback) | ISBN 9781644691137 (adobe pdf)
Subjects: LCSH: Kubrick, Stanley--Criticism and interpretation. | Meaning (Philosophy) in motion pictures
Classification: LCC PN1998.3.K83 C64 2019 | DDC 791.4302/33092--dc23
LC record available at https://lccn.loc.gov/2019022645

ISBN 9781618118363 (hardback)
ISBN 9781644691120 (paperback)
ISBN 9781644691137 (adobe pdf)
ISBN 9781644691144 (ePub)

Book design by Lapiz Digital Services

Academic Studies Press
1577 Beacon Street
Brookline, MA 02446, USA
P: (617)782-6290
F: (857)241-3149
press@academicstudiespress.com
www.academicstudiespress.com

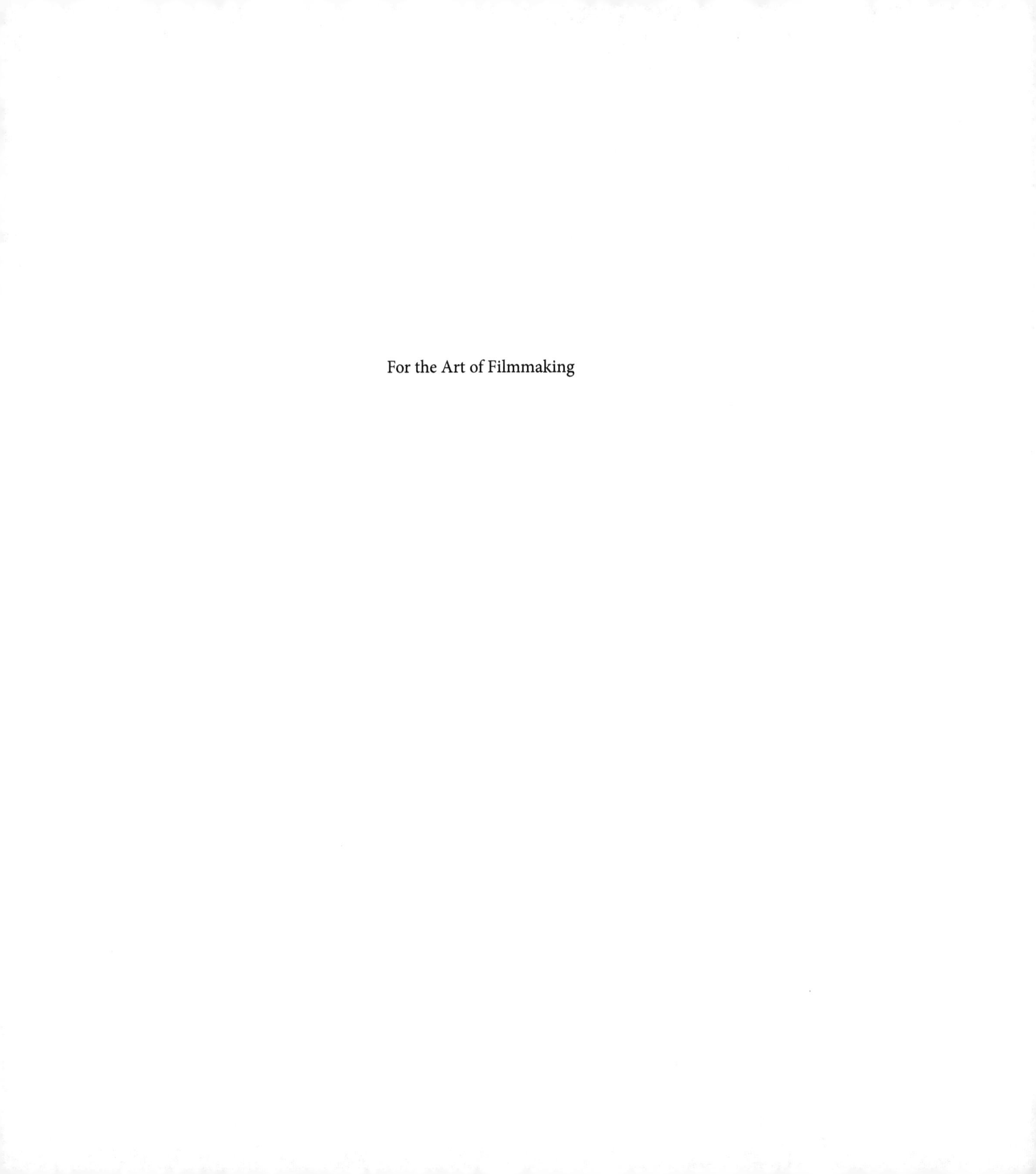

For the Art of Filmmaking

Contents

List of Illustrations

FIGURES

TABLES

Acknowledgments

The author is indebted to:

Academic Studies Press for giving me the opportunity to publish this book.

The University of the Arts London for allowing me access to some of the rich material stored at The Stanley Kubrick Archive.

Prof. Mark Johnson and Prof. Stephen Prince for their helpful suggestions and comments on an earlier draft of the introduction.

The anonymous peer reviewers for their constructive reports.

The University of California Press, for permission to use Rudolf Arnheim's figure of the structural skeleton of the square, figure 3.7.

Mr. Garrett Brown, for permission to use the behind-the-scenes photo of *The Shining*, figure 3.19.

Mr. Martin Pope for sharing, in cooperation with Mr. Filippo Ulivieri, the behind-the-scenes photo of *Paths of Glory*, figure 3.20.

Prof. Jeremy Barham, for permission to use his diagrams of Bartók's *Music for Strings, Percussion and Celesta* as used in *The Shining*, figure 5.6 and figure 5.7.

Anthony Blampied, friend and archivist at Cinematek (Brussels) for his help in obtaining various written sources on Kubrick.

All the scholars listed in the notes and bibliography with some of whom I had the pleasure and honor to discuss my ideas in person. Without their insights this book could not have been written.

Annick for her continuous support, strength and patience throughout the writing process.

Introduction

The Theoretical Context of This Study

Dialogue tends to be employed as the principal means of communication, but I believe that without doubt there is a more cinematic manner of communicating.

—Stanley Kubrick[1]

The goal of this introductory chapter is to establish the theoretical context upon which this book is founded, starting with a discussion of a paradox that lies at the heart of what constitutes the central subject matter of this study, namely meaning in film. Second, we briefly discuss what has been the most influential model in film theory for dealing with this paradox, namely the linguistic model (also known as the film-as-language view). At the same time, we argue why this model is no longer sustainable in the light of the recent "embodied turn" in cognitive science. Third, we show how an embodied view of meaning forces us to address the paradox of cinematic meaning anew, thus prompting the need for a new research agenda. Fourth and last, we will lay out the main intentions and structure of this book as they emerge from the reorientation of the theoretical focus.

1. The paradox of cinematic meaning

This book is about meaning and cinema and the way this relationship is manifested in the films of the great American film director Stanley Kubrick (1928–1999).[2] In this regard, Kubrick's oeuvre can be considered among the finest and most remarkable in film history. With films such as *Paths of Glory* (1957), *2001: A Space Odyssey* (1968), *Barry Lyndon* (1975), *The Shining* (1980) and *Eyes Wide Shut* (1999), he created some of the most engaging cinematic artworks in modern cinema that continue to fascinate audiences and critics today.[3] In attempting to explain this endless fascination with Kubrick's work, scholars have recurrently pointed toward the filmmaker's ability to shape its conceptual content in an almost exclusively visual way. *2001: A Space Odyssey* is perhaps the purest embodiment of this thought. Out of two hours and nineteen minutes of film, there are only a little less than forty minutes of dialogue, yet, the film conveys a richness and complexity of themes rarely equalled in other films. As Michael Benson recently stressed in his book, exactly fifty years after its release: "*2001* is essentially a nonverbal experience, once more comparable to a musical composition than to the usual dialogue-based commercial cinema. . . . It spoke its own language, . . . the authority and power of the images themselves didn't necessitate literal comprehension."[4] This refusal to fit meaning into the "straitjacket of words," as Kubrick calls it, also runs as a red thread throughout the interviews that were conducted with the director over the years.[5] Cited below is one excerpt from Kubrick's comments, as it appeared in 1969 in the magazine *Action*:

> In *Space Odyssey* the mood hitting you is the visual imagery. The people who didn't respond, I now, for want of coming up with a better explanation, categorize as "verbally oriented people." . . . Communicating visually and through music gets past the verbal pigeonhole concepts that people are stuck with. You know, words have a highly subjective and very limited meaning, and they immediately limit the possible emotional and subconscious designating effect of a work of art. Movies have tied themselves into that because the crucial things that generally come out of a film are still word-delivered. There's emotion backing them up, you've got the actors generating feeling, etc. It's basically word communication.[6]

However intuitively true the attribution of themes or meanings to the non-verbal, perceptual level of Kubrick's cinema may sound, the less clear it is from a purely logical and theoretical point-of-view. That this attribution is less evident than it appears at first sight becomes clear once we isolate the premises on which it is founded:

(1) Films present the opportunity to communicate abstract meanings without the traditional reliance on words.[7]
(2) Meaning is a matter of conceptual structure.
(3) Films, as opposed to words, do not connect so easily to concepts.[8]
(4) How, then, can films be capable of communicating conceptual meaning?

So despite the fact that premise (1) sounds intuitively true, it bears a set of premises, (2) and (3), that, apparently, seem to contradict each other. We shall label this logical inconsistency, which leads again to a questioning of the relationship between meaning and cinema (4), the *paradox of cinematic meaning.*

Let us start our investigation of this paradox by considering the question underlying the first premise: On what conditions does successful communication of meaning depend? Perhaps the most straightforward answer to this question has been provided by the British philosopher Paul Grice. In his influential article from 1957 called "Meaning" the author has argued that communication of meaning is successful insofar the perceiver of the representation (e.g., the hearer) understands the representation that is being communicated (e.g., the utterance), that is, and here is where the central claim of his argument becomes manifest, insofar the perceiver recognizes the communicator's intention to represent, and further recognizes that he himself is intended to recognize it. In Grice's own words, "for A to mean something by x, A must intend to induce by x a belief in an audience, and he must also intend his utterance to be recognized as so intended."[9] This aspect is also known as the "self-referentiality" of the intention to communicate and is, as the American philosopher John Searle pointed out fifty years later, "seldom remarked on."[10] The crucial question, then, is this: if successful communication of meaning depends on the audience's recognition of the communicator's intention to represent the meaning, how then can this recognition be achieved? The key to answering this question lies in the representation x.

Here we may quote Noël Carroll, who adds the following note to Grice's analysis: "The intention A intends to be recognized must be discernible in x. Where x is an artwork, the intention the artist means to convey must be discernible in the work."[11] If we further define this intention in terms of mental conceptual structure (let us call this y), it follows that y has to be imposed onto x for it is only when y is embodied in x that the audience will be able to extract y from x, and thus achieve recognition of the communicator's intention.[12]

The conception of meaning and communication just sketched out is not a new one, but it echoes the underlying theoretical assumptions of two different, but neighboring areas of research, namely *cognitive semantics* and *inferential pragmatics*. The first discipline began in the 1970s and initiated a radical critique of the truth-conditional view of meaning in language, as advocated by the Anglo-American tradition in philosophy.[13] This view rests upon the assumption that meaning can be objectively described as a relationship between words and an objective external reality, and that this relationship can be modelled in terms of truth or falsity.[14] Cognitive semantics, as put forth by such scholars as Leonard Talmy, George Lakoff, Mark Johnson and Ronald Langacker, rejects this view, which inevitably leads to an undervaluation of the role of the mind, and asserts instead that semantic structure (i.e., the meanings conventionally associated with words) can be equated with conceptual structure, "the nature and organisation of mental representations in all its richness and diversity."[15] Moreover, cognitive semantics claims that this conceptual structure is fundamentally embodied. This principle is known as the thesis of the "embodied mind" and roughly states that the nature of conceptual content emerges from bodily experiences and interactions with the environment.[16]

The second discipline began to flourish in the late 1970s and 1980s and initiated an alternative to the classical code model of communication, according to which utterances are signals that encode messages and comprehension is achieved by decoding the signals to obtain the messages. On the inferential view, originally suggested by Grice, but further developed by such scholars as Wilson and Sperber, representations such as utterances are not signals, but pieces of evidence about the speaker's meaning, and comprehension is achieved by inferring this meaning from evidence provided by the representation and the context in which it is produced.[17]

What quality, then, does the representation need to possess in order for it to express and externalize the conceptual structure? The general answer is that the representation has to "connect to" the conceptual structure. As for language, the key focus of both cognitive semantics and inferential pragmatics, this connection is inherent to its *symbolic* function. When we use language and write the word "tree," the meaning conventionally paired with it, is not the particular physical object of a tree, but the idea of a tree, that is, the *concept* of a tree.[18] As a result of this pairing of form and concept, language is often taken at face value when discussing the process of transmitting meaning from one entity to another. This is evidenced in the many references people make to language when talking about the phenomenon of communication itself (i.e., our meta-language). Consider, for example, the following list of English expressions, as compiled by the cognitive linguist Michael Reddy:

> Whenever you have a good *idea* practice capturing it *in words*. You have to *put* each *concept into words* very carefully. Try to *pack* more *thoughts into* fewer *words*. Insert those *ideas* elsewhere *in* the *paragraph*. Don't *force* your meanings *into* the wrong *words*.[19]

As Reddy argued, these expressions can be seen as linguistic manifestations of a general metaphor system which he coins the "conduit metaphor." According to this metaphor, people, when communicating, "insert" internal concepts (e.g., ideas, thoughts, emotions) "into" external "containers" (e.g., words, phrases, sentences, etc.) whose contents are then "extracted" by listeners and readers. Because language allows for a symbolic assembly of form and meaning, it is only natural to refer to words and paragraphs as the proper "insides" wherein the meanings can reside. Diagrammatically, this "trajectory" from mind to language might be represented as in figure I.1 by means of an arrow running from one container to another. The first part of the trajectory designates an EXIT path: the conceptual meaning goes from inside the communicator's head (the body as container for the mind) to its outside. The second pattern, by contrast, describes an ENTRY path: the meaning goes from outside the communicator's head to the inside of language.[20] As stated, this ENTRY path is facilitated by the symbolic function of language.

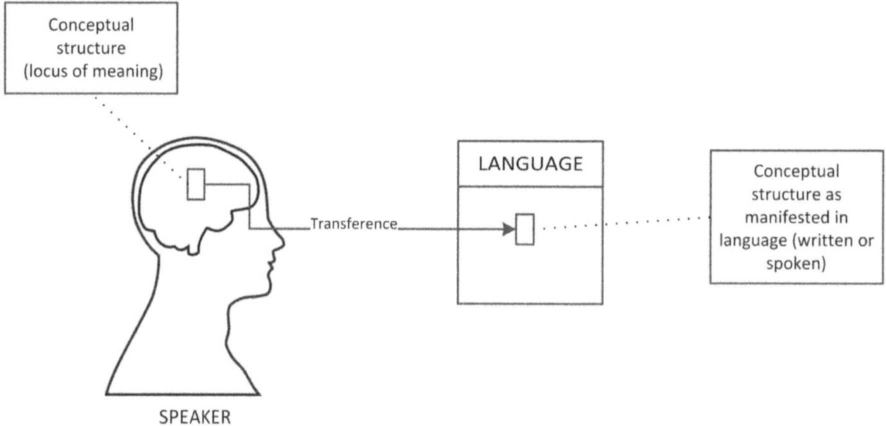

Figure I.1 Language as the "conduit" of conceptual structure.

A look at film, however, reveals a far more complicated picture. First, there is the question of identifying the communicator. Who is the agent who intentionally makes an utterance in a medium that usually implies the contribution of more than one individual? Raising this question brings us to the much-complicated matter of authorship in cinema.[21] As Sellors aptly points out, "authorship is a problem in film studies that simply will not go away."[22] Exploring this debate lies beyond the scope of this book. On a general note, it is sufficient to say that whoever the communicator in film may be, whether it be an individual mind or a collective of minds, it does not change anything to the central principle of cognitive semantics that meaning is equated with conceptual structure. In other words, it is less important to know to which "concrete" individual artist (e.g., filmmaker) the conceptual structure can be attributed than to assume for now that it is the conceptual structure that is being manifested in the representation, whether it be an utterance or, as in our case, a film. Following Turner's book, we may call this general and unspecified mind to which the conceptual structure adheres "the artful mind."[23]

Having said this, Kubrick, however, presents us with a rather unique case in motion-picture history if it comes to defining authorship in cinema. As has been repeatedly stressed in the literature, Kubrick, more than any other major filmmaker working within the context of a studio system, was able to maintain an uncommon high degree of independence and directorial control in the sense of decision-making authority and responsibility with regard to the making and overall design of his films. As Philips writes: "By steadily building a reputation as a filmmaker of international importance, he gained full artistic control over his films, guiding the production of each of them from the earliest stages of planning and scripting through post-production."[24] Because Kubrick stood much closer to his material than almost any other filmmaker working in Hollywood, it is not surprising, as Young already observed in 1959, that there is a "strong feeling of unity and single-mindedness in his films."[25] Although such a result can never be guaranteed given the collective nature of film-making, Kubrick's unique reputation allows us, in other words, to speak of Kubrick as a "cinematic author" or a "filmic author," in the senses defined by Livingston and Sellors, respectively.[26]

The critical reader, however, might object here that we are putting too much emphasis on the filmmaker's or artist's or speaker's intention. Indeed, does the meaning available in films often not exceed the artist's intention? Do we not value the work partly because it enacts possibilities of meaning that go beyond anything that the speaker or filmmaker consciously intends? This is a very good point, and therefore, we have to be very clear from the start about the sort of meaning that this book will be engaged in. To sort this out, we may turn to Bordwell's distinction between "referential and explicit meanings," and "implicit and symptomatic meanings."[27] The former constitute the backbone of narrative comprehension as they fall together with the "apparent, manifest, or direct meanings" of a work.[28] They are close to the bare-plot summaries of the films as they largely result from the viewers' attempts to construct a mental model of the situation in which the narrative action takes place. Van Dyck and Kintsch call this the "situation model."[29] Spectators construe such models by drawing not only on their knowledge about conventions, but also and more profoundly, as chapter 1 will make clear to us, on conceptions of causality, space and time. As Persson points out, it is an important feature of the situation or the referential meaning that it is closely tied to the "spectators' abilities to understand the behavior in terms of character psychology" and to infer "causal relations between events and scenes," which often involve "a character's mental states and traits" (e.g., "Alice is angry with her husband Bill because he did not get jealous when she told him that another man wanted sex with her," "Alex feels sick when he watches violence on the screen," "Wendy is shocked when she sees the word REDRUM in the mirror," "HAL 9000 decides to terminate the astronauts Bowman and Poole because he thinks they want to disconnect him").[30] In the field of philosophy of mind these causal relations involving mental events are known as instances of "mental causation."[31] This concept provides us with a thick and rich level of meaning that is central to our understanding of narratives, including, as we shall see in chapter 1, the narratives of Kubrick's work.

The latter, by contrast, are more "hidden" and "non-obvious," and have to do with the process of interpretation.[32] At this level, we enter a more abstract and symbolic understanding of cinematic meaning. They often contain speculations and claims about "how the film supposedly is bound up with certain ideas, values, or ideologies than in itself is not 'aware of'" (e.g., "The monolith is Kubrick's representation of the cinema screen itself," "*The Shining* is about the genocide of Native Americans," "*Eyes Wide Shut* is rife with Illuminati symbolism").[33] Although these symptomatic meanings or meanings "against the grain" emanate out of the film, many of them operate outside the film's diegetic and fictional world. They "take a step back," as Persson writes, "from the film, investigating its fictional, narrative, communicatory, rhetorical, and societal functions rather than establishing its fictional meaning."[34] As Bordwell and Thompson have stressed, the abstract qualities of such implicit meanings "can lead to very broad concepts often called *themes*."[35] Many of Kubrick's films seem to exhibit the theme of dehumanization. How valuable such descriptions may be, they nevertheless stay very general; they fit for literally hundreds of films. Therefore, Bordwell and Thompson suggest that "the search for implicit meanings should not leave behind the *particular* and *concrete* features of a film. . . . we should strive to make our interpretations precise by seeing how each film's thematic meanings are suggested by the film's total system."[36] A good scholarly example of such a combined incorporation of thematic interpretation and close formal analysis, can be found, for instance, in Robert Kolker's seminal chapter on Kubrick entitled "Tectonics of the Mechanical Man."[37] The work explicitly adopts an ideological and cultural approach, yet the thematic wanderings offered by the author never lose touch with the formal evidence offered by the filmmaker's work.[38]

Although the line between comprehension and interpretation is not always easy to draw, it will be the referential or situational meanings that will be the primary focus of this study for the basic reason that these are concerned with the "overt facts about story or theme that are directly presented as such within the film."[39] In other words, if we wish to show how films are capable of conveying meaning non-verbally, then it is best to focus on the sort of meaning of which we are certain to a confident degree that it is actually intended to be communicated by the films to the viewer. Situational meanings and plot summarization largely meet this condition and are therefore most appropriately fitted to examine the question of meaning in film. Speculations about the philosophical and allegorical meanings of the film, on the other hand, how interesting as they might seem, do not always offer this degree of specificity and are, in this sense, less appropriate. Not surprisingly, the "lowest," literal level of meaning, that of straightforward explanation of the plot, was also the only level of meaning that Kubrick was keen to discuss himself as he rightly felt that a verbal summary of the "deeper" meaning was not only impossible, but also deceptive given the fact that it is intended to involve the audience in an experience. As he once stated in an early interview: "Films deal with the emotions and reflect the fragmentation of experience. It is thus misleading to try to sum up the [deeper] meaning of a film verbally."[40]

By focusing upon intended situational meanings, do we not disregard the emotional and subconscious effects that Kubrick's cinema seem to emphasize? This is correct only if one assumes that the one has nothing to do with the other. As soon will become clear, however, such a distinction is not something that this book intends to maintain. Indeed, it will be one of the key objectives of this book to demonstrate that much of the intended visual situational meanings in Kubrick's film have their roots in bodily and nonconscious meanings that escape any intentional verbal articulation. In other words, the focus upon situational meanings should be seen as a way (and an opportune way at that) to reveal the cognitive unconscious dimensions of meaning-making that so forcefully account for our endless fascination with Kubrick's films.

But we must not run ahead of our argument. Now that we have sorted out the kind of meaning that this book will take as a starting point, let us further stress two more basic observations that may account for a film's complexity. The first one is that film, as opposed to language, can be conceived as a container for many other subcontainers: one for each mode of representation it contains (a visual container, a gestural container, a musical container, a linguistic container, etc.). In other words, the "trajectory" of meaning that runs from the conceptual and mental level to the external level of representation does not develop in one direction as it is the case with language, but in various directions, thus giving rise to many potential ENTRY paths. Moreover, these paths do not co-exist as parallel lines. Belonging to the generic container called "film," they are interconnected thus influencing each other in various ways.

The second observation is that many of these subcontainers have a profoundly different ontological status than language. Take, for instance, the visual subcontainer, the one most relevant to our understanding of cinema. It has been frequently noted in the literature that pictorial representations, as opposed to words, maintain a relationship with the represented reality that is based on resemblance rather than on arbitrary convention.[41] They are what semioticians call *iconic* signs instead of *symbolic* ones.[42] Although iconic signs do not literally possess the properties of the represented or denoted object, they nevertheless seem to "reproduce" some of its properties.[43] In film studies this is often further explicated in causal terms. As Gaut writes, "we speak of a photograph of some object only if that object caused a light pattern to be imprinted on the photographic emulsion."[44] This causal relation, the author points out, is not arbitrary, but "fixed by empirical facts." In other words, if the symbolic function of language facilitates the transference of concepts, and this function is absent from iconic images, how then can these images connect to conceptual structure?

The picture becomes even more complicated when we consider the subcontainer of music ("pure" or "absolute" instrumental music, that is), which appears to be quite different from the standard representational arts, such as (figurative) painting, photography and literature. As Scruton asks himself, "is there anything, other than itself, that music means?"[45] For this reason, because music lacks a clear object or reference, music has often been characterized as "abstract."[46] Consequently, if the representational capability of music is questioned and this capability is conditional for communicating meaning, how then can music become a container for meaning? It is a question frequently posed, but seldomly answered in a manner that is satisfying.

It should be obvious by now, then, that the "entrance" question of meaning is much more complicated in film than it is in language. It is at this point in our argument that we can see how the paradox of cinematic meaning starts to emerge: Film seems to lack the form-concept pairing that makes symbolic language such a suitable container for the storage of meaning, yet scholars and layman alike assume that film, just like language, is capable of conveying meaning. In a diagrammatical way, this may be visualized as in figure I.2.

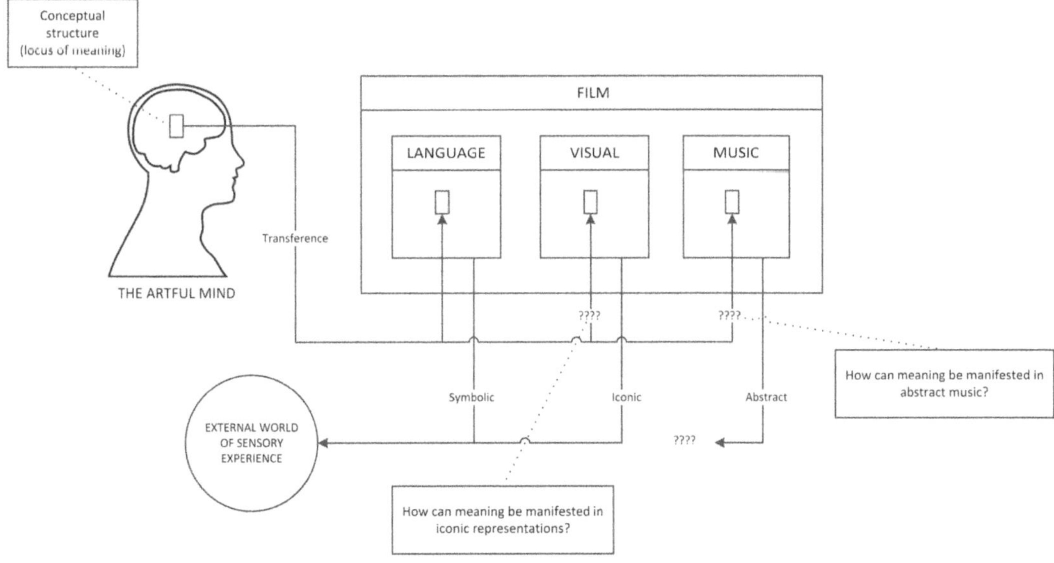

Figure I.2 The paradox of cinematic meaning.

Given this diagram, then, one may argue that the key challenge lies in finding a way to reconcile the conceptual structure of meaning with the distinctive representational structure of film by facing such questions as: How can conceptual structure be bridged to the iconic surface of visual representations? How can music be meaningful while at the same time being non-representational? How do the answers to these questions interact with each other within the generic container called film? Yet, from early on, film scholars have predominantly preferred to evade these questions by pursuing another challenge, one that is not so much motivated by the essential differences between film and language, but by the question of how meaning in film can be modelled upon linguistic, symbolic meaning. The broad metaphor used to describe this linguistic turn in film studies has come to known as the FILM AS LANGUAGE metaphor.

2. The film as language metaphor

Ever since the birth of cinema it has been customary to talk about film as if it were a "readable text" with its own "syntax" and "grammar." References to linguistic terminology can be traced back to the earliest writings on film, to reach its height in the 1970s with the rise of film semiotics.[47] Taken together, phrases such as "the cinematic text," "cinema speech," "the grammar of film" or "the language of film" provide linguistic evidence for the existence of the FILM AS LANGUAGE metaphor.[48] This metaphor presumes a set of cross-domain mappings between the source domain of language and the target domain of film (usually restricted to the visual subcontainer), some of which are summarized as in table I.1.[49]

Table I.1 The FILM AS LANGUAGE metaphor.

Source domain [Language]	*Target Domain [Film]*
Text	Film
Reading	Film comprehension
Words	Shots
Sentences	A montage sequence
Syntax	Principles for combining shots

It is not difficult to see why this metaphor is so appealing. Because most of us assume that film can be meaningful in the same way that language is meaningful, it makes intuitive sense to draw on linguistic terminology to describe our understanding of film. But what does this analogy substantially mean? What does it mean to say that a non-symbolic medium such as film can be compared to a symbolic medium such as language and more importantly what are its consequences for the conception of meaning in cinema? To avoid any misunderstanding, it might be useful to first distinguish, as John Carroll did, between two general ways of interpreting the analogy between film and language, namely as a strong *theoretical* claim or as a weaker *methodological* assumption.[50] The theoretical claim asserts that language and cinema resemble one another directly. They are conceived of as members of the same natural kind. The methodological assumption, by contrast, asserts no such theoretical claim, but instead emphasizes the methodological value of using linguistic models as a means for guiding film theory. The theoretical claim seems hard to defend for a number of obvious reasons which we will not elaborate on here. Therefore we will only limit ourselves to the justification of the methodological argument. To see its appeal, let us consider, for example, the following series of images, as cited from the introduction to Carroll's book:

(1) A close-up shot (i.e., face only) of a man, A, smiling.
(2) A medium-shot (i.e., from the waist up) of two men, A and B, engaged in conversation.
(3) A long-shot (i.e., revealing both men completely) of the two men A and B parting; they wave to one another as they walk off.[51]

The order above implies that the smiling gesture of A in (1) invited the conversation. However, as Carroll further points out, if we should put the same images in a different order, we would get an entirely different meaning: the order (2), (1), (3) suggests that something in the conversation pleased A, whereas the order (2), (3) and (1) suggests A's overall satisfaction with meeting B. This observation led many scholars to believe that the conveyance of meaning in film works quite similar to the conveyance of meaning in language, that is, just like the meaning of a sentence depends on the order of the individual words, so does the meaning of a scene depend on the order of the individual images. Since the discipline of structural linguistics, as it was founded by Ferdinand de Saussure, was considered to be the most sophisticated discipline for analysing a discourse's underlying reality, it was only logical, from a methodological point-of-view, that its conceptual tools should also be extended into the realm of film. Hence, the birth of classical film semiotics.[52] Of major importance in its development were the writings of Christian Metz who, in the 1960s and 1970s, undertook the task of lending the methodological assumption of the FILM IS LANGUAGE metaphor more theoretical weight by modelling film's underlying reality on the rules and structures governing the linguistic sign. As Metz himself put it, "the task of the semiotics of the filmic fact" is "to analyse film texts in order to discover either textual systems, cinematic codes, or sub-codes."[53] It would take us too far afield to consider the methodological issues of such an attempt in detail. For our present purpose, however, it is more important to consider the theoretical implications of such an undertaking for the concept of meaning in cinema. In the previous section, we already assumed that meaning is fundamentally mind-dependent, that is, in order for a representation to be meaningful, the representation has to connect to the internal conceptual structure of the mind (i.e., the representation as the manifestation of conceptual structure). Comprehension occurs when the observer is able to infer this content on the basis of the evidence provided by the representation. This requires a degree of recognition which can only happen if the representation externalizes the conceptual structure. This, in turn, led us to formulate the ontological paradox of cinematic meaning: how can film externalize concepts given that film, for its largest part, does not connect to concepts as language does through its symbolic form? By contrast, the linguistic approach to meaning, such as the one initiated by Metz, is fundamentally mind-independent. Its dependence on the linguistic notion of a sign adheres primarily to a relational and objective conception of meaning according to which meaning is based on *difference*s between signs.

But how, then, can film semiotics provide us with a satisfying account of meaning in cinema, if we assume that meaning is unavoidably tied to the conceptual structure of the mind? The answer here is as follows: a linguistic approach to meaning can only be justified insofar it is supported by a *science* of the mind that similarly puts the arbitrariness of the sign at the centre of its theoretical claims. Such an objectivist approach to psychology was provided in the 1950s with what now is commonly referred to as "first-generation cognitive science" or "the cognitive science of the disembodied mind."[54] Having its roots in artificial intelligence, information-processing psychology, analytic philosophy of mind and language, and Noam Chomsky's idea of an innate grammar, it assumed a view according to which the mind is symbolic and algorithmic.[55] As Johnson writes: "Mind was taken to be a capacity for formal operations and functions that was not dependent on any one particular form of embodiment."[56] Because these formal symbols of the mind bear a relationship with perceptual experience that is arbitrary, the comparison to language was easily made. This idea lies at the heart of Fodor's hypothesis of a "language of thought," which presumes an infinite set of mental representations that "acquire their meaning by being 'about'—or referring to—the states of affairs in the external world."[57] Similarly to how words typically have arbitrary relations to entities in the world, these symbols of the mind have arbitrary relations to perceptual states. It is precisely for this reason that Barsalou calls these symbols "amodal." "Just as the word 'chair' has no systematic similarity to physical chairs, the amodal symbol for chair has no systematic similarity to perceived chairs."[58] As Johnson points out, this (false) idea that all human thinking has the form of a language is deeply entrenched in our ordinary and philosophical discourse.[59] Because it is so common for humans to express their thoughts in language (recall Reddy's "conduit metaphor"), "we are easily seduced into believing that the operations of mind and thought are structured like the operations of written and spoken language."[60] We presuppose, as Lakoff and Johnson label it, the THOUGHT AS LANGUAGE metaphor (see table I.2).[61] This metaphor is evidenced in expressions such as "Let me make a *mental note* of that," "She's an *open book* to me—I can *read* her every thought," "The public *misread* the President's intentions," and "Do you think I'm some kind of mind-*reader*?"

Table I.2 The THOUGHT AS LANGUAGE metaphor (after Lakoff and Johnson).

Source domain [Linguistic Acts]	*Target Domain [Thinking]*
Linguistic activity (speaking/writing)	Thinking
Words	Ideas
Sentences	Complex ideas
Spelling	Communicating a sequence of thoughts
Writing	Memorization

Hence, if the mind is believed to share a formal language consisting entirely of arbitrary symbols, and meaning is conceived to be a matter of the mind, it follows that *all* meaning is linguistic meaning, including meaning in film. As to the definition of linguistic meaning, approaches differ. As we already saw, Saussure viewed linguistic meaning as essentially based on differences *within* language. By contrast, truth-based approaches to linguistic meaning conceive meaning as a relation between words and objective (mind-independent) reality.[62] According to this "objectivist theory of meaning" conventional and arbitrary signs such as words become meaningful insofar they refer to the state of affairs in the world (e.g., things, persons, events). Despite these differences, they nevertheless share one core assumption, namely that meaning is best captured in terms of a conception of human thought that, similar to the arbitrary nature of language, is disembodied, that is, a mind separated from its body and its world.[63]

Consequently, by providing a conception of the mind within the language analysis tradition, first-generation cognitive science provided film semioticians with "the ideal paradigm" for their linguistic method.[64] This can be derived from the following line of reasoning:

(1) Meaning is a matter of conceptual structure.
(2) Like language, this conceptual structure is arbitrary and disembodied (i.e., the THOUGHT AS LANGUAGE metaphor).
(3) Hence, meaning can be equated with linguistic meaning.
(4) If film wants to have true meaning it has to be modelled on linguistic meaning.
(5) Hence, in order to study this meaning, one has to consider the semantic or syntactic rules that govern the non-perceptible system underlying film (i.e., the research aim of film semiotics).

As Buckland has pointed out, the engagement of film semiotics with first-generation cognitive science, in particular Noam Chomsky's transformational generative grammar, has led a number of European film theorists, among them Chateau and Colin, to overcome what he coins the "translinguistics of Metz's film semiotics," that is, "Metz's insistence that film semiotics be based exclusively on the methods of structural linguistics."[65] Buckland refers to this next "maturation" stage of semiotic film theory as the "cognitive semiotics of film."

More importantly, however, from the perspective of this book, first-generation cognitive science and the mind-body dualism that underpins it, provided film semioticians with a scientific and formal argument for overcoming the paradox of cinematic meaning. Since Fodor's language of thought metaphor seduces us to believe that conceptual structure has the form of a language (i.e., not a natural one, but a formal one), it is no longer necessary to consider the mind as the locus of meaning. Rather, it is the linguistic sign that now takes on this role as it becomes the epitaph by which film connects to language. In this sense it can be said that film semiotics provides a solution to the paradox of cinematic meaning. Film is meaningful because its underlying reality is governed by the same disembodied and media-independent rules of meaning-making that are manifest in verbal language (and in all other media for that matter). Schematically, this can be represented as in figure I.3.

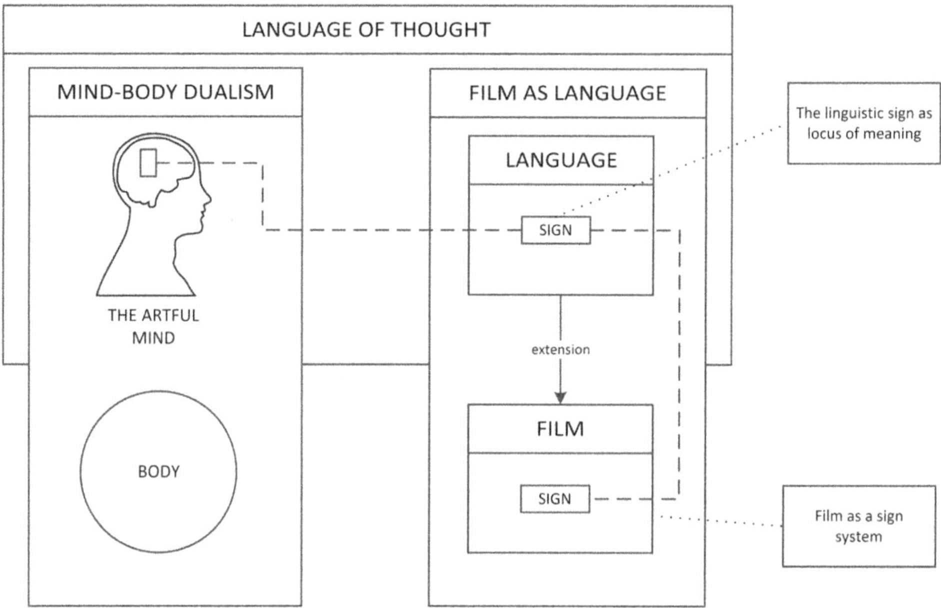

Figure I.3 Evading the paradox of cinematic meaning: The FILM AS LANGUAGE metaphor.

Over the last two decades the linguistic approach to meaning in film has met with increasing criticism, especially from Anglo-Saxon quarters.[66] Part of it has been directed to the strong theoretical claim of a direct resemblance between film and natural language.[67] This point of criticism, however, seems rather ill placed, as Buckland has counter-argued, because Metz himself has repeatedly stated that film is not analogous to natural language ("film is a *language sans langue*").[68] As we have seen, film semiotics was not so much founded on any direct resemblance between film and language, but on methodological grounds, the idea that film's specific, underlying reality could be reconstructed by the methods of structural linguistics. Nevertheless, there seems to me that there are four more fundamental reasons why the linguistic approach seems to fail in providing the scholar with a satisfactory account of meaning in cinema.

The first reason is that the linguistic view of meaning is simply too narrow and too reductionist. As Mark Johnson aptly puts it, "if you assume that meaning is essentially linguistic and tied to concepts and propositions, then anything in art that is not expressible propositionally is ignored or dismissed as meaningless or cognitively insignificant."[69] Noël Carroll echoes this claim when he charges that "it is an error to attempt to model all art interpretation on linguistic models."[70] He coins this charge the "linguistic fallacy," as an antidote to Wimsatt's and Beardsley's most famous slogan of "the intentional fallacy" (i.e., the disregard of author intentions in the interpretation of art).[71] It is a fallacy, he argues, "because most artforms—and, therefore, most of the artworks produced in those artforms—are not governed by the kind of structures we find in language proper. That is, the objects of interpretation with respect to most artforms are not language-like in the sense of possessing the kind of rules that determine things such as word meaning and sentence meaning."[72] Take for example, the pictorial quality of films. Pictures on the whole do not require decoding in order for them to be understood. Comprehension of images is based upon a shared capacity for embodied perception. We grasp the meaning using the same perceptual abilities that enable us to perceive faces and expression in ordinary experience. Consequently, if one defines meaning in film predominantly at the level of the combination of images, as film semiotics does, one misses an important source of meaning.

Secondly, film semiotics may not go as far as to claim that film *is* a natural language, but by analogizing meaning in visual representations to linguistic signification (and by that, imposing conformity), it unavoidably fails to value the differences between film and language. In other words, the problem is not that film semiotics strive to find a deeper structure that is shared by both film and language—in fact, we will see later that the embodied approach to meaning does just the same—but that the structure they propose (the disembodied, linguistic one) is a very limited one because it diverts attention "from those aspects that may be unique to film."[73] In case of film, this implies, above all, that the common structure should be in accordance with, to quote Prince, "a recognition of cinematic images as iconic rather than as symbolic signs, depending on relations of similarity to, rather than difference from, what they represent."[74] It is precisely for this reason that the project of film semiotics eventually fails to account for the paradox of cinematic meaning.

Thirdly, the linguistic turn in film studies put an end to a tradition of film theory where the focus has been on a psychological and scientific explanation of films. This tradition goes back as far as the first achievements in psychological research of the film since its earliest beginnings in the 1910s and includes, among others, the writings of Hugo Münsterberg, Rudolf Arnheim and Albert Michotte.[75] These scholars set themselves the task of describing the psychological mechanisms that explain the perception and comprehension of film. The structuralist or linguistic turn in the 1960s, however, severely undermined the significance of their works by displacing the locus of meaning from the mind to the linguistic sign. This lack of interest in psychology continued unabated in the 1970s and 1980s as film theory began to establish a strong affinity toward interpretative and ideologically driven doctrines. Bordwell calls this development "SLAB theory" as it is mostly based on Saussurean linguistics, Lacanian psychoanalysis, Althusserian Marxism, and Barthian textual theory.[76] It is also more commonly known as "Grand Theory" because of its all-encompassing and totalizing claims.[77] In this tradition theorizing does no longer fulfil the function of explaining. Rather it becomes, to quote Carroll, "the routine application of some larger, unified theory to questions of cinema, which procedure churns out roughly the same answers, or remarkably similar answers."[78] It was not until the 1980s and the 1990s, when the "cognitive turn" took its grip in various fields of knowledge, that a handful of scholars, including, among others, Noël Carroll, David Bordwell, Edward Branigan, Ed Tan, Carl Plantinga, Torben Grodal and Murray Smith, started to restore the interdisciplinary link between film studies and the cognitive sciences. This discipline, known today as Cognitive Film Theory, sets itself apart from Grand Theory in its commitment to "clarity of exposition and argument and to the relevance of empirical evidence and the standards of science (where appropriate)."[79] Especially in the light of the ever-growing influence of evolutionary theory and recent advances in neuroscience, and the increasing prevalence of digital technologies, such a bridging of the divide between the humanities and the natural sciences, what Smiths recently referred to as the building of a "third cultural" or "naturalized" approach to film and art, is more relevant than ever.[80]

Fourthly and perhaps most importantly is that the propositional view of meaning in recent years has lost a great deal of its theoretical weight and rhetorical power as a new paradigm entered the field that took over the place from its intellectual ally, first-generation cognitive science. This shift has been referred to as "second-generation cognitive science" or "the science of the embodied mind."[81] It is precisely through this new paradigm that the paradox of cinematic meaning will come to the surface again as the mind, and not the sign, reclaims its rightful place as the locus of meaning.[82]

3. Toward an embodied view of meaning in cinema

In contrast to first-generation cognitive science, embodied cognitive science treats the mind, concepts, meaning, and rationality as fundamentally embodied, and therefore as not reducible merely to the functional relations and programs of a disembodied machine. Theoretical support for this view is highly disparate and can be derived from various intellectual sources as diverse as linguistics, psychology, anthropology, philosophy and neurophysiology.[83] Despite a great deal of interpretational variety among these disciplines, they nevertheless share, in lesser or greater degree, the thesis that conceptual structure arises from bodily, social and cultural experience, so part of what makes conceptual organization meaningful are the experiences with which it is associated. Two scholars that have contributed considerably to the theoretical and methodological development of the embodied cognition thesis are the cognitivist linguist George Lakoff and the philosopher Mark Johnson.[84] Together they proposed a theory of embodied cognition whose central constituent elements might be isolated in the following condensed form:

(1) Conceptual structures arise from the nature of human bodily interaction with the external world.
(2) This connection is captured, among others, by the theoretical notion of an *image schema*. Image schemas are relatively abstract conceptual patterns that arise directly from our everyday interaction with and observation of the world around us. These patterns are intrinsically meaningful by virtue of their connection to our bodies and our embodied experience. They cannot be characterized adequately by meaningless symbols.
(3) These image schemas, in turn, provide the bodily basis for *conceptual metaphors*. We recruit their concrete inferential logic in order to reason about abstract target domains. These mappings across domains are captured by the form of "a is b."
(4) In addition, the target domains of conceptual metaphors may also be structured by means of *metonymy*. In contrast to metaphor, metonymy only involves one conceptual domain. These mappings within a single domain are captured by the form of "a stands for b."[85]

A thorough clarification of these elements will be reserved for the second chapter of this book. For now, let us consider the general implications of an embodied account of the mind for our conception of meaning in cinema.

First, the embodied cognition thesis leads to a fundamentally new hypothesis on the nature of meaning in cinema (and for that matter, the arts in general).[86] If meaning in film is a matter of conceptual structure, and it is assumed by many that this conceptual structure is not disembodied, but embodied, then it follows that meaning in film is also embodied, that is, "it arises through embodied organism-environmental interactions in which significant patterns are marked within the flow of experience."[87] This has an important consequence: it implies that meaning in film goes far beyond the confines of words and sentences. That is, in order to study meaning in film, one has to look beyond arbitrary semantics and syntax, and instead focus on the ways that the artful resources of filmmaking can be related to significant patterns of bodily experience.

Second, with the formulation of this new hypothesis comes also the need to readdress the central question inherent to the paradox of cinematic meaning, namely, how does film connect to conceptual structure? Film semioticians evaded this question by displacing the locus of meaning from the mind to the linguistic sign. However, since meaning is assumed to be no longer disembodied, the privileged role of language as the centre of meaning becomes problematic, thus prompting the need to go back to the drawing table to re-establish the connection between mind and film anew, this time from the perspective of the MIND IS BODY metaphor, rather than the THOUGHT AS LANGUAGE metaphor.[88] Diagrammatically, this can be represented as in figure I.4.

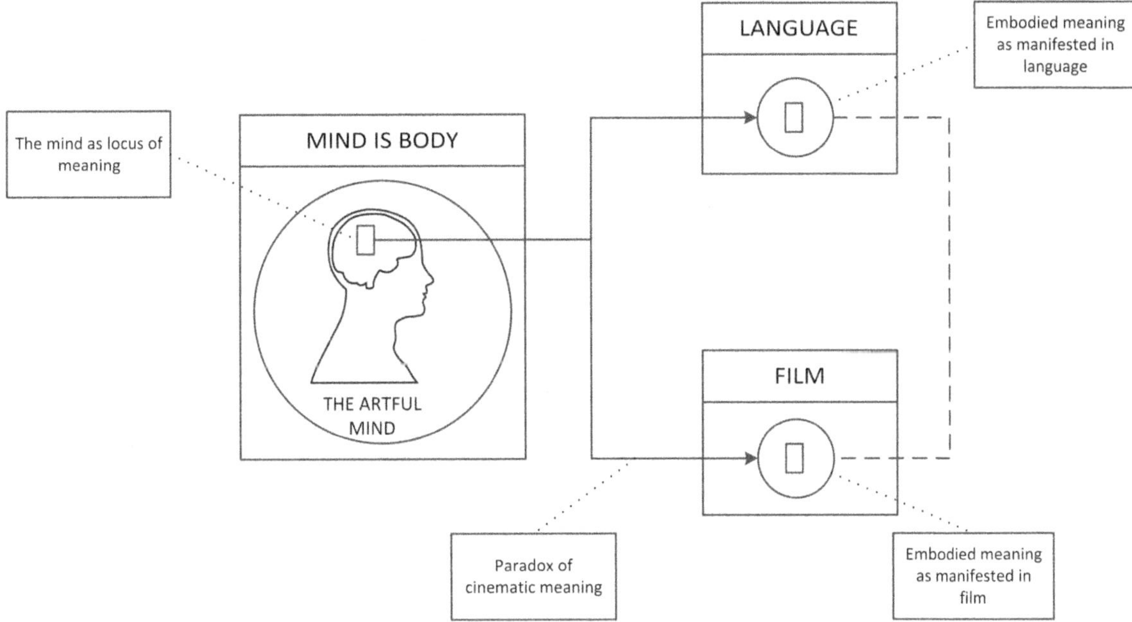

Figure I.4 Readdressing the paradox: The embodied view of meaning in film.

As this figure shows, the harmony between film and language is no longer based on the disembodied linguistic sign, as in figure I.3, but on the notion of embodiment. In this sense it can be said that meaning exceeds linguistic meaning (with the latter being just one part of the former). Language, like film or any other art form for that part, is merely one form of expression in which the embodied meaning manifests itself. Metz said precisely the same thing in relation to filmic codes with the crucial difference that the meaning in his model is disembodied. This is the actual weakness of Metz's work rather than the comparison between film and verbal language.

As a consequence of this, the scholar finds himself faced again with the question as to how meaning (that is, embodied meaning this time) can be expressed in an overall iconic medium such as film. The same question with respect to the symbolic medium of language has been rigorously addressed in the field of cognitive linguistics, where a number of abstract concepts have been subjected to an embodied inquiry. Not coincidentally, these concepts overlap to a large extent with the kind of concepts that define the conceptual structure of mental causation, which in terms of narratives is, as we already mentioned above, a rich level of meaning. These concepts include both event-structure concepts (e.g., events, cause, state) as well as concepts denoting mental states (e.g., emotion, perception, thinking).[89]

Although an increase of interest in embodied metaphor can be discerned in the field of (cognitive) film studies, the same kind of academic scrutiny is still missing.[90] Given Lakoff and Johnson's embodied view of meaning, any systemic account of the question above should at least take into consideration three fundamental tasks. First, to identify the conceptual structure that can be taken as representative of a film's or group of films' intended (situational) meanings. Second, to examine how this structure reflects embodied experience by showing how image-schematic metaphors and metonymies flesh out its literal skeleton. Third, to examine how film reflects this embodied conceptual structure by showing how film may give expression to these image-schematic metaphors and metonymies by its own medium specific tools (e.g., film style, acting, etc.). Baring these three tasks in mind, we can now start to sketch out the structure of this book.

4. The structure of the book

The first chapter takes up the challenge of identifying some of the central concepts that define the meanings of Kubrick's films. Given that we have already determined that the focus of this book will be on the situational and referential meanings and given that these meanings are closely tied to characters and their behaviors, we will locate these concepts within the narrative level of Kubrick's films. We first offer a general, conceptual discussion of the notion of narrative, after which we address the question as to where to locate the bare plot descriptions of Kubrick's films. Knowing where to find these conceptual descriptions, we will be able to provide the reader with thirteen scene descriptions, one for each feature film that Kubrick directed. From these descriptions, we will then derive a conceptual skeletal blueprint, a literal meaning-structure of Kubrick's work, that will be argued to underlie all of the thirteen narratives. As already suggested above, this structure will be referred to as the structure of "mental causation."

This structure, in turn, will provide us with all of the central concepts necessary to move toward the second chapter of this book, which aims to address the question of their embodiment. By virtue of which metaphors and metonymies are the concepts inherent to the structure of mental causation fleshed out by bodily knowledge? Given that image schemas fulfil a fundamental role in describing the answer to this question, a considerable degree of attention will be devoted to a clarification of this concept. A concise survey of the cognitive linguistic literature will eventually lead us to distinguish between two core metaphor systems of human thinking that account for an understanding of mental causation, namely the EVENT-STRUCTURE metaphor and the MIND IS A BODY metaphor.[92]

Together, the first two chapters constitute the "conceptual" part of this book. The next part, by contrast, considers the task of showing how the embodied conceptual structure, as identified in the first chapter, is fleshed out visually in the films of Kubrick. Likewise, this "formal" part will be divided over two chapters.

The third chapter is general and considers the question as to how the constituents of embodied meaning-making, as discussed in chapter 2, can be manifested in film. For practical reasons, and given that the visual level is the most essential to our understanding of cinema, we will narrow down our focus to the iconic surface level of moving pictures. Given the two-fold nature of conceptual metaphor, this task will amount to assessing two key questions: (1) How may image schemas be imposed onto the iconic and representational level of films? and (2) How may moving pictures give rise to target domains to which these image schemas might be extended metaphorically? Answers to these questions will be sought in the notions of *film style* and *acting*, respectively.

It is only once we have successfully dealt with both challenges that we will be able to move to the fourth chapter in which we shall consolidate all of the insights of the previous chapters by exploring the question as to how the films of Kubrick resort to image schemas for the purpose of conveying the stories of mental causation visually. It is in the course of closely analysing various film scenes that we will gradually come to address the paradox of cinematic meaning, as raised at the beginning of this introduction.

Lastly, we take the opportunity of the concluding chapter to assess two theoretical dilemmas that involve the film viewer. The first dilemma takes into consideration the question as to how viewers are able to discover the situational meanings of Kubrick's films given the fact that they, as observers, are not performing the bodily actions that lie at the heart of the visual conveyance of those meanings. In addressing this question, we will stress the importance of embodied simulation mechanisms inside the viewer as they have received considerable attention among various scholars working on the boundary between film art and cognitive science.[93] The second dilemma takes into account the paradoxical relationship between meaning and (film) music as already mentioned above. How can non-representational, instrumental music, as prominently present in Kubrick's films, be experienced as meaningful (e.g., as expressing the emotions of characters), given the fact that musical sounds, unlike words or visual images, do not refer, strictly speaking, to something outside themselves? Following an embodied cognitive approach to musical meaning, we will locate the answer to this question not so much in the music itself, but in the embodied viewer who makes sense of the music. Music may not possess the bodily and spatial properties that are necessary for fleshing out the abstract meaning (e.g., motion, gravity, containment), the people who listen to it nonetheless resort to these properties in order to understand and conceptualize the musical sounds they hear. It is precisely in this sense that we will argue that music can be capable of expressing meaning including the concepts of mental causation. Viewers are able to do so because the embodied tools we use to conceptualize music are similar to the embodied tools we use to understand the meaning.

Notes

1. Ciment, *Kubrick*, 187. This quote is Jeremy Barham's own translation from the original French edition published by Calmann-Lévy. See Barham, "Incorporating Monsters," 141. Strangely enough, these words are not included in Faber and Faber's English translation.
2. The major events in Kubrick's personal life are well documented, so we will not elaborate on them here. Readers interested in Kubrick's biography may find the following readings of interest: Baxter, *Stanley Kubrick*; LoBrutto, *Kubrick*; and Abrams, *Stanley Kubrick*. See in this regard also the documentary made by his long-time assistant and brother-in-law Jan Harlan entitled *Stanley Kubrick: A Life in Pictures* (2001).
3. This can be observed in the flow of publications that continues unabated. Some recent collective works on Kubrick and his films include, among others, Broderick, *The Kubrick Legacy*; Fenwick, *Understanding Kubrick's 2001*; Fenwick, Hunter and Pezzotta, "Stanley Kubrick"; Hunter, "Kubrick and Adaptation"; Ljujić, Krämer and Daniels, *Stanley Kubrick*; and Szaniawski, *After Kubrick*.
4. Benson, *Space Odyssey*, 8.
5. LoBrutto, *Stanley Kubrick*, 277. For a good compilation of interviews taken between 1959–1987, see Philips, *Stanley Kubrick*.
6. Rapf, "A Talk With Stanley Kubrick," 78. Very enlightening in this regard is also Kubrick's own one-page article entitled "Words and Movies," 14. For similar quotations in which the filmmaker criticizes the linguistic view of meaning in cinema, see, among others, Nordern, "Playboy Interview," 47–48; and Belson, *Space Odyssey*, 365.
7. Here we are paraphrasing Kubrick who in an interview with Joseph Gelmis stated that "movies present the opportunity to convey complex concepts and abstractions without the traditional reliance on words." See Gelmis, "The Film Director as Superstar," 90.
8. Later in this book, we will challenge this premise, but for now let us take it as given.
9. Grice, "Meaning," 383.
10. Searle, "Grice on Meaning," 11.
11. Carroll, "Art Interpretation," 119–120. This is very close in spirit to what Paisley Livingston refers to as "the meshing condition", "the intention to mean *q* by saying or otherwise representing *p* is successful just in case the intention to imply *q meshes* sufficiently with what is written, spoken, or otherwise put on display." See Livingston, *Cinema, Philosophy, Bergman*, 99.
12. It is important to keep in mind that although the embodiment of y in x is a necessary condition for the audience's recognition of y, it is not a sufficient condition. The fact that y is embodied in x does not in itself guarantee the audience's discovery of y.
13. See, for instance, Davidson, "Truth and Meaning"; and Searle, *Speech Acts*.
14. For a good recent discussion of truth-based approaches to linguistic meaning, see Iten, *Linguistic Meaning*.
15. Evans and Green, *Cognitive Linguistics*, 156. Among the foundational book-length texts in cognitive semantics are, Talmy, *Cognitive Semantics*; Langacker, *Cognitive Grammar*; Lakoff and Johnson, *Metaphors*; Lakoff, *Women*; and Johnson, *The Body in the Mind*.
16. Lakoff and Johnson, *Philosophy*; Johnson, *Embodied Mind*; Gibbs, *Embodiment*.
17. Wilson and Sperber, *Meaning and Relevance*, 2.
18. Evans and Green, *Cognitive Linguistics*, 7.
19. Reddy, "The Conduit Metaphor," 167.
20. In chapter 2 of this book, when clarifying the notion of embodied cognition, the concept of "container" will be identified as a prototypical example of what Lakoff and Johnson term an "image schema," that is, a dynamic and recurrent pattern of sensory-motor experience. From this perspective, ENTRY and EXIT designate two "dynamic patterns of containment." See also Dewell, "Dynamic patterns," 369–394.
21. For a discussion of cinematic authorship, see Livingston, "Cinematic Authorship," 132–148; and Gaut, "Film Authorship," 149–172. See also Meskin, "Authorship," 12–28; and Sellors, "Collective Authorship," 263–271.
22. Sellors, "Collective Authorship," 263.
23. Turner, *The Artful Mind*.
24. Philips, *Stanley Kubrick*, vii.
25. Young, "The Hollywood War," 7.

26. Livingston, "Cinematic Authorship," 135; Sellors, "Collective Authorship," 266. Sellors prefers "filmic author" to "cinematic author" because the former evokes the medium of film, whereas the latter suggests the institution of cinema. He defines a filmic author as "the agent or agents who intentionally token(s) a filmic utterance, where 'to token' refers to any action, an intended function of which is to make manifest or communicate some attitude(s) by means of the production of an apparently moving image projected on a screen or other surface and a filmic utterance is the result of the act of tokening in this medium."
27. Bordwell, *Making Meaning*, 8–9.
28. Ibid., 2.
29. Van Dijk and Kintsch, *Strategies in Discourse Comprehension*.
30. Persson, *Understanding Cinema*, 31.
31. Kim, *Philosophy of Mind*, 173–204; Robb and Heil, "Mental Causation."
32. Bordwell, *Making Meaning*, 2.
33. Persson, *Understanding Cinema*, 34. The interpretation of the monolith as screen can be credited to Loughlin, *Alien Sex*, 73. For a good discussion of the seemingly endless cycle of interpretations in *The Shining*, see Lovisato, "(Do Not) Overlook."
34. Ibid., 34.
35. Bordwell and Thompson, *Film Art*, 56.
36. Ibid., 56.
37. "Tectonics of the Mechanical Man" is a chapter in the book *A Cinema of Loneliness*, Kolker's classic account of the New Hollywood. See also Kolker, *Extraordinary Image*.
38. Over the last years many Kubrick scholars have adopted a more overt formal approach to Kubrick's films. They include, among others, Coëgnarts, *Stanley Kubrick*; Falsetto, *Stanley Kubrick*; Kuberski, *Kubrick's Total Cinema*; Luckhurst, *The Shining*; McQuiston, *We'll Meet Again*; and Sperl, *Die Semantisierung*.
39. Wilson, "Interpretation," 163.
40. Young, "The Hollywood War," 7.
41. See, for instance, Prince, "The Discourse of Pictures," 16–28.
42. Chandler, *Semiotics*, 36.
43. Eco, "Iconic Signs," 1.
44. Gaut, *Cinematic Art*, 52.
45. Scruton, *The Aesthetics of Music*, 118.
46. Walton, "What Is Abstract," 351.
47. For notable references to language in early film theory, see, among others, Eisenstein, *The Film Sense*, Lindsay, *The Art of the Moving Picture*; Pudovkin, *Film Technique*, xiii–xvii; and Spottiswoode, *A Grammar of the Film*. Important studies within the field of film semiotics include, among others, Bettetini, *The Language and Technique of the Film*; Carroll, *Structural Psychology*; Eco, "Cinematic Code"; Metz, *Film Language*, *Language and Cinema*; and Peters, *Pictorial Signs*. For good reflective discussions of the relationship between film and language, see, among others, Buckland, "Film Semiotics"; Prince, "The Discourse of Pictures"; Pryluck, "The Film Metaphor"; and Stam, "Film and Language."
48. See also Carroll, *Structural Psychology*, 29.
49. We shall see in chapter 5 of this book that the same observation can also be made with regard to music. Johnson calls this the MUSIC AS LANGUAGE metaphor. For a discussion, see Johnson, *The Meaning of the Body*, 235.
50. Carroll, *Structural Psychology*, 31; see also Buckland, "Film Semiotics," 88.
51. Ibid., 1.
52. See also Buckland, "Film Semiotics," 88.
53. Metz, *Language and Cinema*, 150.
54. Lakoff and Johnson, *Philosophy*, 75. For a discussion, see also Johnson, *Embodied Mind*, 16.

55. Chomsky, *Syntactic Structures.*
56. Johnson, *Embodied Mind*, 16.
57. Ibid., 69. For a discussion of this hypothesis, see Fodor, *The Language of Thought.*
58. Barsalou, "Perceptual Symbol Systems," 578–579.
59. Johnson, *The Meaning of the Body*, 202.
60. Ibid., 202.
61. Lakoff and Johnson, *Philosophy in the Flesh*, 244.
62. Iten, *Linguistic Meaning*, 1–6.
63. Johnson, *The Meaning of the Body*, 272.
64. Buckland, *The Cognitive Semiotics of Film*, 18
65. Ibid., 2. Film writings that draw on insights from first-generation cognitive science, include, among others, Chateau, "Generative Model of Film Discourse"; and Colin, "The Grande Syntagmatique Revisited."
66. Carroll, *The Philosophy of Motion Pictures*; Currie, *Image and Mind*; Prince, "Psychoanalytical Film Theory"; and Pryluck, "The Film Metaphor." For a short summary of Carroll's and Currie's critiques, see Sinnerbrink, *New Philosophies of Film*, 24–27.
67. See, for instance, Currie, *Image and Mind.*
68. Buckland, "Film Semiotics," 99.
69. Johnson, "Identity, Bodily Meaning, and Art," 21.
70. Carroll, "Art Interpretation," 117.
71. Wimsatt and Beardsley, "The Intentional Fallacy."
72. Carroll, "Art Interpretation," 122.
73. Pryluck, "The Film Metaphor," 123.
74. Prince, "Psychoanalytical Film Theory," 80.
75. For an excellent overview of their achievements, see Tan, "A Psychology of the Film."
76. Bordwell, "Historical Poetics," 385.
77. Bordwell, "Contemporary Film Studies"; Carroll, "Prospects for Film Theory."
78. Ibid., 41
79. Plantinga, "Cognitive Film Theory," 258. For a good overview of some of the current views and issues within cognitive film theory, see Shimamura, *Psychocinematics*; and Nannicelli and Taberham, *Cognitive Media Theory.*
80. Smith, *Film, Art, and the Third Culture.*
81. Lakoff and Johnson, *Philosophy in the Flesh*, 77. For a discussion, see also Johnson, *Embodied Mind*, 17.
82. The use of the word "new" here is not entirely accurate as the embodied view of the mind is not a completely new paradigm, but rather a continuation, as Barsalou has pointed out, of a tradition of thinking that was considered dominant until the early twentieth century. Its historical roots go back as far as Ancient Greek Philosophy (Aristotle and Epicurus) and includes, among others, the intellectual heir of British empiricism (Locke, Berkeley, and Hume), American pragmatism (John Dewey) and French phenomenology (Merleau-Ponty, Bergson). See Barsalou, "Grounded Cognition," 619.
83. For a good discussion of some of its central claims, see Wilson, "Embodied Cognition."
84. Seminal works include Lakoff and Johnson, *Metaphors*; Lakoff and Johnson, *Philosophy*; Lakoff, *Women*; Johnson, *The Body in the Mind*; and Johnson, *The Meaning of the Body.*
85. Although metonymy has been less extensively investigated by Lakoff and Johnson, it constitutes a fundamental aspect of recent cognitive linguistic literature. See, among others, Evans and Green, *Cognitive Linguistics.* Hence, the reason why we include it in this overview.
86. In contrast to Lakoff, Johnson himself has written a great deal about the relationship between the arts and embodied meaning. Worth reading in this context are Johnson, *The Meaning of the Body*, "Identity, Bodily Meaning, and Art", and more recently, *The Aesthetics of Meaning and Thought.*

87. Johnson, *The Meaning of the Body*, 273
88. Lakoff and Johnson, *Philosophy*, 235.
89. For a discussion of event-structure concepts, see Lakoff and Johnson, *Philosophy*, 170–234. For a pioneering work on the metaphorical conceptualization of emotion, see Kövecses, *Metaphor and Emotion*. Among the influential works on the mental concepts of perception and thinking are Lakoff, "Reflections"; Yamanashi, "Metaphorical Modes"; Lakoff and Johnson, *Philosophy*, 393–399; Yu, "Chinese Metaphors", "The Eyes"; Gibbs, *Embodiment*, 97; and Johnson, *The Meaning of the Body*, 165. We will discuss these and other more in detail in chapter 2 of this book.
90. Studies that apply insights from Conceptual Metaphor Theory to film include, among others, Buckland, *The Cognitive Semiotics of Film*; Branigan, *Projecting a Camera*; Kappelhoff and Müller, "Embodied Meaning Construction"; Fahlenbrach, "Emotions in Sound"; Ortiz, "Primary Metaphors"; Coëgnarts and Kravanja, "Embodied Visual Meaning"; Winter, "Horror Movies." Two edited volumes at the crossroads of CTM and film studies, are Coëgnarts and Kravanja, *Embodied Cognition and Cinema*; and Fahlenbrach, *Embodied Metaphors in Film, Television, and Video Games*.
91. For a discussion of the EVENT-STRUCTURE metaphor, see Lakoff and Johnson, *Philosophy*, 178–194. For a discussion of the MIND IS A BODY metaphor, see Lakoff and Johnson, *Philosophy*, 235–236; and Sweetser, *From Etymology to Pragmatics*.
92. See, among others, Hasson et al., "Neurocinematics"; Grodal, *Embodied Visions*; Gallese and Guerra, "Embodying Movies"; D'Aloia and Eugeni, "Neurofilmology"; Coëgnarts, "Cinema and the Embodied Mind."

Chapter 1

Identifying the Meaning: In Search of the Concepts of Kubrick's Films

The perfect novel from which to make a movie is, I think, not the novel of action but, on the contrary, the novel which is mainly concerned with the inner life of its characters.

—Stanley Kubrick[1]

If it is our goal to demonstrate how the situational meanings of Kubrick's films are communicated visually to the viewer, then, we first have to identify the concepts that constitute those meanings. Before pursuing this task, we will first provide the reader with some insight into the question as to how spectators construct the situational meanings of films. Since an understanding of this question falls together with the way people make sense of stories, the first part of this chapter will be devoted to a clarification of the concept of narrative. Knowing more or less how narrative comprehension is achieved, we will be able to move on to the second part of this chapter which is centred around the question as to where to find the concepts that constitute the situational meanings of Kubrick's films. This question will be explored through a consideration of four distinctive sources of conceptual description: the novel, the screenplay, the film, and the descriptions as formulated by the film viewer. Each level of description will be discussed with respect to Kubrick's unique method of adapting stories into films. Once we know where to find these concepts, we can actually present some conceptual descriptions. This will be done in the third part of this chapter in which we shall provide the reader with thirteen scene descriptions, one for each feature film that Kubrick directed. From these descriptions, we will then extract, in the fourth part, a literal conceptual scheme or skeletal blueprint that will be argued to underlie all of the thirteen narratives. In the fifth and last section, we introduce the challenge of the subsequent chapter by arguing how this conceptual structure poses us with a theoretical problem that necessitates us to consider the significant role of embodiment.

1. What is narrative?

What is narrative? To address this question is to engage in a large and rich body of literature that demands deeper and more detailed study than this chapter can offer.[2] For our purpose, it is sufficient to offer a general understanding of the concept of narrative. As always, the best way to get an idea of something is by comparison with what it is not. Take, for example, the following random string of events:

(1) A general goes mad. A radio is destroyed. A telephone call takes place. A nuclear bomb is dropped.

As Bordwell and Thompson have argued, it is hard to perceive such a list of actions as a narrative.[3] In order for it to be conceived as such, there has to be something holding the individual events together. Consider now the same events, but this time described anew:

(2) A US general goes mad and orders his bomber wing to drop their nuclear bombs on Soviet targets. The Americans are able to successfully recall all of the bombers except but one whose radio equipment has been destroyed by the Soviets. Refusing to become a mass murderer, the American president telephones the Soviet premier to warn him of the impending attack and to help him neutralizing it. This plan, however, fails and the plain succeeds in dropping the bomb after all.

We now have a narrative that many of you will recognize as a very general outline of the plot summary of *Dr. Strangelove*. We are able to grasp it as such because, in contrast to our earlier description, we are able to *connect* the events.[4] Firstly, we are able to situate the events spatially: we infer that the general gave his orders from an air force base somewhere in the United States, that the bombers are heading toward the USSR, that both presidents are probably operating from inside their War Rooms. Secondly, we are able to link the events causally: the general has launched an attack because he has gone mad. The Americans are not able to recall all of the planes because the Soviets have destroyed the radio equipment of one of the bombers, which, in turn, necessitates the president's telephone call. Lastly, we can understand that the three events are temporally related to each other: the order of the attack occurs before the telephone call, which in turn occurs before the dropping of the bomb; all of the action probably taking place in a couple of hours.

A narrative thus arises, as a final product, from an ongoing process of construction: from the events conveyed by the representation (whatever the medium), the perceiver actively construes "a chain of events in cause-effect relationship occurring in time and space."[5] Narrative thus is, to cite Edward Branigan, a perceptual (and therefore mental) activity that organizes data (i.e., spatial and temporal data) into a special pattern (i.e., a cause-effect chain with a beginning, middle, and end) which represents and explains experience.[6]

This conception has an important consequence: it implies that any description of a narrative should avoid a strictly formal and logical definition, but should take into account the mental or cognitive processes active in a perceiver during his or her comprehension of a narrative in an actual situation.[7]

Perhaps the most comprehending theoretical model that has been proposed so far in the literature to account for the cognitive dimension of narrative comprehension is the theory of *situation models* or *mental models*.[8] Central to this theory is the idea that narrative comprehension involves more than what is explicitly described in a text. It involves the construction and retrieval of a mental representation of the verbally described situation or state of affairs, rather than the construction and retrieval of a mental representation of the text itself.[9] To see what is meant by this theoretical claim, let us consider an experiment that was already conducted a decade prior to the coining of the concept of a mental model. In their study on sentence memory, Bransford, Barclay, and Franks have demonstrated empirically that the reader's mental representation of the situation described by the text can have a significant effect on the reader's memory.[10] Assume, for example, that participants are hearing input sentences (1) and (2):

(1) Three turtles rested *on* a floating log, and a fish swam beneath *them*.
(2) Three turtles rested *beside* a floating log, and a fish swam beneath *them*.

Then, afterward, during the recognition test, the same participants are additionally confronted with the same sentences, albeit with the final pronoun *them* changed to *it*.

(3) Three turtles rested *on* a floating log, and a fish swam beneath *it*.
(4) Three turtles rested *beside* a floating log, and a fish swam beneath *it*.

Participants who had heard input sentence (1) frequently confused it with recognition sentence (3), whereas people who had heard input sentence (2) rarely confused it with recognition sentence (4). These findings indicate that the discrepancy cannot be explained by merely differential changes at the textual and formal level. Indeed, sentences (1) and (3) and sentences (2) and (4) only differ with respect to the pronoun (*them* or *it*). How, then, can we account for this difference? As the authors argue, the explanation has to be found in the spatial layout described by the sentences.[11] Sentence (2) offers a description that includes information about a fish swimming beneath the turtles. The description in sentence (1) also contains this information, but it includes something additional as well. As they write: "Since the turtles were on the log and the fish swam beneath them, it follows that the fish swam beneath the log as well."[12] The inferential spatial logic, however, that the fish swam beneath the log, was not included in the input sentences. "It had to come from one's general cognitive knowledge of the world (in this case, knowledge of spatial relations)."[13] Or as Zwaan and Radvansky put it: sentences (1) and (3) are being confused, "because they describe the same situation." By contrast, sentences (2) and (4) "are less likely to be confused because they describe different situations." [14]

The spatial layout of the described events is but one of many aspects of situation models. The *event-indexing model* (henceforth, EI model) proposed by Zwaan, Langston, and Graesser has been introduced to account for the multidimensional set-up of situation models.[15] More specifically, the EI model asserts that perceivers, when construing mental models, monitor connections between events (incoming events with prior events stored in working memory) along various dimensions or indexes including, among others, space, time and causality.[16] Continuity with regard to these aspects, then, is what constitutes a coherent situation model. Table 1.1 enlists the conceptualizations of temporal, spatial, and causal continuity, as provided by Zwaan, Magliano and Graesser.[17]

Table 1.1 Situational continuity along the dimensions of time, space and causality (after Zwaan, Magliano and Graesser).

Temporal continuity	Occurs when an incoming event in a story describes an event, state, or action that occurs within the same time interval as the previous sentence. A sentence is temporally discontinuous with the prior context if there is a time shift.
Spatial continuity	Occurs when the text describes events, states, and actions that take place in the same spatial setting. A spatial setting is a room, scenario, or region that has distinctive features that are discriminable from alternative spatial settings.
Causal continuity	Occurs when there is a direct causal link between the current sentence and prior story information. In the absence of causal continuity, the reader attempts to infer a causal link and this requires extra processing time.

As this table already suggests, analyses of narrative texts typically use a clause or sentence as the narrative unit of analysis with each clause representing an event. These clauses then can be indexed spatially, temporally and so on. Being a visual medium, film, however, lacks this clear-cut segmentation into clauses. This, in turn, raises the question as to which unit of film can be seen as serving the same function as a clause. To overcome this problem, Magliano, Miller and Zwaan have proposed to use the shot as the equivalent unit for the analysis of narrative films.[18] This, however, does not mean that a shot is identical to a clause, far from it. The authors are keen to stress that, where a clause typically conveys only one or two states, events, goals or actions, this is not necessarily true for a shot. Nevertheless, the choice for the shot seems logical and well-motivated from the point of view of *continuity editing*.[19] This system of cutting creates the illusion that a series of shots conveys events that are temporally, spatially, and causally contiguous with each other. In other words, although the shot is not a clause, it does allow us to identify whether or not an incoming shot conveys events or actions that are contiguous or not with the immediately prior shot along the various dimensions of narrative comprehension. This, in turn, has led the authors to define continuity in film along the two most basic dimensions of events, namely: time and space.[20] The authors assumed a shot to be temporally continuous with the previous one "if it depicts events or actions which immediately follow or are concurrent with those of the previous shot." Spatial continuity, in turn, was defined along two aspects: "spatial regions of interactions" and "spatial movement of characters." Continuity in the first aspect "was assumed to occur when a shot depicts a location that is within the same spatial region as the previous shot." Discontinuity takes place "when a shot depicts (1) a new spatial region that has not been shown in any previous shot or (2) a location in a spatial region that has been shown before, but was not the same spatial region depicted in the previous shot." Continuity in the second aspect "was assumed to occur when all the salient characters depicted in a shot were located in the same region as the shot in which they were last seen." Diagrammatically, the EI model in film understanding may be represented as in figure 1.1.

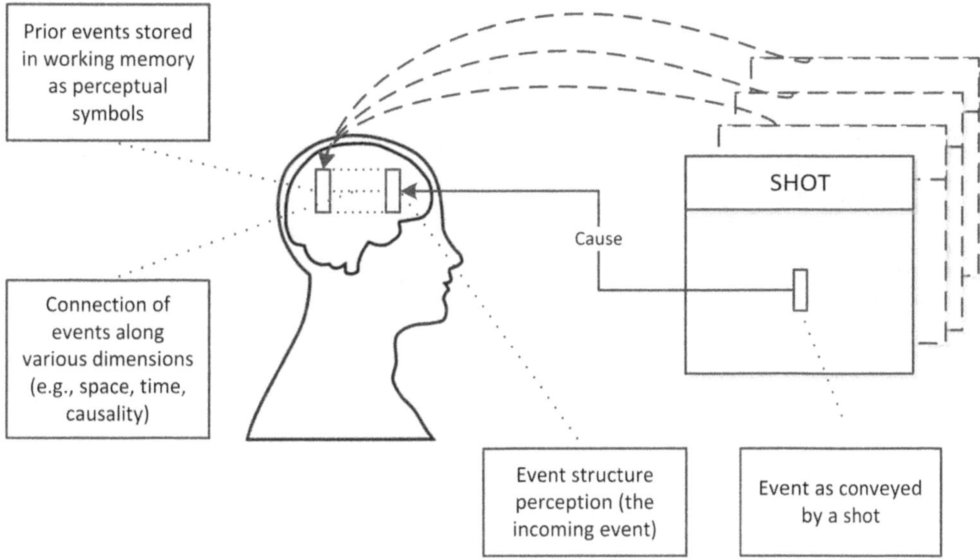

Figure 1.1 Indexing events in film understanding.

We construe a narrative, then, by identifying its events and linking them along various dimensions. As to the nature of these events, Bordwell and Thompson have further pointed out that they can take two forms: either they are presumed and inferred by the viewer or they are explicitly presented in the film.[21] For instance, at the start of *Eyes Wide Shut*, in between credit cards (figures 1.2*A* and 1.2*C*), we see a beautiful woman with her back to the camera letting an elegant black dress dropping to the floor (figure 1.2*B*). She will be later revealed as Alice (Nicole Kidman). After the appearance of the film title, we watch the exterior of an apartment block (figure 1.2*D*). It is night. The traffic with yellow cabs signals us that we are probably in New York. Then we see a handsome man in evening dress looking for something (figure 1.2*E*). The shot is spatially and temporally continuous with figure 1.2*B*. He walks into a bedroom, goes to a small table, picks up keys and a mobile phone and walks to a chest of drawers (figure 1.2*F*). This is Bill Harford (Tom Cruise). He now opens a drawer and takes out a handkerchief (figure 1.2*G*). He utters the words: "Honey, have you seen my wallet?" Off-screen we hear a female voice replying: "Ah . . . isn't it on the bedside table?" Bill walks across to the bedside table and finds his wallet (figure 1.2*H*). He goes around the bed, saying, "Now listen, you know we're running a little late?" and into the en-suite bathroom where Alice is sitting on the loo wearing an evening dress (figure 1.2*I*). On the basis of these cues, we can already draw several conclusions. We assume that Bill and Alice are a married couple who are dressing themselves up for a party, that Alice tried on a dress, but rejected it. We also assume that, before we saw Bill, he also changed clothes. From the look of the interior of the apartment we also infer that they are well-off and that they probably lead a busy professional and social life. In other words, we infer causes, a temporal sequence, even though none of this information has been directly presented. The sum total of both types of events is what constitutes the *story*, that is, "all the events that we see and hear, plus all those that we infer or assume to have occurred, arranged in their presumed causal relations, chronological order, duration, frequency, and spatial locations."[22]

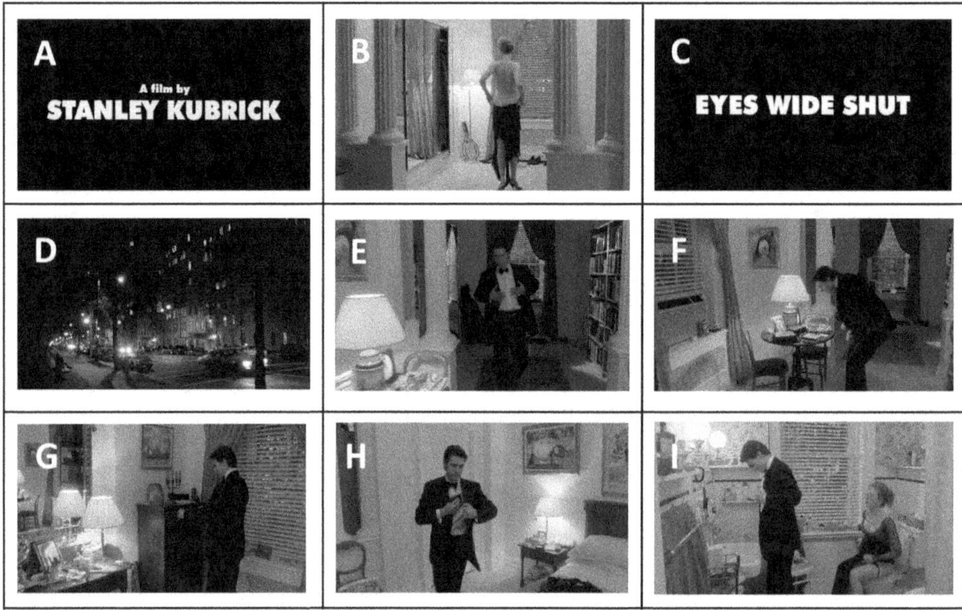

Figure 1.2 The opening scene of *Eyes Wide Shut.*

As viewers, we can only construct a mental model of the situation as conveyed by the film on the basis of what is explicitly and directly presented by the filmmaker. This is called the *plot* which refers to "everything visibly and audibly present in the film before us."[23] This does not only include the events that are directly depicted, but also the elements that are brought in from outside the story, that is, the non-diegetic elements that the characters cannot read or hear such as the film's credits or the soundtrack. For instance, while the opening images of *Eyes Wide Shut* are presented to us, we also hear the *Suite for Jazz Orchestra No. 2* by Dmitri Shostakovich. Initially, the viewer is held to believe that this music is non-diegetic. Later in the scene this perceptive state changes, however, as we watch how Bill turns off the on-screen stereo, thus revealing the surprise that the music was diegetic all along. As such the film announces, to quote McQuiston, "its request to the audience to see and hear the world only as Bill does."[24]

Knowing more or less how spectators come to understand the situational meanings of a film, let us now turn to the question as to where to find the proper conceptual description of those meanings. Finding an answer to this question is crucial for it can be assumed that these descriptions provide us with the concepts that are rendered non-verbally by the films of Kubrick. Indeed, if it is our goal to identify the concepts that constitute the referential or situational meanings of Kubrick's work and these meanings, in turn, are construed by the viewer on the basis of the explicitly presented events of the plot, then it follows that we should provide conceptual (i.e., verbal) descriptions of those meanings in order for us to obtain the concepts.

2. Locating the situational meanings of Kubrick's films

The task of locating the situational meanings of Kubrick's work amounts to considering and comparing various conceptual sources of description. In what follows, we will discuss four of them, as they each can be mapped on the timeline of the filmmaking and film viewing process. They include in successive order: (1) the novels upon which the films are based, (2) the screenplays adopted from these novels, (3) the films themselves, and (4) the spectator's verbal accounts of the films' situational meanings. As figure 1.3 suggests, these sources are not to be treated as independent of each other. Rather, they are interconnected with each later location on the timeline modifying and adapting the situational meanings of the prior location: the spectator tells in verbal terms what the film is about; the film conveys in cinematic terms what is written in the screenplay; and the screenplay modifies what is written in the novel. In what follows, we will discuss each location, in turn, with respect to Kubrick's unique method of adapting novels into films, and with the hope of pinpointing the proper descriptive locations from which, subsequently, to draw some of the concepts that constitute the situational meanings of Kubrick's films.

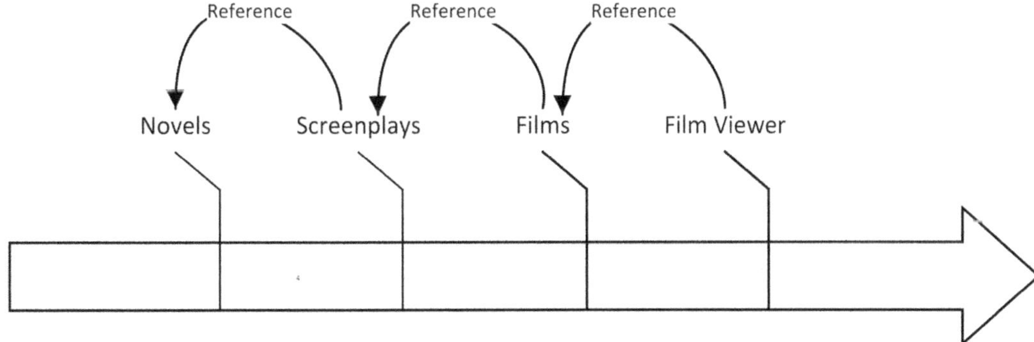

Figure 1.3 In search of the situational meanings of Kubrick's films.

The novels

A first initiative way would be to search for the situational meanings in the novels upon which most of the films of Kubrick are based. As can be seen in table 1.2, Kubrick was a prominent adapter of literature. With the exception of his first two films and *2001*, for which only a short story served as a starting point, all his films were based on pre-existing pieces of writing including such famous works as Vladimir Nabokov's *Lolita*, Anthony Burgess' *A Clockwork Orange* and Stephen King's *The Shining*. His choice of novels was random and depended purely on whether or not he had a "falling-in-love reaction" to the story.[25] As he once told *Rolling Stone* magazine: "I read. I order books from the States. I literally go into bookstores, close my eyes and take things off the shelf. If I don't like the book after a bit, I don't finish it. But I like to be surprised."[26] Nevertheless, despite this absence of an outspoken preference, one may sense a genuine interest for the psychological novel over the novel of action. A clear written statement that backs this claim can be found in the Winter 1960/61 issue of *Sight and Sound* in which the director, in an article of his own, has declared that the former type of novel is "the perfect novel from which to make a movie" for it gives "the adaptor an absolute compass bearing, as it were, on what a character is thinking or feeling at any given moment of the story. And from this he can invent action which will be an objective correlative of the book's psychological content."[27]

Table 1.2 The literary source material of Kubrick's work.

Year	*Film*	*Novel*
1953	*Fear and Desire*	—
1955	*Killer's Kiss*	—
1956	*The Killing*	*Clean Break* (Lionel White, 1955)
1957	*Paths of Glory*	*Paths of Glory* (Humphrey Cobb, 1935)
1960	*Spartacus*	*Spartacus* (Howard Fast, 1951)
1962	*Lolita*	*Lolita* (Vladimir Nabokov, 1955)
1964	*Dr. Strangelove*	*Red Alert* aka *Two Hours to Doom* (Peter Bryant aka Peter George, 1958)
1968	*2001: A Space Odyssey*	*The Sentinel* (Arthur C. Clarke, 1951)
1971	*A Clockwork Orange*	*A Clockwork Orange* (Anthony Burgess, 1962)
1975	*Barry Lyndon*	*The Memoirs of Barry Lyndon* aka *The Luck of Barry Lyndon* (William Makepeace Thackeray, 1844)
1980	*The Shining*	*The Shining* (Stephen King, 1977)
1987	*Full Metal Jacket*	*The Short-Timers* (Gustav Hasford, 1979)
1999	*Eyes Wide Shut*	*Traumnovelle* (trans. *Rhapsody–A Dream Novel*) (Arthur Schnitzler, 1926)

As adaptations, his films unavoidably raise the question as to what degree the depicted events refer back (and thus stay faithful) to the events described in the novels. It is in addressing this question that many Kubrick scholars have pointed toward the various idiosyncratic ways in which his work deviates from the written source material upon which it is based.[28] As Welsh observes: "Kubrick had two 'literary' talents besides his genius for creating visual spectacles: one was for satire, and the other was for transformative adaptation."[29] As to the origin of this distance between the written work and the cinematic work, we may follow Pezzotta and point toward Kubrick's unique and creative method of adapting novels into films.[30] This method roughly consists of two stages: firstly, to break down the written work into a bare and skeletal structure or blueprint that captures the underlying conceptual and emotional essence of the book (rather than the factual, action events) and secondly, to flesh out this structural "compass" by means of the techniques of filmmaking (rather than the techniques of novel writing). Diane Johnson, co-author of the screenplay to *The Shining*, sees precisely in the first stage an important reason why Kubrick favoured adapting existing books rather than working from original scripts, as it allowed him "to gauge the effect, examine the structure, and think about the subject of a book more easily than a script."[31] In further clarifying this structure, we can make the comparison, as Pezzotta did, to the concept of *canovaccio* (canvas or scenario), which in the *commedia dell'arte* was a vague plot outline in which "dialogue was summarized in indirect speech and left to the actors' improvisation."[32] Similarly, one can see a strong resemblance here with what the famous Russian stage director Konstantin Stanislavski labelled the psychological and inner "scheme of the play."[33] The following definition is taken from Gorchakov's *Stanislavsky Directs*, of which Kubrick himself has claimed to be inspired by it:[34]

> The scheme is the bone outline; it is the skeleton which holds together the inner and outer actions of the play. Rehearse along the lines of its inner and outer action, but don't dress it in the mise en scène and effective forms of expression. Keep the characters on the level of the skeleton outline only; don't cover them with the meat and fat of the juicy actors' images. This will come later. Define the characters only in their basic aspirations and rehearse the play only through its main accents. In this way it is possible to play the entire role of Molière in fifteen minutes and the whole play in forty-five minutes, not counting intermissions. When the author sees this living, acting skeleton—the outline of the main situations—he may see his play's omissions.[35]

As Stanislavski, at the early stage of acting, did not want the skeleton to be spoiled by the actor's imagery, so Kubrick, at the early stage of adapting the novel, did not want the skeleton to be corrupted too much by the author's imagery. The "meat and fat" of the conceptual scheme should come from the director, not from the writer. And as Kubrick has repeatedly stressed in interviews, this implies foremost the substitution of the verbal medium of the author by the cinematic and non-verbal medium of the filmmaker, the visual and aural spectacle over the play of words.

Unavoidably, putting such a method into practise sooner or later ends up in creative differences with the writers who now see their own written works (novels and screenplays) to be reduced to mere blueprints. It should be no surprise, then, that the history of Kubrick adaptations reads as a series of polemics between Kubrick, the filmmaker and the creative agency called writership.[36] Telling in this regard is the reaction of Frederic Raphael to the director's own treatment of the script for *Eyes Wide Shut*, which he recalls as follows: "The text is jejune and without literary grace. It is almost gauche in its unpretentiousness. Occasionally it is embarrassing."[37] Several writers have also expressed their disappointment in the way in which the filmmaker modified their original scripts. In the published version of his own film script of *Lolita*, Nabokov commented on this as follows:

> The modifications, the garbling of my best little finds, the omission of entire scenes, the addition of new ones, and all sorts of other changes may not have been sufficient to erase my name from the credit titles but they certainly made the picture as unfaithful to the original script as an American poet's translation from Rimbaud or Pasternak.[38]

This, however, did not seem to affect the writer's positive attitude toward the film as he also adds that "Kubrick was a great director" and that "Lolita was a first rate film with magnificent actors." Others, however, reacted with more resentment. It is well-known that King was not pleased with Kubrick's decision to shift the focus of *The Shining* from the superficial evil of the Overlook Hotel to the psychological evil inside the character of Jack Torrance. Along similar lines, Burgess has expressed his bitterness over Kubrick's choice to exclude the last chapter of his novel ("a vindication of free will"), which would have possibly weakened the sex and violence of the previous parts, and as a result, also the public controversy that followed.[39]

In view of all this, *2001* forms an interesting contrast in that it is the only film of which the novel was conceived after the conceptual blueprint of the film was already established. As Kubrick recalls:

> The novel came about after we did a 130-page prose treatment of the film at the very outset. This initial treatment was subsequently changed in the screenplay, and the screenplay in turn was altered during the making of the film. But Arthur took all the existing material, plus an impression of some of the rushes, and wrote the novel. As a result, there's a difference between the novel and the film. ... In both cases, of course, the treatment must accommodate to the necessities of the medium. I think that the divergencies between the two works are interesting. Actually, it was an unprecedented situation for someone to do an essentially original literary work based on glimpses and segments of a film he had not yet seen in its entirety.[40]

In sum, then, we might conclude that the novel is probably not the best place to look for the concepts that Kubrick's films convey cinematically. Even if the director would have stayed true to the events of the novels, the use of novels would have been controversial since the process of elision, the omission of events, is inherent to any process of adapting novels into films. It is as an issue, as Jenkins has pointed out, "that may and ought to be addressed, probed, weighed, and considered. But, thoroughgoing problem that it is, it can never be fully resolved."[41] Hence, if novels are unfitting, where then do we have to look for the descriptions? Probably the best way is to find them outside the novels and within their corresponding adaptations. This unavoidably brings us to the written work of the screenplay.

The screenplays

A quick look at table 1.3 tells us that from the thirteen feature films that the filmmaker directed, *Spartacus* is the only screenplay he did not take credit for (whether it be partially or completely). He wrote three of them in collaboration with the person who also wrote the original novel (*Lolita*, *2001*, *Full Metal Jacket*), and two of them entirely on his own (*A Clockwork Orange* and *Barry Lyndon*).[42]

Table 1.3 The screenplay credits of Kubrick's films.

Year	***Film***	***Screenplay credit***
1953	*Fear and Desire*	Stanley Kubrick, Howard Sackler
1955	*Killer's Kiss*	Stanley Kubrick, Howard Sackler
1956	*The Killing*	Stanley Kubrick, Jim Thompson (dialogues)
1957	*Paths of Glory*	Stanley Kubrick, Calder Willingham, Jim Thompson
1960	*Spartacus*	Dalton Trumbo
1962	*Lolita*	Vladimir Nabokov, Stanley Kubrick (uncredited)

Continued

1964	*Dr. Strangelove*	Stanley Kubrick, Terry Southern, Peter George
1968	*2001: A Space Odyssey*	Stanley Kubrick, Arthur C. Clarke
1971	*A Clockwork Orange*	Stanley Kubrick
1975	*Barry Lyndon*	Stanley Kubrick
1980	*The Shining*	Stanley Kubrick, Diane Johnson
1987	*Full Metal Jacket*	Stanley Kubrick, Michael Herr, Gustav Hasford
1999	*Eyes Wide Shut*	Stanley Kubrick, Frederic Raphael

Although the screenplay stands much closer to the actual film, occupying a unique place between the existing piece of writing and the cinematic outcome, it nevertheless suffers from a serious limitation that at first sight seems to compromise its capability of serving as a suitable source location for the conceptual descriptions of the films' narrative events. This limitation entails that screenplays, as they are traditionally conceived, do not so much offer descriptions of what is happening as they provide descriptions of what the actors have to say and what they have to do. That is, they consist essentially of *dialogue* and *stage directions* rather than of descriptions of *events*. In other words, screenplays, in their turn, lack precisely that feature that made novels such an appropriate candidate for our descriptive search. This aspect was also of great concern to Kubrick who, according to Johnson, shared the opinion that "novelists were apt to be better writers than screenwriters."[43] Kubrick's scepticism toward the screenplay can also be clearly felt through the following quote:

> The screenplay is the most uncommunicative form of writing ever devised. It's hard to convey mood and it's hard to convey imagery. You can convey dialogue, but if you stick to the conventions of a screenplay, the description has to be very brief and telegraphic. You can't create a mood or anything like that.[44]

Kubrick, however, would not have established his unique reputation as a self-regulating filmmaker, if he would not compensate for this lack of descriptions by challenging the conventions of the classic screenplay format. And indeed, if one looks at some of the formats of the Kubrick screenplays, as available in The Stanley Kubrick Archive, one may find a genuine interest in descriptions over dialogue. For instance, it is the convention of the classic screenplay format to present dialogues in a centered column and the description straight across the page. LoBrutto has noticed, however, that Kubrick, for his screen adaptation of *A Clockwork Orange*, adopted the opposite method, "centering the description so it reads like a poem and running the dialogue from the left margin so the imagery captured the reader's eye."[45] The same observation has also been made by Pezzotta with regard to the screenplay of *Eyes Wide Shut*. At The Stanley Kubrick Archive she analysed a draft script by Raphael, dated "January 26, 1996" that makes use of the same format. Insightful is also the signed message of Raphael preceding the document saying "I am working on at the second half of the script. I hope that I am right in thinking that this is the way you want it to look. It can, of course, easily be 'translated' into the usual script format which you, understandable, are not crazy about."[46] Descriptive evidence can also be found in a typewritten script supplement to an undefined "A" script for

2001: A Space Odyssey, which contains, among others, a basic descriptive outline of the events of each scene that together constitute the wordless "Dawn of Man" sequence.[47]

Another important strategy that Kubrick adopted in order to compensate for the screenplay's lack of descriptions is the inclusion of what is now regarded by many to be one of the director's trademarks, namely the use of the *first-person* or *third-person voice-over*.[48] As can be seen in table 1.4, Kubrick made considerable use of this narrative device throughout his oeuvre.[49]

Table 1.4 The use of narration in Kubrick's films.

Year	*Film*	*Narrator*
1953	*Fear and Desire*	Third-person (anonymous)
1955	*Killer's Kiss*	First-person (Davey/Gloria)
1956	*The Killing*	Third-person (anonymous)
1957	*Paths of Glory*	Third-person (anonymous)
1960	*Spartacus*	Third-person (anonymous)
1962	*Lolita*	First-person (Humbert Humbert)
1964	*Dr. Strangelove*	Third-person (anonymous)
1968	*2001: A Space Odyssey*	—
1971	*A Clockwork Orange*	First-person (Alex)
1975	*Barry Lyndon*	Third-person (anonymous)
1980	*The Shining*	—
1987	*Full Metal Jacket*	First-person (Joker)
1999	*Eyes Wide Shut*	—

Of the thirteen films he made, only three films do not contain explicitly some sort of voice-over narration, whether it be used only briefly such as in *Fear and Desire*, *Paths of Glory*, *Spartacus* and *Dr. Strangelove* or more outspokenly such as in *Lolita*, *A Clockwork Orange*, *Barry Lyndon* and *Full Metal Jacket*.[50] This number would even amount to two if we would include the initial use of a third-person narrator in the early draft scripts of *2001*.[51] Although *2001* and *The Shining* have no voice-overs, they do provide titles which can be seen to serve a similar function.[52] Voice-over commentary distinguishes itself from the dialogue spoken by the characters in that it is overtly more descriptive and informative about the characters' motivation and plot. Notably in this regard is *Barry Lyndon* in which a third-person, omniscient narrator describes, in only a few moments of screen time, what the main character is thinking and feeling. A good illustration of this can be found in the disembodied voice-over that is used over the visuals of Barry seeing Lady Lyndon for the first time:

> Five years in the Army, and considerable experience of the world had dispelled any romantic notions regarding love with which Barry commenced life. And he had it in mind, as many gentlemen had done before him to marry a woman of

> fortune and condition. And, as such things so often happen these thoughts coincided with his setting sight upon a lady who will play a considerable part in the drama of his life: the Countess of Lyndon, Viscountess Bullingdon of England, Baroness Castle Lyndon of Ireland. A woman of vast wealth and great beauty. She was the wife of Sir Charles Lyndon, Knight of the Bath, Minister to George III at several of the Courts of Europe. A cripple, wheeled about in a chair worn out by gout and a myriad of diseases. Her Ladyship's Chaplain, Mr. Runt acted as tutor to her son, the little Viscount Bullingdon, a melancholy little boy, much attached to his mother.[53]

However valuable the screenplays of Kubrick may be from a descriptive and conceptual perspective, their descriptions are only useful insofar they are also manifested in the finished film (whether in verbal or non-verbal form). It is here, in this confirmation of the screenplay's conceptual content by the film's audio-visual content that also lies its limitation as it is rarely the case that one can find, in the screenplay, a corresponding conceptual description for each of the events conveyed by the film. As such we are necessitated to search for an additional descriptive location, one that can account for the descriptions that are missing from the screenplays. Given that the latter limitation results from the inescapable gap between the unfilmed and the filmed, one would be inclined to locate those missing descriptions within the films themselves.

The films

Films, however, yield two other difficulties which were absent so far and which prevent any further lengthy discussion. First, there is the danger of circular reasoning. If our goal is to reveal the process by virtue of which the films of Kubrick are able to convey concepts, but take the films as the starting point for locating the concepts, then we run the risk of jumping ahead in our argument by examining already what is meant to be analysed at a later stage, namely the films themselves. In other words, a discussion of the formal level should follow the discussion of the conceptual level and not the other way around.

Second and most importantly, however, is the fact that films, in contrast to novels and screenplays do not provide descriptions of their own depicted events unless those descriptions are explicitly given by the films themselves through the use of such devices as a narrating voice-over, as discussed above, or the intersection of intertitles. This again touches upon the ontological difference between language and film. As we have already noted in the introduction, language by nature is conceptual and abstract whereas films, due to their iconic nature, essentially are not. However, if it is our goal to locate the films' communicated concepts within the descriptions of the narrated events then we need conceptual descriptions of those events in order to obtain the concepts. A possible way out to this dilemma, then, would be to locate these verbalizations outside the films, and within the experiential domain of the film viewer.

The film viewer

Taking into consideration the descriptive significance of the film viewer would enable us to overcome at least two of the shortcomings mentioned so far. Firstly, since the descriptions offered by the film viewer would be based on the perception of the actual films, we would be able to reduce the gap between the unfilmed and the filmed which antagonized the screenplay. Secondly, because these descriptions are linguistic and conceptual, we would be able to overcome the limitation posed by the medium film. This, however, does not mean that the descriptions of the spectator are free from risks. Aside of the practical difficulty of putting the events, as seen and heard in the film, into words, there lurks the possible danger of interpretation. As we already saw in the theoretical introduction to this book, interpretation distinguishes itself from comprehension in that it is mainly concerned with "implicit" and "symptomatic" meanings rather than "referential" and "explicit" meanings, which are at the centre of this book.[54] As stated, referential meanings are close to the bare-plot summaries of the films, and are therefore most suitable to serve as complementary descriptive sources to the screenplays of Kubrick's films.

In providing the missing descriptions of the films' literal events ourselves (and thus adopting the role of a screenwriter somehow), we will not elaborate on the cinematic techniques and non-diegetic material that helped communicating those events to the viewer. To give you an example, when Moon-Watcher in *2001* discovers that he can use a bone as a weapon, this moment of epiphany is rendered non-verbally through such means as gestural behavior and music. These tools are clearly used with the purpose of cueing the inner event of a cognitive leap forward. Therefore, whenever we have to rely on our own descriptions, we will keep the references to film style to their limit. We will not mention camera movement, editing nor any other stylistic device that helps signalling the event to the viewer, but we will simply restrict ourselves to a bare-plot description of the elicited event. In other words, the focus of the descriptions will be on *what* is communicated, not on *how* it is communicated. A study of the latter question will be reserved for chapters 3 and 4 of this book. In this way, by filtering out the references to film style, we will be able to overcome the risk of circular reasoning, as mentioned earlier.

3. Thirteen films, thirteen narrative descriptions

Having addressed the question of location, we are now in a position to actually offer some of the descriptions of the narrative events of Kubrick's work. To facilitate this provision somehow, we have selected from each of the thirteen films that Kubrick made, a significant scene. A scene can be defined as a segment in a narrative film that is continuous along the dimensions of time and space or that uses crosscutting to show two or more simultaneous actions. We will first situate and contextualize each scene within the general narrative framework of the film, after which we will provide a description of its events. The origin(s) of each description (e.g., screenplay, voice-over, author description) will be specified in the text or the corresponding footnote. Each description will be taken to convey a narrative on its own, that is, a smaller one within the surface story level of the film. The descriptions will pertain to both non-verbal scenes (scenes without dialogue) as well as to verbal ones (scenes with dialogue). Depending on the nature of the scene, some descriptions will appear to be slightly longer or shorter. For each narrative description it should be possible to discuss its events along the various dimensions of situational continuity (time, space, causality), but this will not be the central aim here. The key objective here is to carefully *describe* the referential and situational meanings of the scenes, as these descriptions, a total sum of thirteen, will provide us with the concepts that are presumably communicated visually by Kubrick's films.

Fear and Desire (1953)

Notably refuted and self-criticized by the director himself, who wrote it off, rather harshly, as nothing more than a "bumbling, amateur film exercise," Kubrick's first feature film only recently re-emerged for general audiences after being unavailable for nearly forty years.[55] Set up as an allegory, *Fear and Desire* tells the story of a group of soldiers, lieutenant Corby (Kenneth Harp) and his three men Mac (Frank Silvera), Fletcher (Stephen Coit) and Sidney (Paul Mazursky), who are stuck in a forest behind enemy lines. From the early start of the film we come to know that the war depicted is a fictitious and unspecified one, "not a war that has been fought, nor one that will be, but any war," as the voice-over informs us. Making their way through the woods, they surprise two enemy soldiers whom they attack and slaughter with their bayonets, despite the fact that these men were just harmlessly eating their supper. Soon after this massacre they stumble upon one of the local girls (Virginia Leith). Afraid that she might betray them, they take her prisoner by tying her to a tree. As the other soldiers return to the raft that should take them back to safe territory, Sidney, the youngest and less experienced of the group, is left with the task to guard her. In their absence, however, a situation unfolds, let this to be our first narrative of the series of thirteen, of which its events are quite detailed described in the screenplay as follows:

(1) Sidney comes up from behind her with his hands cupped and filled with water. He is hurrying and water is dripping. He comes around the tree and raises his cupped hands to her face. She lowers her head to his hands and drinks. She pauses and looks up into his eyes. She starts to lower her head and drink again. She continues drinking from his hand. The gulps are clearly heard. Sidney has a very strange expression. He is still holding his hands cupped and she simply looks at him. The girl looks at him and smiles sweetly but as if she has some secret motive. He smiles back insanely. He giggles. The girl lowers her head and licks out the last few drops from Sidney's hand. Sidney sort of moans and sighs. Sidney looks as though he has received a low voltage shock. The girl looks up slowly from his cupped hands. Separating his hands he caresses her face. Her cheeks become streaked with dirt from his hands. The girl badly pretends that she is enjoying it. Her fists are clenched. Sidney grabs her by the arms and presses his face into her hair. Her face reveals her plan is working. Sidney is frantically making love to the girl who is still bond to the tree. Sidney's murmurings are heard. Sidney still making love. His arms are around the girl and the tree. His hands are caressing the tree just above the spot the buckle is. As the hands move around they feel the buckle. Girl looks pleased. Sidney moves away and looks into her eyes. His manner is one of hysterical glee. He walks around behind her. Her smile shows great self-satisfaction that her animal cunning is about to triumph. Sidney's hands undoing the buckle. Sidney has come half way around the tree and is kissing her shoulder as he pulls on the buckle to release her. As the buckle is undone the belt suddenly flies out as the girl tries to break away. Sidney grabs her about two steps from the tree and they struggle. They lose their balance. The girl's face as she looks down at the ground rushing at her. They hit the ground and continue the struggle. Sidney has her pinned to the

> ground. The girl presses her new advantage and struggles her harder. Their feet trashing around. With a sudden burst of strength the girl manages to twist free. Sidney lunges after her leg and gets a fleeting grip on it. The girl just does get away from his sprawling grasp. She stumbles to her feet and starts to run. He pulls his revolver out of his pocket. The girl is running. Sidney aims the gun and fires five times rapidly. The girl lying face down in the grass. Her eyes are open. Sidney is sitting dazed in the same spot. He looks quite mad. Scratches on face. The girl's hand lying in the grass. Sidney is sitting on the ground about thirty feet from the dead girl. Sidney falls down and begins crying. His face is pressed into the ground and sobbing.[56]

Killer's Kiss (1955)

For his second feature film Kubrick turned to the genre of film noir. *Killer's Kiss* tells the story of a welterweight prize-fighter Davey Gordon (Jamie Smith) who falls in love with a young woman, Gloria Price (Irene Kane), who lives in the apartment opposite of his. The night after his big fight against "Kid" Rodriguez, Davey is awakened by her scream as she is being attacked by her tyrannizing boss Vincent "Vinnie" Rapallo (Frank Silvera) who runs the dance hall where she works as a taxi dancer. Running to her room to rescue her, Davey chases after Vincent, who escapes him, and goes back to comfort Gloria. The next morning, they kiss each other and they decide to both collect their pays, he from his manager Albert, she from Rapallo, before taking the train together to Seattle. Vincent, however, is destined to prevent Gloria from leaving him. With the support of two of his hoodlums, he manages to hold the girl captive. Davey hurries to rescue her, but instead is getting captured and beaten up himself. This is followed by a series of actions, let this to be our second narrative under conceptual consideration, of which its bare plot outline may be rendered as follows:

> (2) Davey lies beaten up on the floor of the loft where Vincent and two of his thugs are holding Gloria. He has just been beaten up. Gloria, in a bid to save Davey (or her own future?), gives herself to Vincent. She pleads for her life telling him that she will do everything to please him. They kiss each other. Vinnie, however, reluctant to be taken for a "fourteen karat sucker," becomes mad and starts to shout at Gloria. This distraction gives Davey some time to figure out a way to escape his perilous situation. A solution comes to his mind when he sees the window of the loft which gives entrance to the outside. He looks at the other two hoodlums who are now both distracted by the quarrel between Vinnie and the girl. One of them is standing at his feet, the other is sitting. He manages to master the former one by placing his feet between his legs. As his opponent loses balance and falls, he throws himself through the window. He lands safely on the ground and starts to run away through abandoned city streets and across rooftops, eventually ending up in an abandoned mannequin warehouse where he kills Rapallo in a violent fight.[57]

The Killing (1956)

Also for his next film Kubrick stayed within the genre of crime films by making the hard-boiled heist film *The Killing*, his first of three successful collaborations with producer James B. Harris (the other films being *Paths of Glory* and *Lolita*) and the first of his films to be adapted from a novel. Based on Lionel White's *Clean Break*, *The Killing* recalls the story of Johnny Clay (Sterling Hayden), an ex-convict who gathers a group of men to execute his seemingly fool proof caper to rob a racetrack of $2 million during a race. Although the overall execution of the heist goes smoothly and Johnny succeeds in robbing the cashier's office, the plan ultimately goes wrong in the meeting place where Clay's men are supposed to await the arrival of Johnny and the money. Prior to the robbery, one of Clay's team, racetrack cashier George Peatty (Elisha Cook, Jr.), has told his wife, Sherry (Marie Windsor), about the heist. She in turn has told her boyfriend, Val Cannon (Vince Edwards), who decides to rob Clay's team after the robbery. Our third narrative, then, occurs right after Val and a friend crash in the meeting place. George has started a gunfight during which everyone gets killed except for George himself, who leaves his friend Marvin Unger's apartment badly wounded. The events that follow can be retold as follows:

> (3) Johnny arrives at the meeting place at 7.29, still 15 minutes late. As he stops his car, he sees George walking out of the building. Covered with blood he heads toward his own car. On his way he bumps into Johnny's car, yet without noticing the familiar face behind the wheel. Johnny assumes that something has gone wrong. It had been prearranged and agreed to by all that in the event of an emergency before the split, the money was to be saved by whoever had possession of it at that time without any consideration of the fate of the others, the money to be divided in safety at a later date. After what he had seen, not knowing the cause or the circumstances of the others, Johnny had no choice but to save himself and the money. Sticking to the arrangement he does not hesitate and decides to drive on through. Because of what he has seen, he is now forced to buy the largest suitcase he can find.[58]

Paths of Glory (1957)

Kubrick's second collaboration with producer James B. Harris is an anti-war film based on the novel of the same name by Humphrey Cobb. Set in the trenches during World War I, the film tells the story of Colonel Dax (Kirk Douglas) who is faced with the impossible task of capturing a well-defended German key position called the "Ant Hill." The attack, however, leads to a foreseeable failure as none of his men are able to reach the German trenches. In order to avoid blame, Mireau (George Macready), the general overseeing the attack, accuses the regiment of cowardice in the face of the enemy and orders three of its men to be court martialled. In an attempt to save the lives of his men from execution, Dax volunteers to defend them. The trial proves to be a farce and the three soldiers are executed by a firing squad drawn from their own regiment. With this summary in mind, let us now take a closer look at the scene that initiated the attack and all of its subsequent events, namely the cat and mouse game between General Mireau and General Broulard (Adolphe Menjou) that occurs at the beginning of the film and whose explicit events may be rendered as follows:

> (4) France, 1916. General George Broulard arrives at a gracious eighteenth-century chateau which has been converted into military headquarters. Inside, he is greeted by General Paul Mireau who was awaiting him. The welcome is warm and friendly. They call each other by their first names. Broulard wanders about the room admiringly complementing Paul about the interior decoration. Mireau invites him to sit down. Then the subject of the conversation changes as Broulard has come to see him about something "big." He wants Mireau to take the Ant Hill. Mireau smiles patronizingly calling such an act "close to being ridiculous" and "out of the question." Disappointed by his reaction, Broulard gets out of his chair, circles around and now mentions a potential promotion while he holds the arm of Mireau who is walking next to him. They move to a small bar where Mireau pours himself a cognac. He looks at Broulard with an idle expression that seems to say, "All right, let's suppose I'm interested, what's the next move?" Knowing that Mireau is hooked, he returns to his chair. For a moment Mireau is still reluctant as he starts to talk about the responsibility toward his men, but when Broulard for a second time leaves his chair, Mireau is soon there to safeguard his promotion. He prevents Broulard from exiting by drawing him back into the room and when Broulard reacts favourably to his request for artillery support and possible replacements, he convinces himself he "might do the job".[59]

Spartacus (1960)
After *Paths of Glory*, thirty-year-old Kubrick was originally planned to direct *One-Eyed Jacks* for Marlon Brando. Disagreements over the script and casting decisions, however, forced them to part ways.[60] Ultimately, Brando directed the film himself and Kubrick instead was hired to replace Anthony Mann on *Spartacus*. Many (including Kubrick himself) have pointed to this film as the exception in his oeuvre, labelling it as the only film over which he did not had "absolute control." Although he had no part in writing the screenplay and despite his dissatisfaction with his experience while making it, *Spartacus* is a well-thought-out, if somewhat conventional epic and was both critically and commercially a success. The film tells the story of Spartacus (Kirk Douglas), a Thracian slave who, after being treated as an animal in a school for gladiators run by Lentulus Batiatus (Peter Ustinov), breaks free to become the leader of an army of slaves against Rome. Together with his love Varinia (Jean Simmons) he plans to leave Italy by hiring ships at Brundisium from Cilician pirates who could then take them and their fellow slaves home. Meanwhile, in Rome there is a struggle of power going on between Marcus Licinius Crassus (Laurence Olivier) and his populist opponent Gracchus (Charles Laughton). Gracchus knows that his rival will try to seize control of the Roman army under the pretext of the slave crisis. In an attempt to prevent this from happening, Gracchus grants as much military power as possible to his own protégé, a young senator by the name of Julius Caesar (John Gavin). Although Caesar does not share Crassus's disdain for the lower classes of Rome, he is nevertheless taken in by the man's charm and nobility of character. Thus, when Gracchus tells him that he has arranged for Spartacus to leave Italy by making a deal with the Cilician pirates, Caesar regards such tactics as not worthy of a Roman and he decides to change his loyalty to that of his opponent Crassus. Let us take the scene that anticipates this change to be our fifth narrative:

(5) The interior of a Roman public tepidarium. Caesar is having a talk with Metallius and Laelirus about their recent loss against Spartacus. Crassus enters the tepidarium and asks if he can have a few moments of the commander's time. He assumes the affirmations they instantly give and moves off with Caesar to conduct their own private conversation. The relation is warm and friendly. Crassus has difficulties of understanding why Caesar has left him for Gracchus and his mob. He begs him to go back to his own kind, the patrician party, and to stay loyal to Rome, not the mob. Crassus, however, is his friend and he abandons the idea of betraying him. He stands up and walks away at which point Crassus halts him and puts him before a moral dilemma: "which is worse—to betray Gracchus or to betray Rome?" As Crassus leaves, he is called in by Gracchus who lies on his back on a low bench, his middle-parts covered with a snowy white sheet. Crassus seats himself while Caesar is standing silent between the two rivals. They are negotiating the terms under which Crassus will take up command against Spartacus. After hearing those terms, Gracchus casts a keen glance at Caesar, then peers across to Crassus and chuckles "dictatorship." Crassus, however, calls it "order" whereupon he leaves by asking Caesar to convey his respects to his wife. Now Caesar, starts to talk with Gracchus saying that Crassus is "right." To prevent Crassus from saving Rome from the slave army and thereby assuming dictatorship, Gracchus reveals to Caesar that he has arranged for Spartacus to escape Italy by making a deal with the Cilician pirates. Caesar stares at him in shocked silence and responds with involuntary revulsion: "So now we begin to deal with pirates. We bargain with criminals."[61]

Lolita (1962)

After *Spartacus* Kubrick moved to England where he would remain the rest of his life to make all of his subsequent films, the first one being *Lolita*, an adaptation of Nabokov's celebrated, yet controversial novel about a middle-aged man infatuated with a young girl. Although Nabokov was engaged to write the screenplay, which he also delivered, most of his script, however, was eventually not used by Kubrick.[62] The film tells the story of Humbert Humbert (James Mason), a professor of literature who becomes so obsessed with his landlady's 15–16 year old daughter Dolores Haze (Sue Lyon) that he marries the mother just to be near the girl.[63] When Charlotte Haze (Shelley Winters) is killed in a road accident, he travels with Lolita across the US until Quilty (Peter Sellers), a depraved playwright in pursuit of them, ends up depriving Humbert of Lolita. Let the scene where Humbert meets Lolita for the first time to be our sixth narrative description:

(6) Day—the interior of the Haze house. Humbert arrives in West Ramsdale, looking for lodgings for the Summer. Charlotte Haze shows Humbert around her house. Humbert, however, is obviously not interested in her or the house. In an attempt to hasten his exit, he asks her telephone number. Charlotte, however, insists, and in a final attempt to lure him, she shows him the garden in the

backyard. Now comes the shock of dazzling enchantment. From a mat in a pool of sun, half-naked, kneeling, turning about on her knees, Lolita peers at Humbert over dark glasses. Humbert is hooked. He changes his mind and quickly reconsiders Charlotte's offer to rent a room. Curious about what clinched the deal for him to move into the house, Charlotte asks: "What was the decisive factor? Uh, my garden?" Dodging the truth, Humbert replies, "I think it was your cherry pies."[64]

Dr. Strangelove (1964)

Kubrick's next film *Dr. Strangelove or: How I Learned to Stop Worrying and Love the Bomb* is a black comedy about the Cold War fears of a nuclear conflict between the Soviet Union and the United States. Loosely based on Peter George's thriller novel *Red Alert* (1958), the film starts off when a deranged general by the name of Jack D. Ripper (Sterling Hayden) tells Group Captain Lionel Mandrake (Peter Sellers) that the Soviets have attacked Washington and that they are to go to transmit "Wing Attack Plan R," which authorizes a lower-echelon commander to issue an attack after an enemy's first strike has disconnected the US government. To prevent sabotage, Mandrake is ordered to impound all private radios on the base, but when he notices that all the civilian stations are still operating, he assumes that no bombs have been dropped and that the bombers therefore can be called back. However, when he wants to report this news back to Ripper, a cat and mouse game unfolds between the two men. This scene, our seventh narrative so far, is described quite lengthy in the screenplay as follows:

(7) The interior of Burpelson Air Force Base. Group Captain Mandrake rounds a corner and hurries down a corridor to the open door of General Ripper's office. He enters and crosses directly to the desk, where Ripper sits opposite a large aerial photomural of the base. Ripper leans back in his chair as Mandrake approaches and listens impassively as he speaks. Mandrake switches on the transistor radio he carries in one hand, and its thin, rattling music begins, continuing under the conversation with Ripper. Ripper is still silent and impassive, but he taps very lightly on the edge of his desk with a pencil. Ripper leans forward gravely. Mandrake has fully recovered his breath and his aplomb. He murmurs his words negligently, pleased to be able to report his discovery, but as if it would be bad for him to act as if there were anything more serious involved than some small sporting contretemps. As Mandrake speaks, Ripper rises from his desk and walks across to the door of the office, Mandrake follows. Ripper locks the office door, pockets the key, and returns to the desk. Mandrake switches off the radio but remains standing. He glances at his wristwatch. Ripper lights his cigar. Mandrake is puzzled. He tosses the now-silent transistor radio negligently from one hand to the other and shifts his weight into a rather indolent stance. He speaks with excruciating nonchalance. Now, at last, the staggering significance of what is happening finally hits Mandrake. He may not yet understand the

> Why of it, but the What is clearly out on the table between the two men. Mandrake is silent for a long, long moment. Then he speaks . . . very softly. Ripper, puffing leisurely, advices Mandrake to just take it easy. Again, Mandrake is silent. Thoughtfully, he places the transistor radio on the desk, gives a slow, exceedingly smart, British Military salute, and assumes a very R.A.F. stance to speak his piece, clearly and firmly. Mandrake crosses briskly to the door. Ripper watches impassively as Mandrake tries the door momentarily forgetting it is locked. Mandrake now crosses from the door back to Ripper's desk. The negligent murmur, the nonchalant manner can survive the situation no longer; Mandrake's voice breaks unnaturally. Ripper's face is like stone, like something carved high on Mt. Rushmore. His long cigar juts out like a weapon. Casually, he moves a file folder from his desk, revealing a .45 automatic. Ripper's great stone face speaks . . . and speaks with the voice of rock mountains—heavy, inexorable, crushing. Mandrake's expression is even, yet with a hint of desperation, as he steals a quick glance at the gun on Ripper's desk. Twin pinpoints of light appear in Ripper's eyes. A tiny tremor of pent-up intensity quivers his voice.[65]

2001: A Space Odyssey (1968)

After the success of *Dr. Strangelove* Stanley Kubrick embarked on a highly ambitious project that would become a landmark, science fiction classic and one of the greatest achievements in the history of cinema: *2001: A Space Odyssey*. To help him writing the story, Kubrick called upon the expertise of British novelist Arthur C. Clarke, who was then one of the leading figures in the genre of science-fiction. The two men agreed to co-write a film story entitled *Journey Beyond the Stars*, which was then adapted into *2001*. Both film and book consist of four episodes, three of which are announced on-screen by an intertitle. The first part, "The Dawn of Man," offers a recount of the events that gave birth to men's intellectual leap forward: a primeval ape man, in the story revealed as Moon-Watcher, comes in contact with a mysterious black monolith after which he becomes endowed with intelligence. In the second "part," which is left untitled in the film, we follow Dr. Heywood Floyd (William Sylvester) as he travels to the lunar surface where millions of years later an identical monolith is discovered. In the third part, "Jupiter Mission," a team of five astronauts including Bowman (Keir Dullea), Pool (Gary Lockwood) and three hibernating crew members, are headed toward Jupiter to trace down the origin of the signal transmitted by the monolith. During their journey, however, they fall in conflict with HAL 9000, the computer on board of the ship the Discovery, a struggle that eventually will lead to Poole's death and the shutdown of HAL. In the fourth and last part, "Jupiter and Beyond the Infinite," we follow Bowman, now the only survivor, as he undergoes a mystical and undefinable journey through space and time. There are many memorable scenes to choose from, but let us pick out the scene where Moon-Watcher becomes gifted with intelligence, together with his encounter with the monolith which precedes it, as our eight narrative:

(8) As Moon-Watcher sleeps at night with his cave-mates (woman + child?) he is awakened by a strange sound that has never been heard before (the transparent cube). On the way to the stream next morning the tribe comes upon the cube (15 foot square, transparent). Moon-Watcher examines it (sniffs, touches, tastes). It is not food so he rejects it and the tribe walks on. As Moon-Watcher's tribe is leaving, the cube all at once begins to give off a pulsating light and sound which seem to have an hypnotic effect on the man-apes, who slowly turn and move around the cube and freeze in their places as they watch it. (As they turn toward the cube and come to their positions of watching, their bodies reflect the pulsating light and sound of the cube.) Soon the sound and light stop and the tribe rises and goes on its way as though they have no recollection of what they have seen. (We do not see what the cube is giving off but the narrator tells us what it is teaching them a lesson but does not tell us what the lesson is.). Once again Moon-Watcher and his tribe are walking toward the stream in the morning. Moon-Watcher is passing through an elephant skeleton that they usually pass when he is caught by a strange feeling (it is almost like a magical spell). He is trying to remember something. He picks up one of the elephant bones and begins to swing it about slowly (not violently) almost in a dance-like fashion. As Moon-Watcher moves about he sees a tapir passing. He stops and still as if in a spell brings the bone down on the tapir's head. He is killed instantly.[66]

A Clockwork Orange (1971)

After the critical and commercial success of *2001*, Kubrick was destined to follow up his science fiction epic with a historical and biographical epic about the life of Napoleon. Extensive preparations and logistic arrangements were already far advanced.[67] However, in the time it took Kubrick to finish all the pre-production work and the screenplay, other competing Napoleon projects were already in the pipeline with Dino De Laurentiis' production of *Waterloo* (1970) being the most ambitious one. The film proved to be a box office failure and MGM, cautious of repeating this financial loss, abandoned the project thus turning Napoleon into one of the greatest films never made. Disheartened, Kubrick left the studio for Warner Brothers, where he made *A Clockwork Orange* instead. Adapted from the novel of Anthony Burgess, the film tells the story of Alex (Malcolm McDowell) who is the gang leader of a group of juvenile delinquents which he refers to as his "Droogs." Sharpened up by the consummation of drug-laced milk, "moloko plus," they indulge themselves in acts of "ultra-violence." After getting betrayed by his fellow gang members, Alex eventually ends up in jail where he volunteers to take part in a program that will accelerate his release: the fictional Ludovico Technique, a new type of intense aversion therapy that reprograms people's brains to be physically repulsed by thoughts of lustful sexuality and violence. Let us take the scene where Alex undergoes the treatment to be our ninth narrative. The events are retold over the visual presentation by the film's protagonist himself who assumes the role of a narrative guide:

(9) Where I was taken to, brothers, was like no cine I'd been in before. I was bound up in a straight-jacket and my guliver was strapped to a headrest with like wires running away from it. Then they clamped like lidlocks on my eyes so I could not shut them no matter how hard I tried. It seemed a bit crazy to me, but I let them get on with what they wanted to get on with. If I was to be a free young malchick in a fortnight's time, I would put with much in the meantime, my brothers. . . . The sounds were real horroshow. You could sloshy the screams and moans very realistic and you could even get the heavy breathing and panting of the tolchocking malchicks at the same time. And then, what do you know, soon our dear old friend, the red, red vino on tap. The same in all places like it's put out by the same big firm, began to flow. It was beautiful. It's funny how the colors of the real world only seem really real when you viddy them on a screen. . . . Now all the time I was watching this, I was beginning to get very aware of like not feeling all that well, but I tried to forget this, concentrating on a young devotchka, who was being given the old in-out, in-out, first by one malchick, then another, then another. . . . When it came to the sixth or seventh malchick, leering and smecking and then going into it, I began to feel really sick. But I could not shut my glazzies and even if I tried to move my glazballs about I still not get out of the line of fire of this picture.[68]

Barry Lyndon (1975)

A Clockwork Orange was followed by *Barry Lyndon*, a screen adaptation of William Makepeace Thackeray's 1844 novel *The Luck of Barry Lyndon*. The film is divided into two acts. The first act contains an account of the events leading up to Barry's (Ryan O'Neil) engagement with the beautiful Countess of Lyndon (Marisa Berenson) through whom he will finally acquire the style and title of Barry Lyndon. The second act, by contrast, contains an account of the misfortunes and disasters which befell Barry Lyndon. We first follow the title character as he is forced to leave his Irish home town for the city of Dublin after allegedly shooting the British captain John Quin (Leonard Rossiter) in a set-up duel. This duel was caused by his cousin, the fickle Nora Brady (Gay Hamilton), who had earlier on seduced Barry, but has now left him for the more prosperous British officer. On his way to Dublin he becomes the victim of a robbery which forces him to join the British army. Engaged in a military conflict with the Kingdom of France (i.e., the Seven Years' War), Barry's regiment is sent to fight in Germany whereupon the futility of warfare and the death of his good friend, Captain Grogan (Godfrey Quigley), encourages him to desert the army to seek fortune and stature elsewhere. He seizes the opportunity by stealing the horse and identification papers of a British officer. En route, however, he is exposed by the Prussian Captain Potzdorf (Hardy Krüger) who threatens to turn him over again to the British side (where he faces execution for desertion) unless he joins the Prussian army (an ally of the British). During a skirmish he rescues the life of Potzdorf from a burning building. As a token of gratitude for his loyalty and his service to the regiment he is discharged from the army and put into the secret service of the Minister of Police where he is entrusted with the assignment to watch upon the actions of an Irish gentleman who calls himself the Chevalier du Balibari (Patrick Magee), a noted gambler and libertine whose allegiance is in question. However, when Barry meets the Chevalier the events take a different turn. Let us take this meeting to be our tenth narrative. As with *A Clockwork Orange* the events, as visually presented, are narrated through a voice-over, albeit this time in third-person mode:

(10) It was very imprudent of him, but when Barry saw the splendour of the Chevalier's appearance, the nobleness of his manner, he felt it impossible to keep disguise with him. Those who have never been out of their country know little what it is to hear a friendly voice in captivity and as many a man who would not understand the cause of the burst of feeling which was now about to take place. With tears in his eyes, he confesses to the Chevalier that he is an Irishman named Redmond Barry who was put into his service to serve as a watch upon his actions. Having confessed, Barry starts to cry louder. The Chevalier now stands up from his chair, he walks to Barry and embraces him in a comforting way. The Chevalier was as much as affected as Barry at thus finding one of his countrymen. For he too was an exile from home. And a friendly voice, a look, brought the old country back to his memory again.[69]

The Shining (1980)

Kubrick's next film is a screen adaptation of Stephen King's *The Shining.* The film tells the story of Jack Torrance (Jack Nicholson), a would-be writer who takes on the job of winter caretaker at the Overlook Hotel in the Colorado Rockies which will allow him five months of piece and isolation to write his book. He is, however, not entirely alone as his wife Wendy (Shelley Duvall) and five-year young son Danny (Danny Lloyd) are joining him. Together with the hotel's cook, Dick Hallorann (Scatman Crothers), Danny shares a telepathic gift which enables him to see glimpses of the hotel's horrifying past. During the winter of 1970, the previous winter caretaker, Charles Grady, suffered a complete mental breakdown. He killed his wife and twin girls with an axe before committing suicide. Like his predecessor, Jack gradually succumbs to cabin fever. Becoming increasingly short-tempered and violent, he ultimately degenerates into an axe-wielding maniac and a life-threatening danger to his wife and son. Let us take the scene where Wendy becomes aware of Jack's mental insanity by accidentally finding out what Jack was typing all the time as our eleventh narrative:

(11) Wendy enters the lounge. The room is silent and empty. She walks over to his table and stops near the manuscript which is stacked next to his typewriter. She stands there for a few seconds wondering what to do, when her eye alights upon the page in the typewriter. She leans over to look at it. It reads: "All work and no play makes Jack a dull boy." She sees that this phrase has been typed in single lines, one on top of the other, down the entire page. She stares at it in disbelief for several seconds, and then picks up a few pages from the stack. They all say the same thing: "All work and no play makes Jack a

dull boy." Wendy clumsily leafs through the thick stack and all the pages are exactly the same. "How do you like it?," says Jack. Wendy whirls around and sees Jack, standing, smiling at her. . . . Wendy is terrified and doesn't know what to say. Wendy has a predicament. Considering the monstrous implications of what she's just read, she doesn't know how to proceed. Wendy starts backing out of the room, still holding the soft-ball bat. Jack follows her. . . . He laughs at his joke. Wendy swings the bat in a defensive arc in front of her. . . . She swings bat and hits him on head. He falls down the stairs and out cold.[70]

Full Metal Jacket (1987)

The Shining was followed up by the Vietnam war drama *Full Metal Jacket*. Based on Gustav Hasford's novel *The Short-Timers* the film is divided into two parts. The first part takes place at the U.S. marine boot camp at Parris Island and shows how a group of young men are being trained and turned into a platoon of lethal human killing machines by their abusive and foul-mouthed drill instructor, Gunnery Sergeant Hartman (former drill sergeant R. Lee Ermey). Among the recruits is Private "Joker" (Matthew Modine) who does not take the army very serious, but nevertheless manages to impress the sergeant which earns him a promotion to squad leader and instructor of a tall overweight private called "Gomer Pyle" (Vincent D'Onofrio). Bullied, beaten and dehumanized, Pyle ultimately goes insane and finally commits suicide after first having shot Hartman. The film, then, moves ahead to the second part which focuses on the actual war in Vietnam. Joker is now a war correspondent and has yet to see real combat. That all changes, however, when he is sent on a mission to follow the actions of the Lusthog Squad at Phu Bai. The film ends with Joker performing a mercy-kill on a mortally wounded female sniper who had previously killed three of their men. Let us take this latter scene to be our twelfth narrative:

(12) Joker, Animal Mother, Rafter Man, Donlon and T.H.E. Rock are standing over the female sniper who is lying on the ground badly wounded. She is praying in Vietnamese. At one moment Animal Mother suggests to "get the fuck outta here." These words, however, are met by resistance of Joker who now looks up at Animal Mother replying to him, "What about her?" Animal Mother responds back by saying that they should "let her rot." The young girl utters a deep moan of pain, "Dau qua" ("it hurts"). "We can't just leave her here," Joker returns. Animal Mother becomes more aggressive calling Joker an "asshole who is fresh out of friends now that Cowboy is wasted." He asserts his authority by saying that he is "running the squad now." Joker responds, "I'm not trying to run the squad. I'm just saying we can't leave her like this." The sniper starts to groan in English: "Shoot me, shoot me ..." "If you want to waste her. Go on waste her," says Animal Mother. Joker lifts his .45, aims it carefully and pulls the trigger. Bang! Silence.[71]

Eyes Wide Shut (1999)
Kubrick's long anticipated last film is an adaptation of Arthur Schnitzler's 1926 novella *Traumnovelle* (*Dream Story*). Relocated from early twentieth-century Vienna to 1990s New York City, *Eyes Wide Shut* tells the story of Dr. Bill Harford (Tom Cruise) who after his wife Alice (Nicole Kidman) has confessed to him about a momentary urge she once had to sleep with a naval officer a year earlier, is plagued by the taunting desire to actually commit what she has only imagined in her mind, namely having sex with someone else. He embarks on a nightly journey through the cold winter streets of dreamlike Manhattan, eventually ending up unlawfully in a massive masked orgy of a hidden secret society. When, at the end of the film, he returns to his wife who is asleep, and he sees the mask he had worn the night before lying next to her, he collapses emotionally from guilt. It is now Bill who has to make a confession. Let this scene to be our thirteenth and last narrative:

(13) The interior of Bill's apartment. Night. Bill quietly enters and goes to his study to undress, as he did the night before. He enters the bedroom as quietly as possible. He hears Alice breathing softly and regularly and sees the outline of her head on the pillow. Unexpectedly, his heart is filled with a feeling of tenderness and even of security. Then he notices something dark quite near Alice's face. It has definite outlines like the shadowy features of a human face, and it is lying on his pillow. For a moment his heart stops beating, but an instant later he sees what it is, and he looks at the mask he had worn the night before. All at once he reaches the end of his strength. He utters a loud and painful sob—quite unexpectedly—and sinks down beside her, burying his head in her arms, and cries. A minute later he feels a soft hand caressing his hair. He looks into Alice's worried eyes. Bill says, "I will tell you everything." Bill still crying.[72]

4. Toward a conceptual blueprint of Kubrick's work

What then do these thirteen descriptions tell us about the concepts conveyed by the films of Kubrick? There are two fundamental observations to be made. Firstly, the descriptions contain a lot of words that denote *mental events* of characters and secondly, because they are embedded in narratives, these mental events are *causally* related to other events (both physical and mental), that is, they pertain to a conceptual structure known as *mental causation*. Let us explore each observation more in detail.

Mental events
The first observation is obviously not unique to the cinema of Kubrick. As has been frequently stressed in the literature, readers and viewers understand novels and films primarily by following the "actions" of the minds of characters in the story worlds. Palmer goes even so far as to say that "in essence, narrative is the description of fictional mental functioning."[73] The thirteen descriptions presented here are no different in this regard. Sidney

cannot control his desire for the girl. General Mireau changes his mind about attacking the Ant Hill when he is offered a promotion. The same can be said of Humbert who decides to move into the house after seeing the landlady's daughter. Moon-Watcher's perceptual contact with the monolith is followed by a cognitive leap forward. Joker has an argument with Animal Mother because he cannot bear the sight of the suffering girl. Bill has an emotional breakdown after seeing the mask lying on the pillow next to his wife and so on. These events can all be situated within the fictional being's property domain of "the mind—of the inner life and the personality—of characters."[74] They refer to mental categories such as cognition, perception and emotion which, following Barrett can all be labelled as "ontologically subjective" as opposed to "ontologically objective."[75] Both terms were introduced by Searle to refer to two different modes of existence.[76] Something is labelled as "ontologically subjective" insofar its existence depends entirely on the experience of a human or animal subject. By contrast, something is called "ontologically objective" insofar it has an existence independent of any experience. Extending this distinction, Barrett, then, has argued that mental events are essentially ontologically subjective because the majority of the words we use to describe the psychological categories of the mind such as thoughts, cognitions, memories, emotions and beliefs are all observer-dependent. In contrast to objective entities such as mountains or molecules they do not have an existence independent of perceptual experience. As Barrett points out, "these categories have been formed and named by the human mind to represent and explain the human mind."[77] Take for instance the category of anger. As she writes, "I experience myself as angry or I see your face as angry or I experience the rat's behavior as angry, but anger does not exist independent of someone's perception of it. Without a perceiver, there are only internal sensations and a stream of physical actions."[78]

Characterizing a mental event as ontologically subjective is useful to contrast it with what it is not, but it does not, however, provide us much insight into its internal building blocks. By virtue of which conceptual aspects or components can we define mental events? Here we may turn to Narayanan who has argued that our structuring of all events, concrete and abstract (such as mental events are), arises from the way we structure the movements of our bodies.[79] He provides a rough and ready structure that will serve well as a literal skeleton for our conception of a mental event. Following Narayanan's work, Lakoff and Johnson summarize the stages of this literal skeleton as in table 1.5.[80]

Table 1.5 The literal skeleton for our conception of event structure (after Narayanan).

Initial State	Whatever is required for the event is satisfied
Start	The starting up process for the event
End of Start	The end of the starting up process and the beginning of the main process
Main Process	The central aspects of the event
Possible Interactions	Disruptions of the main process
Possible Continuation of Iteration	The perpetuation or repetition of the main process
Resultant State	The state resulting from the main process

An event thus always involves a change of state from an initial state to a resulting state. It is not difficult to see, then, how this general and literal definition applies to mental events. When a human or fictional being experiences a particular mental event (e.g., perception, emotion, cognition), this experience is seen as a change of the subject's state from an initial state which is the negation of the mental event (not feeling X, not perceiving Y, not knowing Z) to a resultant state which is its confirmation (feeling X, perceiving Y, knowing Z). For instance, when Moon-Watcher was endowed with intelligence his state has changed from a non-cognitive state (e.g., not having the idea of using the bone as a weapon) to a cognitive one (i.e., the idea of using the bone as a weapon). The same can be said of relationship events such as love or friendship. At the beginning, the relationship between General Broulard and General Mireau starts as friendly and amical. This initial state changes, however, as soon as General Broulard mentions the attack on the Ant Hill. The promotion, in turn, can be seen as yet another cause of the change of state of the relationship. Similar examples can be drawn from each of the thirteen descriptions.

Mental causation

Mental events do not operate in isolation. As part of narratives, they are engaged in causal relationships with other events or entities (either physical or mental). Sidney shoots the girl after losing his mental control. Davey throws himself out of the window after first contemplating his escape route. Bill starts to experience an intense emotional state after seeing the mask lying next to his wife. Alex becomes sick when he sees violence. Moon-Watcher starts to "see" the bone as a weapon after first having encountered the monolith. As we already have stressed in the introduction to this book, these causal relations of the mind with the world are in the field of philosophy of mind known as instances of *mental causation*.[81] They are central to our conception of ourselves as agents and often taken for granted in everyday experience and in scientific practice. The suspense you experience when little Danny turns a corner to face the Grady twins causes you to cover your eyes with your hands just like Danny does. Your intention to go and see *2001* on the big screen causes you to get into your car and so on. Depending on the role of the mental event (cause or effect) and the nature of the other event (mental or physical) we may distinguish between three types of mental causation: *physical-to-mental causation*, *mental-to-mental causation* and *mental-to-physical causation*.[82] Let us briefly address each one of them.

Physical-to-mental causation occurs when a physical event is the determining factor (i.e., cause) for a mental event. As Davidson has pointed out, the most fundamental example of this type and at the same time the most important source of knowledge relevant to human understanding of the external world, is perception.[83] Perception occurs when an "ontologically objective state of affairs in the world outside your head" causes an "ontologically subjective visual experience of that state of affairs entirely inside your head."[84] It is not difficult to see how this causality may be applied to the various descriptions. Moon-Watcher perceives the monolith because its appearance has caused him to perceive it. Bill perceives the mask, because the presence of the mask is causally responsible for Bill's perceptual experience of the mask. Diagrammatically, the situation of physical-to-mental causation (the category to which the perceptual scene belongs) can be represented as in figure 1.4 (after Searle).[85]

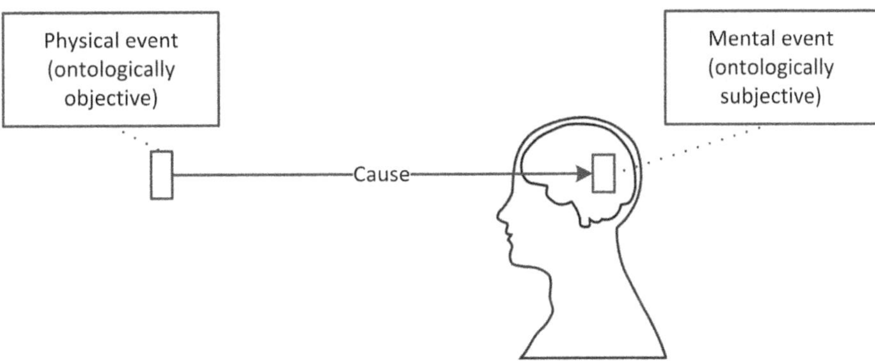

Figure 1.4 A causal theory of perception (after Searle).

Mental-to-mental causation occurs when a mental event is the determining factor of another mental event. As with physical-to-mental causation this type is essential to human experience. The visual sight of the girl causes Sidney to desire her. Bill experiences an intense feeling of sadness after seeing the mask. Barry's perception of The Chevalier causes him to cry. Seeing the sniper suffering, evokes feelings of empathy in Joker and so on. Diagrammatically, the generalizing picture of mental-to-mental causation can be put as in figure 1.5. Notice that the first mental event in the examples above (i.e., perception) always presumes the presence of a physical event (i.e., the object perceived).

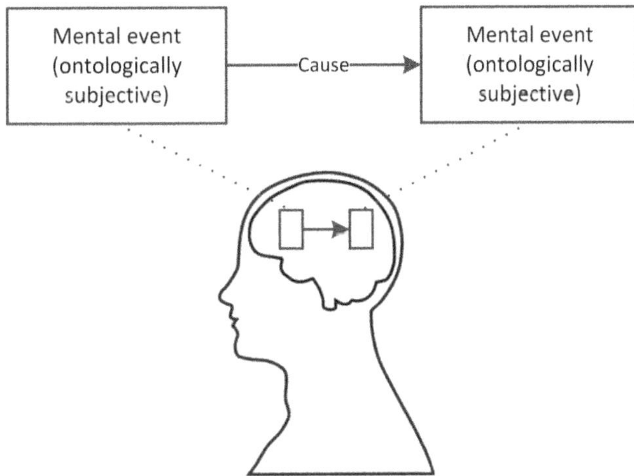

Figure 1.5 Mental-to-mental causation.

Mental-to-physical causation occurs when a mental event further triggers off a physical event. If perception constituted the most obvious example to illustrate physical-to-mental causation, then behaviors and actions are perhaps the most obvious cases to show how causality may run from the mental to the physical. For instance, Sidney shoots the girl out of panic of losing the girl. Mandrake crosses briskly to the door to warn the others that Ripper has gone insane. Alex starts to feel sick when he sees the violence on-screen. Both the characters of Barry and Bill start to cry out of sadness and so on. The two aspects of mental-to-physical causation can be represented diagrammatically as in figure 1.6.

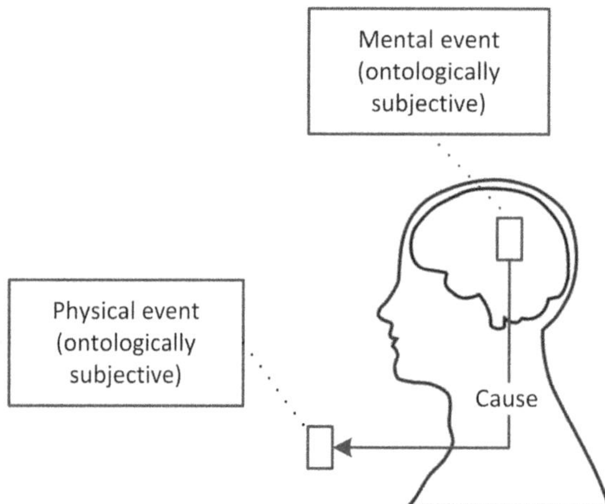

Figure 1.6 Mental-to-physical causation.

Notice the difference in ontological status between the physical event discussed earlier (the object seen) and the physical event under discussion here (behavior). In the case of perception, the physical event was ontologically objective. The entity seen has an existence independent of human experience. The same, however, does not apply to the physical event of behavior. Because behaviors are actions (i.e., descriptions of physical movements) with a meaning that is inferred by an observer, they can be labelled as ontologically subjective.[86]

A flow of mental causation then can be defined as a chain that combines at least two or more of the three types of mental causation above. One such type of chain is known in literature as the "flow-of-emotion scenario" or the "Western folk theory of emotion."[87] This scenario refers to a conceptualization of emotions according to which feelings of emotions are embodied in a larger chain of causation which involves all three types of mental causation discussed above. In the structure of English, the flow-of-emotion scenario may be expressed within the structure of a simple sentence as in: "Bill started to cry at the sight of the mask." Here the causality runs as follows: from the physical (the mask) to the mental (Bill's perception of the mask), from the mental (Bill's perception of the mask) to the mental (Bill's emotional experience), and from the mental (Bill's emotional experience) back again to the physical (Bill's crying). Thus, the flow-of-emotion scenario comprises all three types of mental causation of which its visual diagram may be represented as in figure 1.7.

It is important to stress that this flow-of-emotion scenario is a *folk theory* of mental causation and not a scientific theory. It involves an "intuitive causal explanatory 'theory' of emotion that people construct to explain, interpret, and intervene on the world around them."[88] Therefore it should not be confused with traditional expert theories of emotion such as behaviorist models of emotion or identity approaches to emotion.[89] These theories seek to find the objective criteria for measuring emotions by observing distinct patterns of physical changes such as changes in behavior (e.g., facial expressions), body (e.g., variations in heart rate, blood pressure), or brain (activity in brain circuits). Barrett calls these theories appropriately "materialist theories" in the sense that they, despite their differences in the specifics of how emotions are caused and manifested, have one crucial thing in common: they assume that mental events such as emotional experiences are caused by and therefore can be redefined as nothing but these physical fingerprints.[90]

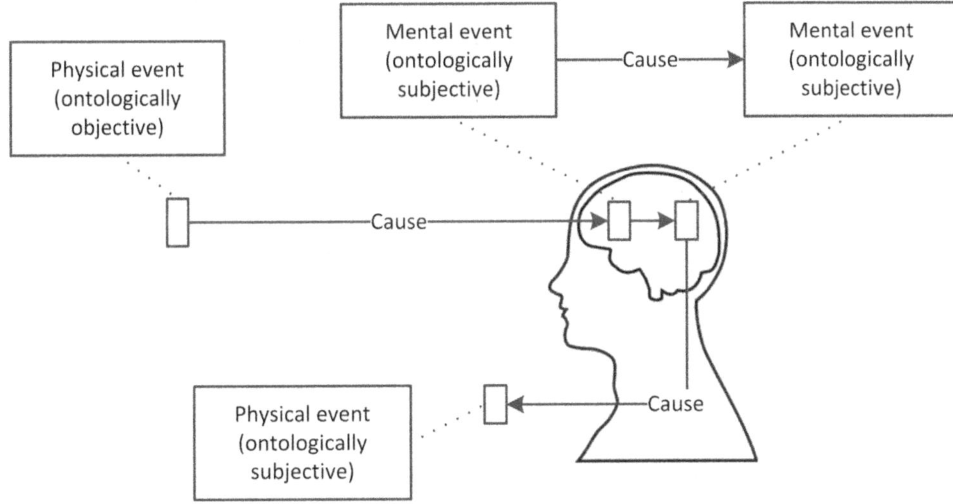

Figure 1.7 The flow-of-mental causation.

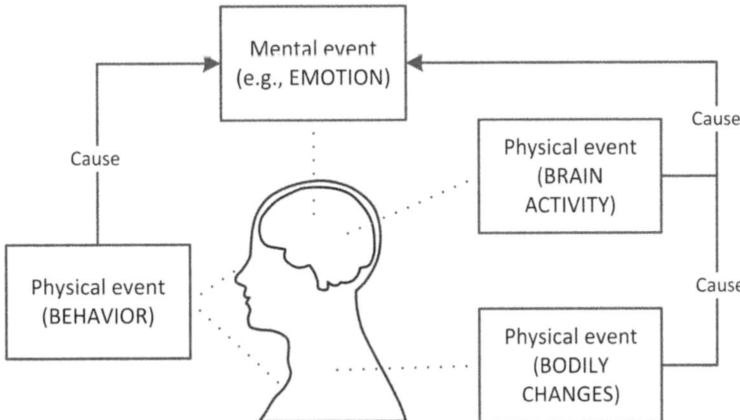

Figure 1.8 The materialist scientific account of mental causation.

It should be emphasized that in this book we are not so much interested in scientific materialist theories of mental causation (descriptions of physical fingerprints), but in the everyday folk stories of mental causation as these are the stories that are construed by the viewer when seeing Kubrick's films.

5. The grounding problem of mental causation

As the reader already may have inferred by now, the nature of the concepts under discussion here poses us with a fundamental theoretical problem which comes to the surface as soon as we connect the conceptual structure of mental causation to the construction of situation models in narrative comprehension, as discussed at the beginning of this chapter. If narrative comprehension depends on the viewer's capability of indexing events along various dimensions, how then can such comprehension be achieved with regard to a type of event that is neither purely physical nor spatially constrained (i.e., the abstract mental event)? Consider, for example, the two causal relations that are inherent to the folk theory of emotion, namely (1) the causal relation between a physical event O and a subject S's perception of O and (2) the causal relation between S's perception of O and S's emotion. Both S's perception of O and S's emotional state are two non-spatial entities. They both describe two inner mental events of a subject S.

Hence, in virtue of what, then, can (1) S's perception of O interact with the outer event O, and (2) S's perception of O interact with S's emotional state? Indeed, if both entities were spatially constrained like two objects, causal interaction could well be achieved by the relative spatial locations of the substances. But if both entities are non-spatial, relative spatial locations are unavailable to attain interaction. The reader may see in this dilemma a further manifestation of what in the field of philosophy of mind is more broadly known as the "pairing problem."[91] The pairing problem refers to the problem of how mental events can be paired with other events given that they, as immaterial substances, lie outside physical space. Kim illustrates this problem with the following thought experiment:

> It is metaphysically possible for there to be two souls, A and B, with the same intrinsic properties such that they both act in a certain way at the same time and as a result a material object, C, undergoes a change. Moreover, it is the action of A, not that of B, that is the cause of the physical change in C. What makes it the case that this is so? What pairing relation pairs the first soul, but not the second soul, with the physical object? Since souls, as immaterial substances, are outside physical space and cannot bear spatial relations to anything, it is not possible to invoke spatial relations to ground the pairing.[92]

Consequently, in order to overcome this problem, one might assume that both mental events have to be spatially grounded. It is here that we may find a solution to this problem in the notion of embodiment. As Kim argues, "what is needed to solve the pairing problem for immaterial minds is a kind of mental coordinate system, a 'mental space,' in which these minds are each given a unique 'location' at a time."[93] If mental events were, like physical events, located in space, causal pairing could be achieved by the relative spatial locations of the substances. Indeed, one can only index a relation between a mental event and another event (mental or physical) as continuous along the dimension of space, if both events have a location (including the mental one). In other words, it is only when the rather impoverished literal structure of a mental event, as discussed earlier, is fleshed out by experiential knowledge, that the spatial pairing can take place, and the events can be indexed by the spectator along the dimensions of causality and time.

By making a claim for the importance of spatial and bodily knowledge in our comprehension of mental causation, we do not yet, however, provide an answer to the question of how this grounding can be realized. How can the situational meaning structure of mental causation be fleshed out by spatial knowledge? Addressing this problem of grounding is of fundamental importance to define the conditions under which viewers perceive causality among mental events in the context of film viewing. That is, viewers can only construe a situation model of mental causation, as conveyed non-verbally insofar (1) this conceptual structure is embodied and (2) this embodied conceptual structure is fleshed out by the visual resources of cinema. It is only when both conditions are satisfied that the viewer will be able to index the events of mental causation along the various dimensions that guide narrative comprehension. Diagrammatically, we might represent both conditions as in figure 1.9.

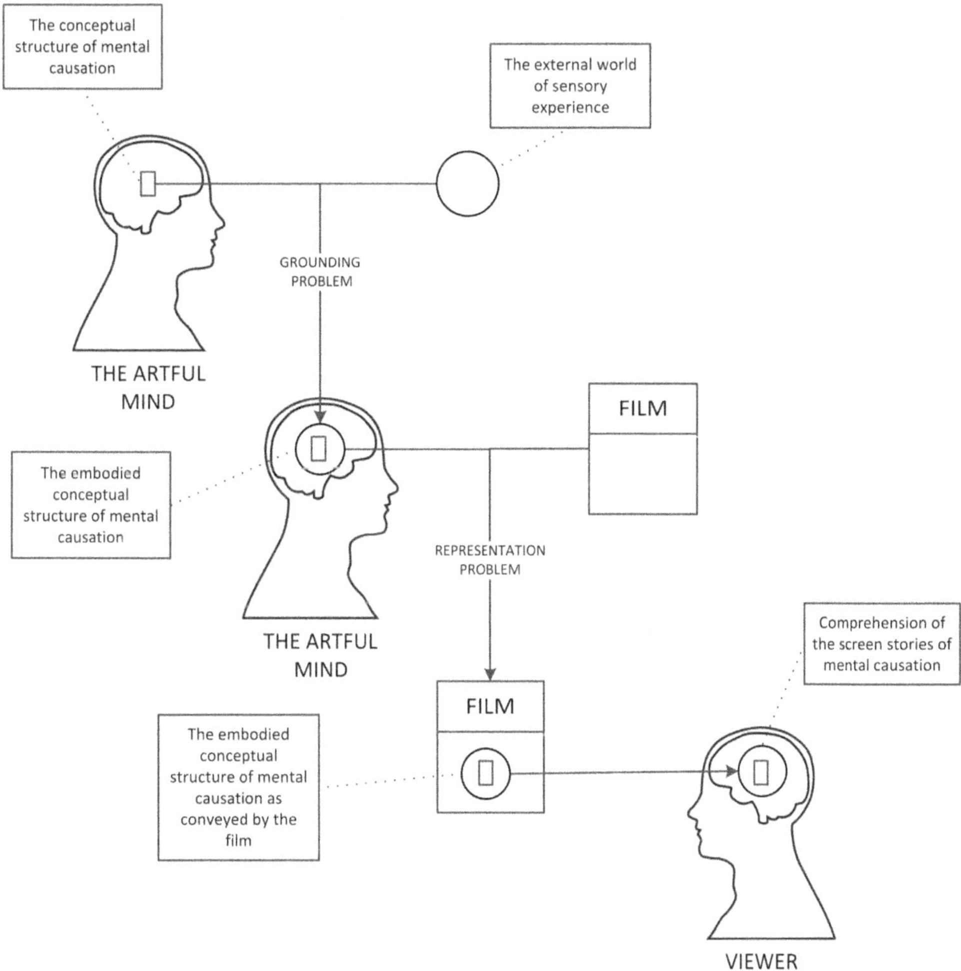

Figure 1.9 The grounding problem of mental causation, followed by its representational problem.

As this figure shows, the grounding problem arises from the relationship between conceptual structure and the external world of sensory experience.[94] As we have seen in the introduction, exploring this relationship has been central to the advocates of the embodied cognition thesis. Hence, the crucial task then will be to show how, more specifically, the conceptual structure of mental causation is informed by bodily knowledge. This problem will be dealt with more in detail in the subsequent chapter of this book in which the thesis of embodied cognition will be clarified through a discussion of three theoretical notions derived from the field of cognitive linguistics: image schema, conceptual metaphor and conceptual metonymy. Once we have established that the conceptual structure of mental causation is fleshed out, in the sense that it is determined by the nature of human embodiment, we can then examine how this embodied conceptual structure can be depicted in film. This problem, let us call it for sake of simplicity, the problem of representation, concerns the nature of the relationship between embodied conceptual structure and film. As stated, this relationship lies at the heart of the paradox of cinematic meaning. The theoretical challenges that go hand-in-hand with a discussion of this relationship will be the topic of the third chapter of this book.

6. Conclusion

The purpose of this chapter was to identify the concepts out of which the situational meanings of the films of Kubrick are constructed. In order to locate these concepts, four levels of conceptual description were proposed: the novel, the screenplay, the film and the recollections of the film viewer. Assessing the conceptual usefulness of each level in relation to Kubrick's unique method of adapting novels into films, allowed us, subsequently, to describe thirteen scenes, one conceptual description for each film that the director made. From these verbal descriptions we were then able to extract a conceptual structure that, with the help of the field of philosophy of mind, was further defined as the general and overarching conceptual structure of mental causation. The nature of this structure, in turn, necessitated us to introduce the crucial role of embodiment, that is, in order for a viewer to construct a situation model of mental causation, two conditions have to be met: (1) the impoverished literal structure of mental causation has to be embodied and (2) this embodied conceptual structure, in turn, has to be conveyed non-verbally to the viewer. The problems to which both conditions unavoidably give rise, were referred to as the grounding problem and the problem of representation, respectively. In the subsequent chapters, we will address both problems successively, starting with the first one.

Notes

1. Kubrick, "Words and Movies," 14.
2. For good conceptual discussions of the notion of narrative in relation to film, we refer the reader to two classical studies in the field: Bordwell's *Narration in the Fiction Film* and Branigan's *Narrative Comprehension and Film.*
3. Bordwell and Thompson, *Film Art*, 69.
4. Ibid., 69.
5. Ibid., 69.

6. Branigan, *Narrative Comprehension*, 3.
7. Ibid, 12.
8. Two books, both published in 1983, were pivotal for the development of this perspective. They are Johnson-Laird, *Mental Models*; and Van Dijk and Kintsch, *Strategies in Discourse Comprehension*. For a good review of research on the use of situation models, see also Zwaan and Radvansky, "Situation Models."
9. Zwaan and Radvansky, "Situation Models," 162.
10. Bransford, Barclay and Franks, "Sentence Memory." For a discussion, see also Zwaan and Radvansky, "Situation Models," 162–163.
11. Ibid., 191.
12. Ibid., 195.
13. Ibid., 195.
14. Zwaan and Radvansky, "Situation Models," 163.
15. Zwaan, Langston and Graesser, "The Construction of Situation Models." In addition to Zwaan and Radvansky, "Situation Models," 162–163, see also Zwaan, Magliano and Graesser, "Situation-Model Construction"; and Zwaan, "Situation Models."
16. The concept of *working memory* is a theoretical concept central to cognitive psychology and neuroscience and can be construed as a cognitive system with a limited storage capacity that runs perceptual simulations of the things just perceived or about to be perceived (e.g., language, visual experiences). From the perspective of perceptual symbol theory, this system is inherently modal, meaning that the symbols stored in this system share the same perceptual systems that gave rise to them. For a discussion, see Barsalou, "Perceptual Symbol Systems," 604.
17. Zwaan, Magliano and Graesser, "Situation-Model Construction," 387.
18. Magliano, Miller and Zwaan, "Indexing Space and Time," 535.
19. Bordwell and Thompson, *Film Art*, 310–333.
20. Magliano, Miller and Zwaan, "Indexing Space and Time," 535.
21. Bordwell and Thompson, *Film Art*, 70.
22. Ibid., 505.
23. Ibid., 71.
24. McQuiston, *We'll Meet Again*, 57–58. See also Gengaro, *Listening to Stanley Kubrick*, 232.
25. Cahill, "The *Rolling Stone* Interview," 196.
26. Ibid., 195.
27. Kubrick, "Words and Movies," 14.
28. For good discussions of Kubrick's work from the perspective of adaptation, see, among others, Pezzotta, *Stanley Kubrick*; Welsh, "A Kubrick Tribute"; Jenkins, *Stanley Kubrick*; and Stuckey, "Re-Writing Nabokov's *Lolita*." See also the special issue, Hunter, "Kubrick and Adaptation."
29. Welsh, "A Kubrick Tribute," 253.
30. Pezzotta, *Stanley Kubrick*, 17–33.
31. Johnson, "Writing *The Shining*," 56.
32. Pezzotta, *Stanley Kubrick*, 27.
33. Gorchakov, *Stanislavsky Directs*, 353–359.
34. Gelmis, "The Film Director as Superstar," 103. For other Kubrick references to Stanislavski, see also Strick and Houston, "Modern Times," 64 and Ciment's interview with Kubrick's early collaborator James B. Harris in Ciment, *Kubrick*, 202.
35. Gorchakov, *Stanislavsky Directs*, 356.
36. For a good history of these polemics, see Pezzotta, *Stanley Kubrick*, 15–33.
37. Raphael, *Eyes Wide Open*, 177–179.
38. Nabokov, foreword to *Lolita*, xii-xiii.

39. Burgess, *You've Had Your Time*, 244–245. See also Pezzotta, *Stanley Kubrick*, 30.
40. Gelmis, "The Film Director as Superstar," 95–96.
41. Jenkins, *Stanley Kubrick*, 8.
42. As to the question of accessibility, scholars today find themselves very fortunate as since 2007 various script versions of almost all of Kubrick's films can be consulted at the University of Arts London (UAL). This was made possible by the Kubrick Estate who, under supervision of Jan Harlan, the director's executive producer and brother-in-law, donated the accumulated material at the Kubrick family home "Childwickbury" near St Albans, to the university. This archive, known as *The Stanley Kubrick Archive*, is collected and stored in boxes on over 800 linear metres of shelving and includes, among others, draft and completed scripts, research materials, set plans and production documents. As to the quantity of screenplays available in the archive, the total amount of scripts is divided unequally over the thirteen feature films. Kubrick's departure from the United States in the early 1960s thereby marks a striking breach. From the archive catalogue we can infer that the highest amount of available documents is reserved for those films that Kubrick made when he lived and worked in the UK (i.e., after *Spartacus*). To give you an idea. There is only one screenplay to be consulted for *Paths of Glory*, whereas the number of screenplays available for *2001* amounts to more than ten. One might postulate many possible reasons for this, but probably the most likely explanation is the economic one: as his status as a major director grew, he could afford more time, and hence more draft versions of the screenplay.
43. Johnson, "Writing *The Shining*," 56.
44. Rapf, "A Talk With Stanley Kubrick," 78–79.
45. LoBrutto, *Stanley Kubrick*, 340.
46. Pezzotta, *Stanley Kubrick*, 27.
47. See appendix, ref. no. SK/12/1/2/5.
48. For a good discussion and characterization of this device in the work of Kubrick, see Falsetto, *A Narrative and Stylistic Analysis*, 85–103.
49. In *Eyes Wide Shut*, when Bill is observing his wife Alice while she helps her daughter with her homework, we hear Alice's voice-over like an echo of Bill's thoughts. Because this voice-over is a repetition of dialogue that was previously uttered by Alice in the film, we do not include it here.
50. For a good discussion, see also Kolker, *A Cinema of Loneliness*, 167–171.
51. See, among others, reference numbers SK/12/1/2/3 and SK/12/1/2/4.
52. See also Kolker, *A Cinema of Loneliness*, 168.
53. It is interesting to note here that in the early versions of the screenplay (e.g., ref. no. SK/14/1/11) the narration was not written in the third-person mode, but, as in the Thackeray novel, in the first-person mode with Barry providing the autobiographical voice-over. Many of the character names were also different to those in the final film version. For instance, Barry's character was named Roderick.
54. Bordwell, *Making Meaning*, 8–9.
55. LoBrutto, *Stanley Kubrick*, 91.
56. Extract taken from "An Untitled Screenplay" by Howard Sackler and Stanley Kubrick. See appendix, ref. no. SK/5/2/3.
57. Author description. No screenplay to be consulted at The Stanley Kubrick Archive.
58. Author description includes the third-person voice-over which can be heard in the film. No screenplay to be consulted at The Stanley Kubrick Archive.
59. Author description with only some small parts adopted from the screenplay available at The Stanley Kubrick Archive (ref. no. SK/8/1/3).
60. Phillips and Hill, *The Encyclopaedia of Stanley Kubrick*, 33.
61. Author description with only some small parts adopted from the screenplay (ref. no. SK/9/1/2/2).
62. Nabokov published his own script in 1974 as *Lolita: A Screenplay*.
63. In the book, as opposed to the film, Lolita is portrayed as a 12-year-old girl.
64. Author description with only some small parts adopted from the screenplay (ref. no. SK/10/1/26). It is interesting to note that in the screenplay the scene continues with Lolita inviting Humbert to sit next to her on the grass and asking him "You going to live with us?"

A vivid description, not included in the film, but worth mentioning here runs as follows: "She lies back and turns her face up to the sun. Humbert's shadow falls across her. He stares as she shifts and shuttles. Finally she opens her eyes and looks at him, cat-like, deliberate. Humbert seems unable to move. She smiles at him lazily and makes a face."

65. Description taken from the screenplay (ref. no. SK/11/1/26).
66. Description taken from the "Dawn of Man Script" (ref. no. SK/12/1/2/5), a supplement to "A" script containing proposed changes, cast, and a basic outline of action. This description does not completely conjoin with what we see and hear in the film. For instance, the description makes notice of a narrator which is excluded from the film. Nevertheless, it gives a good verbal account of the meaning that is conveyed by the scene to the film viewer.
67. From his production notes we know that he envisioned a three-hour epic, with a 150-day shooting schedule. For the many battle sequences Kubrick hoped to enlist a "large number of extras" hired from either Romania where he could get a "maximum of 30,000 troops at $2 per man" or Yugoslavia which could "provide up to the same numbers at $5 per man." He considered using "large numbers of expensive sets" planning to shoot his palace interiors in France and Italy, where "authentic Palaces and Villas of the period" could be rented for $350–750 per day, "and in most cases are completely furnished, requiring only the most minor work on our part before shooting." For the title role of the Emperor he considered "new faces" such as David Hemmings and Jack Nicholson. For Napoleon's aides, staff officers and Marshals he considered a list of "great actors" including, among others, Ian Holm, Alec Guinness, and Laurence Olivier. He offered the then semi-retired actress Audrey Hepburn the role of Josephine who, in a letter, however, politely turned down the offer hoping that he will keep her in mind for future projects. In addition, Kubrick kept an enormous file cabinet, with cards detailing day by day and year by year every known fact of Napoleon's life.
68. Description taken from the first-person voice-over as heard in the film.
69. Description taken from the third-person voice-over as heard in the film, complemented by the author's own description of the visual action on-screen.
70. Description taken from "The Shining Screenplay" (ref. no. SK/15/1/38).
71. Mainly author description with only a few verbal references to the screenplay (ref. no. SK/16/1/22). In the script (not the film) the girl's death is preceded by the following voice-over of Joker: "I try to decide what I would want if I were down, half dead, hurting bad, surrounded by my enemies. I look into her eyes, trying to find the answer. She sees me. She recognizes me. I am the one who will end her life. We share a bloody intimacy."
72. Description taken from an early script entitled "Eyes Wide Shut: Stanley Kubrick Project" (ref. no. SK/17/1/11). See also the description in the published version of the screenplay: Kubrick and Raphael, *Eyes Wide Shut*, 94–95.
73. Palmer, *Fictional Minds*, 12.
74. Eder, "Understanding Characters," 24.
75. Barrett, "The Future of Psychology," 327.
76. Searle, *The Construction of Social Reality*, 8.
77. Barrett, "The Future of Psychology," 329.
78. Ibid., 328
79. Narayanan, "Embodiment in Language Understanding."
80. Lakoff and Johnson, *Philosophy in the Flesh*, 176.
81. Davidson, "Mental Events," 207–224; Kim, *Philosophy of Mind*, 173–204; and Robb and Heil, "Mental Causation."
82. Kim, *Philosophy of Mind*, 173.
83. Davidson, "Mental Events," 208.
84. Searle, *Seeing Things as They Are*, 17.
85. In analytical philosophy, the condition according to which perception cannot take place without a causal relation between perception and the object seen is referred to as the "Causal Theory of Perception." This view has been advocated by such scholars as Grice, "The Causal Theory of Perception," 224–247; Pears, "The Causal Conditions of Perception," 25–40; Searle, *Seeing Things as They Are*; and

Strawson, "Causation in Perception," 73–99. Originally developed by the British philosopher Paul Grice, and further advanced by Pears, Strawson and Searle, this theory consists roughly of the claim that there must be a causal relation by which the physical object in reality causes the subject's visual experience. As Strawson (quoted by Hyman, "The Evidence of Our Senses," 235) puts it more formally: "It is a conceptual truth that when a subject S [perceives] an external object O, O is causally responsible for S's [perceptual] experience." The necessity of this condition becomes especially clear when we consider so called cases of contrivance in which a mere correspondence between what a person takes himself to see, and what is there before his eyes, does not by itself establish that he sees what he thinks he sees. For instance, suppose that: (a) I seem to see a pillar at a certain distance and direction, (b) there is actually such a pillar at that distance and direction, but (c) unknown to me, there is a mirror interposed between myself and the pillar that reflects a numerically different though similar pillar. As Grice argues, it would certainly be incorrect to say that I saw the pillar behind the mirror—because the object of the pillar is not causally responsible for my experience, I do not see it—and correct to say that the second pillar (i.e., the reflection) causes my visual experience. In other words, the difference is a causal one: your perceptual experience is caused by a reflection of the pillar, not by the pillar itself.

86. Here we follow Barrett, "The Future of Psychology," 328.
87. Dirven, "Emotions as Cause and the Cause of Emotions," 55–86; Heider, *Landscapes of Emotion*, 6; Kövecses, *Metaphor and Emotion*, 64; and Radden, "The Conceptualisation of Emotional Causality," 273–294.
88. Gelman and Legare, "Concepts and Folk Theories," 379.
89. For a discussion, see Barrett et al., "The Experience of Emotion," 374.
90. Only recently, Barrett has criticized this prevailing traditional view of the mind arguing that it is a categorical mistake to reduce the content of an ontologically subjective event such as an emotional experience entirely to the ontologically objective descriptions of physical fingerprints. She finds support in John Searle's philosophical framework of "biological naturalism" according to which it is wrong to confuse the evidence that we have about a subject matter for the subject matter itself. The subject matter of psychology is the human mind, and human behavior is evidence for the existence and features of the mind, but it is not itself the mind. An adequate account of the mind therefore requires more than just a description of the neurobiological events that constitute the conscious states, it also requires a description of the phenomenological content of the conscious states themselves. For a discussion, see Barrett et al., "The Experience of Emotion," 375.
91. Kim, "Causation," 217–236. See also Kim, *Philosophy of Mind*, 44–48.
92. Kim, *Philosophy of Mind*, 46.
93. Ibid., 46.
94. As already stated in the introduction, this relationship is of fundamental concern for cognitive semantics. For a discussion, see also Evans and Green, *Cognitive Linguistics*, 157.

Chapter 2

Embodying the Meaning: The Role of Image Schemas, Metaphors, and Metonymies

There is no severing, separation from, or bleaching out of the bodily dimensions of meaning. Mind is embodied, meaning is embodied, and thought is embodied in this most profound sense.

—George Lakoff and Mark Johnson[1]

The goal of this chapter is three-fold. First, to show how conceptual structure derives from embodiment by providing the reader with a general introduction to three theoretical notions that are central to the cognitive linguistic approach to embodied cognition, namely image schema, metaphor and metonymy.[2] Second, to show how these guiding principles of embodied cognition play a crucial role in the grounding of the conceptual structure of mental causation that, as we have seen in the previous chapter, underlies the narrative organization of Kubrick's work. Third and last, to introduce the next chapter by outlining some of the theoretical challenges that arise when one attempts to connect the embodied conceptual structure to the formal structure of film.

1. Embodiment and conceptual structure

1.1 Image schemas

The notion of an *image schema* was jointly introduced by Mark Johnson and George Lakoff in their now classic 1987 monographs *The Body in the Mind* and *Women, Fire, and Dangerous Things*. With this notion both authors attempted to explain how the nature of human conceptual organization arises from the nature of human bodily interaction with the external world (i.e., the embodied cognition thesis). An image schema, as the name suggests, is a composite of two terms that, at first glimpse, seem to contradict each other. The term *image* suggests concreteness and refers to the type of experience upon which image schemas are founded, namely *imagistic* or *sensory* experience. Although the ordinary usage of the term *image* might favour the sensory domain of vision, it has a much broader application context in psychology and in cognitive linguistics, where it is used to denote all types of sensory-perceptual experience, some of which Evans and Green summarize as in table 2.1.[3]

Table 2.1 Some sensory-perceptual systems (after Evans and Green).

System	*Sensory experience*	*Physical location*
Visual system	Vision	Eye, optic nerve
Haptic system	Touch	Beneath the skin
Auditory system	Hearing	Ear/auditory canal
Vestibular system	Movement/balance	Ear/auditory canal

The term *schema* suggests abstractness and refers to the nature of the concepts that derive from these imagistic experiences. Despite the fact that image schemas arise from perceptual interactions with the world, image schemas are not concrete concepts, but rather "abstract concepts consisting of patterns emerging from repeated instances of embodied experience."[4]

Perhaps the easiest way to make sense of this conception of an image schema is with an illustration. Consider, for example, the following extract, as provided by Johnson, which describes only a small fraction of the many daily experiences of physical containment:

> You wake *out* of a deep sleep and peer *out* from beneath the covers *into* your room. You gradually emerge *out* of your stupor, pull yourself *out* from under the covers, climb *into* your robe, stretch *out* your limbs, and walk *in* a daze *out* of the bedroom and *into* the bathroom. You look *in* the mirror and see your face staring *out* at you. You reach *into* the medicine cabinet, take *out* the toothpaste, squeeze *out* some toothpaste, put the toothbrush *into* your mouth, brush your teeth *in* a hurry, and rinse *out* your mouth. At breakfast you perform a host of further *in-out* moves—pouring *out* the coffee, setting *out* the dishes, putting the toast *in* the toaster, spreading *out* the jam on the toast, and on and on.[5]

What the recurrent use of the expressions *in* and *out* in this example shows, is not just a play with words. Rather, it suggests that a significant amount of daily activities can be organized around the same repeatable structure of experience (i.e., a schema). This recurrent pattern consists of a boundary distinguishing an interior from an exterior and constitutes what Lakoff and Johnson refer to as the image schema of CONTAINER.[6] It is a gestalt structure in the sense that the parts only make sense with a whole. The meaning of one part depends on the relation to the other parts. There is only an outside if there is also a boundary and an inside, an inside if there is also an outside and a boundary, and a boundary if there are also sides.

Having an example of an image schema in mind, let us now explore its properties more in detail by looking into three fundamental assertions that are commonly put forward in relation to image schemas and that can be listed as follows:

- Image schemas are pre-conceptual and inherently meaningful.
- Image schemas have a logic.
- Image schema are inherently dynamic and come in clusters.

The discussion that follows, draws significantly from a cross-reading of several authoritative sources in image schema research. In addition to the classic works of Lakoff and Johnson, these sources include, among others, Hampe's excellent edited volume on the importance of image schemas in cognitive linguistics and Evan and Green's outstanding summary of the properties of image schemas in their general introduction to cognitive linguistics.[7]

Image schemas are pre-conceptual and directly meaningful

The first assertion stems from the fact that image schemas, such as the CONTAINER schema discussed above, are directly grounded in sensory experience.[8] As the first concepts to emerge in the early stages of human development, they occupy a rather distinct status among other concepts. Because they are the foundations of the human conceptual system, they do not require understanding through other concepts. For instance, we come to understand a concept such as containment simply in virtue of human embodiment. Of course, we still have to learn that, in English language, words such as *in* and *out* designate this concept, but the concept itself needs, as it were, no further explication or reflection. The same can be said, for example, of such concepts as *front* and *back* which only make sense for beings with fronts and backs. As Lakoff and Johnson observe, "if all beings on this planet were uniform stationary spheres floating in some medium and perceiving equally in all directions, they would have no concepts of *front* or *back*."[9] Because image schemas are pre-conceptual, they typically operate beneath the level of our conscious awareness. They are part of the category that Lakoff and Johnson refer to as the *cognitive unconscious*.[10]

As such, image schemas present us with two challenges. The first challenge is to identify them. Indeed, if image schemas exist as patterns beneath conscious awareness, how then can we bring them to the conscious level? As our example of the CONTAINER schema already indicated, one way to identify them is by way of what Johnson calls "a phenomenological description."[11] The term *phenomenological* is here used not in the sense of Husserl's method of "transcendental reduction," but rather in the sense of a reflective interrogation of your own embodied experiences. As Johnson writes, "ask yourself what the most fundamental structures of your perception, object manipulation, and bodily movement are" and "certain obvious patterns immediately jump out at you."[12] It is precisely by applying such a method that cognitive linguists over the years have identified a number of image schemas. Two provisional lists of them can be found in the works of Hampe and Evans and Green.[13] Table 2.2 shows the list of Evans and Green as they were compiled by the authors from various sources, including, among others, Lakoff and Johnson. The image schemas are grouped according to the nature of the experiences that ground them.

Table 2.2 A partial list of image schemas (after Evans and Green).

SPACE	UP-DOWN, FRONT-BACK, LEFT-RIGHT, NEAR-FAR, CENTRE-PERIPHERY, CONTACT, STRAIGHT, VERTICALITY
CONTAINMENT	CONTAINER, IN-OUT, SURFACE, FULL-EMPTY, CONTENT
LOCOMOTION	MOMENTUM, SOURCE-PATH-GOAL
BALANCE	AXIS BALANCE, TWIN-PAN BALANCE, POINT BALANCE, EQUILIBRIUM

Continued

FORCE	COMPULSION, BLOCKAGE, COUNTERFORCE, DIVERSION, REMOVAL OF RESTRAINT, ENABLEMENT, ATTRACTION, RESISTANCE
UNITY/MULTIPLICITY	MERGING, COLLECTION, SPLITTING, ITERATION, PART-WHOLE, COUNT-MASS, LINK(AGE)
IDENTITY	MATCHING, SUPERIMPOSITION
EXISTENCE	REMOVAL, BOUNDED SPACE, CYCLE, OBJECT, PROCESS

The second challenge is to represent them. Because image schemas derive from experience, they are represented as *analogue representations.*[14] The term *analogue* refers to a type of relationship in which the representations of the mind are analogically related to the sensory experiences or perceptual states that produced them. The American psychologist Lawrence Barsalou also calls these analogue representations *perceptual symbols.*[15] They are contrasted with *amodal symbols* which, like words, are characterized by a type of relationship that is only arbitrarily related to the perceptual states that gave rise to them. Consequently, if image schemas are not represented in symbolic forms such as words, how, then, can we represent them? As the reader may have already noticed, most semantics, including cognitive linguists, use precisely symbolic forms such as words from natural language to represent pre-linguistic elements of meaning. For instance, in the field of cognitive semantics it is common to represent image schemas by using words in small capitals (e.g., CONTAINER). Another strategy that cognitive linguists often use to represent image schemas is by means of pictorial representations such as diagrams.[16] A diagram has the advantage of representing concepts independently of language. For example, the three-part structure of the basic CONTAINER schema might be diagrammed by any bounded geometrical figure. Here, and henceforth, we will use the figure of a rectangle as the diagrammatical means to represent the CONTAINER schema:[17]

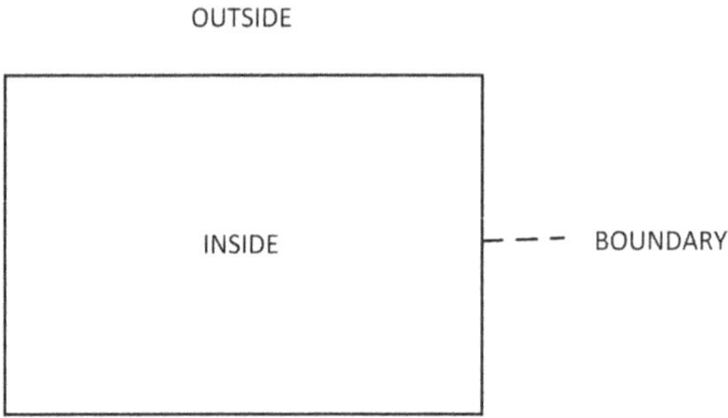

Figure 2.1 The CONTAINER image schema.

It is important to stress, however, that these drawings are not the image schemas themselves. We use these diagrams simply as a meta-language to characterize "some of the properties of the schemas" and "to get some idea of what they are like."[18]

Image schemas have a logic

Together with the image-schematic structure comes also its own logic.[19] Consider, for example, what follows if you put some object X in your wallet (container A) and you then place your wallet in your pocket (container B). By virtue of the internal spatial logic of containment, as diagrammed in figure 2.2 (X is in A and A is in B), it follows self-evidently that the object in your wallet is also in your pocket (X is in B).[20]

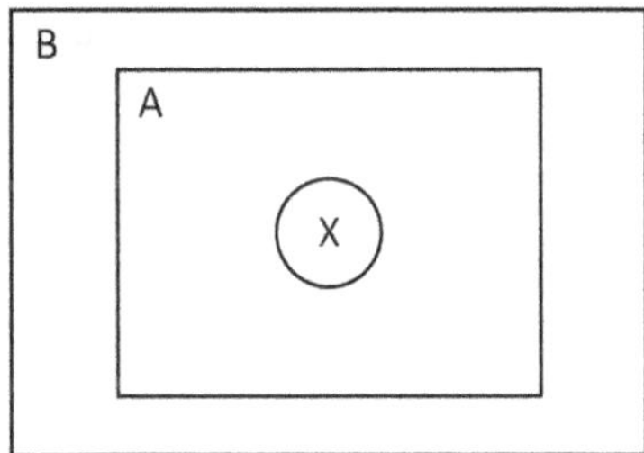

Figure 2.2 The CONTAINER image schema logic (after Lakoff and Johnson).

As Johnson points out, such apparently trivial spatial logic is by no means trivial. On the contrary, it is precisely this kind of spatial and bodily logic that allows us "to make sense of, and to act intelligently within, our ordinary experience."[21]

As a second example, consider the spatial logic of the SOURCE-PATH-GOAL image schema.[22] Like the CONTAINER schema, this schema is one of the most fundamental schemas in our conceptual system. It underlies our basic experience of motion and is characterized by a trajector (henceforth, TR) that moves from one source location (the starting point) to another goal location (the ending point).[23] Diagrammatically, its structure can be represented as in figure 2.3.[24]

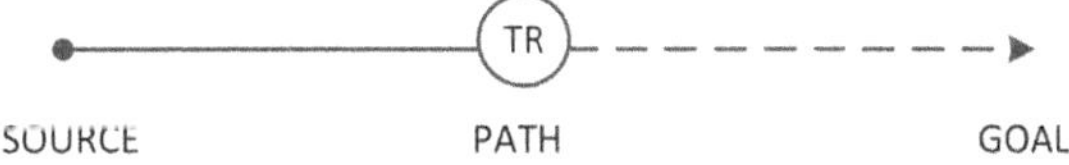

Figure 2.3 SOURCE-PATH-GOAL image schema (after Lakoff and Johnson).

As with the CONTAINER schema, one can draw an internal "logic" from the spatial relations inherent in this structure. According to Lakoff and Johnson this runs something as follows:

- If you have traversed a route to a current location, you have been at all previous locations on that route.
- If you travel from A to B and from B to C, then you have travelled from A to C.
- If there is a direct route from A to B and you are moving along that route toward B, then you will keep getting closer to B.

- If X and Y are travelling along a direct route from A to B and X passes Y, then X is further from A and closer to B than Y is.
- If X and Y start from A at the same time moving along the same route toward B and if X moves faster than Y, then X will arrive at B before Y.[25]

Image schemas are inherently dynamic and come in clusters
A last important aspect that should be emphasized, is that image schemas are dynamic and highly flexible rather than fixed and static. Image schemas do not operate on their own, but they influence each other in various ways through processes of combination and superimposition, thus resulting in more complex and dynamic forms of image-schematic structures. A good illustration of this can be found in the interaction of the SOURCE-PATH-GOAL image schema with the image schema of FORCE. As we saw above, the first schema underlies our understanding of entities in motion. Entities, however, do not move on their own accord. As Johnson argues, entities move because "something with power" causes them to move.[26] A ball moves into the goal because my foot made it move from outside the goal to the inside of it. This is where the notion of *force* comes into being. A force is that what imparts a directionality or vector quality on the moving entity.[27] According to Johnson, FORCE schemas are typically held to consist of six properties.[28] First, they are commonly experienced through *interaction*. For example, by bumping into the edge of a table, you experience the interactional character of force. Second, they have a *vector* quality in the sense that they usually involve the movement of some object (mass) through space in some direction (e.g., when I move my hand to grasp something, there is force exerted in a direction). Third, as a result of this vector quality, they typically involve a *single path of motion*. Fourth, they have *sources* or *origins* and because they are directional, they have *targets*. As Radden further explicates, these origins may be either *internal* as when people are guided by their intentions when moving their bodies, or *external* as when motion is brought about by physical laws (e.g., wind, water, physical objects, other people).[29] Fifth, they have a *degree of power or intensity*. One force can be stronger or weaker than another force. And sixth and last, they always involve a *structure or sequence of causality*, a consequence of having all the preceding properties (e.g. the door closes because I acted on it to cause it to shut).

Given these properties, then, one may distinguish between several schemas of motion and their associated force vectors. Johnson identifies no less than seven force schemas, two of which are illustrated in figure 2.4.[30]

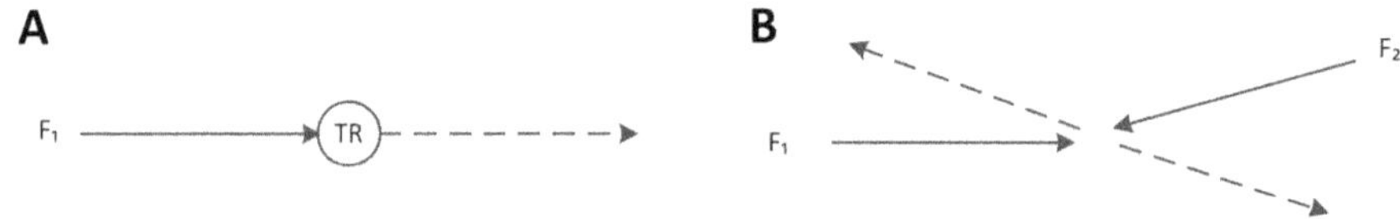

Figure 2.4 *A*, COMPULSION and *B*, DIVERSION schema.

The COMPULSION schema emerges from our experience of being brought in motion by an external force (e.g., being blown away by the wind, being pushed by other people). The DIVERSION schema occurs when our previous course of motion is being diverted by our encounter with another entity (e.g., swimming against a strong current).

When the FORCE schema involves an interaction between two entities, such as is the case with the schemas above, we might also speak of a *force dynamic pattern*. This notion was introduced by the cognitive linguist Leonard Talmy to account for the various ways force interactions between entities might be conceptualized.[31] Force dynamic expressions such as "The ball kept rolling because of the wind blowing on it" typically involve a role difference between two force entities: one entity that is in focus and another entity that is opposing it. Talmy calls these entities the *agonist* (abbreviated Ago) and the *antagonist* (abbreviated Ant), respectively.[32] In the expression the ball is the agonist and the wind is the antagonist. Force entities also have an *intrinsic force tendency*, either toward *action* or toward *rest*. In the example, the ball has a tendency toward rest. Another basic feature is the *balance of strength* between the two forces. The forces are out of balance by definition; if the two forces are equally strong, the situation is not interesting from a force-dynamic point of view. One force is therefore stronger or weaker than the other. In the example, the wind has a great power, since it overcomes the resistance of the force tendency of the ball (i.e., toward rest). Depending on the balance between the forces and the intrinsic force tendencies of the entities, there is also a *resultant*, either toward action or inaction (or rest). In the example, the ball moves and thus is not able to manifest its tendency toward rest.

FORCE and SOURCE-PATH-GOAL schemas, in turn, might be combined with other schemas such as the CONTAINER schema. This gives rise to what Robert Dewell labels "dynamic patterns of containment."[33] Depending on the moving entity or trajector we focus upon (object and container, respectively), we might distinguish between several such patterns. Figure 2.5 shows two of them as they were discussed by Dewell. ENTRY refers to the experiential pattern according to which a smaller entity capable of motion moves from the outside toward the interior of a container, thus becoming the contained object (e.g., people walking into houses and rooms, people inserting things into jars or glasses). Figure 2.5*A* represents the final stage of this path type whereby the dashed arrow corresponds to the prior locations of the trajectory.

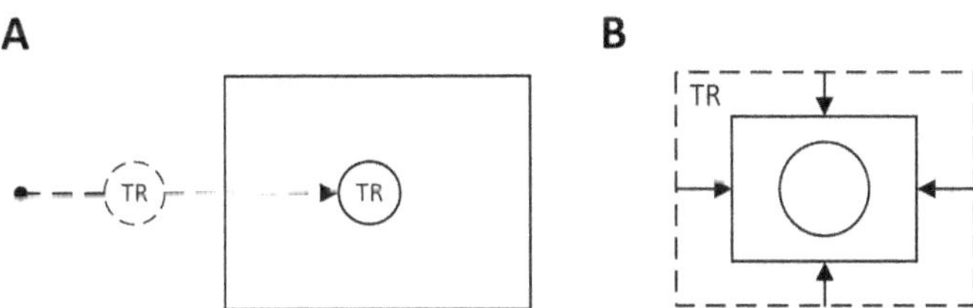

Figure 2.5 *A*, ENTRY and *B*, ENCLOSING.

In ENCLOSING, by contrast, the container is the moving figure that closes in on the stationary object so as to exclude the free space that resides between the boundary of the container and the object inside of it (e.g., grasping hand, a wrapping napkin). Figure 2.5*B* represents the final stage of this path type whereby the arrows represent the forces that are imposed on to the contained object by the container, thus eventually enclosing the object completely.

As we shall see in the next chapter, patterns such as these will be revealed to play a fundamental role in structuring the visible reality in front of the camera.

1.2 Metaphor and metonymy

Having an idea of what image schemas are, let us now turn to a discussion of two assertions that further built on this notion and that, as we will see in the next part of this chapter, are of crucial importance in explaining how the conceptual structure of mental causation underlying Kubrick's work can be fleshed out by spatial knowledge. These assertions have to do with two other cognitive processes and might be put as follows:

- Image schemas provide the concrete basis for conceptual metaphors.
- Image schematic metaphors interact with metonymies.

As above, let us consider each statement in turn.

Image schemas provide the concrete basis for conceptual metaphors
Probably most important in the light of this book is the assertion that image schemas provide the bodily basis for the metaphorical nature of abstract concepts.[34] This idea is central to what is now more broadly known as Conceptual Metaphor Theory (CMT). First proposed by Lakoff and Johnson in their now classic publication *Metaphors We Live By*, this theory makes the basic claim that metaphor is not simply a rhetorical tool of language, but a pervasive and essential feature of human thought.[35] That is, conceptual structure is partly organized in terms of cross-domain mappings or correspondences between conceptual domains. A *domain* can be conceived of as a "body of knowledge that organizes related concepts."[36] The conceptual domain that is being described in metaphorical terms is called a *target domain* and is usually abstract in nature. It involves concepts such as those identified in the preceding chapter (that is, concepts such as emotion, perception and causation which are all hard to understand without the assistance of metaphor). The conceptual domain that is used in order to describe the abstract target domain is called a *source domain* and is usually concrete in nature.[37] The significance of image schemas, then, is that they can provide the concrete basis for these source domains.[38] Their imagistic structure and inferential logic make them highly suitable for "fleshing out" the non-imagistic (i.e., abstract) realms of human experience. As such, conceptual metaphors have an experiential basis: they are grounded in the nature of our everyday experiences, or as Lakoff and Johnson so eloquently put it, they are "metaphors we live by." As a way of illustrating the mechanism of conceptual metaphor, let us consider the following statement about the effect that Kubrick's films have on the viewer, as it was expressed by Garreth Brown, inventor of the Steadicam and Kubrick's camera operator for *The Shining* (own emphasis):

> Stanley Kubrick *brought* you *into* spaces in a really interesting way. His storytelling shots *walked* you *in*, and *moved* you *into* places that were memorably beautiful, beautifully lit, or strikingly presented in some way. But there are no ordinary spaces in his films.[39]

What is striking about this quotation, is that it represents an everyday way of talking about being "absorbed" in a film narrative.[40] There is nothing stylized or overtly poetic about it. However, it is clearly non-literal. Kubrick cannot literally "bring" the spectator "into" the spaces of his films. Yet, Brown uses his own bodily knowledge (about forced movement into a container) in order to conceptualize his experience of seeing a Kubrick film (the target domain).

It is important to stress that the motivation for this metaphor resides at the conceptual level and not at the linguistic level. The linguistic metaphorical expressions are merely the manifestations of an underlying conceptual association between the concrete source domain and the abstract target domain. Therefore, as with image schemas, we are obliged to rely on language in order to communicate about conceptual metaphors. In the literature it is common to formalize the latter by making use of the shorthand notion "a is b" often in combination with the use of small capitals (e.g., CHANGE OF STATE IS MOVEMENT). This is simply a formal way to designate a series of discrete conceptual mappings which licence a range of linguistic examples.

Given that CMT provides us with a suitable theoretical tool for addressing abstract target domains and given that the conceptual structure underlying Kubrick's work (i.e., mental causation) can be characterized as highly abstract, it is plausible to assume that people also use the mechanism of conceptual metaphor to "flesh out" the latter. Addressing this hypothesis will be the central goal of the next section of this chapter. Before moving into this discussion, however, let us first consider the importance of another cognitive operation that has been emphasized by some scholars at least as important as conceptual metaphor in terms of providing structure to the human conceptual system (including abstract thought). In cognitive linguistic literature this mechanism is known by the name of *conceptual metonymy.*

Image-schematic metaphors interact with metonymies

Like metaphor, metonymy is claimed to be not just a purely linguistic device, but essentially a conceptual phenomenon that is central to human thought.[41] Yet, despite this similarity, metonymy is also argued to be fundamentally different than metaphor. For instance, several authors have pointed out that metonymy, unlike metaphor, is not defined in terms of cross-domain mappings.[42] Instead, it is defined by mappings within a single domain in which "one conceptual entity, the vehicle, provides mental access to another conceptual entity, the target."[43] Visually, this distinction might be represented as in figure 2.6.

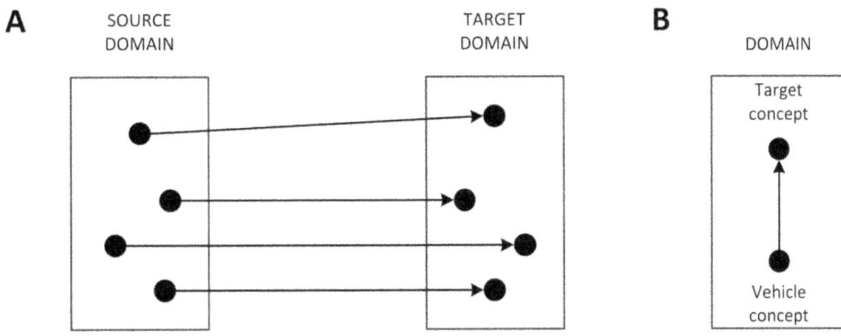

Figure 2.6 *A*, metaphor versus *B*, metonymy.

To illustrate the mechanism of metonymy, consider, for example, the following expression as taken from the screenplay of *Eyes Wide Shut* (the vehicle is italicized):

> Unexpectedly, his *heart* is filled with a feeling of tenderness and even of security.[44]

The reason why the vehicle in the expression above represents an instance of a metonymy is because both the target (tenderness and security) and the vehicle (heart) belong to the same conceptual domain (emotions).[45] The heart is conceived of as a container that stands for its content (the feelings of tenderness and security). As this example indicates, metonymy is based on continuity or conceptual proximity rather than on conceptual distance, as it is the case with metaphor. Other examples of metonymies that have been cited in cognitive semantic literature, include, among others, PLACE FOR EVENT ("*Iraq* nearly cost Tony Blair the premiership") PLACE FOR INSTITUTION ("*Downing Street* refused comment") and PART FOR WHOLE ("My *wheels* are parked out the back").[46]

In theory there seems to be little confusion about the distinction between metaphor and metonymy. In practice, however, both mechanisms are often blended together in close association. As Barcelona states, "they seem to be points on a continuum of mapping processes."[47] Given that metaphor and metonymy are both conceptual, and given that they may in principle both relate to the same conceptual domains, questions arise concerning the interaction of metaphor and metonymy within the conceptual system.[48] Consider, for example, the following expression as offered by Velasco:

> She made every effort to attract him, and finally she has *won* his *heart*.[49]

Likewise, this example incorporates a metonymical mapping (HEART FOR LOVE), but this relationship is now also embedded in a metaphorical one in which obtaining someone's love is understood in terms of winning a prize (LOVE IS A PRIZE). In this metaphor, attaining someone's love is understood in terms of obtaining a reward whereby the lover must overcome some barriers in order to gain the prize of love.[50] As such, both the vehicle and the target concept of the metonymical relationship are part of the same target domain of the metaphorical relationship. Schematically, this interaction might be diagrammed more generally as in figure 2.7.

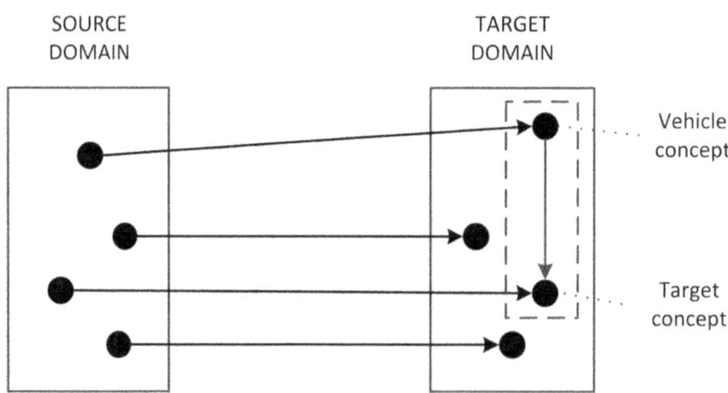

Figure 2.7 Metaphor-metonymy interaction.

2. Fleshing-out the conceptual structure of mental causation

The discussion presented so far involved a general and brief introduction to the theoretical concepts that are central to the view of embodied cognition as developed within the field of cognitive linguistics. The central aim of this part is to illustrate them more concretely by applying them to the kind of abstract concepts that, in the previous chapter, were argued to constitute the literal, conceptual skeleton of Kubrick's narratives and that fall under the general category of mental causation. Figure 2.8 recalls these concepts as they together constitute the Western folk theory of emotion.

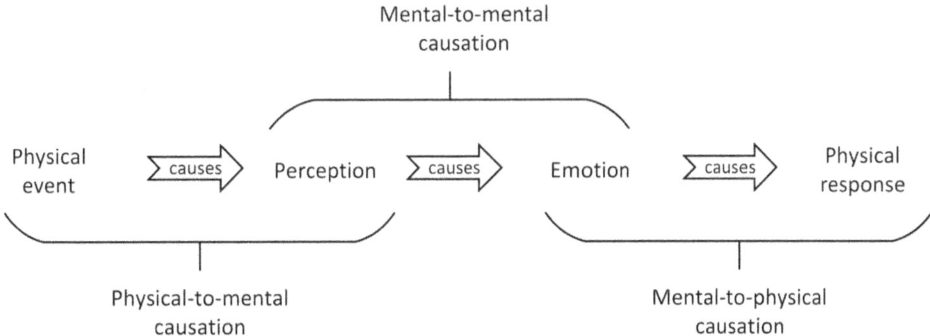

Figure 2.8 The Western folk theory of emotion.

Depending on the abstract concepts inherent in this figure (i.e., perception, emotion and causation), one may formulate three questions of conceptualization:

(1) How is *perception* conceptualized?
(2) How is *emotion* conceptualized?
(3) How are *causes* conceptualized and how does the answer to this question relate to the conceptualizations of *perception as cause* and *emotion as cause*?

For each of the three questions above, cognitive linguists have proposed a number of metaphors and metonymies. In what follows, we will discuss them, concept by concept. As with the previous part, the discussion is based on a cross-reading of several authoritative sources in the cognitive linguistic literature.[51]

2.1 Metaphor and perception

In addressing the first question, cognitive linguists have proposed two different ways of analysis. The first way considers perception as a *target domain* in need of metaphorical clarification.[52] By contrast, the second way considers perception as a *source domain* in its own right for the conceptualization of other target domains. Thereby scholars have particularly emphasized the importance of the domain of perception for the conceptualization of the domains of *cognition* and *time*.[53] This subsection is structured in such a way as to reflect this distinction.

2.1.1 Perception as a target domain

How do people conceive and talk about perception? In addressing this question cognitive linguists have emphasized the workings of at least two metaphors and one metonymy, all of which may be diagrammed as in figure 2.9. Let us go through them, one by one.

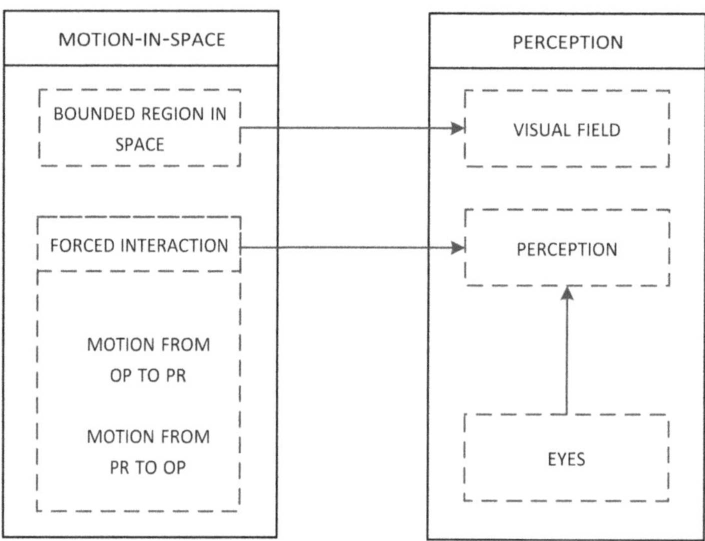

Figure 2.9 Metaphors of perception.

Visual fields are containers

The first metaphor relates to our concept of a visual field. A visual field refers to all the objects and state of affairs that come into view when you open your eyes in a certain direction.[54] As the word *into* in this definition already suggests, our most fundamental understanding of what visual fields are, comes from a metaphor in which a visual field is conceptualized as a bounded region in space or a container. This metaphor, which Lakoff and Johnson call, the VISUAL FIELDS ARE CONTAINERS metaphor, is licensed by such expressions as "The ship is *coming into* view" or "I have him *in* sight." Inferential evidence for this metaphor is provided by the systematic relationship between the logic of bounded regions in space and the logic of visual fields (see table 2.3).

Table 2.3 The inferential correspondences between bounded regions and visual fields.

Inferences true of bounded regions	*Inferences true of visual fields*
If you're *in* a bounded region, you're not *out* of that bounded region.	If you're *in* my visual field, you're not *out* of my visual field.
If you're *out* of a bounded region, you're not *in* that bounded region.	If you're *out* of my visual field you're not *in* my visual field.

Perception is a forced interaction between perceiver and object perceived

If a visual field defines that area in space that we see, then, the target domain of perception involves the process of perceiving itself.[55] Perception may be defined as the process by which the perceiver (abbreviated PR), becomes aware, through his or her perceptual organs, of the objects and states of affairs (abbreviated OP) around him or her. Likewise, when we ask how this process is conceptualized in language, metaphor quickly shows up. The source domain that has been argued to play a fundamental role in this regard is the source domain of *spatial interaction*. Since interaction is commonly brought about by forced movement (i.e., movement caused by a force), we can further distinguish between two subcases: (1) one metaphor in which the interaction between the PR and the OP takes place through forced movement from the OP to the PR, and (2) an opposite metaphor in which the interaction between the PR and the OP is instantiated by forced movement from the PR to the OP. Following Lakoff, the former type may be described as the PERCEPTION IS RECEPTION metaphor, the latter as the PERCEIVING IS TOUCHING metaphor.[56]

(1) One way to conceive of the first type is by retrieving the VISUAL FIELD AS A CONTAINER metaphor and relating it to the earlier discussed dynamic pattern of ENTRY. This gives rise to an embodied conceptual structure in which the OP, motivated by an internal or external force, enters a bounded region of spatial interaction that coincides with the PR's visual field. This is evidenced in such expressions as "He *came into* my visual field." In this case the interaction is based on the logic of the containment schema. The OP or trajector (TR) moves from a position *outside* the PR's visual field or landmark (LM) to occupy a location *inside* the LM. Spatial interaction or perception, then, takes place as soon as the OP *enters* the visual field of the PR. Visibility increases with the increase of substance (i.e., the OP) inside the container (e.g., "He is *full in* view").

The spatial link can also take on a more physical form as when the OP actually makes contact with the PR. Consider, for example, the expression "That view blew me away." Underlying it is the force schema of COMPULSION in which the PR is brought in motion due to the force tendency of the OP, or to use Talmy's distinction between the agonist (Ago) and the antagonist (Ant), as discussed earlier: the PR (Ago) undergoes the effect of the OP (Ant) because the intrinsic force tendency of the OP is stronger than the intrinsic force tendency of the PR.

(2) By contrast, in the second type, perception occurs "when the perceiver moves his organs of perception to the thing perceived and touches it."[57] Usually this type of interaction is licensed by the use of such words as *on* and *from . . . to* as can be illustrated by the following two expressions taken from the screenplay of *Eyes Wide Shut*:

> He puts his hands in his pockets and his eyes wander about the room until they finally rest again *on* Marion.
>
> His eyes wander *from* voluptuous bodies *to* slender bodies, *from* delicate *to* richly developed figures.[58]

Underlying these expressions is a conceptual metaphor in which the target domain of vision is conceptualized in terms of the source domain of limbs. The word "eyes" thereby designate the "visual limbs" that wander, just as the word "gaze" can designate such visual limbs (e.g., "My gaze *is out over* the bay"). Following Lakoff, we may summarize the inferential correspondences that go on between both domains as in table 2.4.[59]

Table 2.4 The inferential correspondences between limbs and vision.

Inferences true of limbs	*Inferences true of vision*
Limbs can be directed.	Vision can be directed.
A limb can go in only one direction at a time.	Vision can go in only one direction at a time.
Limbs can extend from the body to other objects.	Vision can move from the body to other objects.
Tactile perception occurs when a limb touches an object.	Visual perception occurs when the eye-gaze touches an object.
Limbs can pick out objects.	Vision can pick out objects.

It is interesting to see how all the perception expressions cited so far focus mainly on the cause of perception (movement => interaction) rather than on the effect of perception (interaction => effect). An exception to the rule, as we shall see more clearly in the next section, is the expression "That view *blew* me away" that focuses more on the emotional effect of the interaction rather than on the coming about of the interaction itself.

Depending on the type of movement (reception versus touching) and the origin of the force that causes the movement, one might distinguish between several metaphorical ways of conceptualizing perception. The origin or source of the force may be located inside the moving entity itself as when an entity moves by using its intention as an internal force. Or the origin of the force may be located outside the moving entity as when the entity is brought in motion by an external force. Combining these elements with the two entities of perception, this leads us to a matrix which might be represented as in table 2.5.

Table 2.5 Perception and forced movement.

Type of movement	*Origin of the force that causes the movement*	*Linguistic examples*
PR => OP	OP	"My eyes are *pulled toward* the building."
PR => OP	PR	"My gaze is *out* over the bay."
OP => PR	OP	"A comet came *into* my sight."
OP => PR	PR	"She was pulled *into* his gaze."

Eyes for seeing

Lastly, as some of the linguistic examples cited so far already illustrated, there is also a metonymical relationship at work within the conceptual target domain of perception according to which one entity in the schema of perception (i.e., the perceptual organ) is taken as standing for the schema as a whole (i.e., the concept of perception). Consequently, given that seeing and hearing are two of human's core senses, this general mapping further designates two special cases, namely the conceptual metonymy EYES STAND FOR SEEING (e.g., "Keep an eye on him," "Keep your eyes open"), and the conceptual metonymy EARS STAND FOR HEARING (e.g., "I cannot believe my ears," "Walls have ears"). Since both organs are directly related to their function, they also adhere to the more general conceptual metonymy THE INSTRUMENT USED IN AN ACTIVITY STANDS FOR THE ACTIVITY or THE PERCEPTUAL ORGAN FOR FUNCTION OF THE PERCEPTUAL ORGAN.[60]

2.1.2 Perception as a source domain

The metaphorical system just sketched out deals with a conceptual system in which perception is addressed as an abstract target domain. From the opposite side, scholars have also pointed toward a conceptual system in which perception in its own right serves as the source domain for the conceptualization of other abstract target domains such as cognition and time.

Cognition

It has been argued in the cognitive linguistic literature that metaphor plays an essential role in how people reason about the concept of thinking. Thereby scholars have stressed the importance of a very general metaphor which centres on the idea that the MIND IS A BODY.[61] This metaphor, in turn, gives rise to a submetaphor according to which the mental faculty of thinking is understood in terms of physical functioning.[62] One special case of this submetaphor is the metaphor THINKING IS PERCEIVING or UNDERSTANDING IS SEEING.[63] Considered by many as one of the most common and basic metaphors across the world's languages, this metaphor has a complex set of mappings some of which may be summarized as in figure 2.10. As can be seen in this figure, this metaphor now relocates the conceptual domain of perception from the right side of the table (as target domain) to the left side (as source domain).

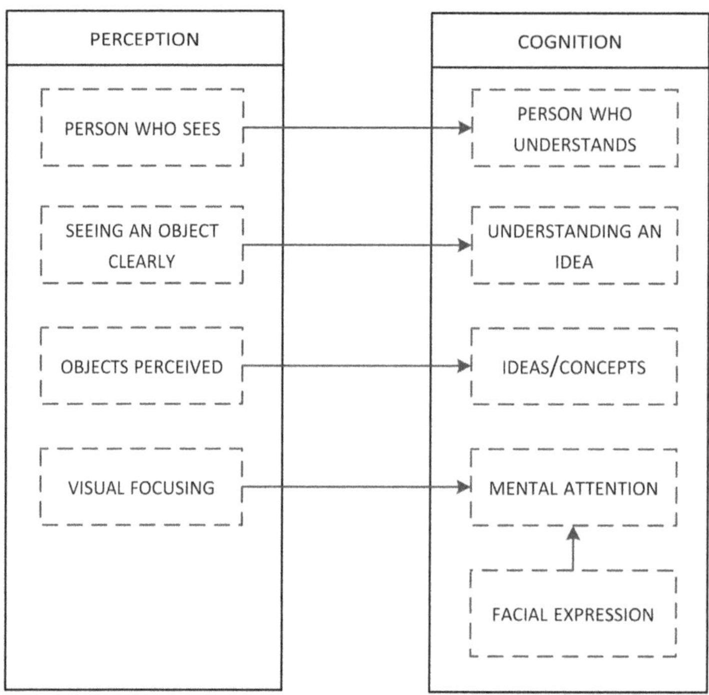

Figure 2.10 Metaphors of cognition.

Hence, when discussing a person's understanding, it follows that someone who apprehends an idea or concept "sees it," whereas someone who is ignorant or incapable of apprehending an idea is "blind" or is "in the dark."[64] Given that perception, as we have seen above, is conceptualized in a metaphorical way, it also follows that the concepts used to conceptualize perception may also be used to conceptualize cognition. This is, for example, how we come to understand thinking similarly in terms of forced movement ("My mind was *racing*," "I *came* to that idea"). Likewise, one may identify the existence of a metonymical relationship within the target domain of cognition in which the facial expression of the thinking person is seen as standing for the mental activity of thinking. For instance, several experimental studies demonstrate that facial expressions are not only indicative of emotions, but also of cognitive processes.[65] Frowning, for example, has been argued to signal hard thinking as when we encounter difficulties in problem-solving.[66]

Time

Many studies in the field of cognitive linguistics relate the conceptual domain of perception to our conceptualization of time.[67] In identifying the significant elements within this source domain, scholars have stressed not so much the significance of the activity of perceiving itself, as they have emphasized the essential role of the space around the perceiver. For instance, Lakoff and Johnson have argued that the most basic submetaphor of this general TIME IS SPACE metaphor "has an observer at the present who is facing toward the future with the past behind the observer."[68] They refer to this metaphor as the Time-Orientation metaphor. This metaphor, which may be represented as in figure 2.11, is motivated by such linguistic expressions as "That's all *behind* us now" or "We're looking *ahead to* the future." In these mappings the space in front of the perceiver (i.e., the space inside the visual field) is related to the future whereas the space behind the perceiver (i.e., the space outside the visual field) is related to the past.

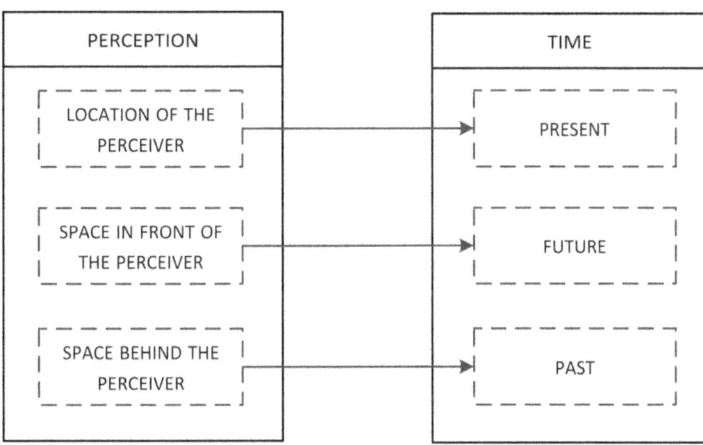

Figure 2.11 The Time-Orientation metaphor.

An exception to this rule, however, was found in the language of Aymara, a Chilean language of the Andes. As research conducted by Núñez and Sweetser revealed, Aymara speakers put the past in front of the observer and the future behind.[69] As a possible explanation model for this discrepancy both authors refer to the strong emphasis Aymara language put on the KNOWING IS SEEING metaphor.[70] As we saw above, this metaphor underlies the mapping according to which the object seen by the viewer is mapped onto the idea or concept that constitutes the knowledge.[71] Consequently, because the past and the future are usually conceived as known and unknown, respectively, it follows, that the past and future are placed in front of and behind the viewer, respectively.

The reason, then, why English speakers still retain a different configuration, despite the fact that they also share the universal KNOWING IS SEEING metaphor, is that both cultures base their temporal conceptions on slightly different aspects of human experiential correlations between time and space.[72] That is, in contrast to the Aymara speakers, English speakers do not conceive the observer as a static one, but as a moving one.[73] This implies that what is known has already been seen and remains behind us, while what is unknown has yet to be seen and remains in front of us. As both authors argue, moving persons do not only share the division between "what I can see in front of me" and "what I cannot see behind me" but also the division between "places I haven't yet been to – and thus haven't seen and don't know about" and "places I've been to already – and have thus seen and gained some knowledge about."[74] Consequently, the metaphorical pair here is not KNOWN IS IN FRONT and UNKNOWN IS IN THE BACK, but rather KNOWN IS BEHIND and UNKNOWN IS AHEAD.

It is exactly the notion of motion that let many scholars to distinguish further between two dominant metaphorical models for time in English that usually are integrated with the Time-Orientation metaphor. These are the Moving-Time metaphor and the Moving-Ego metaphor, respectively.[75] This distinction is basically the same as the duality that we already observed in the metaphorical system of perception. Both models involve movement, "but in one the observer is stationary and time is moving, while in the other the observer is moving and time is stationary."[76] Often this distinction is visualized using the image of a time-line. In the first metaphor a time-line is conceived of as a river or conveyor belt on which the perceived object in time is moving toward the perceiver (e.g., "Christmas is *coming up*"). In the second metaphor the perceiver's point of view moves along the time-line toward the perceived object in time (past or future) (e.g., "We are *coming up on* Christmas").

2.2 Metaphor and emotion

Having discussed the concept of perception and its metaphorical entailments, we can now ask the same question with respect to the concept of emotion. In contrast to perception, emotions have been solely treated as a target domain in need of conceptualization and elaboration. Sketching out some of these metaphors, will be the central aim of the first subsection. In the second subsection, we briefly discuss the conceptualization of a concept that is considered by many to be strongly tied to emotions, namely the concept of relationship (e.g., love, friendship).

2.2.1 Emotion as target domain

When considering the question of how people talk about emotions, Zoltan Kövecses' book *Metaphor and Emotion* stands as a hallmark study in the field of cognitive linguistics. In this book the author illustrates, through detailed cross-linguistic analyses, how many of the concepts we use to reason about emotions reflect widespread metaphorical patterns of thought. As with the metaphors of perception, these emotion metaphors are considered by the author to be deeply rooted in our concrete sensory-motor knowledge. It would be beyond the scope of this book to address all the metaphors identified by Kövecses. We therefore limit ourselves to a discussion of three conceptual relationships, two metaphors and one metonymy, that have been argued to play a crucial role in our conceptualization of emotions. Schematically, they may be represented as in figure 2.12. Likewise, let us consider them each in turn.

Emotions are containers

We already saw in the previous section how the CONTAINER image schema provided a suitable source domain for conceptualizing a visual field. The same can be said of emotions because one of the most natural ways to talk about emotional states is by making reference to bounded regions in space. Thus, in English it is common to say "I'm *in* love," "He's *in* a rage" or "She is *in* a depression," when one attempts to describe his or her experience of "being in an emotional state."[77] As Kövecses rightly observes, this metaphor coincides with what Lakoff and Johnson more generally coin the STATES ARE LOCATIONS metaphor.[78] As they point out, this metaphor is fundamental for our understanding of states in that it is difficult not to speak about them without making reference to such features of the CONTAINER schema as an interior and an exterior. This becomes particularly evident in the use of the expressions *in*, *out*, *deep*, and so on. As was the case with perception, inferential evidence for this metaphorical mapping can be found in the systematic relationship between the logic of bounded regions in space and the logic of (emotional) states. Following Lakoff and Johnson, this mapping might be summarized as in table 2.6.[79]

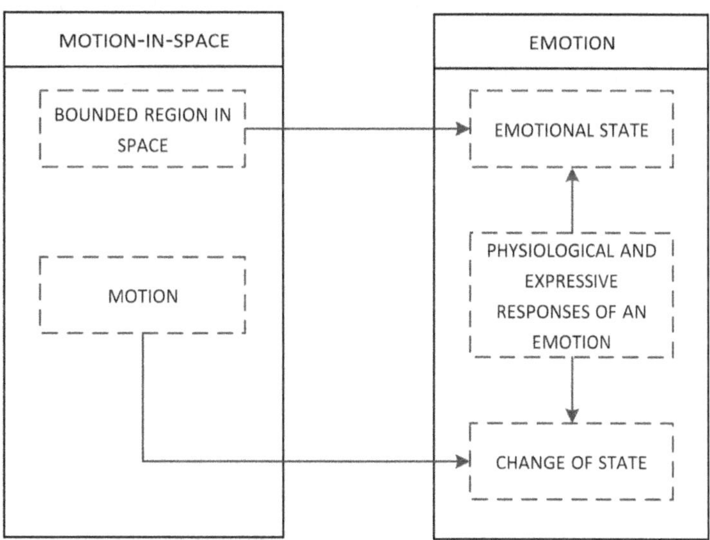

Figure 2.12 Metaphors of emotion.

Table 2.6 The inferential correspondences between bounded regions and (emotional) states.

Inferences true of bounded regions	*Inferences true of states*
If you're *in* a bounded region, you're not *out of* that bounded region.	If you're *in* a state, you're not *out* of that state.
If you're *out* of a bounded region, you're not *in* that bounded region.	If you're *out* of a state you're not *in* that state.
If you're deep *in* a bounded region, you are far from being *out* of that bounded region.	If you're deep *in* a state, you are far from being *out* of that state.
If you are *on the edge of* a bounded region, then you're *close to* being in that bounded region.	If you are *on the edge of* a state, then you are *close to* being *in* that state.

Change of state is change of location or motion

The second metaphor conceptualizes a person's change from a nonemotional state to an emotional one as motion from one bounded region in space to another.[80] Linguistic manifestations of this metaphor can be found in such expressions as "I came *out of* my depression," "He *went* crazy" or "She *entered* a state of euphoria." Similarly, this metaphor coincides with what Lakoff and Johnson label more generally the CHANGES ARE MOVEMENTS metaphor or the CHANGE OF STATE IS CHANGE OF LOCATION metaphor.[81] This metaphor maps each of the inferences true of the logic of movement (i.e., the inferential logic of the SOURCE-PATH-GOAL schema) into the corresponding inferences true of a change-of-state. Following Lakoff and Johnson, this mapping might be summarized as in table 2.7.[82]

Table 2.7 The inferential correspondences between movements and changes (after Lakoff and Johnson).

Inferences true of movements	*Inferences true of changes*
If someone *moves from* Location A to Location B, it is first *in* Location A and later *in* Location B.	If something *changes from* State A to State B, it is first *in* State A and later *in* State B.
If something *moves from* Location A to Location B over a period of time, there is a point at which it is *between* Location A and Location B.	If something *changes from* State A to State B over a period of time, there is a point at which it is *between* State A and State B.

Physiological and expressive responses of an emotion stand for the emotion

Lastly, as was the case with perception, one may identify a general metonymical association within the target domain of emotions. Kövecses calls this metonymy THE PHYSIOLOGICAL AND EXPRESSIVE RESPONSES OF AN EMOTION STAND FOR THE EMOTION. This metonymy, in turn, adheres to an even more general metonymy, THE EFFECTS OF A STATE FOR THE STATE metonymy. Table 2.8 shows some of the most common source concepts in this metonymy as they were listed by Kövecses.[83]

Table 2.8 Physiological and expressive responses of an emotion for the emotion.

Source concept	*Linguistic example*
Body heat	"He did it *in the heat of* passion."
Change in heart rate	"He entered the room *with his heart in* his mouth."
Change in respiration	"She was *heaving with* emotion."
Change in the color of the face	"She *colored with* emotion."

As we already have seen in the previous chapter, physiological changes such as the ones listed above have received a great deal of emphasis in several expert theories of emotions. Advocates of these theories conceive of emotion as being primarily constituted by physiological processes and expressive reactions. Seminal research in this regard is Paul Ekman's extensive work on the relationship between facial expressions and emotions.[84] The author illustrates, through a number of cross-cultural experiments, how various members of different cultures seem to judge the emotions shown in particular facial expressions in an identical way. This led him to categorize facial expressions with six basic emotions: anger, disgust, fear, happiness, sadness and surprise. Happiness, for instance, is typically symbolized by raising of the mouth corners (an obvious smile) and tightening of the eyelids; whereas sadness is symbolized by lowering of the mouth corners, the eyebrows descending to the inner corners and the eyelids drooping. More recently, however, this materialist view of emotion as a universal construct has been criticized in the literature.[85] This discussion, however, is a scientific matter and does not influence the folk theory of emotions according to which people have a natural tendency to refer to facial expressions when talking about emotions.

2.2.2 Human relationship as target domain

Let us conclude the section about emotions by uncovering three metaphors that underlie the domain of human relationships. Following Kövecses our focus will be on the interpersonal relationship of friendship.[86] Although friendship is viewed by many to be an emotion, it is also a rather atypical one. The reason why we tend to associate friendship with emotion is that it appears to involve at least two clear members of the category of emotion, namely, intimacy and affection. As Kövecses' study indicates, people use various metaphors to conceptualize both concepts. In this section, we restrict ourselves to a discussion of three metaphorical ways of conceptualizing the intimacy aspect of friendship. These ways may be summarized as in figure 2.13. As before, let us consider each metaphor in turn.

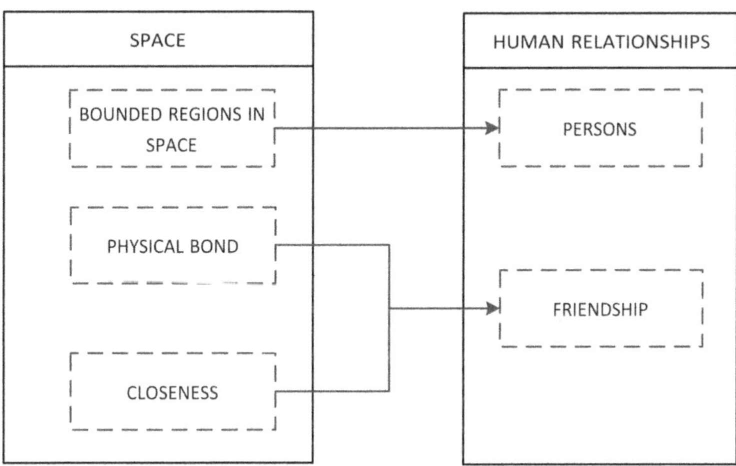

Figure 2.13 Metaphors of human relationships.

Persons are containers

From the metaphors analysed so far, it should be clear by now that the CONTAINER image schema constitutes one of our most fundamental embodied sources for conceptualizing abstract domains. Friendship forms no exception on this rule as many people share the belief that a friend is someone who we can confide *in*. Underlying the notion of confiding is the metaphor A PERSON IS A CONTAINER. As Kövecses has pointed out, this metaphor assumes the existence of two selves: a true one which corresponds to a person's "deepest part" where the real person resides, and a superficial one which corresponds to the person's superficial part. This distinction is evidenced in such sentences as the one below (quoted from Kövecses):

> The difference between a best friend and a good friend is a great degree of honesty, complete renunciation of facades and masks which consequently leads to them being themselves in a very natural way—it's not something contrived, or planned, rather it's a very natural state of being.[87]

The form of a mask also connects to another metaphor, LIFE IS A PLAY. To hide your true self in life is to wear a mask, to play a role. The mask serves as the outermost layer of the person that hides the most significant aspects of the self. By contrast, to be your real, true self in life, is to renounce this mask. Friends, then, are containers that do not wear masks, but instead open up to each other so they can experience each other's own true selves and reach a level of intimacy. As we shall demonstrate later in this book, this metaphorical mapping plays a key role in *Eyes Wide Shut*, where the form of the mask is integrally part of its visual imagery.

Friendship is a physical bond

Another common way to understand the intimacy of human relationships is through the source domain of physical links or connections. Consider, for example, the following statements about friendship as they were collected by Kövecses during an interview of native speakers of American English (author's emphasis):

> True friendship is a *bond that can weather the storms of life*. . . . [In] real friendship somehow or other you make the other person feel and they make you feel what *connects* you is that you have this *common, heavy, heavy link* in many areas, not that you were just working in the same field or what have you.[88]

Underlying these linguistic expressions is the metaphorical extension of the LINK image schema toward the domain of friendship. As Johnson has argued, the LINK image schema consists of two entities and a physical bond between them.[89] In the metaphor, then, the two entities are mapped onto the two friends, the physical bond onto the emotional bond and the strength of the bond onto the stability of the relationship. A strong positive emotional relationship is a relationship whose bond is very strong. The opposite is true of a strong negative emotional relationship. Obviously, this metaphor is not limited to friendships alone. As Kövecses stresses, human relationships in general are commonly conceived of as connections, links, ties, bonds, and so on.

Friendship is closeness

So far we have conceptualized the aspect of intimacy inherent to friendship in two distinctive ways, through the openness of a container and through the strength of a physical bond. A third and last way would be to conceptualize it through the spatial distance between two entities (e.g., two people), in particular, the absence of it, which may be termed *closeness*. This metaphor, FRIENDSHIP IS CLOSENESS, is grounded in the high-level metaphor AN EMOTIONAL RELATIONSHIP IS A DISTANCE BETWEEN TWO ENTITIES and is motivated by such linguistic examples as "*Close* friends," "We were *tight* as a glove," "They were *bosom* buddies," and "They are as *thick* as thieves."[90]

2.3 Metaphor and causation

If it comes to explaining how concepts are metaphorical, causation probably serves as one of the best illustrations. In chapter eleven of *Philosophy in the Flesh*, Lakoff and Johnson have argued that this concept, together with concepts such as events, changes, states, actions, and responses, which are all central to philosophy, are not reflections of a mind-independent reality.[91] Instead they are fundamentally human concepts. We reason about them by making use of metaphors that arise from everyday bodily experience. One such metaphor is what they refer to as the LOCATION EVENT-STRUCTURE metaphor.[92] This very general metaphor can be conceived of as a single complex mapping with a number of submappings that allow us to understand the main abstract concepts of the target domain of events (e.g., states, change, cause) metaphorically in terms of our more familiar concepts of motion in space (i.e., physical space, force, and motion). We already addressed the first two of them as they were associated with the conceptualization of emotion (i.e., STATES ARE BOUNDED REGIONS and CHANGES ARE MOVEMENTS). The two subsequent submappings of the "state" part of the LOCATION EVENT-STRUCTURE metaphor involve the conceptualizations of CAUSES AS FORCES and CAUSATION AS FORCED MOVEMENT. These metaphors typically come to the surface by the use of verbs that denote forced movement such as *bringing*, *throwing*, *driving* and *pulling*. They are licensed by such expressions as "He *drove* her crazy" or "That experience *pushed* him over the edge." As Lakoff and Johnson point out, in their literal sense, these verbs point to instances of physical movement.[93] Yet, in these expressions they are used metaphorically in order to designate abstract causation. Following the authors, the inferential logic true of forced movement may be mapped onto the inferential logic true of mental causation, as in table 2.9.[94]

Table 2.9 The inferential correspondences between forced movement and causation.

Inferences true of forced movement	*Inferences true of causation*
The application of the force precedes or accompanies the movement.	The occurrence of the cause precedes or accompanies the change of state.
The movement would not have occurred without the application of a force.	The change of a mental state would not have occurred without a cause.
The force impinges on the entity that moves.	The cause impinges on the entity that changes state.

The question that immediately arises, is of course, how the CAUSES ARE FORCES metaphor applies to the concepts of perception and emotion. Given that the Western folk theory of emotion theorizes both concepts as causes, we might conceptualize them as forces as well: perception as the force that brings about an emotion (the force of perception) and emotion as the force that brings about a behavioral response (the force of emotion) (see figure 2.14). Let us take a closer look at each submapping. As was the case with perception and emotion, we conclude our discussion with a discussion of a metonymy within the target domain of events, namely the EFFECT FOR CAUSE metonymy.

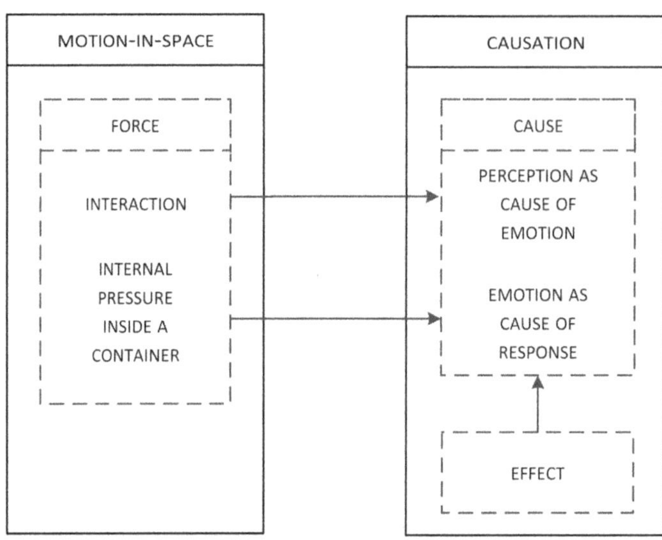

Figure 2.14 Metaphors of causation.

The force of perception

We already saw above how perception can be conceptualized as a force interaction between a perceiver and an object perceived. Hence, given that perception is the cause of emotion and causes are forces, it follows that the force interaction between the PR and the OP might be viewed as a physical force in its own right that may produce an effect in the perceiver (i.e., the effect of becoming emotional). From the cause of perception (movement => interaction) we are now shifting away to perception as cause (interaction => effect). This gives rise to what Kövecses labels the CAUSE OF EMOTION IS A PHYSICAL FORCE metaphor.[95] In contrast to the interaction metaphor for perception that has to do with the way perception arises, this metaphor primarily emphasizes the way emotions arise. Linguistic examples include such expressions as "He *blew* me away," "When I found out, it *hit* me *hard*" or "That was a terrible *blow*." Following Kövecses, we might make the underlying metaphorical mappings vivid, as in table 2.10, by means of adopting the basic concepts of Talmy's force dynamic model as discussed earlier.[96]

Table 2.10 The cause of emotion is a physical force.

Force schema	*Source: Physical force*	*Target: Emotion*
Agonist	Physical object	The rational self
Antagonist	Physical force	The cause of emotion
The intrinsic force tendency of the Antagonist	To produce effect in object	To cause self to become emotional
The intrinsic force tendency of the Agonist	To remain unaffected by the force	To remain unemotional

The force of emotion

When it comes to conceptualizing the second part of the folk scenario (emotion as cause of a response), Kövecses has argued that the general-level metaphor EMOTION IS A FORCE might be instantiated by several specific-level metaphors.[97] One of the best known and most studied metaphors in this regard is what the author labels the EMOTION IS INTERNAL PRESSURE INSIDE A CONTAINER metaphor. In this metaphor people are conceptualized as containers for emotions with the substance inside the container corresponding to the emotion. The substance exerts an internal pressure on the container. When there is very little substance in the container, the pressure is low and thus emotion is at low intensity. In that case, there is little motivation for the self to undertake action (i.e., to respond emotionally). By contrast, with an increase of the substance, the pressure becomes higher, and thus also the intensity of the emotion. The higher the intensity of the internal pressure to bring about an effect, the higher also the intensity of the self's motivation to respond emotionally. If the intensity of internal pressure increases to the point that the substance goes out of the container, an external effect on the container takes place. In that case, the self performs an emotional response. This effect, however, might be prevented insofar as the container is able to keep the substance inside, that is, in case the self succeeds in controlling the emotional response. Likewise, one may lay out these mappings, as in table 2.11, by making use of Talmy's force dynamic model.

Table 2.11 Emotion is a pressure inside a container.

Force schema	*Source: Internal pressure*	*Target: Emotion*
Agonist	The container-entity that is affected by the pressure	The rational self that is affected by the emotion
Antagonist	The substance with pressure inside the container	The emotion (= motivation for action)
The intrinsic force tendency of the Antagonist	Substance-pressure on the container	The emotion causing the self to respond
The intrinsic force tendency of the Agonist	The container-entity attempts to resist the pressure (= attempts to keep the substance inside)	The rational self attempts not to respond (= attempts to control the emotional response)

Effect for cause

Although Lakoff and Johnson exclude metonymy from their discussion of the LOCATION EVENT-STRUCTURE, other scholars such as Radden and Kövecses make mention of the existence of a general metonymy within the target domain of events, namely the EFFECTS FOR CAUSES metonymy.[98] In their study both scholars argue that effects, as opposed to causes, serve more often as a metonymical vehicle. They find support for their claim in several subtypes of the EFFECTS FOR CAUSES metonymy. This list includes, among others, the metonymy PHYSICAL/BEHAVIORAL EFFECT FOR EMOTION, as was discussed earlier in the subsection about emotions (e.g., "She was upset"). Since perception and emotion can be conceived of not only as causes, but additionally as effects (i.e., the first as effect of the object perceived and the second as the effect of perception), one may conceptualize two additional subtypes of the EFFECTS FOR CAUSES metonymy. Following Radden and Kövecses, they may be referred to as THE PERCEPTION FOR THE OBJECT PERCEIVED (e.g., "What a sight") and the EMOTION FOR THE CAUSE OF EMOTION (e.g., "She is my joy").

3. From embodied conceptual structure to film: The challenge of going beyond language

Having examined how the conceptual structure of mental causation is embodied, we are now in a position to address the relation between embodied conceptual structure and film. As was already mentioned in the introduction, film, as opposed to language, can be seen as a medium that blends various modes of expression, including not only linguistic modes, but also (and above all) non-verbal modes of expression such as pictures and music. As far as cognitive linguistics is concerned, language has always been the centre of attention to provide empirical support for the thesis of embodied cognition. One merely has to consider all the linguistic examples that were cited in this chapter to back the underlying metaphorical and metonymical mappings. Given that this book is about film, however, we are not so much interested in the various ways image-schematic driven metaphors and their interactions with metonymies are licenced by linguistic manifestations, as we are interested in the ways they are manifested at the audio-visual level of films. Motivation for this widening of scope can be found in the nature of conceptual metaphor itself. As we have seen earlier, metaphor and metonymy are considered properties of the *mind* rather than exclusively properties of *language*. The latter is merely the surface level in which the embodied conceptual structure is manifested. Given this assertion, it is therefore plausible to assume that language is not the only form of representation which permits the cognitive mechanisms of metaphor and metonymy. Addressing this assumption allows one to avoid an often raised critique against Conceptual Metaphor Theory. This fallacy roughly consists of the claim that cognitive linguists tend to fall in a practice of circular reasoning in which the central proposition (i.e., metaphor is a conceptual phenomenon rather than a linguistic one) is proven by referring back to language.[99] Indeed, if research on conceptual metaphor is restricted to language, opponents might contend that there is no difference between the conceptual level and the linguistic level, which in turn would significantly jeopardize the theoretical validity of CMT. As Forceville and Jeulink argue:

> If CMT is correct in emphasizing the centrality of the MIND IS BODY metaphor in human conceptualizing, it should be difficult or even impossible to find non-metaphorical conceptualizations of abstract phenomena. . . . The focus on verbal manifestations of the postulated conceptual metaphors is no help here: detractors might object that the conceptual and the verbal levels are actually the same thing. If this should be the case, CMT claims about the central role of metaphor in cognition would of course be seriously undermined.[100]

Going beyond language, however, confronts us with a set of new theoretical challenges that, precisely because of the primacy of language in the literature, has been often overlooked. As has been revealed in the introduction, they involve such questions as to how embodied conceptual structure can be reconciled with the *iconic* nature of pictures, and how embodied conceptual structure can be bridged to the *non-representational* nature of musical sounds? The focus of the two subsequent chapters will be on addressing the first question. This task will be divided over two chapters. In the first chapter, chapter 3, we will address the question as to how moving pictures can elicit the source tools of embodied meaning-making, in particular, image schemas (as the bodily source of metaphors) and the vehicle concepts of metonymies. In the second chapter, chapter 4, we will illustrate, through various examples, how Kubrick's films make use of these tools in order to convey in visual terms the kind of stories of mental causation as identified in the first chapter.

4. Conclusion

In the previous chapter we have identified a conceptual structure that can be seen as representative of the conceptual structure underlying the narratives of Kubrick's films. Following the terminology used in the field of philosophy of mind, we referred to this structure as mental causation. The goal of this chapter, then, was to explore the question as to how mental causation is embodied. In order to do so, we first had to clarify three theoretical concepts that are central to the embodied cognition thesis as put forward by the advocates of cognitive linguistics. These concepts were identified as: image schema, metaphor and metonymy. Having learned about these tools, we were able to show how people use them unconsciously in their everyday linguistic interactions to reason about such concepts as perception, cognition, time, emotion and causation; all of which are central to mental causation. We ended this chapter by raising some of the challenges that arise when one attempts to connect the notion of embodied conceptual structure to the formal level of film. In the next chapter we will consider one of them as we will demonstrate, through an analysis of Kubrick's work, how moving pictures are able to elicit the embodied tools of meaning-making, despite their iconic nature.

Notes

1. Lakoff and Johnson, "Why Cognitive Linguistics," 249.
2. Due to the abundance of literature on these topics, the task of covering them will be unavoidably schematic and synthetic. For further understanding, we refer the reader to the works quoted in this chapter.
3. Evans and Green, *Cognitive Linguistics*, 179.
4. Ibid., 179. As Johnson put it, "image schemas are not to be understood either as merely 'mental' or merely 'bodily,' but rather as contours of what Dewey called the 'body-mind.'" See Johnson, "The Philosophical Significance," 22.
5. Johnson, *The Body*, 30–31. For a discussion, see also Evans and Green, *Cognitive Linguistics*, 179; Lakoff, *Women*, 271.
6. Lakoff and Johnson, *Philosophy*, 31–32. See also Lakoff, *Women*, 271.
7. Hampe, *From Perception to Meaning*; Evans and Green, *Cognitive Linguistics*, 179–189.
8. Evans and Green, *Cognitive Linguistics*, 180.
9. Lakoff and Johnson, *Philosophy*, 34.
10. Ibid., 9–15. See also Johnson, *The Meaning of the Body*, 139.
11. Johnson, "The Philosophical," 19.
12. Ibid., 20.
13. Hampe, *From Perception to Meaning*, 2; Evans and Green, *Cognitive Linguistics*, 190.
14. Evans and Green, *Cognitive Linguistics*, 184.

15. Barsalou, "Perceptual Symbol Systems," 577–609.
16. Evans and Green, *Cognitive Linguistics*, 180; Johnson, *The Body in the Mind*, 23.
17. Lakoff and Johnson, for example, use the figure of a circle. See Lakoff and Johnson, *Philosophy*, 32.
18. Lakoff, *Women*, 45. For a discussion, see also Correa-Beningfield et al. "Image Schemas vs. Complex Primitives," 348.
19. Johnson, "The Philosophical," 22; Johnson, *The Meaning*, 139.
20. After Lakoff and Johnson, *Philosophy*, 32.
21. Johnson, *The Meaning*, 139.
22. See, among others, Gibbs, *Embodiment*, 91; Lakoff and Johnson, *Philosophy*, 32–34.
23. The concept of a *trajector* (abbreviated TR) derives from Langacker's theory of Cognitive Grammar and relates to the entity in the scene that is typically capable of motion. The entity with respect to which the TR moves, is called the *landmark* (abbreviated LM). In cognitive linguistic literature it is also common to refer to both entities as the *subject* and *object*, respectively. Both terms are also closely related to the principle of Gestalt psychology known as *figure-ground segregation*. The *figure* is the entity that is typically privileged in the spatial scene, perhaps due to a definite contour or prominent coloring. It stands out against the *ground* or *reference object* which is the entity that is given less prominence in the spatial scene. For a discussion, see Evans and Green, *Cognitive Linguistics*, 69, 541.
24. After Lakoff and Johnson, *Philosophy*, 33.
25. Lakoff and Johnson, *Philosophy*, 33–34.
26. Johnson, *The Body in the Mind*, 43.
27. Radden, "Motion Metaphorized," 436.
28. Johnson, *The Body in the Mind*, 43–44.
29. Radden, "Motion Metaphorized," 437–438.
30. Johnson, *The Body in the Mind*, 45–47. For a discussion of these schemas, see also Evans and Green, *Cognitive Linguistics*, 187–189.
31. Talmy, "Force Dynamics," 49–100.
32. Ibid., 53.
33. Dewell, "Dynamic patterns," 369–394.
34. For a good survey and evaluation of this claim, see Gibbs, *Embodiment*, 90.
35. Lakoff and Johnson, *Metaphors We Live By*.
36. Evans and Green, *Cognitive Linguistics*, 190.
37. For a list of common source and target domains, see Kövecses, *Metaphor: A Practical Introduction*, 17–32.
38. Evans and Green, *Cognitive Linguistics*, 190.
39. "*The Shining*: Kubrick's Masterpiece of Suspense, Symbolism, Sets & Steadicam," accessed October 14, 2018, https://selvedgeyard.com/2017/03/10/the-shining-kubricks-masterpiece-of-suspense-symbolism-sets-steadicam/
40. We will elaborate more on the concept of "narrative absorption" in chapter 5.
41. For a discussion, see, among others, Dirven and Pörings, eds., *Metaphor and Metonymy*; Lakoff and Johnson, *Metaphors We Live By*; Kövecses and Radden, "Metonymy"; and Radden and Kövecses, "Towards a Theory of Metonymy."
42. Lakoff and Turner, *More Than Cool Reason*, 103; Radden and Kövecses, "Towards a Theory of Metonymy," 21.
43. Radden and Kövecses, "Towards a Theory of Metonymy," 21.
44. See ref. no. SK/17/1/11, 119 in the appendix.
45. See also Ruiz de Mendoza Ibánez, "Metaphor, Metonymy," 293.
46. Evans and Green, *Cognitive Linguistics*, 313–314.
47. Barcelona, *Metaphor and Metonymy*, 16.
48. Goossens, "Metaptonymy," 323–340; Ruiz de Mendoza Ibánez, "Metaphor, Metonymy"; Velasco, "Metaphor, Metonymy, and Image-Schemas," 47–63.
49. Velasco, "Metaphor, Metonymy, and Image-Schemas," 52.

50. Ibid., 54.
51. These sources include, among others, Lakoff, "Reflections," 133–144; Yamanashi, "Metaphorical Modes," 157–175; and Yu, "The Eyes," 663–686 (as far as the concept of *perception* is concerned); Kövecses, *Metaphor and Emotion* (as far as the concept of *emotion* is concerned); and Lakoff and Johnson, *Philosophy in the Flesh*, Chap. 11 (as far as the concept of *causation* is concerned).
52. Lakoff and Johnson, *Metaphors We Live By*, 30; Lakoff, "Reflections," 133–144; Yamanashi, "Metaphorical Modes," 157–175; Yu, "The Eyes," 663–686.
53. For studies that focus on cognition see, among others, Gibbs, *Embodiment*, 96–99; Johnson, *The Meaning of the Body*, 165; Lakoff and Johnson, *Philosophy in the Flesh*, Chap. 12; Yu, "Chinese Metaphors of Thinking," 141–165. For studies that focus on time see, among others, Boroditsky, "Metaphoric Structuring," 1–28; Evans, *The Structure of Time*; Gentner, "Spatial Metaphors in Temporal Reasoning," 203–222; Gentner, Mutsumi and Boroditsky, "As Time Goes By," 537–565; Lakoff and Johnson, *Philosophy in the Flesh*, Chap. 10; and Núñez and Sweetser, "With the Future Behind Them," 401–450.
54. Searle refers to this commonsensical definition of a visual field as the "objective visual field." He distinguishes it from what he calls the "subjective visual field," that area of visual consciousness in front of your face that one experiences when closing your eyes. As he states, in the former "everything is seen or can be seen, whereas in the latter "nothing is seen nor can be seen." See Searle, *Seeing Things as They Are*, 4. This characterization of the visual field, coming from the philosophical tradition of conceptual analysis, differs fundamentally from the conception offered by such neuroscientists as Smythies who defines the visual field more ambiguously as "the spatial array of visual sensations available to observation in introspectionist psychological experiments." See Smythies, "A Note on the Concept of the Visual Field," 369. The difference in definitional criteria thus reflects the intellectual divide that separates the advocates of Direct Realism from the scientific advocates of the representative theory of perception.
55. Like most authors who write about the subject of perception, we will concentrate on vision.
56. Lakoff, "Reflections," 139; see also Yu, "The Eyes," 676.
57. Lakoff, "Reflections," 139.
58. See ref. no. SK/17/1/11 in the appendix.
59. Lakoff, "Reflections," 139.
60. See also Barcelona, *Metaphor and Metonymy*, 249.
61. Lakoff and Johnson, *Philosophy*, Chap. 12; Sweetser, *From Etymology to Pragmatics*.
62. Gibbs, *Embodiment*, 97.
63. Ibid., 97; Johnson, *The Meaning of the Body*, 165; Lakoff and Johnson, *Philosophy in the Flesh*, Chap. 12; Yu, "The Eyes"; Yu, "Chinese Metaphors."
64. Lakoff and Johnson, *Philosophy in the Flesh*, 239.
65. See, for instance, Scherer, "What Does Facial Expression Express?" 139–165.
66. Kaiser and Wehrle, "Facial Expressions," 287.
67. See, for example, Gentner, "Spatial Metaphors," 203–222; Gentner, Imai and Boroditsky, "As Time Goes By," 537–565; Evans, *The Structure of Time*; Lakoff and Johnson, *Philosophy in the Flesh*, Chap. 10.
68. Lakoff and Johnson, *Philosophy*, 140.
69. Núñez and Sweetser, "With the Future Behind Them," 401–450.
70. Ibid., 438–439.
71. Johnson, *The Meaning of the Body*, 165.
72. Núñez and Sweetser, "With the Future Behind Them," 438.
73. Ibid., 439.
74. Ibid., 439.
75. Gentner, "Spatial Metaphors," 203–222; Gentner, Imai and Boroditsky, "As Time Goes By," 537–565; Evans, *The Structure of Time*; Lakoff and Johnson, *Philosophy*, Chap. 10.

76. Lakoff and Johnson, *Philosophy in the Flesh*, 141.
77. Kövecses, *Metaphor and Emotion*, 52.
78. Ibid., 55; Lakoff and Johnson, *Philosophy in the Flesh*, 180.
79. Ibid., 181.
80. Kövecses, *Metaphor and Emotion*, 55.
81. Lakoff and Johnson, *Philosophy in the Flesh*, 180; see also Radden, "Motion Metaphorized," 425.
82. Ibid., 183.
83. Kövecses, *Metaphor and Emotion*, 134.
84. See, for instance, Ekman and Friesen, *Unmasking the Face*; Ekman, Friesen and Ancoli, "Facial Signs," 1125-1134.
85. See, in particular, the criticism voiced by Barrett in *How Emotions are Made.*
86. Kövecses, *Metaphor and Emotion*, 87.
87. Ibid., 90.
88. Ibid., 94.
89. Johnson, *The Body in the Mind*, 117–119.
90. Kövecses, *Metaphor and Emotion*, 92.
91. As stated in the introduction, Lakoff and Johnson refer to these concepts as "event-structure concepts." See Lakoff and Johnson, *Philosophy in the Flesh*, 170.
92. Ibid., 179.
93. Ibid., 194.
94. Ibid., 185.
95. Kövecses, *Metaphor and Emotion*, 83.
96. Ibid., 84.
97. Ibid., 65.
98. Radden and Kövecses, "Towards a Theory of Metonymy," 39.
99. See, among others, Forceville, "Non-verbal and Multimodal Metaphor," 19–42; Forceville and Jeulink, "The Flesh and Blood of Embodied Understanding," 37–59; Gibbs and Perlman, "The Contested Impact of Cognitive Linguistic Research," 211–228; Pecher, Boot and Van Dantzig, "Abstract Concepts," 217–248. Another related criticism has to do with the methods of cognitive linguists. It concerns the scepticism that many cognitive scientists (notably psychologists) feel toward the strategy of making conclusions about the conceptual structure on the basis of the individual analyst's own intuitions. To avoid this criticism, it is required that the findings of cognitive linguists are further validated by evidence obtained from convergent operations such as empirical studies. For a more detailed discussion of some of these studies that are supportive of CMT, see Gibbs, *Embodiment*, 118–121.
100. Forceville and Jeulink, "The Flesh and Blood of Embodied Understanding," 39.

Chapter 3

Setting the Conditions of Embodied Meaning-Making in Film: The Role of Film Style and Acting

The most powerful conveyor of meaning is the immediate impact of perceptual form.

—Rudolf Arnheim[1]

The goal of this chapter is to examine how the building blocks of conceptual metaphor, as discussed in the previous chapter, can be manifested at the visual level of moving pictures. First, we lay out the two challenges that are inherent to the examination of this question, namely: (1) the challenge of demonstrating how image schemas may be imposed onto the iconic and representational level of films and (2) the challenge of demonstrating how moving pictures, in a non-verbal and metonymical way, may give rise to target domains to which these image schemas might be extended metaphorically. To each of these challenges the two subsequent parts of this chapter will propose an answer. The answer to the first challenge will be sought in the notion of film style. Using many examples taken from the films of Kubrick, we will show how film, through the application of various cinematic devices, may structure the reality in front of the camera in such a way as to elicit the ostensive appearance of image schemas. The answer to the second question will be sought in the notion of acting. Through an analysis of some of the performances in Kubrick's films, we will demonstrate how actors, through their body language, are able to convey the concepts of mental causation metonymically. It is only once we have successfully dealt with both challenges that we will be able to show, in the next chapter, how the films of Kubrick resort to these image schemas in order to flesh out the structure of mental causation visually.

1. Image schemas and target domains: A twofold challenge

In the previous chapter we used linguistic expressions for the purpose of showing how the conceptual structure of mental causation is embodied through the mechanism of metaphor. In these expressions it was not difficult to identify the two elements that make up the "a is b" relationship of metaphor. For instance, in a sentence such as "I'm *in* love," one can directly and unambiguously recognize the image schema and the target domain that are responsible for creating the metaphor. We arbitrarily use the words "in" and "love" to refer to the concepts of containment and love, because we have learnt to do so. Our shared knowledge about the code makes it easy for the communicator to represent them and easy for the reader to interpret them. However, if it is our goal to examine how the films of Kubrick communicate stories of mental causation visually and non-verbally, then, we have to examine how both elements can be elicited in moving pictures, not sentences. Moving pictures, however, do not share the arbitrary nature of language. As we already saw in the introduction, pictures, as opposed to words, bear a relationship to reality that is based on resemblance rather than on arbitrary convention, that is, they are iconic rather than symbolic. This, in turn, raised the question as to how the embodied conceptual nature of metaphor can be reconciled with the iconic nature of pictures. Given the two-fold nature of metaphor, any attempt to address this challenge amounts to answering two sub-questions: (1) How can moving pictures instantiate image schemas? and (2) How can moving pictures give rise, in a non-verbal way, to the conceptual target domains to which these image schemas can be extended metaphorically?

It is not hard to see how the second question may be resolved on an intuitive basis. As we saw in the previous chapter, abstract target domains may not only be accessed through metaphor, but also through metonymy. Metonymies, as opposed to metaphors, operate through source vehicles that refer to perceptually rich entities in the concrete world. As such they can also be represented pictorially. Let us recall, for example, the source vehicles that were used to address the target domains inherent to the structure of mental causation. They included concrete concepts such as eyes, facial expressions and bodily behavior. It is in the search for the means to represent these concepts, then, that acting quickly comes to the forefront as it is through the bodily performance of the actor or actress, that we may assume that viewers get access to the target domains of mental causation. Assessing this claim, will be the aim of the third section of this chapter in which we shall draw upon insights from cognitive theorists of acting to assess the relationship between performance and concepts.

The first question, by contrast, poses more of a challenge. As we know from the previous chapter, image schemas, as opposed to the source vehicles of metonymies, do not refer to concrete entities in the physical world, but to abstract gestalt structures of sensory-motor experience. The visual reality that is not yet rendered pictorially on-screen, however, is not abstract, but concrete. This, in turn, raises the question as to how film may organize this reality in such a way as to allow for the ostensive appearance of unifying schematic patterns that are salient in our everyday experience?

It is in the search for an answer to this question that we may turn to Rudolf Arnheim's gestalt approach to static art works such as paintings, drawings and sculptures.[2] Challenging the dominance of the linguistic view of meaning and the dualistic habit of separating the intuitive from the cognitive, Arnheim put forward the view that images of art (the domain of perception) offer more than merely illustrations of events or things. Like words, they are capable of giving form to concepts (the domain of thought). This assumption has led the author to identify and advance his famous concept of "visual thinking." At the core of this concept lies the following line of reasoning:

(1) Thinking calls for images.
(2) Images contain thought.
(3) The visual arts consist of images.
(4) Therefore, the visual arts are a homeground of visual thinking.[3]

To trace visual thinking in images, Arnheim argued, "one must look for well-structured shapes and relations" because it is through these patterns, which underlie the perception of form, that the specifiable themes or concepts of the work are spelled out.[4] To see how the structural skeleton of a work's composition may reflect the work's content, let us consider two paintings that the author discusses in his work: Jan Vermeer's *Woman Holding a Balance* (aka *Woman Weighing Gold*) and Paul Cézanne's portrait of his wife, *Mme. Cézanne in a Yellow Chair* (see figure 3.1).[5]

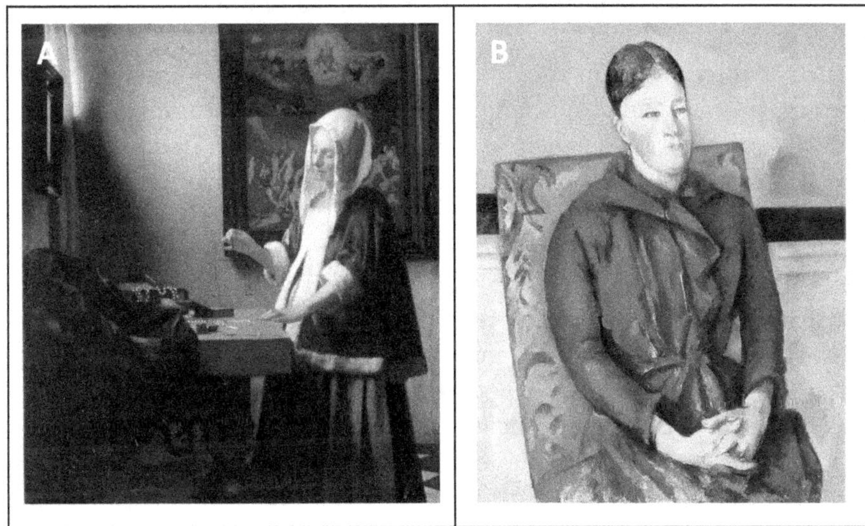

Figure 3.1. *A*, Jan Vermeer's *Woman Holding a Balance* (ca. 1664), Courtesy National Gallery of Art, Washington, and *B*, Paul Cézanne's *Mme. Cézanne in a Yellow Chair* (1888–90), Courtesy Art Institute, Chicago.

The first painting depicts a young woman who holds an empty pair of scales in her right hand while she stands before a painting of the Last Judgment of which its content contrasts with the valuable, golden objects lying on the table in front her. It is an allegory that invites the viewer to contemplate about the importance of resisting the temptations of the world and living modestly in order to find salvation. As Arnheim argues, this intellectual theme is expressed visually by the descending dark, rigidly vertical ledge of the frame in the very center of Vermeer's composition which takes hold of the woman's hand thus suspending its movement.[6] As he writes, "by this device the worldly scene of the foreground is arrested, while a light from above, stronger than the mundane glitter of the jewelry, causes the woman's eyes to close."

The second painting shows a seated, middle-aged woman who, despite its stability and external tranquility, nevertheless is loaded with energy and strong potential activity. As Arnheim so eloquently describes, this subtle blend of serenity and vigor, of firmness and disembodied freedom, which constitutes the theme of the painting, is achieved by various stylistic choices of the artist.[7] First, there is the upright format of the picture which reinforces the upright character of the figure, the chair and the head, thus creating a scale of increasing slimness running from the background over the chair to the figure in the foreground. This vertical quality, however, is counterpointed by the dark band on the wall which divides the background into two horizontal rectangles. Yet, the balance is restored again by the fact that the lower rectangle is taller than the upper one. At the same time, the pattern of dark rectangles is counteracted by the oval figures formed by the shoulders and arms, on the one hand, and the bright face, on the other hand. This dominant rightward movement is also enhanced by the way the figure is asymmetrically placed in relation to the chair. The fact that the figure is occupying mainly the right half of the chair, with the head being drawn toward the upper border of the frame, adds much to the painting's overall effect of lightness and suspension in space.

With examples such as these Arnheim attempted to show that works of art are more than illustrations of particular events. Through their structural conceptions they embody the meaning that the artist, consciously or unconsciously, intended to convey. It is here then, in Arnheim's emphasis on "hidden skeletal structures," that we may observe a close resemblance to Lakoff and Johnson's concept of an "image schema," as discussed in the previous chapter. This is acknowledged by Johnson himself who, in his own work, draws significantly on Arnheim's analysis of balance in the visual arts to develop his own conception of the image schema of BALANCE.[8] Hence, if visual works of art are capable of representing meaning through hidden structural patterns (or, as in our case, image schemas), as Arnheim illustrates so vividly, then we might assume that moving pictures are equally capable of expressing conceptual content by means of film form. In this way, we would be able to overcome the challenge posed by iconic images. Before exploring this hypothesis further in the next section, it should be stressed that Arnheim himself was rather sceptical about bringing his model for analysing compositional patterns in static media to film analysis. Arnheim believed that film was more restricted than other arts.[9] As to the reason why, he refers to the fundamental difference in viewing experience that exists between viewing static media such as a painting and viewing mobile media such as a film. In *The Power of the Center* he states this problem as follows:

> Depending on the film viewer's attitude, the experience of watching a film is much less or much more self-centered than that of looking at a painting. Either he finds himself comfortably seated with the screen as his frame of vision, imposing an immobile structure upon the passing action of the film, or he is captured by the plot so completely that he moves along with it. . . . A painting never belongs as much to the viewer as does the framed film screen, which is an instrument of his vision. . . . Visual composition reveals itself more readily in the quiet detachment from time, found in the immobile works of painting or sculpture.[10]

There is no doubt a certain truth in what Arnheim here writes. Narrative cinema deals with a rapid flow of images and an emphasis on character engagement that at first sight seems to impede the kind of absorbed contemplation that characterizes our visual experience of a painting's composition. Arnheim believed that when we are engaged in a filmic experience, we can only "react to the brutal signals of immediate satisfaction."[11] In such a setting our eyes and ears are prevented from perceiving structures, which are critical for perceiving meaning (given the dependence of the latter on the former). However, as Scott Higgins recently has pointed out, the gap between the two modes of viewing may be smaller than Arnheim's words above seem to suggest. In his own anthology devoted to bridging Arnheim's body of thought to film scholarship, he comments on this as follows:

> Classical continuity privileges attentional patterns used to follow individuals through space; that is, we tend to watch characters rather than compositions. Yet, some filmmakers overly compose their frame and drive attention around it in a way more tune with Arnheim's aesthetic observation. Moreover, where directors do not offer an invitation to contemplate a long take, they can build patterns from shot to shot, or from camera movement to camera movement, in a manner functionally equivalent to a grand compositional scheme.[12]

The author finds support for his claim in the work of the American film director Vincente Minnelli whose color design, he argues, "rewards both practically and compositionally oriented viewing, both contemplation and sensual engagement."[13] In the next section, we will follow Higgin's approach by equally bringing Arnheim's way of thinking to the domain of film studies. Using many examples as taken from Kubrick's oeuvre, we will show how his films, through their visual style, impose several dynamic image schematic structures onto the visual reality.

2. Image schemas and a film's visual style

To structure our discussion, we will first say a few words about form. Among the scholars who have studied the concept most extensively are David Bordwell and Kristin Thompson.[14] In their seminal introduction to the analysis of cinema both authors broadly refer to film form as "the overall system of relations that we can perceive among the elements in the whole film."[15] Pivotal to this definition is the perceptual condition, that is, there has to be a person perceptually experiencing the film in order for the concept of film form to come into existence. Without the perceiver, a film is merely a lifeless object, patterns of light and darkness projected on a screen. Moreover, in order for this perceiver to perceive the overall system of a film, the film itself has to possess a quality. It has to prompt the viewer to see the orderly relations among the parts of the film, for in the absence of it, the viewer will not be able to exercise his or her gift for bringing order to chaos and for constructing wholes out of parts. This, in turn, begs the question of principles. By which principles of film does film help create the relationships among the parts? Bordwell and Thompson answer this question by emphasizing the significance of two interacting systems of film: the *formal system* and the *stylistic system*.[16]

The formal system refers to the discursive function that determines the organization of a film's images and sound. We already discussed one type of formal system in the first chapter of this book, namely *narrative* form. Although this type appears to be the most common one typically associated with fictional, live-action cinema it is not the only one. In addition, the authors identify four other systems: two types of form that are often used in documentaries (*categorical* and *rhetorical* form) and two types of forms that are characteristic of experimental films (*abstract* and *associational* form). Although these categories may be mapped onto genres, they are not mutually exclusive, meaning that an individual film or a genre may incorporate many types of filmic organization.

The stylistic system refers to the "unified, developed, and significant use of particular technical choices."[17] Here, the authors identify four areas of cinematic techniques: two techniques of the shot (mise-en-scene and cinematography), the technique that relates shot to shot, editing, and the relation of sound to film images. The film's stylistic system cannot be studied in isolation from the film's overall form. The pattern that emerges from the film's style, may be designed to serve one of the formal systems. For instance, techniques can function to facilitate the purpose of narrative form, that is, to advance the cause-effect chain.

It is through the second system of film style, then, that we will now argue that films are capable of structuring the spatial and visible world in such a way as to elicit image schemas. Given that this chapter is about visual images, the emphasis will be on those cinematic techniques that have a visual effect on the viewer (e.g., cinematography, mise-en-scene and editing). The discussion will be structured in three parts. First, we consider the role of image schemas in our visual perception of a *static shot*. A static shot is here defined as a shot that does not evoke the visual effect of moving objects on-screen (i.e., static mise-en-scene) nor the visual effect of a mobile frame as elicited by camera movement. Consequently, this part will be significantly indebted to Arnheim's pre-existing work on structural patterns in static visual art, as briefly discussed above. Here, the emphasis will be on the cinematic technique of framing. Second, we consider the role of image schemas in our visual perception of a *dynamic shot*. A dynamic shot is here defined as a shot that does consider either one or both of the two effects above. Hence, the primary focus of this part will be on the cinematic techniques of fixed-frame movement and mobile framing. Third and last, we consider the role of image schemas in our visual perception of relations among shots. This part can be linked to the cinematic technique of editing. Each of the techniques under discussion will be illuminated through various examples taken from Kubrick's oeuvre.

2.1 The static shot

2.1.1 The CONTAINER image schema

In his Wittgensteinian-inspired book *Projecting a Camera*, film theorist Edward Branigan has argued that the concept of a "frame" is a *polysemous* word meaning that it is a word that has "distinct, though related, meanings, or at least meanings that are fairly close."[18] To illustrate this, he identifies no fewer than fifteen different, though related, ways of employing the word "frame" in the critical discourse about film.[19] Here, we adopt the first way which is probably the most commonly accepted definition of a frame as experienced by the film viewer:

> The frame is the *real edge* of an image on the screen that has resulted from limits imposed on celluloid inside a physical camera and projector so that, for example, a projected image can be said to be "in frame" or "out of frame" on the screen. A spectator, however, is not really seeing an actual edge. The edge of an image onscreen is not the edge of an individual exposed frame from inside a film camera but, at least, a composite edge that is made up of a number of exposed frames, because in watching a film a spectator does not see each individual frame halted on the screen as if a series of slides were being shown.[20]

Regardless of the polysemy of the word frame, there seems to be a general structure underlying *all* ways of reasoning about frames. It is clear from our language about frames, as evidenced by the expressions "in frame" and "out of frame" in the quotation above, that the structure inherent to our perception of the filmic frame is that of the

CONTAINER image schema.[21] Evidence of this congruence can be found in the way the inferences true of bounded regions, as already discussed in chapter 2, also hold for frames (see table 3.1).

Table 3.1 The frame as container.

Inferences true of bounded regions	***Inferences true of frames***
If you're *in* a bounded region, you're not *out* of that bounded region.	If you're *in* a frame, you're not *out* of that frame.
If you're *out* of a bounded region, you're not *in* that bounded region.	If you're *out* of a frame you're not *in* that frame.
If you're deep *in* a bounded region, you are far from being *out* of that bounded region.	If you're deep *in* a frame, you are far from being *out* of that frame.
If you are *on the edge of* a bounded region, then you're *close to* being *in* that bounded region.	If you are *on the edge of* a frame, then you are *close to* being *in* that frame.

But what do these inferences mean? What does it mean to say that something is "in a frame" or something is "out of a frame"? To answer these seemingly basic questions is to take a look at the nature of the image projected on the screen (henceforth, the film image). A film image is essentially a *two-dimensional* image with a creation of an illusion of *depth* on it. This definition suggests the existence of three orientational axes. The word "two-dimensional" suggests a horizontal axis X (a LEFT-RIGHT schema) and a vertical axis Y (a TOP-DOWN schema), whereas the word "depth" suggests an illusionary depth axis Z (a FRONT-BACK schema). From this conception of a film image, we may draw six zones of off-screen space. Following Noël Burch, these can be identified as: (1) the space *left* of the frame, (2) the space *right* of the frame, (3) the space *above* the frame, (4) the space *below* the frame, (5) the space *behind* the set and (6) the space *behind and near* the camera (see figure 3.2).[22] Together they comprise what Bordwell and Thompson describe as the "six areas blocked from being visible on the screen but still part of the space of the scene."[23]

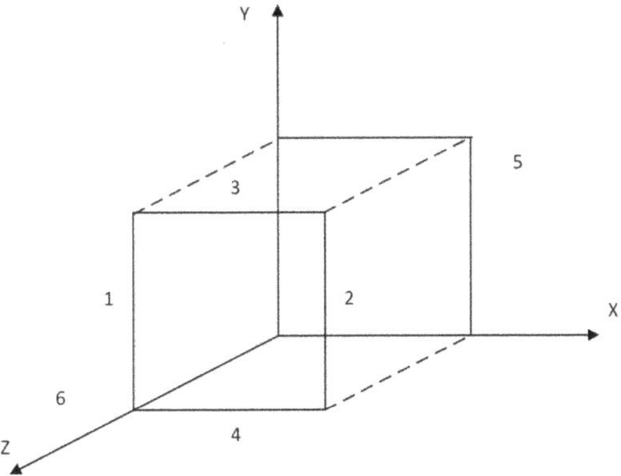

Figure 3.2. The six zones of off-screen space (after Burch).

Inherent to these six zones are three different boundaries: (1) the boundary of the frame, (2) the boundary of the set and (3) the boundary of the camera.

The first boundary provides us with the criteria for defining the "inside" and the "outside" of a frame. Something is inside the frame if it is present within the four edges of the frame. By contrast, something is outside the frame if it lies outside these edges, that is, if it is excluded from the inside space of the frame. Naturally, it is only the inside of the frame that is also on-screen.[24] This assertion is self-evident from the spatial logic built into the CONTAINER schema:

- Given two containers, the film frame, A, and the screen, B, and an object, X, if A is *in* B and X is *in* A, then X is *in* B (i.e., X is on-screen).

Underlying this spatial logic is a static conception of the CONTAINER schema of which its visual diagram (figure 3.3) is similar to the figure discussed earlier in chapter 2 (see figure 2.2). It is a "static" diagram because there is no movement ("an arrow") linked to either one or both of the two central figures (i.e., the containers and/or the visual object).

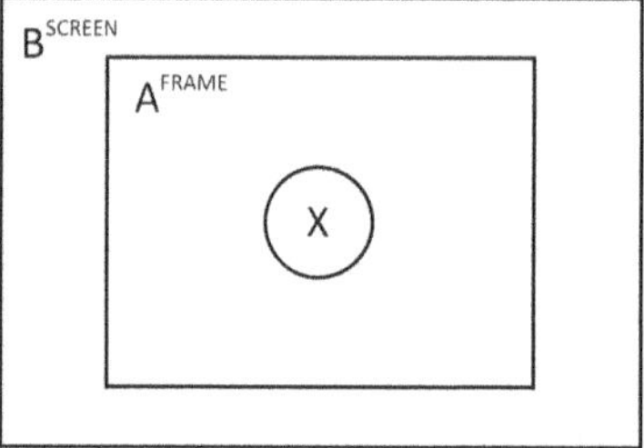

Figure 3.3. The static conception of the CONTAINER schema as applied to the filmic terms, frame and screen.

The amount of space *in* the screen that is occupied by the inside of the frame depends on the *aspect ratio*, that is, the relationship of the frame's width to its height.[25] In the original ratio known as Academy ratio, the frame was 1.33 or 1.37 as wide as it was high, later the width was normalized at 1.66 times the height for the European film market and 1.85 times the height for US and Asian markets. Table 3.2 gives you an idea of the aspect ratios of Kubrick's films. It compares the original aspect ratios of their theatrical releases with the aspect ratios of today's DVD and Blu-ray versions (the versions used for capturing the screenshots for this book are marked in italics).

Table 3.2 The aspect ratios of Kubrick's films

Year	*Film*	*Gauge*	*Theatrical ratio*	*DVD ratio*	*Blu-ray ratio*
1953	*Fear and Desire*	35mm	1.33:1	1.33:1	*1.37:1*
1955	*Killer's Kiss*	35mm	1.33:1	1.33:1	*1.37:1*
1956	*The Killing*	35mm	1.33:1	1.33:1	*1.66:1*

Continued

1957	*Paths of Glory*	35mm	1.66:1	1.33:1	*1.66:1*
1960	*Spartacus*	70mm	2.21:1	2.20:1	1.85:1/*2.21:1*
1962	*Lolita*	35mm	1.66:1	1.66:1	*1.66:1*
1964	*Dr. Strangelove*	35mm	1.66:1	1.66:1	*1.66:1*/1.78:1
1968	*2001: A Space Odyssey*	70mm	2.20:1	2.20:1	*2.20:1*
1971	*A Clockwork Orange*	35mm	1.66:1	1.66:1	*1.66.1*
1975	*Barry Lyndon*	35mm	1.66:1	1.59:1/1.66:1	*1.66:1*/1.78:1
1980	*The Shining*	35mm	1.66:1	1.33:1	*1.78:1*
1987	*Full Metal Jacket*	35mm	1.85:1	1.33:1	*1.78:1*
1999	*Eyes Wide Shut*	35mm	1.85:1	1.33:1	*1.78:1*

As this table indicates, most of Kubrick's films were shot in the Academy ratio.[26] The two exceptions are *Spartacus* and *2001* which were both shot in wider aspect ratios (2.21 times the height for the 70 mm release prints). Unfortunately, as many home theatre fans of Kubrick have remarked, some of today's DVD versions, especially those versions of his later films, do not represent the aspect ratios in which they were screened.[27]

The second boundary refers to the boundary between what is part of the set of the film (i.e., the scenery and props as arranged for shooting a film) and what is not (e.g., wooden supports holding up the walls, the lighting stands, electrical cords, camera men). Naturally, in narrative cinema this boundary should be preserved in order for a viewer to perceive the story as real and not as artificial. Consequently, this entails that a revelation of the outside space of the set should be avoided at any cost, unless it is the filmmaker's intention to do so, for otherwise the shot would call attention to the fictional nature of the film. Given that what we see on-screen depends on what is *in* frame, it follows that the inside of the frame should always overlap with the inside of the set. The boundary of the film set may be located outside the filmic frame, yet its content should at all time be the content of the filmic frame. An inclusion of the space beyond the set within the frame would reveal the scenery as artificial. Again, we may draw on the logic of the CONTAINER schema to infer these conclusions:

- Given two containers, the film frame, A, and the set, B, if the whole inside of A is *in* B, then the fictional nature of the film will be preserved.
- Given two containers, the film frame, A, and the set, B, if a part of the outside of B is *in* A, then the fictional nature of the film will be revealed.

Disregarding the container of the screen, we may illustrate and diagram this distinctive logic as in figure 3.4 (*A* and *B*, respectively). Naturally, making-of documentaries or behind-the-scenes are good means to expose the fictional nature of the film. Figure 3.4*B* shows a look behind the scenes of *The Shining* as it was shot by Kubrick's daughter Vivian.[28]

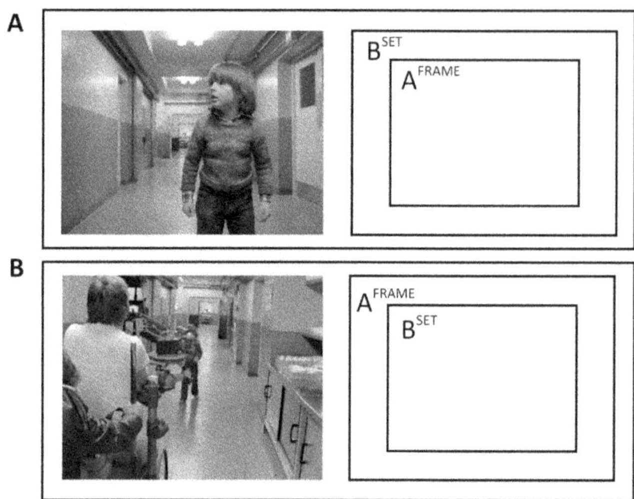

Figure 3.4. *A*, preserving fictional reality versus *B*, revealing fictional artificiality.

Moreover, given that the scenery is made up of the same material that inhabits our visible world, it follows that the scenery itself may give rise to physical instantiations of the CONTAINER schema (e.g., rooms, objects). A film may restrict such instantiations as when the scenery does not contain bounded regions (e.g. shots of endless dark matter of the universe as it is the case in *2001*), but it rarely may abandon them completely. If the setting consists of a bounded region, this bounded region may open up to the viewer. A character may open a window, thus revealing to the viewer a glimpse of the space outside the room. In such a case, the revealed space, although still termed the "outside" relative to the visible inside of the room, becomes, in turn, part of the visible inside space of the film set and the film frame. Again, this simply follows from the logic of the CONTAINER schema:

- Given three containers, the film frame, A, the film set, B, an unspecified bounded region, C, and an object, X, if A is *in* B and C is *in* A and X is *in* C, then X is both *in* A and B.

Figure 3.5 shows a striking filmic manifestation of this logic. Taken from *Killer's Kiss*, it shows the character of Gloria (X), standing in her apartment, as she is hooked in the mirror image of Davey's apartment (C). This visual containment is emphasized even more by the presence of the framework of the window of her apartment inside the mirror image. She is literally caught in a series of frames. Here, we may already give an impression of the next chapter as this "lack of freedom to move" might be extended metaphorically to the conceptual and narrative level of the film, that is, to Gloria's intense emotional state of mind which overpowers her to the extent that she is no longer in control of her free actions.

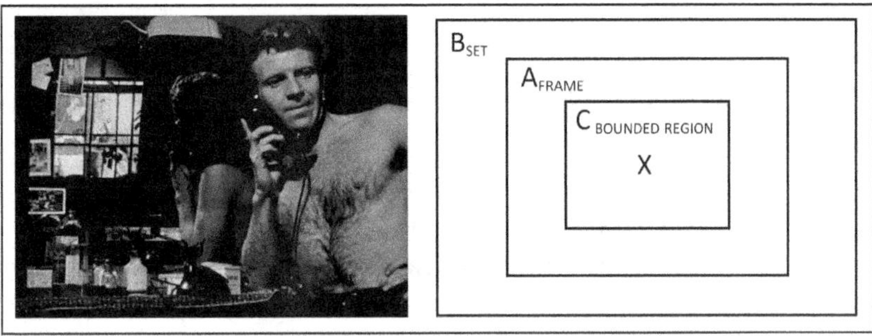

Figure 3.5. Frame-within-frame configuration in *Killer's Kiss*.

The third boundary may be considered as a somewhat awkward boundary because of its causal relationship with the material inside the boundary of the frame (i.e., the scene that is filmed). That is, the inside visual content of the filmic frame would not have occurred without the application of the camera. This has an important implication for our interpretation of the sixth zone of off-screen space. It entails that this zone can never be recorded. Just as our eyes cannot see the space in the back of our heads, so the camera can never record the space behind itself. Sometimes, however, a film may draw attention to this boundary as when, for example, the camera apparatus is treated as a physical entity within the off-screen space that objects within the frame may collide with. Two examples of such contact are illustrated in figure 3.6. In the first series of images (*A-C*), taken from *Killer's Kiss*, we see the character of Vincent Rapallo throwing a glass at two grinning figures reflected in the glass of a picture. Because the camera, however, is located at the position of these figures, it looks as if the camera lens is shattered. In the second iconic series of images (*D-F*), taken from *The Shining*, we see a river of blood approaching and eventually splattering the static camera lens, thereby blurring our vision. Underlying both examples is a dynamic pattern of containment that will be later identified in this chapter as the image schema of APPROACHING.

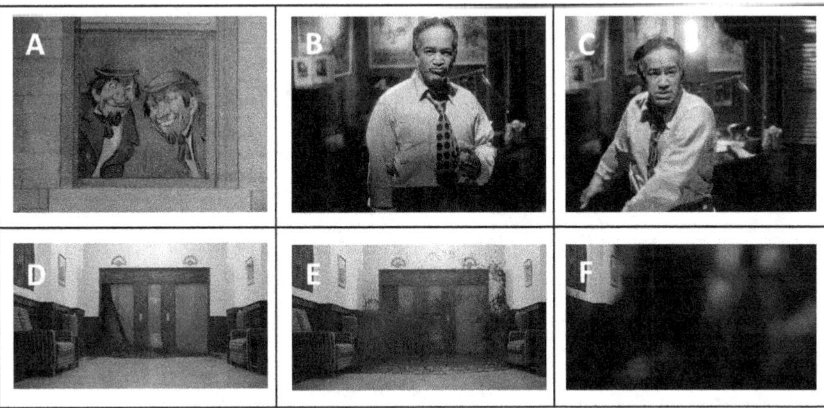

Figure 3.6. Drawing attention to the boundary of the camera in *A-C*, *Killer's Kiss* and *D-F*, *The Shining*.

2.1.2 The BALANCE image schema

Having shown how the inferential logic of the CONTAINER schema is inherent to the filmic frame, we are now in a position to identify the workings of another schema that involves the way the container of the filmic frame, in turn, relates to its visual content. To start off our discussion of this schema, let us return to the visual representation of the logic of the CONTAINER image schema, as diagrammed in figure 3.3. As we know from the previous chapter, diagrams such as this can be misleading for image schemas are not diagrams on a page, nor are they tied to particular images. We use these figures simply as a means to reason about them. However, by providing a pictorial representation of what essentially is not an image, the picture itself becomes part of our perceptual experience (i.e., it becomes an object of visual perception). As such we may rely on other image schemas of our embodied experience in the world to conceptualize our experience of seeing it. Such a projection occurs when we take a look at figure 3.3 from above in which our perception of the object in the centre of the container (a location that was not specified by the logic of the schema) may best be understood and verbalized in terms of the image schema of BALANCE, *visual* balance that is, not physical balance. As Johnson has stressed, the use of balance here is metaphorical in the sense that we project structure from one domain (our bodily experience of physical balance) onto another domain of a different kind (spatial organization in visual perception).[29]

Given this observation, then, one might even go further and explore, as Arnheim did, the effects of replacing the object on a viewer's experience of visual balance or lack of visual balance.[30] Through various informal explorations he found out that, notwithstanding the location of the object within the canvas, it will be affected by the "forces" of an underlying "hidden structure." He refers to this structure as the "structural skeleton of the square."[31] Within this skeleton the centre establishes itself through the crossing of four main structural lines: the central vertical and horizontal axes and the two diagonals (see figure 3.7).

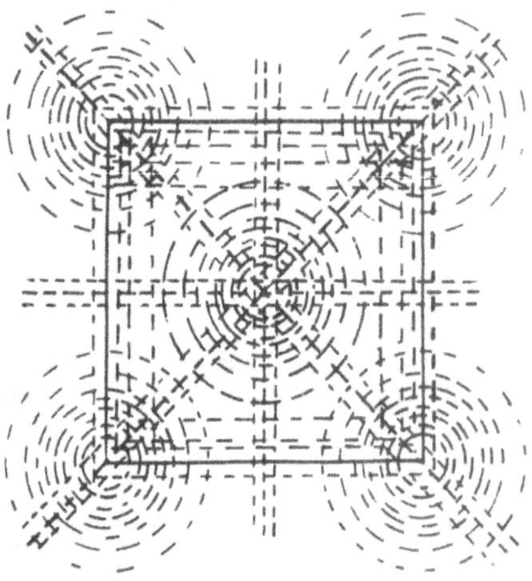

Figure 3.7. The structural skeleton of the square. *Art and Visual Perception: A Psychology of the Creative Eye*, by Rudolf Arnheim, © 2004 by the Regents of the University of California. Published by the University of California Press.

As to how to interpret this structure, Arnheim gives the following explanation (what he terms the disk is the object in our discussion):

> Wherever the disk is located, it will be affected by the forces of all the hidden structural factors. The relative strength and distance of these factors will determine their effect in the total configuration. At the center all the forces balance one another, and therefore the central position makes for rest. Another comparatively restful position can be found, for example, by moving the disk along a diagonal. The point of balance seems to lie somewhat closer to the corner of the square than to the center, which may mean that the center is stronger than the corner and that this preponderance has to be offset by greater distance, as though corner and center were two magnets of unequal power. In general, any location that coincides with a feature of the structural skeleton introduces an element of stability, which of course may be counteracted by other forces.[32]

Following Johnson, there are two important points to be made about Arnheim's structural skeleton.[33] First, it is important to emphasize that this hidden structure only exists in relation to the viewer of the image. That is, balance does not exist objectively *in* the frame. The object seen "is only balanced in *our acts of perception*." However, as Johnson points out, since all spectators more or less are equipped with the same perceptual tools, "it will usually make perfectly good sense to speak of the balance being in the perceived object." It is precisely for this reason then that Johnson considers balance to be an image schema because it operates as a recurring structure or pattern of perceptual activity that is instantiated in a number of different bodily and perceptual experiences. For Johnson, then, the prototypical image schema of BALANCE may be represented by an axis or a point in relation to which some force vectors are symmetrically or proportionally arranged.

The second key point that Johnson makes, is that Arnheim, when talking about "force," "tensions" and "hidden structures," is not actually talking about gravitational or physical forces of the sort that we discussed in the previous chapter (i.e., forces that act upon bodies). Instead, he is talking about what Johnson calls "*psychological* or *perceptual* forces."[34] In other words, he uses the terms "forces" and "weights" metaphorically in order to structure and understand our experience of perceiving balance in visual configurations. Consider, for example, the metaphorical elaboration of the concept of "weight." In its literal and physical sense weight refers to the strength of the gravitational force pulling objects downward. By contrast, the elements in two-dimensional pictures such as film images, do not have mass and, therefore, do not have any physical weight. As Arnheim writes, "there are no known physical forces that would tend to push an eccentrically placed patch of printer's ink in the direction of the center of the square."[35] Yet, we use the concept of weight in a very genuine way to make sense of our experience of perceiving these images (i.e., to express the "force" that an element inside the frame exerts to attract the eye). As Johnson writes, "we have some complex *metaphorical* (but very real) experience of *visual* weight and force."[36] As to the question which factors influence visual weight the most and thus determine our experience of visual balance, Arnheim distinguishes between several factors, some of which are listed as in table 3.3.[37]

Table 3.3 List of factors that influence force and weight relations (after Arnheim).

Factor	*Observation*
Location	A "strong" position on the structural framework can support more weight than one lying off-centre or away from the central vertical or horizontal.
Spatial depth	The greater the depth an area of the visual field reaches, the greater the weight it carries.
Size	Other factors being equal, the larger object will be the heavier.
Color	Red is heavier than blue, and bright colors are heavier than dark ones.
Intrinsic interest	The very tininess of an object may exert a fascination that compensates the slight weight it would otherwise have.
Isolation	An isolated object is heavier than an object of similar appearance surrounded by other objects.
Shape	The regular shape of simple geometrical figures makes them look heavier.
Knowledge	No knowledge on the part of the observer will make a bundle of cotton look lighter than a lump of lead of similar appearance.

As this table shows, the location of the object inside of the frame is only one aspect of many aspects that have to be taken into consideration when assessing the overall balance of a visual work of art. Naturally, a discussion of each of these aspects would take several chapters on their own. There is, however, one aspect that is worth emphasizing here as it will be revealed later on to play an important role in the non-verbal communication of stories of mental causation. This is the aspect of the *size* of the object. In film studies, this aspect is related to the *distance* of framing.[38] The *distance* of framing, also known as *shot scale*, refers to the apparent distance between the camera and the mise-en-scene elements inside the container of the frame. Film scholars usually measure this distance in relation to the human subject. This gives rise to a typology of shot sizes that alternates between an extreme close-up (a view of a portion of the subject) and an extreme long shot (a view of the whole subject as well as his surroundings). The greater the distance, the smaller the object and the "emptier" the frame, and vice versa, the shorter the distance, the bigger the object and the "fuller" the frame. Here one may notice the dynamic interaction of the EMPTY-FULL image schema with the NEAR-FAR image schema.[39] Naturally, this image schematic interaction also influences the visual weight of an object. In the absence of any counterbalancing effect, the object that is nearer and thus larger will have more weight than an object that is farther and thus smaller.

How does visual balance relate to *visual symmetry*, that other concept often associated with it? Especially in the light of the prevalence of symmetrical compositions in the work of Stanley Kubrick such a question is worth raising.[40] Unquestionably, both concepts are closely related suggesting, quite misleadingly, that balance *is* symmetry, of the form exemplified by Johnson:

> Any X is balanced when it is symmetrical, that is, where there are equal elements, with equal weights, in equal locations, one on each side relative to the axis or centre point, or where there is an equal distribution of weight and forces relative to the axis.[41]

Although it is true that symmetry supports balance, it is not true that balance requires symmetry.[42] Arnheim is keen to point out that one can have an experience of visual balance without observing symmetry in the image.[43] Asymmetrical formal relations may well be capable of expressing order and balance as long as the "forces" within the work counterbalance each other. To illustrate this, let us compare two images as taken from *Barry Lyndon* (see figure 3.8). *A* is an example of symmetry of the sort that one often encounters in the work of Kubrick. If you would split the image in two at the height of the mountain in the background of the image, you could see that whatever is on the left of the vertical axis seems to be mirrored in size and relative position on the right also. By contrast, composition *B* does not evoke this symmetry. We do see some symmetry between the characters, but this does not apply to the whole of the image. Yet, we do experience the right image as balanced. How does this come about? A part of the explanation lies precisely in the factors listed by Arnheim. The darker area on the right half of the image is counterbalanced by the brighter area on the left half of the image. Moreover, the isolated and smaller object of the fallen chair on the left, an unconcealed reference to William Hogarth's second satirical painting *The Tête à Tête* from his *Marriage à-la-mode* series, poses a counterweight to the visual weight of the larger group of people on the right. The result is a balanced composition in which all factors are mutually determined in such a way that, to quote Arnheim, "no change seems possible, and the whole assumes the character of 'necessity' in all its parts."[44]

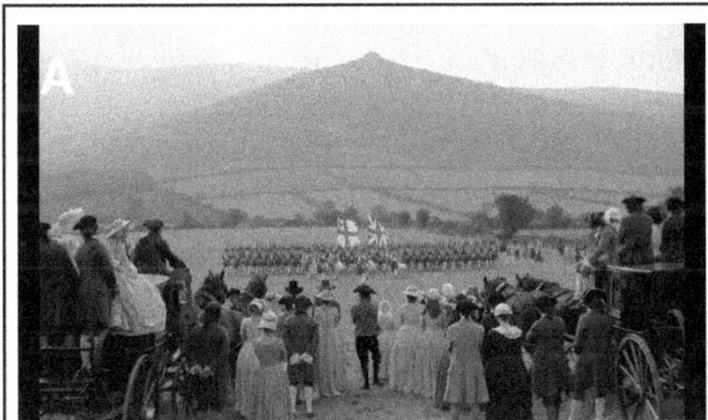

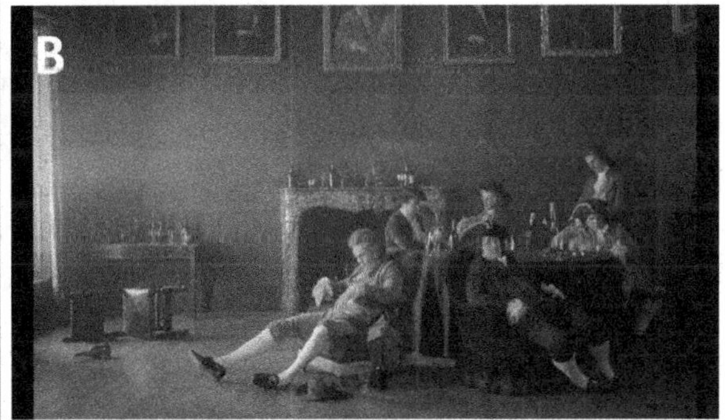

Figure 3.8. Visual balance in *Barry Lyndon*: *A*, symmetry versus *B*, asymmetry.

As a viewer, we are able to infer these aesthetic thoughts because the duration of the shot allows for a kind of artful contemplation that is normally more associated with the experience of watching a static work of art such as a painting. Contemplative static shots, however, if present at all, usually occupy only a small fraction of the total amount of images of an entire film. What distinguishes our experience of watching a film from our experience of watching a still picture, is precisely the observation of motion. In other words, what underlies film is not a static, but a dynamic conception of the CONTAINER schema that comes into being once we attribute motion to either both or one of the two central entities, that is, once the frame and/or the visual object become(s), to use a term from the previous chapter, a trajector. This gives rise to a number of patterns which, as we have seen in the previous chapter, may be identified as "dynamic patterns of containment." Depending on the moving entity, we may distinguish between two subgroups of dynamic patterns: one subgroup in which the container is the relatively moving figure and another subgroup in which the contained object is the relatively mobile entity. Following film terminology, both subgroups may be referred to as the "dynamic patterns of fixed-frame movement" and the "dynamic patterns of mobile framing or camera movement," respectively. In what follows, we address each subgroup separately before turning toward their interaction.

2.2 The dynamic shot

2.2.1 Dynamic patterns of fixed-frame movement

How many ways are there for an object, either motivated by an internal force or an external force, to *go into* or to *go out of* a fixed frame? Again, the answer to this question lies in the nature of the film image. Given the three axes of the film image, as discussed above, fixed-frame movement can take three forms: (1) *lateral* (left-right or top-down movement), (2) *in-depth* (movement toward or away from the camera), or (3) *diagonal* (a combination of lateral and in-depth movement). As Boggs points out, "purely lateral movement creates the impression of movement on a flat surface (which the screen is) and therefore calls attention to one of the medium's limitations: its two-dimensionality."[45] Consequently, if the cinematographer wants to create the illusion of three-dimensionality, he has to choose in-depth movement and diagonal movement over purely lateral movement. Combined with Burch's six zones of off-screen space, then, an object may enter or exit a frame in the following ways: (1) from the left edge of the frame, (2) from the right edge of the frame, (3) from the top edge of the frame, (4) from the bottom edge of the frame, (5) from the space beyond the set or (6) from the space behind and near the camera. The direction of the movement has a major influence on the force dynamics of a shot or any other visual representation. According to Arnheim this is a logical consequence of the force of gravity which makes us live in "anisotropic space, that is, space in which dynamics varies with direction."[46] This is how, for instance, we come to experience upward movement differently than downward movement. As Arnheim observes, "to rise upward means to overcome resistance—it is always a victory. To descend or fall, is to surrender to the pull from below, and therefore is experienced as passive compliance."[47] Similarly, the art historian Heinrich Wölfflin has observed that the diagonal running from left to top right is commonly perceived as ascending, while the other is seen as descending.[48] Notwithstanding the direction of the movement, each instance of entry or exit can be seen as a concrete manifestation of one of the two dynamic patterns as diagrammed in figure 3.9*A*-*B*.

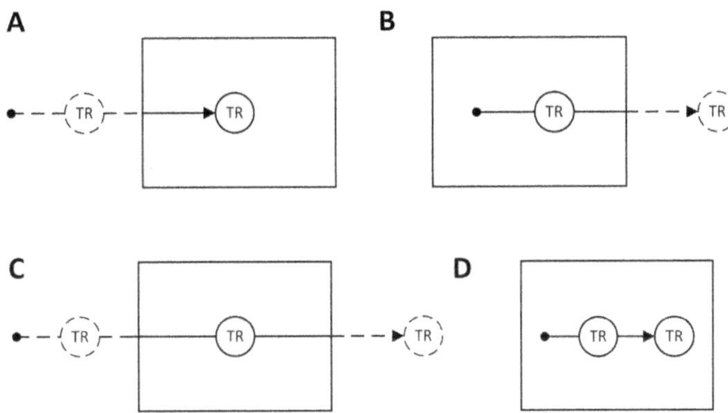

Figure 3.9. *A*, ENTRY, *B*, EXIT, *C*, ENTRY and EXIT, and *D*, no ENTRY nor EXIT.

Both patterns have opposing source-goal locations. In figure 3.9*A* the source of the TR is located outside the container and the goal is located inside the container, whereas in figure 3.9*B* the source is located inside and the goal is located outside. We may also combine both patterns. In that case both source and goal are located outside (figure 3.9*C*). If both entities are located inside, then the notions of entry and exit do not apply (figure 3.9*D*).

As Dewell remarks, pictorial representations such as in figure 3.9 are deceptive in several ways though, making the images appear less schematic and less dynamic than they really are.[49] For instance, figure 3.9*A-B* gives the impression of representing a single entry or exit event while they actually give expression to the whole range of image schema transformations. The container may be instantiated in the frame or it may be instantiated in the set (e.g., a room) or any other bounded region within the set (e.g. a mirror). Moreover, both images are schematic with respect to the path arrows. Although they run horizontal, they can be freely rotated so that the entry and the exit could be through any side of the container.

Within these diagrams we might also discern the workings of two other patterns of sensory-motor experience, namely that of VISUAL BLOCKAGE and THE REMOVAL OF VISUAL RESTRAINT (see figure 3.10). The logic of both patterns can be connected to the force image schemas of BLOCKAGE and REMOVAL OF RESTRAINT, respectively.[50] The former pertains to our everyday encounter of obstacles that block or resist physical force, the latter to our everyday experience of the removal of a barrier or the absence of some potential restraint. This schema thus suggests an open way or path. Here, however, we are not speaking of physical blockage, but of visual blockage, just as Arnheim was not referring to physical balance when discussing balance in visual works of art. VISUAL BLOCKAGE occurs when a visual object is "blocked" from our vision (see figure 3.10*A*). REMOVAL OF VISUAL RESTRAINT accounts for the removal of this blockage (see figure 3.10*B*). The arrows in both figures do not represent a trajectory of an entity, but an entity's transition from a state of invisibility to a state of visibility (and vice versa). Depending on which entity is charged with movement, there are two means to achieve the latter. Either the visual object that is blocked from our vision seeks an alternative pathway of motion so as to enable visualization. This is what happens with ENTRY.

The object moves from a location blocked from our vision (i.e., the space off-screen) to a location visible to us (i.e., the space on-screen). The opposite occurs with EXIT. Alternatively, visualization can be achieved not by moving the object, but by moving the obstacle itself. In our case, this would entail the movement of the boundary of the container (i.e., the frame). By moving the camera (and thus achieving the effect of the mobile frame) one would be able to include the object into the perceiver's visual field. This discussion, however, will be reserved for the next section of this chapter.

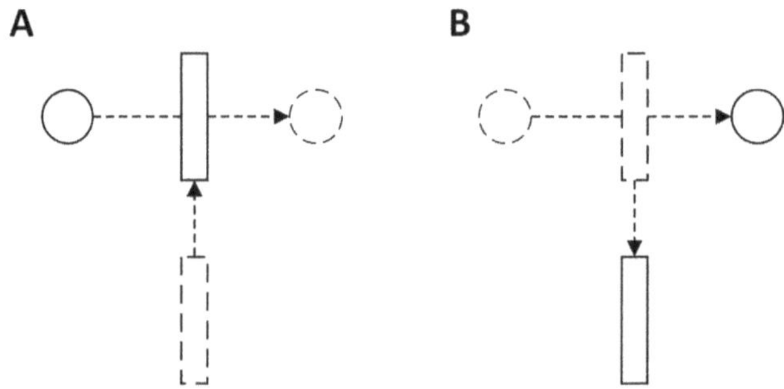

Figure 3.10. *A*, VISUAL BLOCKAGE versus *B*, REMOVAL OF VISUAL RESTRAINT.

Together with the structural elements of the CONTAINER schema, this leads us to map the space outside the container (i.e., off-screen) onto the invisible and the space inside the container (i.e., on-screen) onto the visible. As figure 3.9 above already suggests, this may be processed diagrammatically by using a dashed line for the invisible space and a straight full line for the visible space. Thus, it follows that the dynamic pattern of ENTRY marks the transitional pattern of APPEARING whereas EXIT marks the transitional pattern of DISAPPEARING.

As a way of illustrating the patterns of ENTRY and EXIT, let us consider some examples as selected from Kubrick's films. For instance, figure 3.11 shows a cinematic manifestation of figure 3.9*C* in which both patterns are elicited by lateral fixed-frame movement. The space pod, operated by Bowman inside of it, enters from the left edge (figure 3.11*A*). It carries the lifeless body of Frank Poole into the frame. Inside the frame, the pod sets the body free (figure 3.11*B*). Due to the loss of gravity in space, Poole now floats inside the frame, to exit it again from its right edge (figure 3.11*C*).

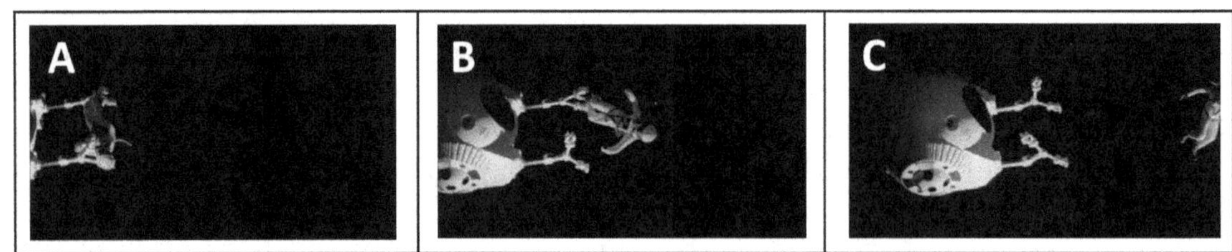

Figure 3.11. ENTRY and EXIT elicited by lateral fixed-frame movement in *2001*.

In this example, Poole's body enters and leaves the frame, not on his own accord, but by an external force imposed upon him by another entity. Let us now consider two variations on the same theme, one in which the character enters the frame by using his intention as an internal force and another in which the other entity, imposing the external force, is blocked from our vision. Figure 3.12 shows an instance of the first variation and a cinematic manifestation of figure 3.9*A*. It shows the character of Jack Torrance as he rises triumphantly upward into the frame after just having axed his opponent Dick Hallorann to death, a gesture which is mirrored at the musical level by Penderecki's excerpt of *Utrenja* which articulates a similar "ascending motion."

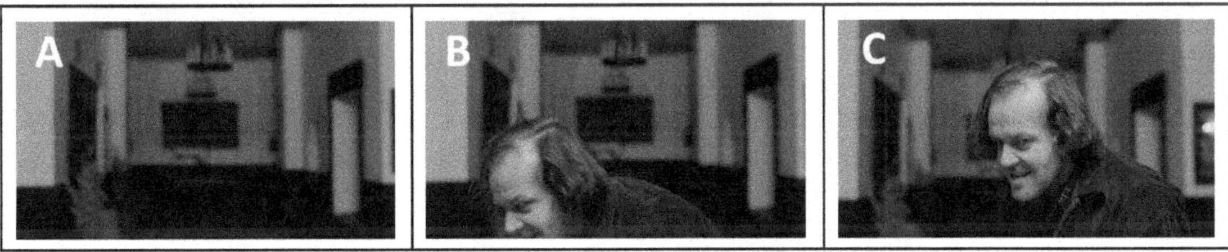

Figure 3.12. ENTRY by upward fixed-frame movement in *The Shining* (visible origin of force).

The second variation is exemplified in figure 3.13. It shows a high-angle shot of a tennis ball rolling into the frame from its below edge until it halts in the centre of the image where little Danny is residing (figure 3.13*A-B*). However, the shot, being a high-angle shot, prevents the spectator from seeing (and thus knowing) the origin of the force that sets the ball in motion. This, in turn, raises the question as to where the ball is coming from? The next semi-subjective shot, taken from behind the boy, attempts to answer this question by showing the space in front of his eyes (figure 3.12*C*). Alas, the only thing we see is an empty corridor. As such the film succeeds in keeping the mystery and suspense intact.[51]

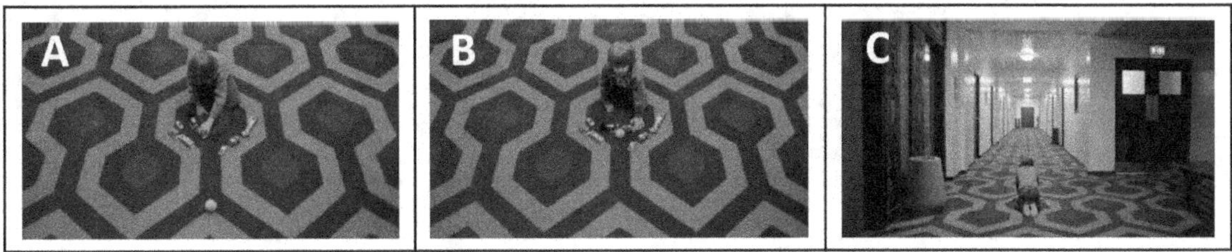

Figure 3.13. ENTRY by upward fixed-frame movement in *The Shining* (invisible origin of force).

In the examples discussed so far at least one or more of the four edges of the frame are being crossed by the actual movement of the object. By contrast, the fifth way, entry through the set, does not necessarily involve this intersection of the boundary of the frame. For instance, a character may enter or exit the inside of the frame from behind the set without intersecting one of its edges. The former occurs, for example, when a character enters the frame by coming in through a door in the back of the image. A good manifestation of this can be found, for instance, in the scene from *A Clockwork Orange* when Alex frightens the Cat Lady by entering her room uninvited (see figure 3.14). What we see here is a manifestation of figure 3.9*A* in figure 3.5, whereby the pattern of entry is not related to container A (the frame), as was the case in the previous examples, but to container C (a bounded region within the set).

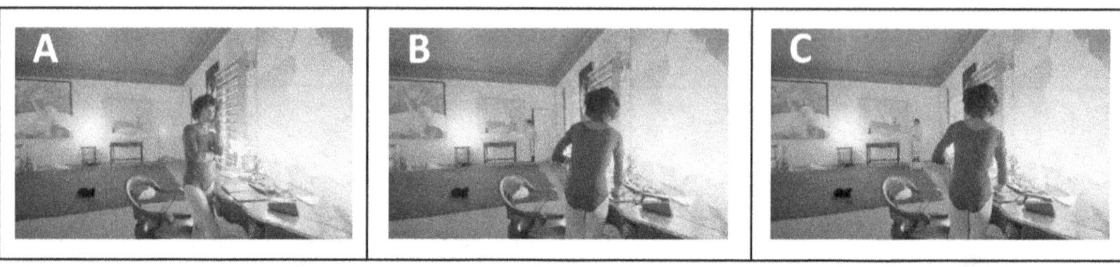

Figure 3.14. ENTRY through a bounded region in the set in *A Clockwork Orange.*

Moreover, visual objects may also appear in a static frame or disappear from its inside without actually entering or exiting it. This is the case when the patterns of VISUAL BLOCKAGE and REMOVAL OF VISUAL RESTRAINT are manifested inside the visual content of the frame itself. A vivid example of appearing without entry through the removal of visual restraint can be found in the scene from *Spartacus* where a group of gladiators (including Spartacus himself) are awaiting their duel until death inside a wooden cabin (see figure 3.15). As the door of the cabin slides open, two new parties are revealed into the frame: in the top background, the Roman audience sitting on a balcony waiting for the gladiators to enter the arena, in the center middle, the arena itself taken in by their brutal trainer Marcellus.[52]

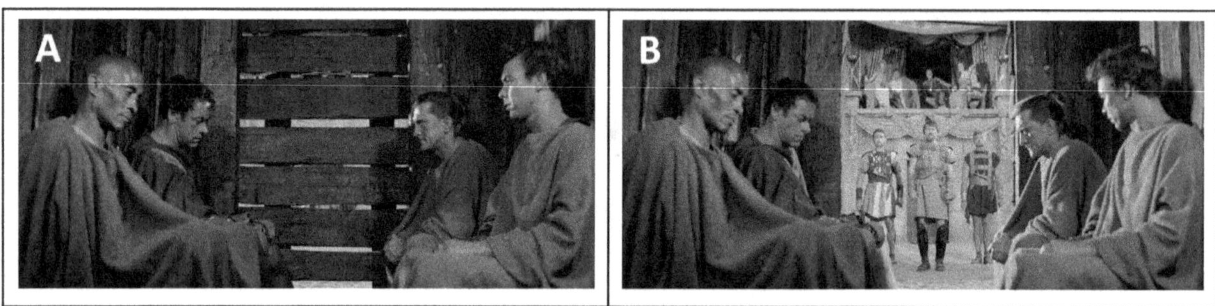

Figure 3.15. Appearing without ENTRY in *Spartacus.*

From the examples of ENTRY and EXIT (via the frame) we may also draw another finding, namely that the amount of intersection points of the TR with the boundary of the frame depends on the *distance* of framing. As a general rule one can say that the greater this distance, the fewer the amount of intersection points with the frame, and vice versa, the smaller this distance, the higher this amount. For instance, if the TR would exit the fixed frame by moving, along the depth axis, forward to the space near the camera (i.e., the sixth zone of off-screen space), all edges of the frame will be crossed.

The distance does not only influence the *amount of intersection points*, but also the *amount of space* inside of the frame that is being occupied by the TR. The framed TR may be far from the camera, but moving in the camera's direction. In that case the amount of space occupied by the TR will gradually increase. By contrast, the TR may also be close to the camera, but moving away from the camera's location. In that case the amount of space occupied by the TR decreases. Two dynamic patterns that we can naturally capture as an APPROACHING schema and a DISTANCING schema, respectively.[53] The greater the distance, the smaller the TR and the "emptier" the frame, and vice versa, the smaller the distance, the larger the TR and the "fuller" the frame. Both patterns might be diagrammed as in figure 3.16. The dashed circle represents the TR's starting location whereas the full lined circle represents the TR's ending location.

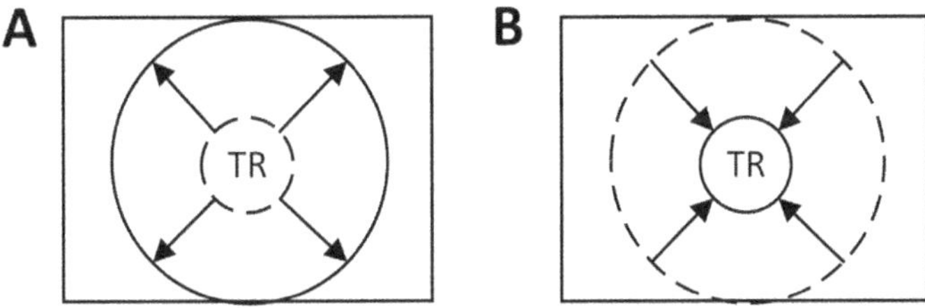

Figure 3.16. *A*, APPROACHING versus *B*, DISTANCING.

We already encountered two cinematic manifestations of the first pattern in figure 3.6. Another example can be found, for instance, in *2001* when the space pod rapidly approaches Frank Poole, whose lifeless body resides off-screen in the area behind the camera (see figure 3.17). The pod gradually evolves from a little, almost unnoticeable dot in the centre of the frame (*A*) to a full blown-up figure occupying almost one third of the image (*B*).

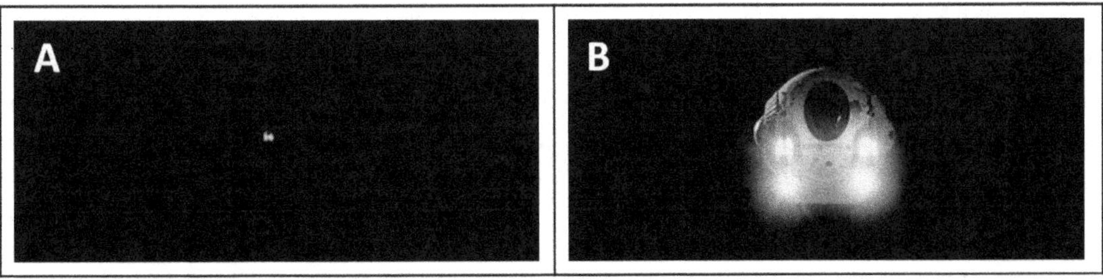

Figure 3.17. Approaching in *2001*.

The shot from *Fear and Desire*, as shown in figure 3.18, illustrates a striking example of the second pattern. It starts with a close-up of the face of Sidney (*A*), the private who was left behind to guard the young peasant girl whom the soldiers have apprehended. As he turns around and walks away from the camera, the girl is revealed inside the frame, as she is bound to a tree (*B-C*). As with figure 3.15 this shot exemplifies a case of appearing through the removal of a visual restraint, albeit this time the revealing is instantiated by a pattern of DISTANCING elicited by the blocking entity (i.e., Sydney).

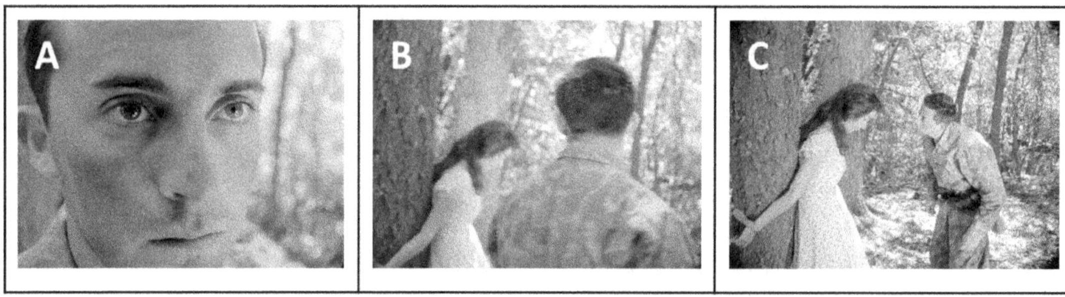

Figure 3.18. Appearing by distancing in *Fear and Desire.*

2.2.2 Dynamic patterns of mobile framing

Having addressed some of the dynamic patterns of containment that are inherent to fixed-frame movement, let us now shift our attention to the frame as trajector as captured by the concept of "mobile frame." This concept may be defined as the *effect* on the space inside the frame as a result of *actual or apparent camera movement* caused by *external forces* exerted on the camera. As a starting point, let us first define what we mean by the term "actual or apparent camera movement"? It refers to a distinction within the general category of camera movement between two types of movement.

We speak of "actual" camera movement when we can attribute literal movement to the physical entity of the camera. One may further divide this type into two subtypes, that is, the effect of the mobile frame may be elicited either (1) by a camera that has its body moving from a fixed physical location, or (2) by a camera that has its body moving from one physical location to another. The first subtype of camera movement is reminiscent of the head and eye movements of a stationary human body and further designates two camera techniques: *panning* in which the camera's line of sight moves in a horizontal plane to the left and right and *tilting* in which the camera's line of sight moves in a vertical plane, up and down.[54] The second subtype of camera movement has the camera travelling along a pathway (either predetermined or not). If the camera moves alongside the photographed object(s) it is called a *tracking shot*. By definition, this movement allows for numerous possibilities including in-and-out movement (i.e., closer/further away from the subject) as well as side-to-side movement.

In addition, the effect of the mobile frame might be created without requiring any literal movement of the camera. Hence, the term "apparent" camera movement. This type commonly coincides with the use of *zoom lenses*.

Consisting of a series of lenses that keep the image in constant focus, the zoom lens allows a stationary camera to glide fluidly toward or away from the subject.[55]

Notwithstanding these distinctions, camera movement can only occur insofar there is an *external force* that causes the camera to move (either literally or apparently). This brings us to the second part of the definition. As the term "external" suggests, this part excludes the possibility of any internal force. This marks a fundamental difference with lively subjects such as actors to which both forces may apply. An actor may move itself into the frame by using its intention as internal force or he may be moved into the frame by an external force (e.g., he can be pushed into the frame by another entity). In the case of camera movement, however, the force is always external, meaning that a camera, being a lifeless mechanical device, cannot move on its own. In other words, the camera has an intrinsic force tendency toward rest. As such it can only be moved by means of the application of an external force. This external force is the concept by virtue of which we understand the cause of camera movement. Inferential evidence for this metaphorical mapping can be found in the systemic relationship between the logic of forced camera movement and the logic of causation (see table 3.4). As the reader may notice, this table is identical to table 2.9 from the previous chapter except for now the moving entity is specified as the camera.

Table 3.4. The inferential correspondences between forced camera movement and causation.

Inferences true of forced camera movement	*Inferences true of causation*
The application of the external force precedes or accompanies the camera movement.	The occurrence of the cause precedes or accompanies the effect.
The camera movement would not have occurred without the application of an external force.	The change of state would not have occurred without a cause.
The external force impinges on the camera.	The cause impinges on the entity that changes state.

It is in locating the origin of this external force that the role of the camera operator or cameraman comes into prominence as he or she is the person responsible for exerting a force onto the camera (i.e., the target to which the force is directed) causing it to move, literally or apparently, so as to achieve the effect of the mobile frame. Schematically, this causal relationship might be put as follows (where the double arrow denotes "leads to"):

> Force acting upon camera => Camera movement => Effect of the mobile frame

The application of the force onto the camera might take several forms of which its variety might best be understood in terms of verbs of forced movement such as "moving," "pushing" or even "throwing." A vibrant application of the latter verb can be found in *A Clockwork Orange*. When Kubrick in an interview with *Sight & Sound* was asked how he managed to create the subjective shot of Alex jumping out of the window, the director answered (italics mine):

> We bought an old Newman Sinclair clockwork mechanism camera (no pun intended) for £50. It's a beautiful camera and it's built like a battleship. We made a number of polystyrene boxes which gave about 18 inches of protection around the camera, and cut out a slice for the lens. We then *threw the camera off* a roof. In order to get it to land lens first, we had to do this six times and the camera survived all six drops. On the final one it landed right on the lens, and smashed it, but it

> didn't do a bit of harm to the camera. This, despite the fact that the polystyrene was literally blasted away from it each time by the impact. The next day we shot a steady test on the camera and found there wasn't a thing wrong with it. On this basis, I would say that the Newman Sinclair must be the most indestructible camera ever made.[56]

As Lakoff and Johnson have pointed out, it is interesting to see how various verbs seem to specify different kinds of forced movement.[57] The verb "throw" describes a situation in which the camera operator applies a force instantaneously or for a very short time, and the movement of the camera occurs after the removal. As the example above already suggests, throwing is a rather unorthodox way for a camera operator to move a camera from one location to another. In the majority of times, the camera operator will simply move the camera by *moving* its position. As a verb of forced motion, "move" describes a situation in which a force is applied constantly rather than temporally. The application of this verb may be illustrated through the workings of three cinematic techniques which all occupy a significant place in the work of Kubrick: the *Steadicam*, the *dolly* and the *hand-held* camera.

The Steadicam is a portable, one-person camera with a build-in gyroscope device that prevents or compensates for rough camera movements (i.e., camera shake). The result is a smooth shot, even when the person carrying the camera is running over an irregular surface. In order to achieve this weightless effect, the camera is mounted on to a spring-loaded arm, which is attached to a frame, which is in turn strapped to the operator's shoulders, chest and hips. Kubrick used the Steadicam technique ever since *The Shining*, when he hired Garrett Brown, its inventor, to shoot the fast, flowing camera movements in the maze (see figure 3.19).

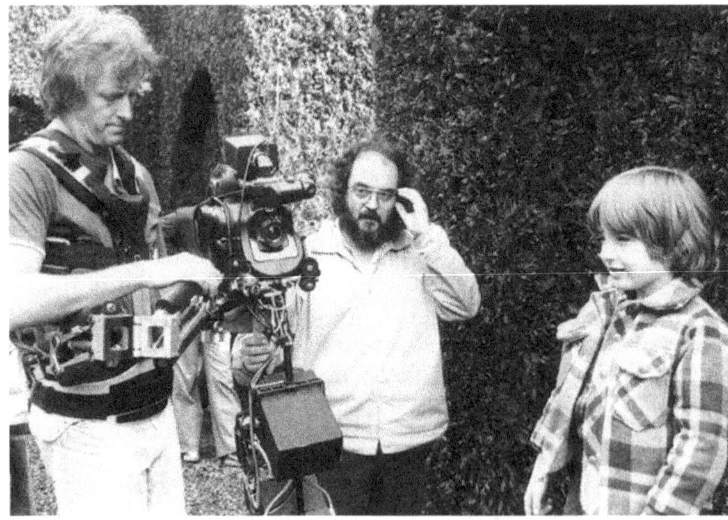

Figure 3.19. Garrett Brown with his Steadicam on the set of *The Shining*. Courtesy of Garrett Brown.

In an interview with French film critic Michel Ciment about the making of this film, the director commented on the technique as follows (an excerpt from it):

> The Steadicam allows one man to move the camera any place he can walk -- into small spaces where a dolly won't fit, and up and down staircases. We used an Arriflex BL camera, which is silent and allows you to shoot sound. You can walk or run with the camera, and the Steadicam smooths out any unsteadiness. It's like a magic carpet. . . . The only problem with the Steadicam is that it requires training, skill and a certain amount of fitness on the part of the operator. You can't just pick it up and use it. But any good camera operator can do useful work even after a few days' training. He won't be an ace but he'll still be able to do much more than he could without it. I used Garrett Brown as the Steadicam operator. He probably has more experience than anyone with the Steadicam because he also happened to invent it.[58]

Before the introduction of the Steadicam, a director had two choices for moving the camera from one location to another. One time-consuming and less practical way was to mount the camera on a wheeled cart, the so-called dolly. The person who operates the dolly is called a dolly grip. Likewise, the position of dolly grip can be considered a highly skilful one as he or she has to *push* and *pull* the cart and usually a camera operator and camera assistant as riders. So here we have the interaction of two forces causing the camera to move: the force exerted on the dolly by the dolly grip and the force exerted on the camera by the camera operator. Examples of tracking shots using in-out dolly movement can be spotted in the early work of Kubrick. Notable in this regard are the dolly shots in the trenches from *Paths of Glory* (see figure 3.20).

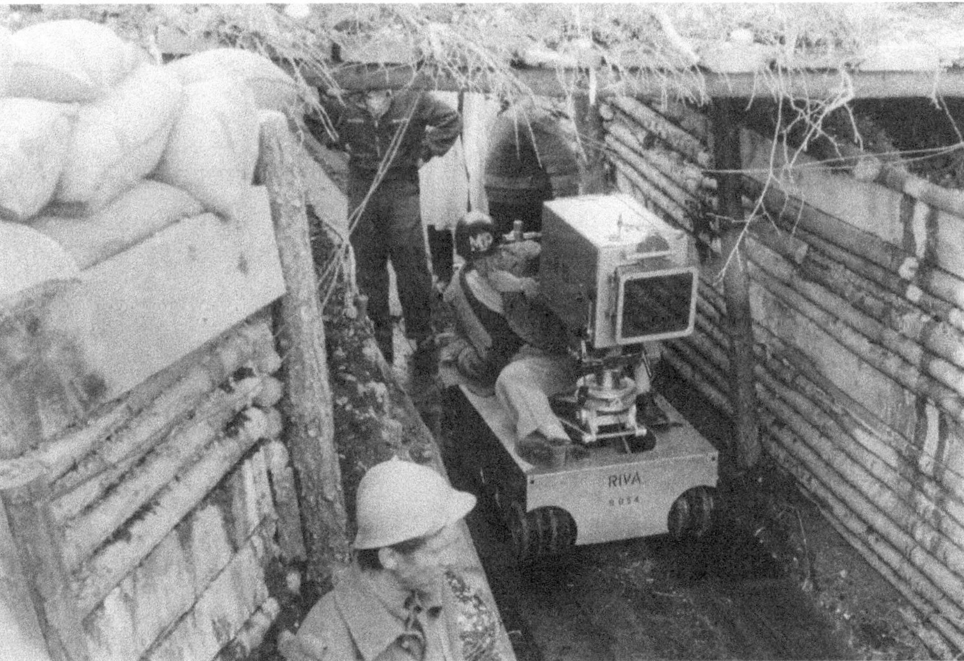

Figure 3.20. A young Stanley Kubrick surveilling the trenches scene from atop a dolly during the filming of *Paths of Glory*. Photograph presumably taken by Lars Looschen. Courtesy of Bryna Productions, United Artists.

The other way, less impractical and less time consuming, but even more sensitive for camera shakes, would be simply holding the camera in your hands while moving from one location to another (i.e., hand-held shooting). Likewise, the camera operator has to exert a force continually on the camera in order to prevent it from falling. Interestingly, in locating the origin of the hand-held camera work in his films, one may point to the director himself as many, if not all of the hand-held shots are his. In the same interview with *Sight & Sound* as above, he motivated this choice as follows: "In addition to the fun of doing the shooting myself, I find it is virtually impossible to explain what you want in a hand-held shot to even the most talented and sensitive camera operator."[59] Given its tendency toward shaking, hand-held camera footage has been traditionally used for the shooting of documentaries, news, reportage, live action, or the evocation of authentic immediacy or *cinéma vérité* during dramatic sequences. This is not any different in Kubrick's work where the hand-held camera has been used to shoot, among others, the U.S. army's attack of Burpelson Air Force Base in *Dr. Strangelove*, the astronauts' approach of the monolith in *2001*, Alex's brutal beating and rape of Mr. Alexander and his wife as well as his fight with the Cat Lady in *A Clockwork Orange*, and, as can be seen in figure 3.21, Redmond's bare-knuckle fight scene with troublemaker Toole in *Barry Lyndon*.

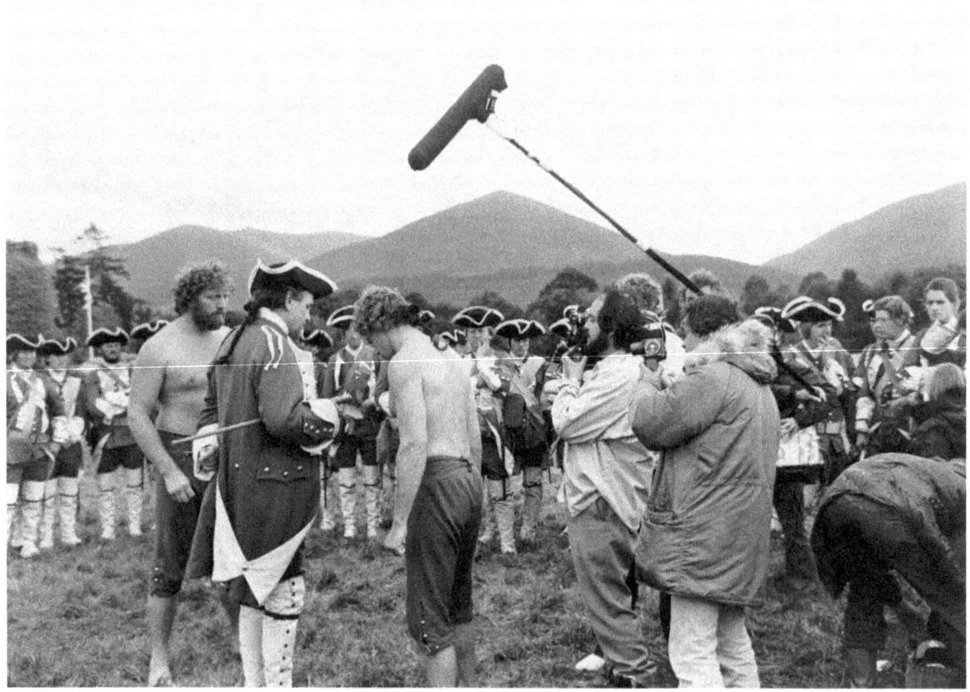

Figure 3.21. Stanley Kubrick while hand-held filming Redmond's bare-knuckle brawl with troublemaker Toole at the army encampment. Courtesy of Alamy Stock Photo.

It is only when an external force acts upon the camera that camera movement (i.e., the effect of the force) comes into being and the camera seems to acquire an existence detached from the force that triggered it. This is evidenced in our language about camera movement which considers such expressions as "the camera zooms in," "the camera moves" or "the camera dollies in." Each of these expressions takes the camera as an independent entity that, much like a human being, is capable of moving on its own by using its intention as an internal force.

With the effect of the camera movement comes also the effect of the mobile frame. As the definition of the mobile frame above already suggests, this effect is measured in terms of the relationship between the movement of the camera and the change of space inside the frame that results from it. Likewise, we might discuss this effect by distinguishing between several dynamic patterns of containment. Here, we will discuss four of them as they can be referred to as (1) INCLUSION, (2) EXCLUSION, (3) ENCLOSURE and (4) EXPOSURE, respectively. They correspond to the four patterns of fixed-framed movement (ENTRY, EXIT, APPROACHING and DISTANCING) with this crucial difference that now the container is the trajector and the visual object is the relatively stationary entity.

INCLUSION occurs when the container includes a new visual object *into* the frame. Disregarding the force that instantiates the camera movement, this may be represented as in figure 3.22*A* whereby the dashed-lined rectangle represents the initial starting point of the container's movement and the full-lined rectangle represents its ending point. By contrast, EXCLUSION, as diagrammed in figure 3.22*B* occurs when the container excludes a visual object from its inside content.

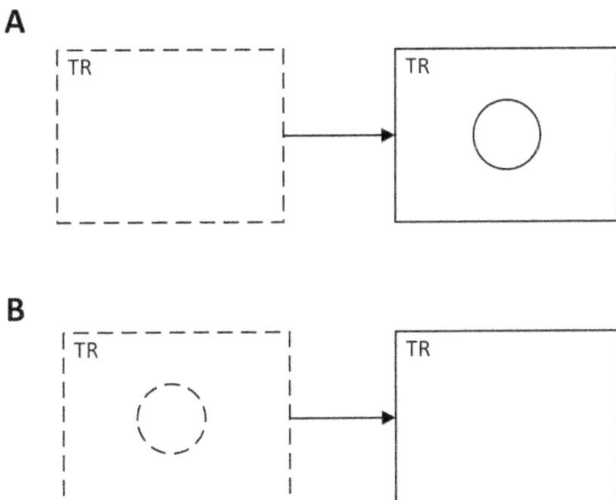

Figure 3.22. *A*, INCLUSION and *B*, EXCLUSION.

Again, it must be stressed that these diagrams are representations of dynamic image schematic structures. As such they can be instantiated in various camera movements, including not only the lateral horizontal movement, as suggested by the diagrams, but also the lateral vertical and the diagonal camera movement.

Despite the fact that both patterns are clearly distinguishable from one another, they are nevertheless constantly and simultaneously at work meaning that the inclusion of one visual object always entails the exclusion of another visual object and vice versa. As a way of illustrating this, consider the following lateral camera movement from *Barry Lyndon*, as shown in figure 3.23. The shot starts with the camera already in motion showing us a group of three people (O1) (*A*). As they approach the balcony, the camera slowly pans to the right, thus gradually relocating the group to the off-screen space. Simultaneously, as they disappear, a sleeping man appears (O2) (*B*). As with the previous group, this screen appearance, however, is short-lived as the camera does not halt, but continues his path along the horizontal line of the balustrade until it includes its two leading characters (O3), Redmond Barry and the Chevalier du Balibari, into the frame (*C*).

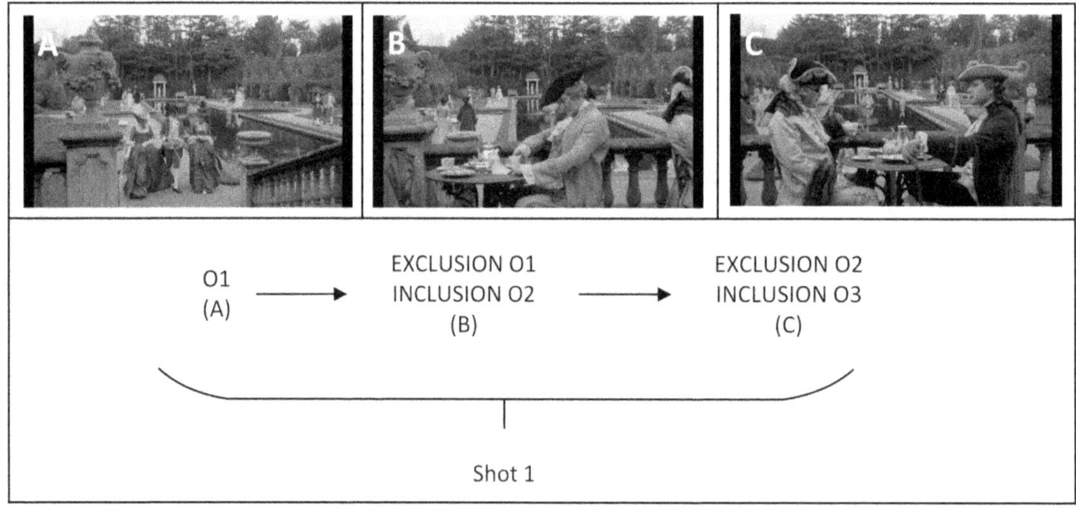

Figure 3.23. INCLUSION and EXCLUSION by lateral camera movement in *Barry Lyndon.*

The patterns of INCLUSION and EXCLUSION, as diagrammed in figure 3.23, are given expression through lateral camera movement. Figure 3.24, taken from *Eyes Wide Shut*, shows us an example in which the same effect is achieved, but this time through a semi-circular camera movement. The camera shows the front of Alice (O1) as she is standing stationary and without her husband Bill at the Ziegler's Christmas party (*A*). The camera then slowly and graciously moves around her left side thus gradually excluding her face (O1) and including her back (O2) (*B*). Simultaneously, as the semi-circular camera movement has come to an end, the increasing distance between the camera and Alice allows for the inclusion of a new character, the flirtatious Hungarian Sandor Szavost (O3) who, in the events that follow, will attempt to hit on her (*C*). Here, one already may anticipate the goal of the next chapter as this camera movement might be extended metaphorically through the PERSON IS A CONTAINER metaphor. Annoyed by her husband's absence and giddy on champagne, which weakens the boundary of marriage, she lays herself more "open" toward other men.

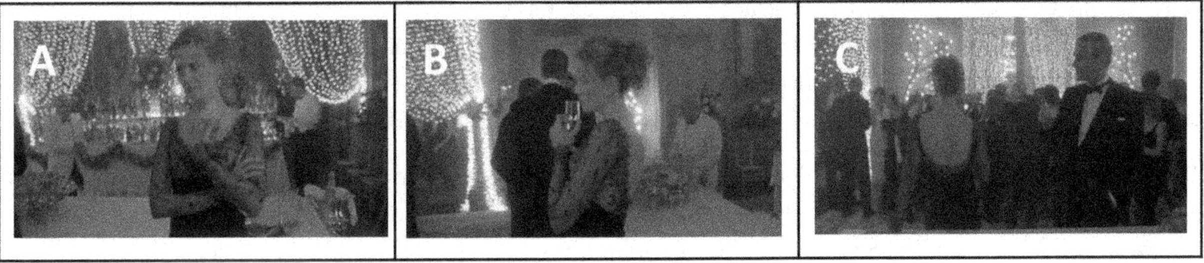

Figure 3.24. EXCLUSION and INCLUSION by semi-circular camera movement in *Eyes Wide Shut.*

A visual object X will not be included nor excluded when the frame shifts to keep that object X on-screen. This is the case, as other examples will show us later on, with a *following shot*.

ENCLOSURE occurs when the container closes in on the visual object so as to exclude the free space that resides between the boundary of the container and the object inside of it. This can be diagrammed as in figure 3.25*A*. Naturally, this pattern is inherent to in-depth camera movement in which the camera moves, apparently or literally, toward the object. By contrast, EXPOSURE occurs when the distance between the boundary of the container and the object increases so as to permit the inclusion of more space inside of it. Consequently, the arrows are pointing outward rather than inward (figure 3.25*B*). Likewise, this pattern is inherent to in-depth camera movement in which the camera moves, apparently or literally, away from the object.

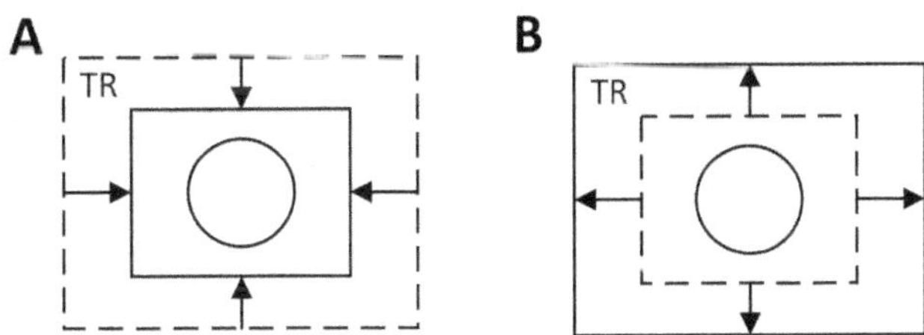

Figure 3.25. *A*, ENCLOSURE and *B*, EXPOSURE.

Both patterns are expressed through what is perhaps one of the trademarks of Kubrick's stylistic system, namely the use of the *zoom lens*. As already stated, movement elicited by this device can be seen as a rather unusual type of camera movement in that the camera does not physically move from one location to another. Yet, as with literal camera movement the camera has to be forcefully controlled in order for it to achieve the effect of the mobile frame. This is also expressed by the English cinematographer John Alcott who collaborated four times with Kubrick (*2001*, *A Clockwork Orange*, *Barry Lyndon* and *The Shining*). When, in an interview with the journal *American Cinematographer*, he was asked about the use of the zoom lens in *Barry Lyndon*, he answered:

> Oh, yes—we used it a great deal. The Angenieux 10-to-1 zoom was used on the Arriflex 35BL, in conjunction with Ed DiGiolio's Cinema Products "Joy Stick" zoom control, which is an excellent one. It starts and stops without a sudden jar, which is very important, and you can manipulate it so slowly that it almost feels like nothing is happening. This is very difficult with some of the motorized zoom controls. I find that this one really works.[60]

Shots that result from the forceful use of this "joy stick" zoom control are abundant and can be found in almost each of Kubrick's films. Figures 3.26 and 3.27 compile a selection of two zoom movements (one for each pattern) as they were gathered from *The Shining* and *Barry Lyndon*, respectively. As shall become clear in the next chapter, the speed in which these patterns unfold should be seen in function of the subject matter (e.g., slow movement for contemplation and fast movement for abrupt and suspenseful perceptions).

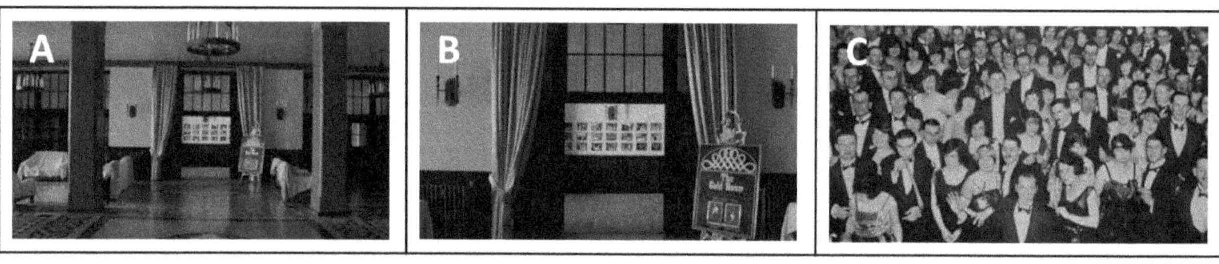

Figure 3.26. ENCLOSURE as elicited through the use of the zoom-in lens in *The Shining*.

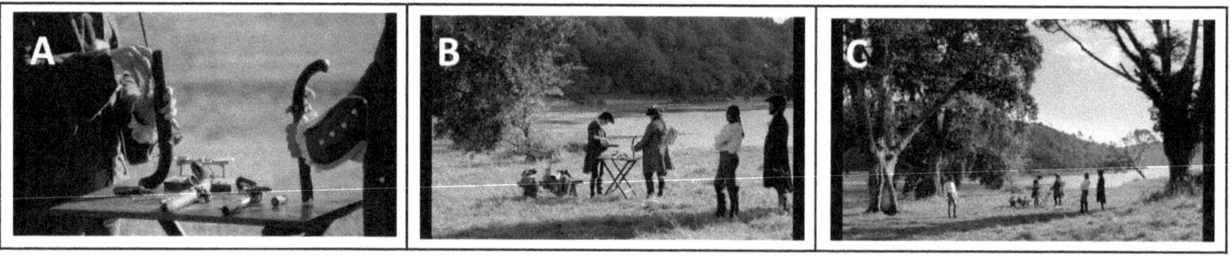

Figure 3.27. EXPOSURE as elicited through the use of the zoom-out lens in *Barry Lyndon*.

In the manifestations of both patterns we may also observe the workings of another image schema, that of PART-WHOLE.[61] As with the CONTAINER image schema, this schema is grounded in the experience of our bodies (i.e., as wholes with parts). Consisting of the structural elements of a whole, parts, and a configuration, we may follow Lakoff and articulate its basic logic according to the following postulates: "If A is a part of B, then B is not a part of A. . . . If the parts exist in the configuration, then and only then does the whole exist."[62] From this it follows that "if the parts are destroyed, then the whole is destroyed." Given this brief description, then, one may define ENCLOSURE as a specific case of EXCLUSION where its starting point delineates the whole and its ending point a part of that whole. By contrast, EXPOSURE can be defined alternatively as a specific case of INCLUSION where its starting point conjoins with a part of the whole and its ending point with the whole. Again, we might turn to the logic of CONTAINMENT to draw these inferences. Figure 3.28 diagrams this logic as applied to figures 3.26 and 3.27, respectively.

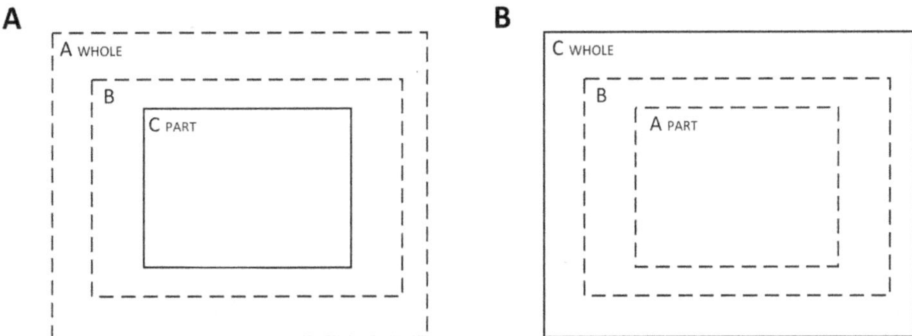

Figure 3.28. The inferential logic of CONTAINMENT as inherent to the dynamic patterns of *A*, ENCLOSURE and *B*, EXPOSURE.

It is here that we may discern a fundamental difference with the example as illustrated in figure 3.23. The image that serves as the ending point of the camera movement in this figure does not constitute a part of the image that serves as the starting point of that same movement (and vice versa).

2.2.3 Linking dynamic patterns in one shot: The long take

Having discussed and illustrated both groups of dynamic patterns in isolation, let us now turn toward the question of their interaction. Which dynamics arise from the pairing of dynamic patterns in a single shot? Since film unfolds in time and space, the filmmaker has the possibility of structuring the visible world in such a way as to create a complex and structured whole in which two or more dynamic patterns are *bonded* together in temporal succession through a LINK schema. As we already saw in the previous chapter, a LINK schema is an image schema that consists of two or more entities, connected physically or metaphorically, and the bond between them. Naturally, the unfolding of such links of dynamic patterns in one and the same shot depends on the duration of the shot. The longer the shot lasts, the more likely that more than one dynamic pattern will unfold in the shot. This brings us to the technique of the *long take*.[63] The long take is a shot that lasts much longer than the conventional editing pace either of the film itself or of films in general. As such, it has the potential for eliciting a series of dynamic patterns. Again, Kubrick's work is highly illuminating in showing how this might unfold cinematically. To illustrate this, let us consider the underlying image schematic structures of two long takes taken from *The Killing*.

The first long take occurs just before Johnny Clay, the leader of the gang, enters the back office to steal $2 million from the money-counting room. The second long take occurs afterward when the conspirators are gathered at an apartment where they are to meet Johnny and divide the money. In both long takes Kubrick manages to connect various group members by eliciting a series of dynamic patterns. To structure the analysis somehow, we first provide a schematic and formal outline of the linkage of dynamic patterns underlying the long take. In this overview the various dynamic patterns are grouped by an underbrace representing the single shot. Moreover, each dynamic pattern will be illustrated by one still image of the film. For practical reasons we will show the reader only a snapshot of the moment that accords with the ending point of the SOURCE-PATH-GOAL image schema as embedded in the movement of either the character or the camera. For example, if the pattern is INCLUSION, the letter associated with it, will correspond with a screenshot showing the included visual object (as opposed to a screenshot of the empty frame).

Having said this, the underlying structure of the first long take might be represented as in figure 3.29.

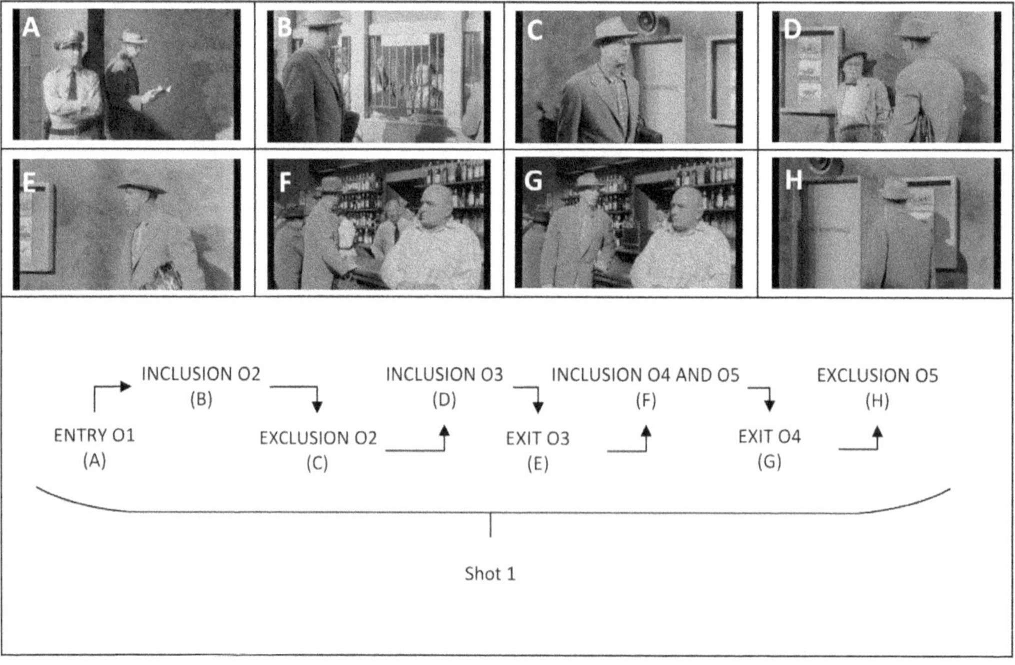

Figure 3.29. Linking various dynamic patterns of containment via the long take in *The Killing* (case one).

The schema reads as follows: Johnny Clay (O1) enters the frame from behind the set (*A*). The camera follows him as he walks toward the clerk George Petty (O2) who is now included as a stationary entity by the movement of the camera (*B*). The camera excludes him again as soon as Johnny continues his walk figure (*C*). He then makes a turn as he recognizes Marvin Unger (O3), the bookkeeper of the group (*D*). Again, the character is included by the movement of the camera. However, this time the character himself exits the frame rather than the camera excluding him (*E*). Johnny continues his walk, this time toward the bar where Mike O'Reilly (O4), the track bartender, and Maurice Oboukhoff (O5), the wrestler, are awaiting his signal to start off the distraction scene (*F*). Mike leaves the frame by exiting it from the right side of the frame (*G*). Maurice is excluded as Johnny now walks toward the door that gives entrance to the back office where the race track money is hidden (*H*). The label "no admittance" clearly signals that entry here is strictly forbidden. Later in the film, when Maurice has caused a quarrel thus attracting the cops, George will open the door for Johnny to come in and rob the place.

After the successful robbery the group members are gathered at the apartment where they are anxiously awaiting the arrival of Johnny. Similarly, the scene is rendered in one single take in which various characters are introduced by the camera following one character, in this case, the nervous clerk George Petty. Likewise, the dynamic structure underlying this long take might be represented as in figure 3.30.

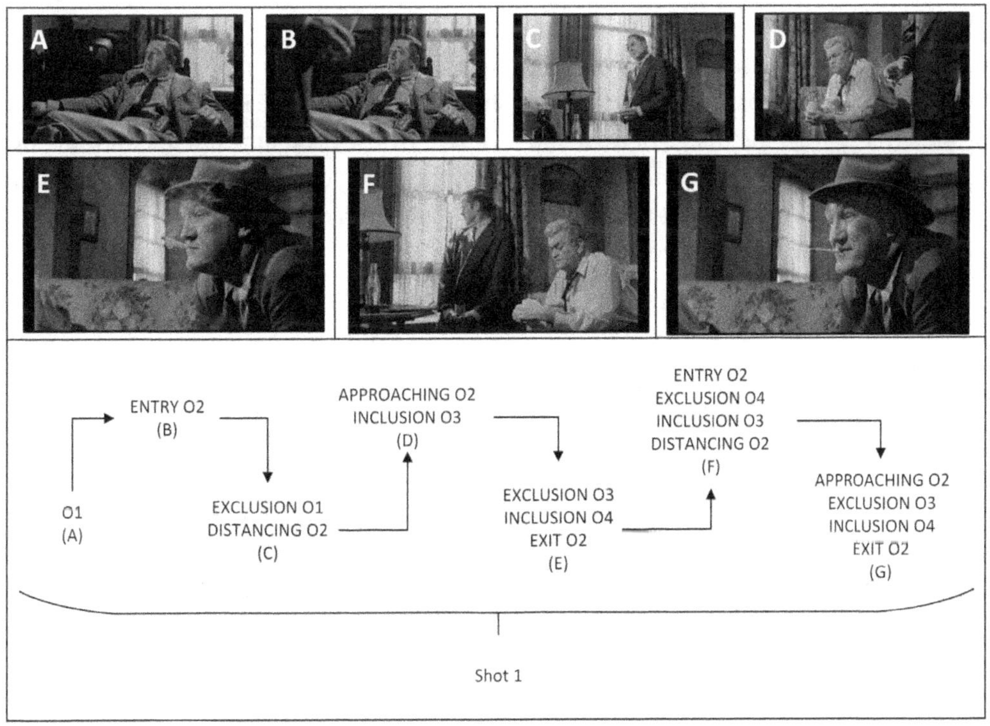

Figure 3.30. Linking various dynamic patterns of containment via the long take in *The Killing* (case two).

The chain of dynamic patterns starts off with a shot of the corrupt policeman Randy Kennan (O1) sitting in a sofa smoking his cigarette (*A*). As his eyes move up, George (O2) enters the scene from the left side of the frame (*B*). Because he is close to the camera, we can only see a part of him. Randy is again excluded from the frame as George distances himself from the camera by walking toward the window (*C*). He holds still for a few seconds, only to move again this time diagonally in forward direction. As he approaches the camera, Marvin (O3) is revealed (*D*). From the right side of the frame George then turns away from Marvin, thus excluding him and revealing the face of Mike (O4) while he himself exits the frame from the right side of the frame (*E*). George then enters the frame once more to position himself again near the window next to Marvin (*F*). The long take ends by repeating the same pattern of figure 3.30*E* (*G*).

2.3 The relation among shots

2.3.1 Linking dynamic patterns through editing

The long take connects the dynamic patterns of containment together in one shot that is continuous along the dimensions of time and space. Another way of linking these patterns would be by means of connecting the individual shots together. In other words, through the technique that is unique to film, namely editing. Because we are dealing with relations among individual shots, those links may well be temporally and/or spatially discontinuous. There is probably no better way to illustrate this distinction than with what is perhaps the most iconic film cut in film history, the bone to satellite transition from *2001*. Before starting, let us first mark our territory of analysis. The film cut may be considered a part of a series of four shots starting with the image of the ape-man throwing the bone in the air and ending with the image of a satellite in space whose orbit appears to continue the bone's downward trajectory.[64] How brief the moment may be in the film, the total duration only lasting 120 seconds, a look at its underlying conceptual structure betrays the workings of a number of dynamic patterns of containment of which its schematic structure may be summarized as in figure 3.31.

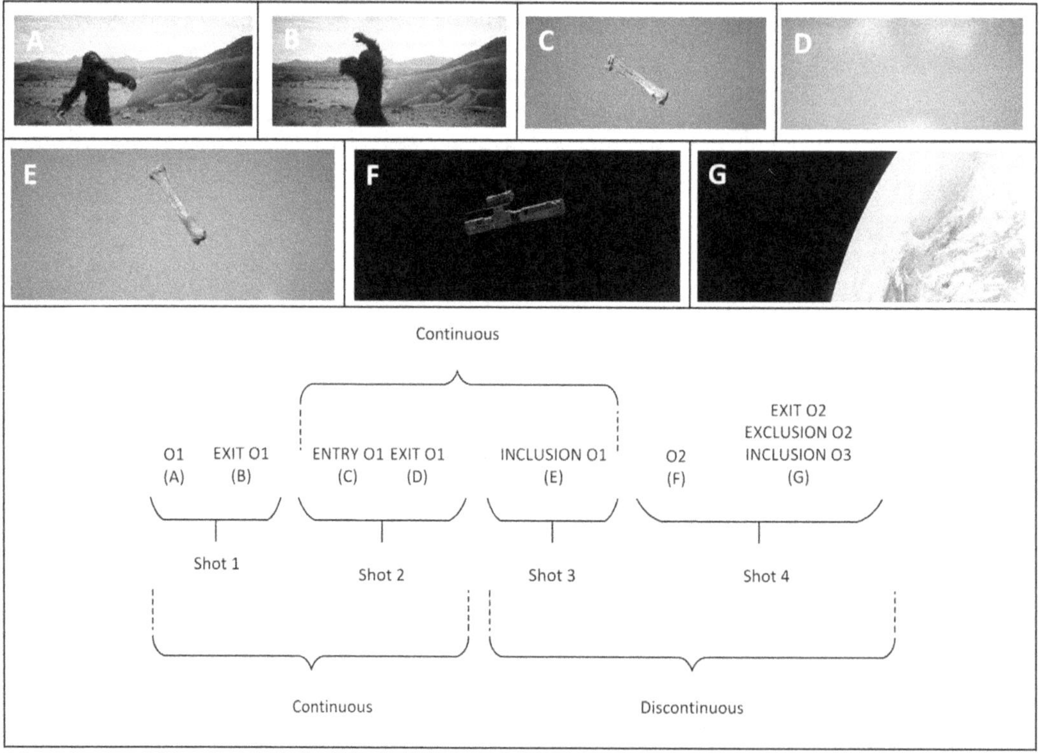

Figure 3.31. Linking dynamic patterns of containment through editing: the bone-satellite match-cut in *2001*.

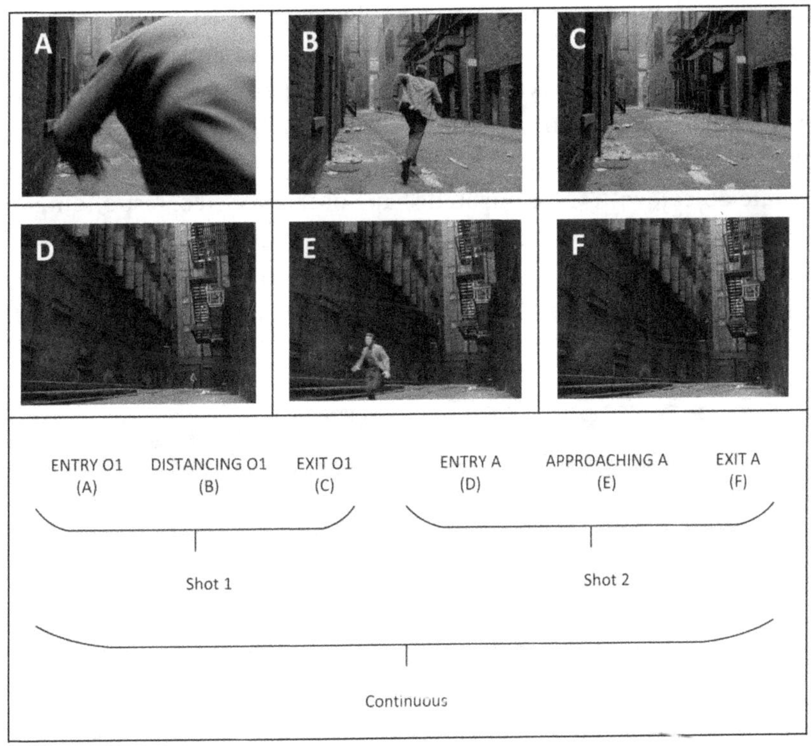

Figure 3.32. Linking dynamic patterns of containment through editing (example taken from *Killer's Kiss*) (part one).

In the first shot (*A*), the ape-man throws the bone (O1) up in the air causing it to exit the frame from the top side (*B*). The film, then, cuts to the second shot which shows the same bone now whirling into the frame from the bottom side (*C*). For a couple of seconds the camera follows the bone (hence, no inclusion or exclusion). However, because the bone moves faster than the camera following it, the bone exits the frame from the top side for a second time (*D*). The film, then, cuts almost unnoticeable to the third shot. No entry this time, as it is the camera now (i.e., the frame) that picks up again what it has left in the previous shot (*E*). The camera continues to follow it as the bone falls downwards. It is in the course of this downward movement, then, that the film breaks its continuity by cutting to a shot of a new object, a satellite in space (O2), that is both spatially (earth versus space) and temporally (million years ago versus modern times) detached from the previous shots (*F*). These discontinuities, however, are counterbalanced by a graphical and formal resemblance between the two objects (O1=O2) which, in turn, prompts the viewer to see the bone and the satellite both as part of "the same, human history of domestication and exploitation of the physical world."[65] From the perspective of cognitive linguistics, we might term this match-cut an example of what Lakoff has coined an *image metaphor*.[66] Image metaphors differ from the type of conceptual metaphors most commonly theorized in the literature (see also previous chapter) in that they do not map complex conceptual structures in a source domain onto conceptual structure in a target domain (e.g., EVENT-STRUCTURE metaphor, MIND IS A BODY), but instead "map conventional mental images onto other conventional mental images by virtue of their internal structure."[67] As Lakoff and Turner write, they are "one-shot metaphors, relating one rich image with one other rich image."[68] Likewise, then, we might understand the match-cut as an image mapping in which one concrete object is linked to another concrete object, with the elongated shape of the bone corresponding to the elongated shape of the space vessel.[69] What we then perceive is a combination of both EXIT and EXCLUSION: due to the loss of gravity in space, the object slowly moves to the bottom left corner of the frame while at the same time, the camera moves to the right. As a result the satellite is no longer visible and a new visual object of the planet Earth appears on-screen (O3) (G).

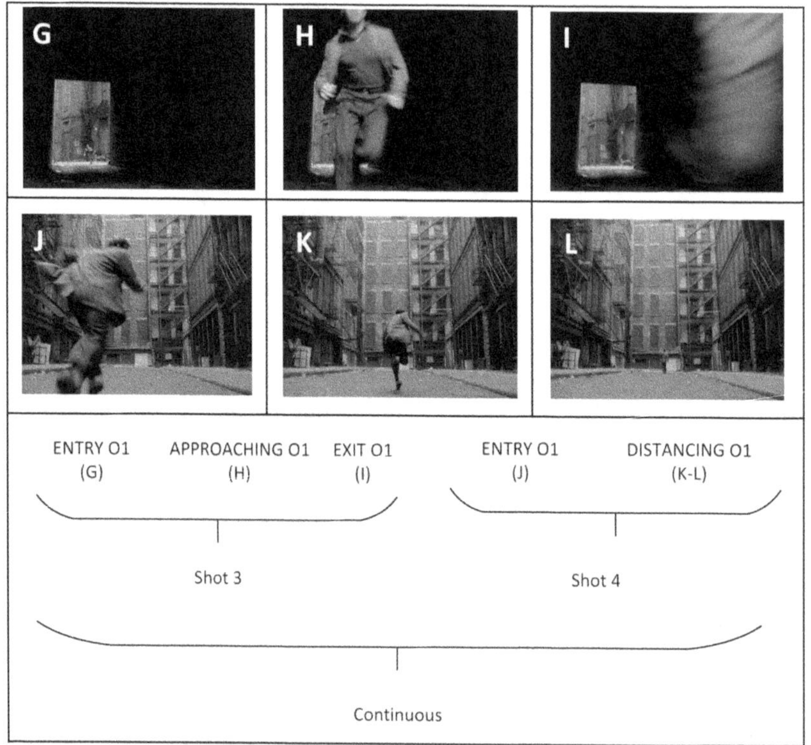

Figure 3.33. Linking dynamic patterns of containment through editing (example taken from *Killer's Kiss*) (part two).

A vigorous montage involving the dynamic patterns of DISTANCING and APPROACHING can be found in the chase scene near the end of *Killer's Kiss* when the lead character Davey Gordon tries to outrun his pursuers. The scene consists, among others, of a series of four static shots whereby each shot gives expression to a pattern of DISTANCING or APPROACHING, whether or not preceded and or followed by a pattern of ENTRY and EXIT, respectively. In the first shot (figure 3.32*A-C*) Davey runs into the frame from the right edge of the frame, from a place behind and near the camera, thus crossing three edges of the frame and filling almost the total amount of empty space inside the frame (*A*). Empty space takes over again as Davey runs toward the back of the image, thus distancing himself from the camera (*B*). He exits the frame by disappearing behind the corner of the building (i.e., not by crossing any edges of the frame) (*C*). By contrast, the second shot (figure 3.32*D-F*) maintains the opposite structure as Davey now appears from behind the corner of the same (?) building (*D*). He then runs forward in a diagonal way (E) across the camera's field of vision, exiting the frame from its left edge (*F*).

The same structure is repeated in the following shot (3.33*G-I*), albeit now the movement runs from left to right and more straight to the camera. The movement continues in the next shot (figure 3.33*J-L*) as Davey enters the frame from the left side (*J*). He distances himself by running away from the camera toward the background of the image figure (*K*), where he halts and contemplates a way out by spotting the fire escape figure (figure 3.33*L*). The shot thus ends with no exit. Without moving the camera and with the help of continuity editing the film thus creates a highly dynamic structure, a ballet of physical movement, elicited by the repetitious juxtaposition of the patterns of APPROACHING and DISTANCING.

2.3.2 Eliciting dynamic patterns by means of editing

Until now the shot was treated as a container for at least one or more dynamic pattern(s). However, an impression of a dynamic pattern may also be *created* after a juxtaposition of shots. In this case, the dynamic pattern is holding the shots together rather than the shot holding the dynamic patterns together. Schematically, this difference between two distinctive organizational templates might be represented as in figure 3.34.

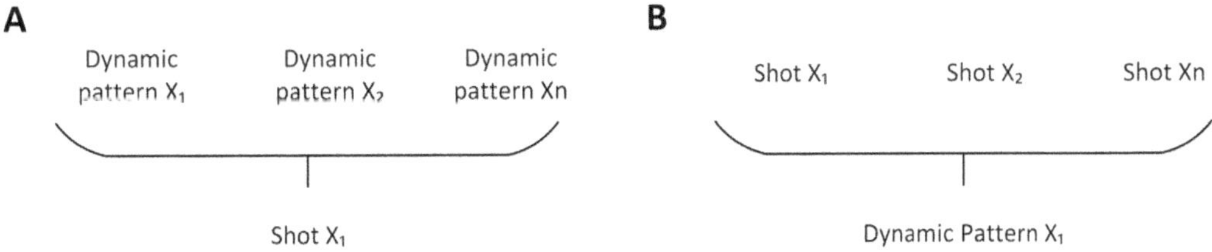

Figure 3.34. *A*, the shot as organizational principle, versus *B*, the dynamic pattern as organizational principle.

One prototypical example of a dynamic pattern that might be provoked by way of editing is the WHOLE-TO-PARTS transition, as we already encountered in relation to the pattern of ENCLOSURE. In film this spatial change might be evoked by one of the most common techniques of the continuity editing system, namely the technique of cutting from an establishing shot, which delineates the overall space of a location, to a shot of a part of this space.[70] Consider, for example, figure 3.35 which shows a series of shots as taken from *The Shining*. The first shot, *A*, establishes the spatial whole of the men's restroom and the positions of Jack and Grady inside of it. This shot is followed by a second one, *B*, which is part of that space, albeit taken from across the centre line or the 180° line, thus turning the second shot into a mirror image of the previous one. Jack now occupies the place in the image that Grady occupied in the previous shot (and vice versa). Also here we may already precede the next chapter as this alteration might be metaphorically linked to the subject matter of the conversation which suggests an identity between Jack, the current caretaker of the Overlook Hotel, and Grady, its previous caretaker. Once the whole is laid out for us, the space is analytically broken down into its components. Shot *B* is followed by two medium shots, *C* and *D*, which are both spatially continuous with the two previous shots. Here again we may see the logic of containment unfolding itself. Given that shot *B* is part of shot *A* and shots *C* and *D* are part of shot *B*, it follows that shots *C* and *D* are also part of shot *A*. Once the 180° line has been established by shot *B*, Kubrick relies on the technique of the shot/reverse shot to join shots *C* and *D* and to cut back and forth from Jack to Grady.

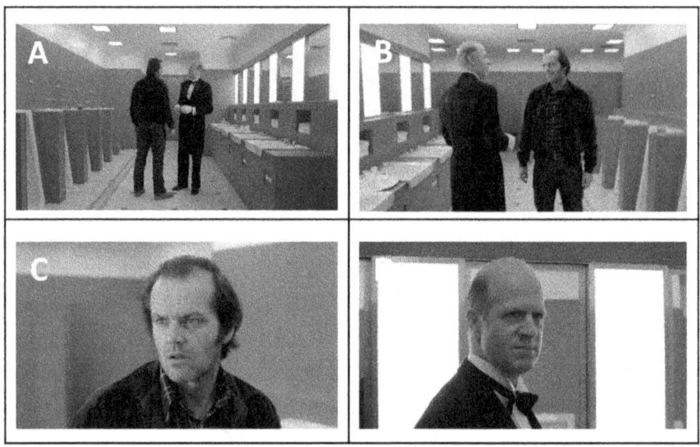

Figure 3.35. The WHOLE-TO-PARTS transition as elicited by editing (example taken from *The Shining*).

As the reader may notice, the pattern that results from this editing technique is quite similar to the pattern of ENCLOSURE, as discussed earlier, except for now the pattern is elicited by editing as opposed to camera movement. The fundamental difference here is that the viewer does not see all of the intermediary locations between the starting point and the ending point of the camera movement. In other words, the pattern is created through a process of *elimination* rather than through a process of *showing*. In this particular case, however, it would have been practically difficult to provoke the same effect by means of camera movement given that the camera angle differs in each shot. For instance, in order to arrive at the same image of shot *B*, starting from shot *A*, it is not only sufficient that the camera moves closer to the actors, but also that it makes a circle of 180°. If the angle would stay unchanged in each of the separate shots, the effect would be quite similar to the pattern of ENCLOSURE that results from forward and perpendicular camera movement (e.g., zoom-in). Such an example can be found in *2001* as illustrated in figure 3.36.

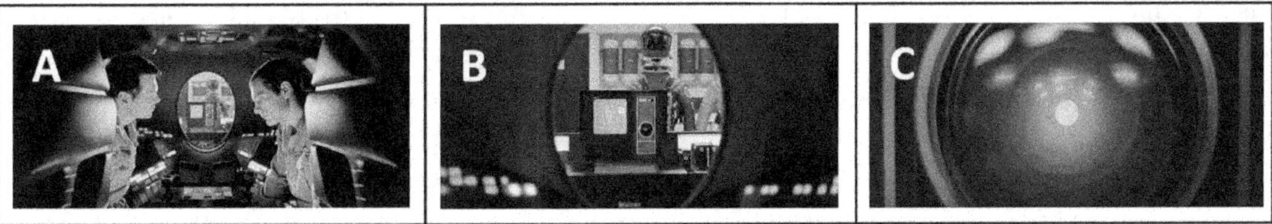

Figure 3.36. ENCLOSURE as elicited by editing (example taken from *2001*).

In the two examples above, the rhythm of the editing is significantly held slow, that is, the shots that designate the parts and the wholes are left on-screen deliberately lengthily with the duration of the "whole" shots being somewhat longer than the duration of the "part" shots. However, the director might, for instance, speed up the tempo by adjusting the length of the shots in such a way as to evoke a more dynamic and impressionistic effect. A good example of this can be found, for example, in *A Clockwork Orange* in the fast editing pattern that is shown near the beginning of the film when Alex, in his bedroom, is listening to a cassette of Beethoven's 9th. Figure 3.37 shows the first eight shots of this pattern of a total amount of twenty shots, the whole only lasting fifteen seconds. As with our previous example, the editing alternates between the whole, here composed of four Christ figures who have their arms intertwined like a chorus line, and parts of this whole. Yet, here the cutting is so fast that the effect is excitement rather than slowness. Again, we might relate this stylistic choice to the filmmaker's desire to express the content of the story which, in this particular case, overlaps with Alex' arousal when hearing Beethoven's music. Or as our male hero puts is: "O bliss, bliss and heaven, oh it was gorgeousness and georgeosity made flesh."

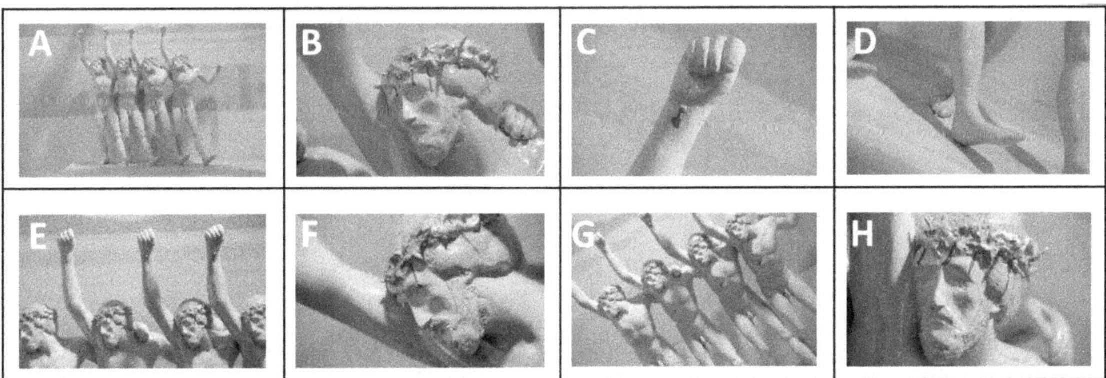

Figure 3.37. Rhythmic editing in *A Clockwork Orange*.

In all of the three examples discussed so far the structural element of the whole is clearly visible on-screen. Alternatively, the filmmaker could elicit the PART-WHOLE schema without even showing the whole. This assumption of spatial coexistence of parts in the absence of a whole (i.e., an establishing shot) is known among film scholars as the *Kuleshov effect*.[71] According to this effect, viewers infer a spatial whole on the basis of seeing only the component parts. A good example of this technique can be found, for example, at the end of *Fear and Desire*, in the scene where Corby finishes off the General who looks just like him. Throughout the whole scene both opponents are never shown together. Yet, through editing and the organization of the visual elements on-screen, the viewer infers a spatial and causal relationship among the individual shots. As shown in figure 3.38*A*, we first see Corby approaching the scene in long shot. Next, we see a medium shot of the face of the wounded General as he shouts, "I surrender," immediately followed by a close-up of Corby while he shoots the General (*B-C*). We do not see the gun, but only hear the gunshot. The General's head falls down to the ground (*D*). This juxtaposition of faces is repeated a couple of times, as partially exemplified in figure 3.38*E-F-G*, in order to stress the bodily likeness between the two men and Corby's own recognition of this resemblance. The scene ends as they leave the area again (*H*).

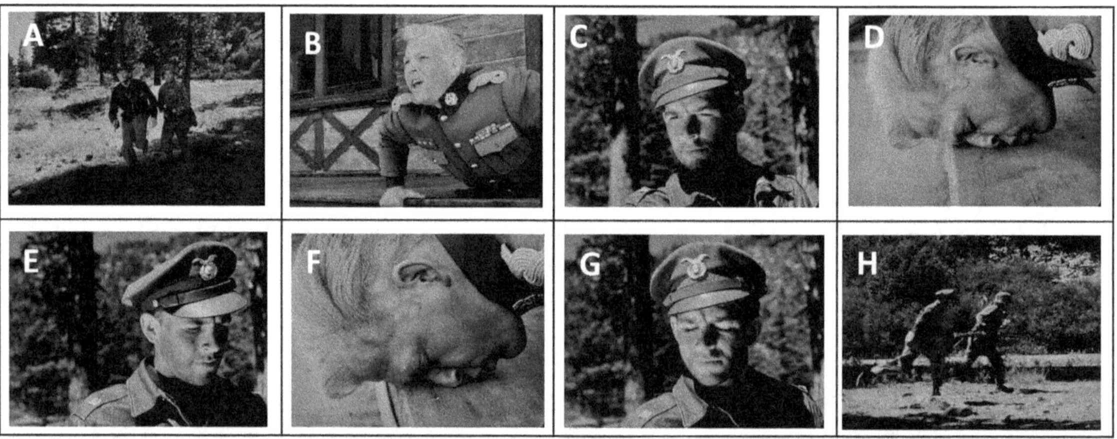

Figure 3.38. Inferring a spatial whole on the basis of seeing only its parts (example taken from *Fear and Desire*).

3. Target domains and acting

We now have discussed and illustrated some of the principle ways in which cinematic resources may arouse the same kind of image-schematic patterns as they were identified by cognitive linguists in our prototypical mode of communication, language. In the next chapter we will see, through a visual analysis of Kubrick's work, how the inferential logic of these patterns may, in turn, be retrieved metaphorically in order to flesh out the inferential logic of the target domains that make up the conceptual structure of mental causation (e.g., perception, cognition, emotion). Before starting this discussion, however, we first have to consider the question as to how these target domains may be elicited non-verbally in film. Addressing this question is of fundamental importance for if there is no target domain, there is no narrative object of meaning for which the image schemas may be appropriated. In the beginning of this chapter, we already put forward the assumption that these target domains may be elicited wordlessly through the metonymical resource of acting, especially given the close association between performance and non-verbal behavior. In this section we would like to elaborate this relationship more in detail, starting with a brief description of an epistemological problem which lies at the heart of the relationship between acting and the identification of others' mental states. It is only once we have a clear notion of this problem, which in the literature is referred to as the "other minds problem," that we can adequately characterize the rhetorical role of acting in classical narrative cinema (and Kubrick's position within it). In the second section, then, we will illustrate more concretely through a discussion of some examples of Kubrick's work, how actors' bodies can be employed to intend the concepts of mental causation. This clear conveyance of mental concepts through the actor's physical behavior, however, can also be undermined and complicated by the filmmaker. Kubrick's work in this regard can be seen as an excellent exemplar of this point. Illustrating this will be the subject matter of the remaining section.

3.1 The other minds problem, performance, and Active Analysis

In chapter 2 of this book we already saw how people have a natural tendency to attribute mental states to physical behavior and perceptual organs. This formed the basis of such conceptual metonymies as FACIAL EXPRESSIONS FOR EMOTIONS, EYES FOR SEEING and HEAD FOR THINKING. In this sense, one might say that these metonymies presuppose the capacity of observing another's mind without having direct perceptual access to it. In other words, they take for granted the ability to overcome a problem which in the philosophy of mind is known as "the other minds problem."[72] Following Thomas Nagel we might roughly distinguish between two philosophical versions of this problem.[73] The first is *epistemological* and asks how we can know for certain that others have a mind. The second is *conceptual* and deals with the question as to how we know if the minds of others are like our own. As stated, both problems follow naturally from the ontological distinction between visible behavior and inaccessible experience, that is, "one's direct observation of the former does not presuppose one has or can have direct knowledge of the latter."[74] As with the paradox of cinematic meaning, we are thus challenged to overcome a logical inconsistency which leads again to a questioning of our capability of attributing mental states to others. This paradox, let us coin this the *paradox of mental attribution*, may be articulated more formally as follows:

(1) People have a natural cognitive tendency to attribute mental states to others.
(2) It is an ontological truth that we cannot have direct access to the mind of others.
(3) How, then, can we attribute mental states to others?

If we, however, want to further assert that the actor's body forms a vital means for expressing the target domains of mental causation, we must first cope with this problem to some extent. Where then lies the solution to this dilemma? In what sense, could we attribute inner, mental experience to others? As the metonymies of mental causation, as discussed in the previous chapter, already suggest, the answer to this question has to be found in the relationship between mental experience and bodily behavior. It is true that we cannot observe other minds directly, but from this observation it does not follow, as the other minds problem assumes, that inner experience and bodily behavior are distinct and that bodily changes are separate from feelings. Aaron Taylor, a film theorist specialized in screen acting, sums up two important reasons why this latter assumption is mistaken.[75] The first reason is that the relationship between bodily changes and feeling is not random. As he writes, "experience of these changes belongs both to the subject who feels it and the object in which the feeling is experienced (i.e., the body)."[76] Here, we may point again toward some of the stories of mental causation as exemplified in chapter 1. Recall, for instance, the Ludovico technique from *A Clockwork Orange*. In a way, this technique represents the strong interdependency of body and mind as Alex' retching and his physical struggling against his straight jacket cannot be detached from his experience of seeing the violence. Taylor himself gives the example of the various training sequences in *Full Metal Jacket* which the author considers to represent the absurdity of trying to "produce robotic behavior that is autonomous from the experience of feeling."[77]

Secondly, the other minds problem does not take into account the important fact that we make use of our bodies to communicate our mental states to others. As the author argues, "you intentionally direct a sense of your experience to another via bodily signals, and others are able to intuit your state of mind through observation even if 'another cannot have your bodily feeling or experience' directly."[78] There are good evolutionary and functional reasons for this. Inferences such as these allow us to understand and predict the behavior of others in order to adjust and update our own (social) behavior. In the concluding chapter of this book, we will see, how embodied simulation processes allow for such inference processes to occur on a neurological level, but for now let us take such faculties for granted.

This brings us to the essence of our argument, namely that the other minds problem is no so much of a problem for those living in the practical world—we are capable of making inferences about others mental states quite easily—as it is an intriguing, albeit abstract and theoretical puzzle for philosophers. Therefore, the "real" problem, as Taylor dubs it, is not so much a question of plausibility (can we attribute mental states to others?), but a question of pragmatics (to what degree can we accurately identify others' mental states?).[79]

It is at this point in our inquiry that we can make the link to acting, and in particular to its function within the rhetorical system of classical narrative cinema, as it is said that one of the main characteristics of performance in this category of cinema is to provide the viewer with a performance that allows him or her to identify the character's interiority in a way that is "comprehensible and unambiguous."[80] In other words, the function of performance in classical cinema is primarily to inform, that is, to reinforce "the narration's aim to provide optimal narrative clarity for viewers."[81]

If the actor's body is one of the chief expressive means to achieve the goal of "transparent signification," which, then, is the technique of acting to be best employed?[82] Academic inquiries into performance usually align classical cinema's urge toward clarity with a type of acting technique that is "realistic" and "natural." Scholars usually line up these features with Stanislavskian modes of acting as opposed to the Brechtian techniques of modernist or postmodern narratives which are characterized by elements such as "estrangement and episodic structures that lack of motivation and causal relationships."[83] Although this distinction does give us some broad theoretical insight, it is unavoidably too oversimplified in several respects. Firstly, classifying an actor's work as belonging to either one of the two categories fails to capture the complexity of an actor's work. As Carnicke points out: "The final performance on screen tells you virtually nothing about the acting technique used during filming. What reads as realistic might arise from any variety of acting techniques, including those of Stanislavski, Brecht, Delsarte, Suzuki, and so on."[84] The author sees the actor more as a flexible performer who is capable of adapting him- or herself to the needs of the director, to give him, as Jack Nicholson once put it, "what he wants ultimately, no matter what it is."[85] Secondly, the distinction overlooks the complexity of the two theoretical systems of acting themselves. For instance, Carnicke is eager to point out that Stanislavski did not only direct realistic plays, but also plays that resisted coherent development and thus are more in tune with the Brechtian system of acting.[86]

Having said this, where does the cinema of Kubrick fit into this distinction? Categorizing the performances of his films as either realistic or non-realistic would be equally over-simplifying things. Broadly speaking, it is safe to say that the director saw performances chiefly in function of the demands of the narrative. Here, we may turn, as we already did in chapter 1, toward the significant influence of Stanislavski on the filmmaker's approach to performance. The director himself has repeatedly stressed in interviews that Gorchakov's *Stanislavsky Directs* has guided him in his thinking about how to work with actors.[87] As Carnicke writes: "Emulating late Stanislavskian technique, Kubrick developed a clear focus on the link between actor and narrative."[88] The same observation has also been made by Falsetto who considers the creation of character in Stanley Kubrick's films as "complex and intimately linked to the various thematic and stylistic operations at play."[89] This link between narrative and acting is best captured by Stanislavski's method of "Active Analysis" which forms the subtext of Gorchakov's book. A close analysis of this method falls beyond the scope of this book, but generally speaking Active Analysis "makes the actor aware of the play's narrative structure through repeated improvisations that function as drafts of the final performance."[90] The embodied notion underlying this method is that actors are able to leak information about the inner world of the human being (i.e., the conceptual demand of the narrative) through gesture, body language and facial expression; all of which can be seen and interpreted by others, on the outside.[91] As various theorists of acting have pointed out, the Active Analysis Method thus bears a close resemblance to the thesis of embodiment as advocated by second-generation cognitive science.[92] Clare, for instance, sees in the principles of Stanislavski's actor training an implementation of the central proposition of Lakoff and Johnson that our concepts are formed through the body. As she writes: "Their view literally and figuratively incorporates the subjective; Stanislavsky shows how to do this in practice for the purpose of acting."[93]

It is in the light of this method, then, that we should understand and justify Kubrick's legendary emphasis on performative repetition.[94] The director did not let his actors repeat a scene merely for the sake of repetition. He wanted his actors to reach the conceptual and emotional core of the narrative structure, or "scheme of the play," as Stanislavski called it, and repetition was one means to achieve this aesthetic goal.[95] That is, through repetition actors become familiar with their dialogue to the extent that they do not have to be concerned anymore about the words they have to say when performing the scene. Repetition thus neutralizes the actor's focus on "knowing the lines" that otherwise would distract from the emotional essence of a scene. In his own words, Kubrick has stated this as follows:

> You cannot act without knowing dialogue. If actors have to think about the words, they can't work on the emotion. So you end up doing thirty takes of something. And still you can see the concentration in their eyes; they don't know their lines. So you just shoot it and shoot it and hope you can get something out of it in pieces.[96]

It is also interesting to note here how repetition also resonates throughout the actors' dialogues. As Pezzotta convincingly has demonstrated through a discussion of various examples, many spoken lines in Kubrick's films, notably *The Shining*, are full of repetition with actors often repeating in their responses sentences and words that were already uttered by the speech of others.[97] This repetition should not only be regarded as a way for actors to easily memorize their dialogue—and thus reach the conceptual essence more effortlessly—but also as a symptom of Kubrick's aesthetic resistance against the propositional and linguistic view of meaning, as elaborated in the introduction. By including these verbal reiterations, Kubrick manages to stress the materiality of the speech. As such, words are deprived of their semantic content and the attention is drawn away from their linguistic meaning and toward the purely bodily and acoustic aspects of the performance, precisely those aspects through which meaning is communicated non-verbally. That this may result to the extent that the effect is even comical, can be illustrated, for example, with the dialogue that accompanies the scene where Jack finds out that Wendy is reading his manuscript:[98]

JACK: How do you like it? How do you like it? What are you doing down here?

WENDY: I just wanted to talk to you.

JACK: Okay. Let's talk. What do you want to talk about?

WENDY: I can't remember.

JACK: You can't remember.

WENDY: No, I can't.

JACK: Maybe it was about Danny?

WENDY: Maybe it was about him. I think we should discuss Danny. I think we should discuss what should be done with him.

JACK: What should be done with him?

WENDY: I don't know.

JACK: I don't think that's true. I think you have some very definite ideas about what should be done with Danny. And I'd like to know what they are.

WENDY: Well I, I think maybe he should be taken to a doctor.

JACK: You think maybe he should be taken to a doctor? When do you think maybe he should be taken to a doctor?

WENDY: As soon as possible?

JACK: As soon as possible?

WENDY: Please.

JACK: You believe his health might be at stake.

WENDY: Yes.

JACK: And you are concerned about him. And are you concerned about me?

WENDY: Of course I am.

JACK: Of course you are! Have you ever thought about my responsibilities?

WENDY: What are you talking about?

JACK: Have you ever had a single moment's thought about my responsibilities? Have you ever thought for a single moment about my responsibilities to my employers?

Kubrick's work reveals yet another strategy for undermining the meaning of linguistic expressions, one that is not so much defined by repetition, but by a gap between the utterance and the situational context. This argument is central to Kolker's account of *Dr. Strangelove*. "What Kubrick, Terry Southern, and Peter George do in their script and what Kubrick does in his direction," he argues, "is create a series of linguistic and visual reductions, giving the characters utterances that defeat meaning."[99] He illustrates the workings of this process of "linguistic subversion," as he coins it, by analysing various fragments of character speech, including an excerpt from the dialogue of Major Kong (Slim Pickens).[100] He is the commander of the aircraft that is ordered to drop a nuclear bomb on Russia. When he prepares for "nuclear combat, toe to toe with the Russkies," he pulls out a cowboy hat, and tells his men:

> I reckon you wouldn't even be human beings if you didn't have some pretty strong personal feelings about nuclear combat. . . . If this thing turns out to be half as important as I figure it just might be, I'd say that you're all in line for some important promotions and personal citations when this thing's over with. And that goes for every last one of you, regardless of your race, color, and your creed.

It is precisely this clash between the seriousness of the situation, on the one hand, and the banality of the cowboy image, on the other hand, that makes the scene so surprisingly funny and frightening at the same time. As Kolker argues: "The serious is made light of and the ridiculous is made serious. The language circles upon itself; it has no subject or object, no detachable meaning. The meaning is the utterance itself and its own perfectly logical irrelevance and banality."[101]

Turning back again to Kubrick's relation to Stanislavski, there is, however, one crucial difference that separates the two artists. This has to do with the way they worked with actors. Where the Russian stage director, in the stage of rehearsals, allowed for typical actor-director discussions about character psychology and a shared understanding of the play's goals and intentions, Kubrick did not encourage such explanatory collaborations.[102] Taylor coins this the technique of "strategic improvisation," that is, "the actors' limited and calculated creative additions to or deviations from scripted dialogue or action."[103] Such a tactic allows actors an uncommon creative and collaborative freedom, yet at the same time it leaves the actors deliberately ignorant and bewildered about the characters' motivations.

If we assume, on the basis of this brief characterization of Kubrick's unique approach to acting, that performance should reflect the needs of the conceptual structure of the narrative, in what sense, then, do the performances in his films accurately reflect the concepts as inherent to the structure of mental causation? Considering his work, we may respond to this question in a twofold manner. On the one hand, we may discern various examples of acting, especially in his earlier work, of which it can be stated with a degree of certainty, that they are intended to communicate minded characters. On the other hand, it would be a categorical mistake to treat all of the acting in Kubrick's work as merely an illustration of transparent signification. Following Taylor, we may also argue that a significant number of examples seem to resist the presumed communicative function of classical cinema. Acting thus becomes a symptom of what the author calls "sceptical classicism," "a mode of narration in which our natural ability to conceptualize and engage with character's mental states is impeded."[104] Let us consider each part of the answer more in detail.

3.2 Mental causation, performance and film style

How are viewers able to interpret the bodily performance of an actor as standing for the content of the narrative or, as in our case, the content of mental causation? As a starting point for investigating this question, let us consider Daniel Richter's wordless performance as Moon-Watcher in the epiphany scene from *2001*, as verbally described in chapter 1. At the beginning of the scene, as shown in figure 3.39*A*, Moon-Watcher's physical behavior signals to us an animal in search of food. He is surrounded by many devoured bones of an antelope skeleton, but he does not seem to care much about them as he is too occupied digging the ground for food, his visual field being fully occupied by the dry soil upon which he stands. The emphasis of the performance is clearly on the action. Then, suddenly, as if in a burst of bright light, something happens. He suspends his instinctive need and lifts up his head (*B*). The performance turns into a static appearance. His eyes are no longer directed toward the soil that he was so eagerly inspecting. It is as if the film, through this gestural change, wants to suggest that the object of his perception lies somewhere else. The next shot seems to confirm this hypothesis as a quick, almost subliminal image appears that is spatially discontinuous with the previous shot. It reveals the celestial alignment with the monolith that has been shown before in relation to an earlier experience of Moon-Watcher (*C*). Through the image schema of LINKAGE, elicited by editing, the film thus suggests a relationship between Moon-Watcher's facial gesture and the appearance of the monolith (is Moon-Watcher remembering this image?).

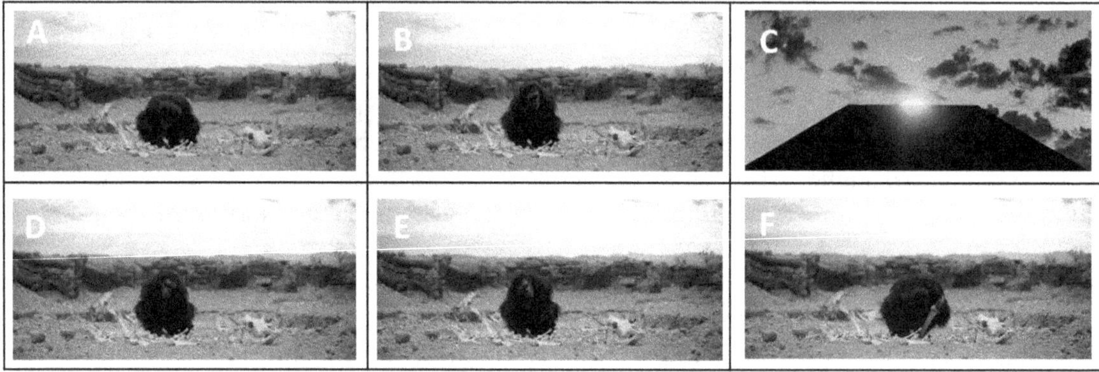

Figure 3.39. HEAD FOR THINKING in *2001* (part one).

The film, then, turns back again to Moon-Watcher as he now directs his gaze toward the bones in front of him (*D*). He moves his head a couple of times from left to right, thus suggesting the metonymy HEAD FOR THINKING (*E*). The mental image of the alignment seems to have conveyed an idea to his mind. Soon after, this idea is materialized into action as Moon-Watcher picks up one of the bones and starts to play with it (*F*). Thinking gives rise to behavior. Slowly realizing that he can use the bone as a weapon, he crashes the bone down repeatedly on the skeletal remains at his feet, first hesitantly and then more forcefully. He raises the bone high and mighty in the air, an act which is captured on-screen as an ENTRY path into a static frame filled with blue sky (figure 3.40*G*). As he forcefully crashes the bone down onto the head of the skeleton (*H*), another subliminal image appears, this time of a live tapir taking a dive (*I*). Is it a future image of what will be the logical consequence of his cognitive progression? As to visually emphasize the importance of this discovery, the physical act as a whole is analytically broken down to its essential parts in very fast and repeated succession (e.g., *J-K-L*), thus forming a formal and aesthetic contrast with the previous "thinking" images. From now on the man-ape will be able to hunt for food. The primate has evolved from a vegetarian to a tool-using carnivore.

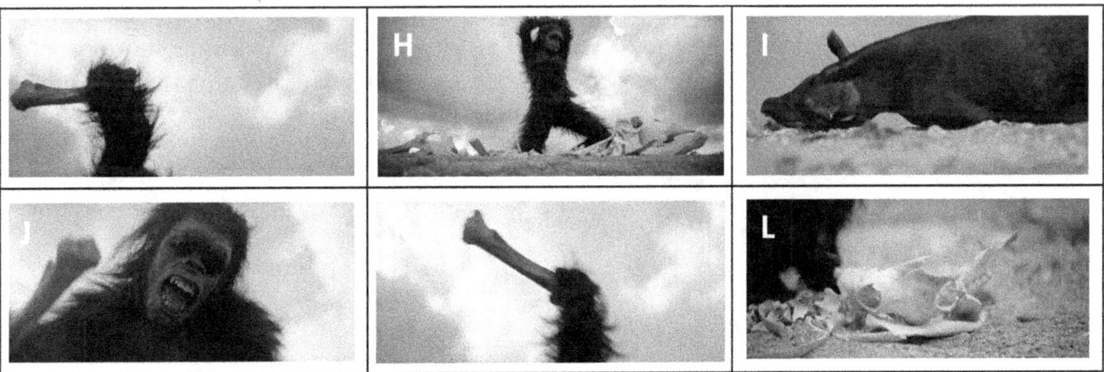

Figure 3.40. Mental-to-physical causation in *2001* (part two).

Notice also the way this cognitive leap-forward, as expressed through Richter's bodily performance, is not only accentuated stylistically through the musical accompaniment of Strauss' *Also sprach Zarathustra*, which now reaches its monumental heights, and, as in our example from *A Clockwork Orange*, through a radical acceleration of the editing pace, but also through the change of the angle of framing. At the beginning of the scene, the angle is straight-on, thus emphasizing Moon-Watcher's downward relationship with the earth surface. At the highpoint of Moon-Watcher's moment of insight, however, this common angle has changed into a low-angle which positions us as looking up at Moon-Watcher who is now no longer framed against a background of earthly landscape, but against a wall of bright light (the natural light of the mind?). Here, again, we may already anticipate the next chapter, as the properties of the image schema of UP-DOWN are extended metaphorically in order to meet, in a purely visual manner, the demands of the narrative content, which were already made clear for us through Richter's bodily performance.

So what does this example tell us? Above all, it informs us that there is a high degree of (metonymical) correlation between the actor's performance and the narrative structure of mental causation. Just by watching Moon-Watcher's body language we can infer a line of causation that runs from the mental to the physical.

To support this claim with one more example, consider Ryan O' Neal's performance in *Barry Lyndon*, as illustrated in figure 3.41. It shows Redmond as he "sees" an opportunity to escape his six-year commitment to the British army by stealing the clothes and steed from an officer who is embracing another man in a lake.

As with our example from *2001*, an image lies at the cause of the protagonist's mental act of thinking, but this time the image is not attributable to the character's memory, but to the character's actual perception. This is illustrated in figure 3.41*A* in which Barry notices the uniforms hanging on a branch of a tree. He, then, turns his head back toward the viewer after which he looks around a couple of times (*B-E*). This series of left to right movements of the head gestures to us something along the lines of "Barry is checking out whether or not the coast is clear to steal the clothes." When he reaches the positive answer to this question, he stops his head and much like Moon-Watcher, he gazes fixedly in front of his eyes. Barry thus "turns his attention to his own consciousness," as Wittgenstein would call it.[105] This mental act is also given form visually through camera movement as the camera slowly zooms in on the subject's head, thus entirely ENCLOSING it (*F*). As a result, the space surrounding Barry's head is EXCLUDED and the HEAD FOR THINKING metonymy is once more prompted to us. Millions of years separate Barry from Moon-Watcher, but in essence they are the same minded subjects whose actions are outer tokens of inner processes.

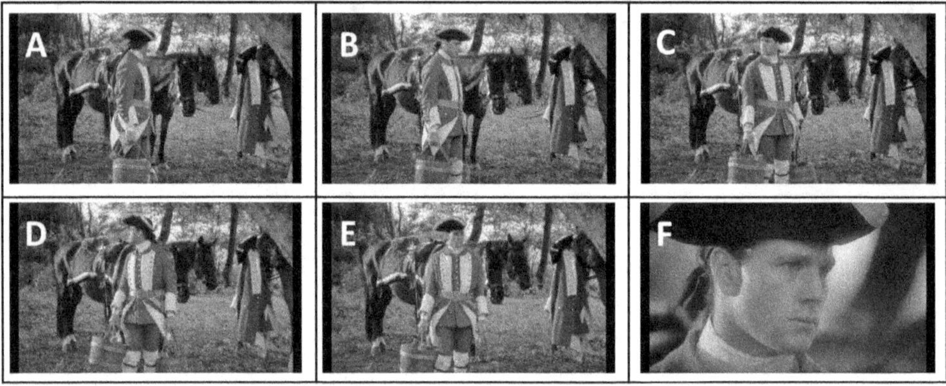

Figure 3.41. HEAD FOR THINKING in *Barry Lyndon.*

If performance can signal cognitive processes, what, then, about emotions? What does an actor's performance reveal us about the emotional states of a character? As we already alluded to in chapter 2, one may draw here upon the work of Paul Ekman whose studies have systematically explored the relationship between facial expressions and emotion concepts, a connection that we saw captured through Kövecses' metonymy FACIAL EXPRESSION FOR EMOTION.[106] For instance, Ekman and Friesen have identified six basic emotions (happiness, sadness, anger, fear, disgust and surprise) and their corresponding descriptions of the facial muscles involved in the formation of them.[107] They are often called "universal emotions" as they are believed to be recognized across different cultures.[108] These descriptions often read as instructions for actors to communicate emotions via eye movements and complex patterns of expression. For instance, happiness is characteristically described by tense lower eyelids, raised cheeks and lip corners pulled up, whereas sadness is described by inner eyebrows raised and drawn together and lip corners pulled down. It is not difficult to find exemplars of these descriptions in each of Kubrick's films.

Figure 3.42 shows three of them, as they are expressed in *Paths of Glory* (sadness), *A Clockwork Orange* (disgust) and *The Shining* (fear). By this, however, we do not wish to imply that emotions in Kubrick's films are always that clearly readable from the actors' facial expressions, on the contrary. We will see in the next section how some of the performative techniques applied in his films exactly seem to complicate this human ability to conceptualize and engage with characters' emotions.

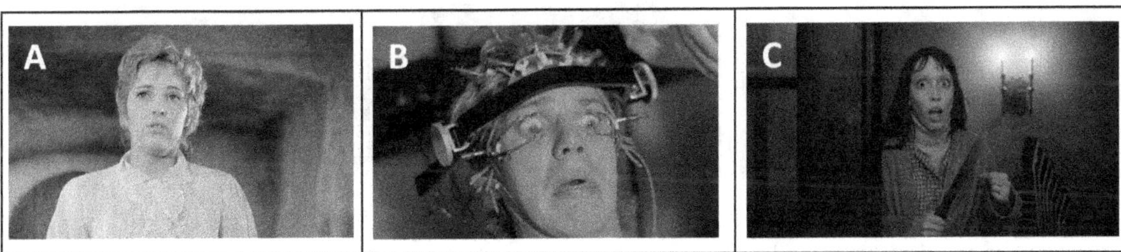

Figure 3.42. Basic emotions: *A*, sadness in *Paths of Glory*, *B*, disgust in *A Clockwork Orange*, and *C*, fear in *The Shining*.

Looking solely at the bare physical behavior of an actor, tells us much about the kind of mental activity that the character is engaged in (e.g., perceiving, thinking, feeling), but it does not tell us much, however, about its *content*. Toward which object is the perception directed? Which image or idea in the character's mind triggered the physical behavior? Why is a character feeling sad or disgusted? Raising these questions, brings us to the second important observation, namely that for a viewer to be able to answer these questions, and thus infer stories of mental causation, he or she has to be able to relate the performance to an object or event that is either located inside or outside the character's mind. If this object is located outside the character's mind, as with perception, this object can be easily visualized. If, however, the object is located inside the character's mind (e.g., memory, fantasy, thought), other means of expression have to be sought.

As our example of *2001* already suggests, one solution would be to treat the internal object as an external object that can be perceived by the viewer. By placing the memory of the monolith outside the protagonist's mind (thus making it observable), and linking it to the outer performance, through editing, we quite effortlessly establish a causal relation between the mental and the physical. The application of the same tactic can also be found, for example, in *Eyes Wide Shut* as when Bill sits in the cab thinking about what Alice has told him (see figure 3.43*A-B*). Later in the film, the same fantasy image returns to haunt Bill as he, aimlessly walking along the street, sees a young couple up against a shop front kissing passionately, oblivious of all around them (*C-E*). As he continues walking, he beats his fists in anger over his fantasy (*F*). From this chronological juxtaposition of images one can infer, quite effortlessly, a flow of mental causation that runs from the sight of the couple toward the fantasy in his mind and up toward his physical reaction. Consequently, as we shall see in the next section, withholding certain images would impede the ease with which we make such causal inferences.

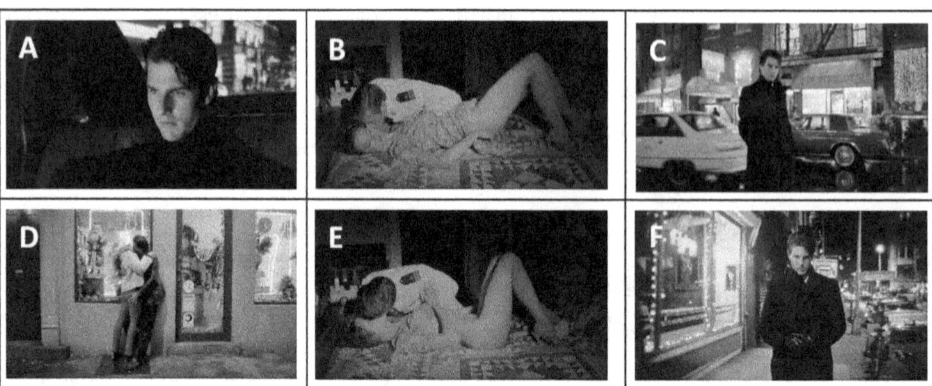

Figure 3.43. Mental-to-physical causation in *Eyes Wide Shut.*

The choice for editing as a means to establish the connection between performance and the inner object is not incidental, but necessitated by the narrative context. In both *2001* and *Eyes Wide Shut*, the film images represent mental images of spatial locations that are distinct from the locations where the characters are residing at the moment of them performing the mental act. Moon-Watcher recalls an image of an event that he has seen before and Bill visualizes in his mind a hypothetical sexual experience that was conveyed to him verbally by his wife. Hence, what is required, is a tool such as editing that enables to connect two locations that are spatial discontinuous to each other. Such a connection cannot be achieved simply by moving the camera from a location A to a location B. The tool, however, may change with the context. Take character perception, for example. It is conditional of (normal) visual perception that the object of perception shares the same spatial region as the perceiver, for otherwise, the perceiving character would not be able to see it. Indeed, fictional beings (at least those existing in a realistic context) can only see, much like human beings, what is in his or her visual field. Thus, the filmmaker may opt to instigate the relationship between perceiver and object by simply showing both entities in the same shot, or, as we shall see in the next chapter, by relying on the dynamic patterns of fixed-frame movement and camera movement; all of which are able to connect spatial continuous locations perfectly well.

Another way of establishing the inner object non-verbally would be not by visualizing it, but by evoking the object indirectly in the mind of the viewer on the basis of what the character perceives. Take again our example of *Barry Lyndon*. On the basis of Barry's visual perception of the uniform, we infer that he is thinking about stealing it for the purpose of deserting the army, but we do not see this *idea* visualized in the same way as Moon-Watcher's memory or Bill's fantasy were visualized. What we do get to see, is the *physical implementation* of the idea by the actor soon after its conception (e.g., we see Barry *stealing* the uniform). The same holds, for example, for the idea of using the bone as a weapon that comes to the mind of Moon-Watcher. We see Moon-Watcher thinking, but we do not see what he is thinking. This becomes only clear to us after he makes use of the bone.

In both *2001* and *Barry Lyndon* the perceptual relationship between the PR and the OP is captured objectively in a single shot. An even more effective means to render the same effect, however, would be by separating both entities over two distinctive shots. This division lies at the centre of what is commonly known in film theory as the *point-of-view shot* (POV).[109] It is usually established by being intersected between a shot of the actor's performative act of looking at something, and a shot showing the actor's reaction (i.e., a shot-reverse-shot). Through the image schema of LINKAGE the inside property of the frame (i.e., the container) thus becomes a metaphorical expression of the character's visual field. To illustrate how this technique can be used to facilitate inferences about the thought process of characters, consider, for instance, the visual way in which Davey's escape plan from *Killer's Kiss*, as described in chapter 1, is induced in the viewer's mind. At first we see a static shot of Davey's face, as it lies on the ground (figure 3.44*A*). This is followed by a semi-subjective shot, showing the character in relation to the window he is looking at (*B*). Through static framing both parts are thus blocked as a whole in which the properties of the FRONT-BACK image schema are extended in order to structure the relationship between the PR (front) and the OP (back). From this spatial whole the film cuts to one of its parts as now only the window is shown from the (relative) point-of view of Davey (*C*). A dynamic pattern, reminiscent of ENCLOSURE, unfolds itself as a result of editing. The film, then, cuts back again to Davey's facial expression (*D*). He now moves his eyes away from the window and toward one of his opponents whose attention is drawn to the quarrel between Vinnie and the girl (*E*). Next, we see a medium shot of the other opponent's feet which are standing between those of Davey (*F*). Likewise, his eyes are directed toward the quarrel (*G*). The moment has come for Davey to escape. He overmasters the opponent after which he runs toward the window to throw himself out of it (*I*). Thus, as with *2001* and *Barry Lyndon*, the film shows the materialization of an idea that the viewer already has inferred on the basis of the prior juxtaposition of images.

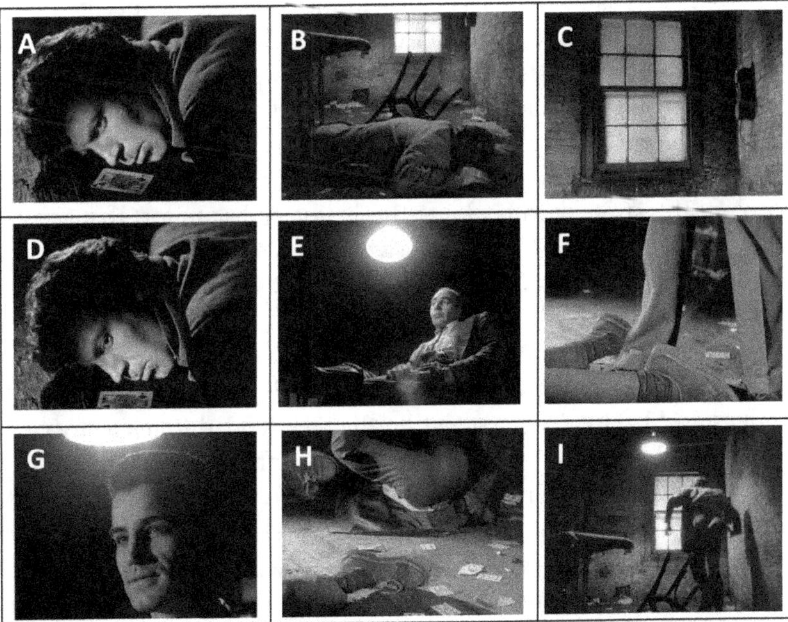

Figure 3.44. Mental-to-physical causation in *Killer's Kiss*.

What this example shows, is that a filmmaker does not always have to resort to an act of showing in order to elicit the thoughts of a character. The latter can equally be brought to the viewer's mind by embedding the actor's facial expression in a dynamic image schematic pattern that is intended to structure the perceptual relationship between the PR and the OP.

3.3 Performative and stylistic impediments to transparent signification

Having presented some of the performative aspects of conveying stories of mental causation, thereby already anticipating the next chapter by emphasizing the significance of dynamic patterns and film style, let us now turn toward that other question: how may this transparent signification of mental causation be obstructed? From the insights provided above, we can already make a few assumptions.

If it is said that character perception facilitates the construal of stories of mental causation, as discussed above, then one can easily assume that these stories can be obstructed by impeding this perception. As Kubrick's work reveals, one way to achieve this is by showing the face of a perceiving character that does not, however, draw attention to a perceptual object. The result is a facial expression in isolation, an effect without a cause, a perceiver without an object perceived. Taylor, in a similar sense, coins this strategy the strategy of "artificially immobilized expressions."[110] Because the facial expression does not signal any object, the subject becomes itself objectified. Take, for instance, the petrified glare of Alex during the opening zoom-out from *A Clockwork Orange* (see figure 3.45*A-C*). The zoom-out evokes a dynamic pattern of containment—what we specified earlier as EXPOSURE—but paradoxically this movement is not intended to reveal the object of Alex' perception. We do get to see his fellow "droogs," but the object of Alex's perception is withheld from the viewers' knowledge during the entire length of the shot. The direction of Alex' gaze contributes a lot to this effect. In *Killer's Kiss*, the close-up of Davey's facial expression was clearly directed toward one of the edges of the frame, thus suggesting the presence of an object outside the frame, but still inside the diegetic world. Here, Alex' eyes are directed toward us, the viewer who is detached from the story told on-screen. This strategy adds a lot to the feeling of discomfort that accompanies our experience when watching the scene. As Taylor writes: "His expressive paralysis is horrific because it appears to indicate an objectified subject, one who takes in nothing from the subjects around him nor from his immediate environment, remaining unchangeable and impenetrable."[111]

A similar example, but this time with a zoom-in movement, can be found in *The Shining* (see figure 3.45*D-F*). The zoom-in recalls the transition from figure 3.41*E* to figure 3.41*F* from our example of *Barry Lyndon*, yet, this time the movement is not embedded in a larger structure that is intended to tell a story of mental causation. For instance, the shot is not preceded by a shot of Jack looking at something that could have motivated the zoom-in, nor the shot is followed by a physical implementation of the idea that arose in his mind. Aided by the metaphor CHANGE OF STATE IS MOVEMENT, here elicited by the dynamic pattern of ENCLOSURE, we assume as a viewer that something is happening in his mind (the turning point from sanity to insanity?), but that is about the only thing we can do. As with *A Clockwork Orange*, the result is silent and enigmatic communication, the emblematic, impenetrable "Kubrick stare," as so many scholars have dubbed it, "head tilted downward, heavy-browed eyes looking upward."[112]

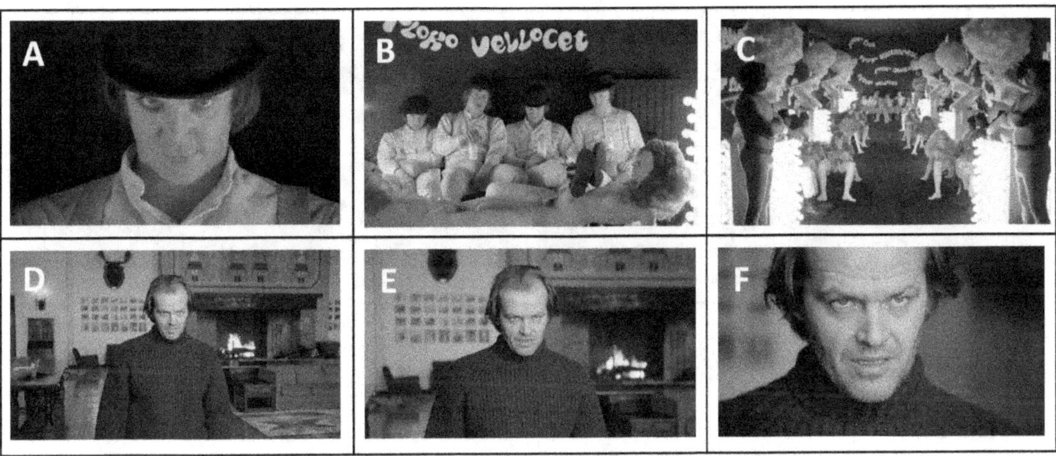

Figure 3.45. The Kubrick Stare in *A-C*, *A Clockwork Orange* and *D-F*, *The Shining*.

A second way in which a filmmaker may impede the transparent signification of mental causation, is to provide viewers with bodily performances that are expressive, but keep them in the dark about the events that are causally responsible for prompting this physical behavior. To illustrate this, let us consider, for example, the scene at the beginning of *The Shining* that shows Jack behind the wheel driving his family to the Overlook Hotel. Already from the first image of the scene, we infer on the basis of the intense expression on his face that he is outwardly annoyed about something (see figure 3.46*A*). When Danny, seemingly unaware of his father's awkward behavior, harmlessly mentions that he is hungry, Jack responds in a way that betrays his inner frustration. When the boy asks about the Donner party and Jack is forced to mention the subject of "cannibalism," "a perverse glee" appears on his face.[113] When Danny tries to take away his mother's concern by saying, "Don't worry mom, I know all about cannibalism, I saw it on TV," Jack repeats his son's lines while simultaneously rolling his eyes upward and arching his eyebrows (*B*). What this example shows, is that there is no "arch," as King critically remarked, through which we can understand Jack's behavior. As King stated, "as far as I was concerned, when I saw the movie, Jack was crazy from the first scene."[114] What King here refers to as the absence of an arch is nothing more than the absence of a story of mental causation. His frustration, as a viewer of the cinematic adaptation of his own book, comes out from the impossibility to make the kind of causal relations involving mental events that he allowed his readers to make when reading his novel. The effect of this strategy is that the attention is drawn toward the presentational facet of Jack's performance. Taylor dubs this the strategy of "excessive ostensiveness."[115] Because we are hampered to make such connections, "we are unable to conceptualize the represented individual as being 'minded' in a recognizable way." As Taylor writes, "their ostensive display acts as a resistant surface that belies a withheld experience (i.e., they are perceived only as a performing body)."[116]

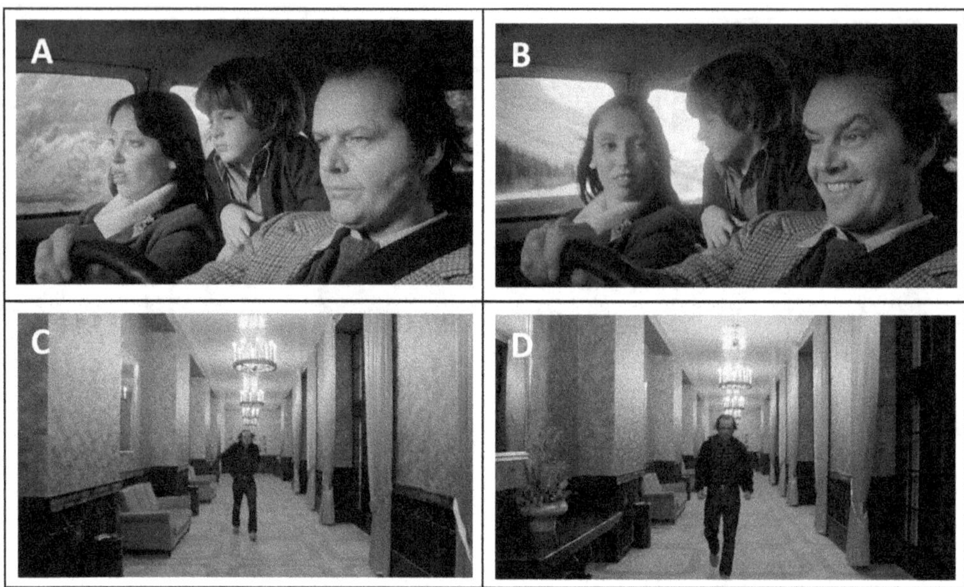

Figure 3.46. Excessive ostensiveness in *The Shining.*

To illustrate this strategy with another example, let us compare the scene from *Eyes Wide Shut*, as illustrated in figure 3.43, with the scene where Jack is hysterically and wildly strolling down the corridor that gives entrance to the Gold Room (see figures 3.46*C-D*). In the former scene there was a clear causal relationship between Bill clapping his hands out of frustration and the fantasy that caused him to express such behavior. In the latter scene, however, we see Jack behaving erratically, punctuating the air with his fists and talking to himself, but we are not allowed to see the inner events that caused him to react as such. As Falsetto describes: "Nicholson communicates the madness and seething anger of the character by the insistent thrusting of his arms down the sides of his body and into the air, as if striking at some unknown assailant."[117] We can assume on the basis of the previous scene that the devil inside of him must have been prompted by his wife's accusation of harming little Danny, but the certainty by which we infer this causal relation is of a significantly lesser degree when compared to the example of *Eyes Wide Shut.*

A third and last way of obstructing the viewer's construal of stories of mental causation on the level of acting, would be to suggest exactly the opposite: establish a clear perceptual relationship between perceiver and object, but neutralize the physical expression that comes with the effect that the perception of the object has on the perceiver. In this way the viewer would be denied making the conceptual link between body and mind that lies at the core of the metonymy FACIAL EXPRESSIONS FOR EMOTION. Taylor in similar terms speaks of the strategy of "expressively neutral action." As he writes, "Kubrick's actors frequently adopt affectless facial expressions that are nearly impossible to scan in order to intuit identifiable mental states."[118] *2001* is perhaps the clearest personification of this strategy. When astronaut Poole (Gary Lockwood) celebrates his birthday with a long-distance video message from his parents, he reacts to it with complete apathy (figure 3.47*A*). Similarly, Falsetto has compared Ryan O' Neal's performance of Barry to that of a "mannequin," one who "lacks interiority" and whose physical movements are "deliberately slow, artificial and stylized."[119] Taylor cites in this regard the climatic pistol dual with his stepson, Lord Bullingdon, as an exemplary case (figure 3.47*B*), with Barry registering "no discernible reaction whatever to the distress of his nemesis, even as his peers avert their eyes from the vomiting dualist in disgust."[120] Often this lack of expression in one performance is further enlarged by virtue of the abundance of expression in one's other performance. Here one may cite Carnicke's exquisite analysis of the stylistic distinction between Cruise's and Kidman's performances in *Eyes Wide Shut*. As a way of illustrating this distinction, she turns to a description of the scene in which Alice confesses her desire for another man:

> Cruise maintains an unchanging look and pose [figure 3.47C]. His face has already become the inexpressive mask he will later wear. Cruise accomplishes this feat by doing literally nothing. In contrast, Kidman's face changes rapidly with the story she tells and in reaction to her husband. Her high level of interactivity is naturalistically embedded in the emotional situations and relationships through which her character moves.[121]

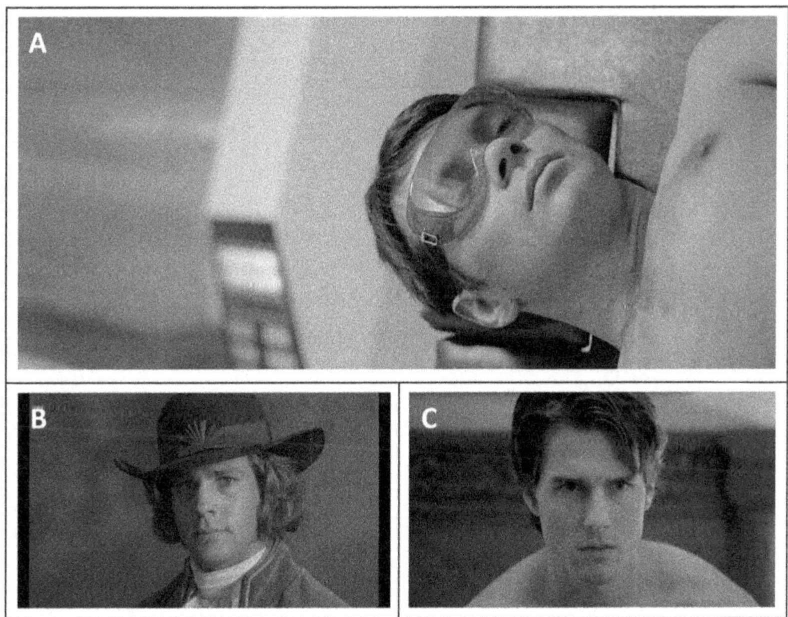

Figure 3.47. Expressively neutral action in *A*, *2001*, *B*, *Barry Lyndon*, and *C*, *Eyes Wide Shut*.

4. Conclusion

The goal of this elaborative chapter was to establish the conditions under which the medium of film can elicit the cognitive tools of embodied meaning-making, as they were elucidated in the previous chapter. This task was divided into two parts. The first part comprised a discussion of how film style can give rise to the same kind of dynamic image-schematic structures that were responsible for structuring the concept of mental causation in language. The second part comprised a discussion of the role of bodily performance in eliciting the abstract target domains of mental causation. Consequently, the next logical step is to demonstrate how the films of Kubrick, much in the same way as the linguistic expressions cited in the previous chapter, rely on these image schematic patterns in order to give form to the kind of stories of mental causation as they were identified in the first chapter. Exposing the richness of these metaphorical inferences will be the primary aim of the fourth chapter in which Kubrick, the filmmaker, will be revealed as a genuine artist of embodied and non-verbal meaning-making.

Notes

1. Arnheim, *The Power of the Centre*, xi.
2. Two important works in which Arnheim has developed this approach are *Art and Visual Perception: A Psychology of the Creative Eye* and *Visual Thinking*.
3. Arnheim, *Visual Thinking*, 254. See also Arnheim, "A Plea for Visual Thinking," 489–497.
4. Ibid., 254.
5. Arnheim's analysis of Vermeer's painting can be found in *Visual Thinking*, 270–271. For his analysis of Cézanne's painting, see *Art and Visual Perception*, 37–41.
6. Arnheim, *Visual Thinking*, 270.
7. Arnheim, *Art and Visual Perception*, 39.
8. Johnson, *The Body in the Mind*, 76–80.
9. Two works in which Arnheim's reservation toward cinema is manifested are *Film as Art* and *The Power of the Center*.
10. Arnheim, *The Power of the Center*, 214.
11. Arnheim, *Film as Art*, 7.
12. Higgins, "Deft Trajectories For the Eye," 113. See also the other contributions in this excellent volume.
13. Ibid., 113.
14. Bordwell and Thompson, *Film Art*.
15. Ibid., 49.
16. Ibid., 175.
17. Ibid., 175.
18. Branigan, *Projecting a Camera*, 101. Polysemy stands in contrast to another type of ambiguity which is called *homonymy*. In this case "two words spelled in the same way possess unrelated, or at least very distant, meanings (thus, separate lexical entries)."
19. Ibid., 103–115.
20. Ibid., 103.
21. Branigan suggests something similar when he writes: "Container schemata variously structure our thinking within the 15 domains of framing in film. Although every frame encloses like a 'container,' what is 'inside' (the contents) and the nature of the 'enclosure' (the criteria for the containing thing) are different for each of the 15 domains. The manner in which a container schema is applied to a domain will determine how inferences are drawn and conjectures made about what is framed." Ibid., 121–122.
22. Burch, *Theory of Film Practice*, 17.
23. Bordwell and Thompson, *Film Art*, 504.
24. Through its edges the frame thus actively defines what is visible for the viewer. For this reason, the frame is not a neutral border. As Bordwell and Thompson observe, "the frame imposes a certain vantage point onto the material within the image. . . . From an implicitly continuous world, the frame selects a slice to show us, leaving the rest of the space off-screen." Ibid., 252, 258.

25. Bordwell and Thompson, *Film Art*, 253–258.
26. For a good discussion of the aspect ratios of Kubrick's films, see also Appelt, "The Craft of Seeing," 255–256.
27. This has erupted considerable consternation and controversy among the online DVD community. For a discussion, see also Bill Hunt's interview with Kubrick's long-time assistant Leon Vitali who supervised the high definition DVD transfers (Hunt, "Vintage Bits Interview").
28. *The Making of The Shining*, directed by Vivian Kubrick (1980; Burbank, CA: Warner Home Video, 2007), Blu-ray.
29. Johnson, *The Body in the Mind*, 80.
30. Arnheim, *Art and Visual Perception*, Chap. 1.
31. Ibid., 13.
32. Ibid., 13–14.
33. Johnson, *The Body in the Mind*, 79–80.
34. Ibid., 79.
35. Arnheim, *Art and Visual Perception*, 6.
36. Johnson, *The Body in the Mind*, 80.
37. Arnheim, *Art and Visual Perception*, 23–26.
38. Bordwell and Thompson, *Film Art*, 262–263. Three other important aspects of framing that are here excluded, but that are equally important in influencing the balance of a visual scene are: (1) the *angle* of framing, (3) the *level* of framing, and (4) the *height* of framing. Following Bordwell and Thompson they may be defined as follows: The angle of framing is the position that the frame takes in relation to the object X inside the frame. The camera can look down at the object (a high-angle), be on the same level as the object (a straight-on angle), or can look up at the object (a low angle). The level of framing pertains to the gravitational forces governing the filmed material and the frame. If the framing is level, the horizon inside the frame will be parallel to the horizontal edges of the frame and perpendicular to the vertical edges of the frame. If the horizon is a diagonal line, the frame is canted. The height of framing relates to the distance of the camera above the ground. The material inside the frame is filmed at low (high) height when the camera is positioned close to (far from) the ground. Note that the height of framing does not necessarily coincide with the angle of framing. For instance, the camera can be at low height while the angle is straight-on.
39. These image schemas are included in Hampe, *From Perception to Meaning*, 2.
40. For a discussion of symmetrical compositions in Kubrick's photographic and filmic work, see Mather, *Stanley Kubrick at Look Magazine*, 237–241. As Lakoff has pointed out, the concept of symmetry can also be connected to the logic of the LINK image schema: "If A is linked to B, then B is linked to A." For his discussion, see *Women*, 274.
41. Johnson, *The Body in the Mind*, 81.
42. As Kolker has pointed out, the balance so naturally implied by a symmetrical composition may, in turn, be challenged by the type of lens that is used to shoot the composition. The author refers especially to Kubrick's use of a wide-angle lens that "tends to confound center and periphery in a way that *unbalances* the composition." He also connects this use to the narrative level: "Rather than balance, these compositions suggest a collapse; they signify not order but a fall into the abyss that awaits all his characters, a stasis in which the uncanny perfection of the image promises ultimate undoing, along with the characters caught within it." For a further discussion, see Kolker, *A Cinema of Loneliness*, 119.
43. Arnheim, *Art and Visual Perception*, 21–22.
44. Ibid., p. 20.
45. Boggs, *The Art of Watching Films*, 90.
46. Arnheim, *Art and Visual Perception*, 30.
47. Ibid., p. 30.
48. Wölfflin, "Ueber das Rechts und Links im Bilde," 82–96. See also Arnheim, *Art and Visual Perception*, 33–36.
49. Dewell, "Dynamic Patterns," 374.

50. Johnson, *The Body in the Mind*, 46–47. Gibbs and Colston in similar terms speak of the BLOCKAGE-REMOVAL image schema transformation. For their discussion, see "Image Schema," 252.
51. Earlier in the film, however, we do see Jack, Danny's father, throwing around a tennis ball in the lobby of the Overlook Hotel. Could he, then, be the external source that sets the ball in motion?
52. For a discussion of the composition of this shot and the way it relates to the narrative content of the film, see also Mather, *Stanley Kubrick at Look Magazine*, 240 and Appelt, "The Craft of Seeing," 256–257.
53. Both schemas are dynamic extensions of the static NEAR-FAR schema. For a discussion of APPROACHING, see also St. Amant et al., "An Image Schema Language."
54. For a discussion of these techniques, see also Boggs, *The Art of Watching Films*, 90–91.
55. Ibid., 92.
56. Strick and Houston, "Interview with Stanley Kubrick," 64–65. See also Philips, *Stanley Kubrick Interviews*, 133.
57. Lakoff and Johnson, *Philosophy in the Flesh*, 185.
58. Ciment, *Kubrick*, 189–190.
59. Strick and Houston, "Interview with Stanley Kubrick," 64.
60. Lightman, "Photographing Stanley Kubrick's *Barry Lyndon*," 321.
61. For a discussion of this schema, see Lakoff, *Women*, 273–274.
62. Ibid., 273.
63. For a discussion of this technique, see also Bordwell and Thompson, *Film Art*, 284–289.
64. For a discussion of this match-cut from the perspective of embodiment and metaphor, see also Caracciolo, "Bones in Outer Space."
65. Ibid., 78.
66. Lakoff, "Image Metaphors," 219. For two more recent discussions, see Gleason, "The Visual Experience of Image Metaphor"; and El Refaie, "Reconsidering 'Image Metaphor.'"
67. One linguistic example which Lakoff cites as a typical illustration of an image metaphor is the following expression of André Breton: "My . . . wife whose waist is an hourglass." Ibid., 219.
68. Lakoff and Turner, *More Than Cool Reason*, 99.
69. Here, one may also observe the influence of what the Soviet filmmaker Sergei Eisenstein termed the "montage of attractions." Often used for expressive and conceptual purposes, this technique relates two separate images to one another on the basis of visual and contextual similarities.
70. Bordwell and Thompson, *Film as Art*, 313.
71. Ibid., 305. Named after the Sovjet filmmaker Lev Kuleshov whose experiments in cutting during the 1920's famously showed that when people viewed the same neutral face of an actor in juxtaposition with various other shots, they assumed not only that the actor's expression changed depending on what he was viewing, but also that the actor was reacting to things present in the same space as himself.
72. For a good summary of this problem, see Hyslop, "Other Minds."
73. Nagel, *The View from Nowhere*, 19–22.
74. Taylor, "Blind Spots and Mind Games," 9.
75. Ibid., 9–10.
76. Ibid., 10.
77. Ibid., 10.
78. Ibid., 10.
79. Ibid., 10.
80. Bordwell, Staiger and Thompson, *The Classical Hollywood Cinema*, 3.
81. Taylor, "Blind Spots and Mind Games," 5.
82. Ibid., 6.
83. Carnicke, "Screen Performance," 46.

84. Ibid., 46.
85. Sherman, ed., *Directing the Film*, 191.
86. Carnicke, "Screen Performance,"46.
87. Gelmis, "The Film Director as Superstar," 103.
88. Carnicke, "Screen Performance," 53.
89. Falsetto, *Stanley Kubrick*, 149.
90. Carnicke, "Screen Performance," 53.
91. Clare, "Stanislavsky's System," 48.
92. The number of studies that use the (embodied) cognitive sciences to inform scholarly and practical explorations in theatre and performance studies is rapidly growing and include, among others, Blair, *The Actor, Image, and Action*; Blair and Cook, *Theatre, Performance and Cognition*; Clare, "Stanislavsky's System"; and Kemp, *Embodied Acting*.
93. Clare, "Stanislavsky's System," 52.
94. Anecdotes abound in this regard. For instance, it is rumoured that Shelley Duvall had to perform the baseball bat scene from *The Shining* 127 times. It still stands as a record for the most retakes of a single movie scene with spoken dialogue.
95. Gorchakov, *Stanislavsky Directs*, 353.
96. Cahill, "The Rolling Stone Interview," 201.
97. Pezzotta, *Stanley Kubrick*, 104–107.
98. Ibid., 105–106.
99. Kolker, *A Cinema of Loneliness*, 134.
100. Ibid., 135.
101. Ibid., 135.
102. See also Carnicke, "Screen Performance," 53; Taylor, "Blind Spots and Mind Games," 17.
103. Ibid., 17.
104. Ibid., 5.
105. Wittgenstein, *Philosophical Investigations*, 131.
106. Ekman's work can be situated within a research history that began with the publication of Darwin's book *The Expression of the Emotions in Man and Animals* (1872/1998). For a good discussion of the history of facial expression research, see Frank, "Facial expressions," 5230–5234.
107. Ekman and Friesen, *Unmasking the Face*.
108. For a good discussion, see also Kohler et al., "Differences in Facial Expressions," 235–244.
109. Bordwell and Thompson, *Film Art*, 264. For a good conceptual description of the elements of the POV shot, see Branigan, "Formal Permutations of the Point-of-View Shot," 54–64.
110. Taylor, "Blind Spots," 23.
111. Ibid., 23.
112. Ibid., 23. See also, for example, Nolan, "Seeing is Digesting," 192.
113. Falsetto, *Stanley Kubrick*, 161.
114. Greene, "Stephen King."
115. Taylor, "Blind Spots and Mind Games," 19.
116. Ibid., 19.
117. Falsetto, *Stanley Kubrick*, 163.
118. Taylor, "Blind Spots and Mind Games," 22.
119. Falsetto, *Stanley Kubrick*, 154–157.
120. Taylor, "Blind Spots and Mind Games," 22.
121. Carnicke, "Screen Performance," 60.

Chapter 4

Fleshing Out the Embodied Meaning Visually: The Art of Kubrick

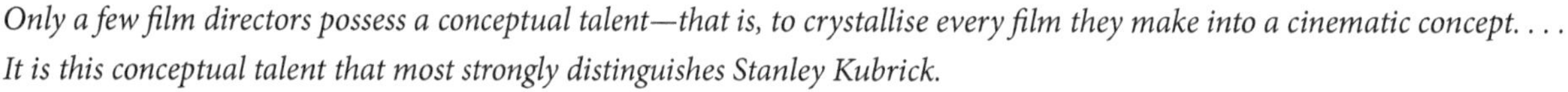

Only a few film directors possess a conceptual talent—that is, to crystallise every film they make into a cinematic concept. . . . It is this conceptual talent that most strongly distinguishes Stanley Kubrick.

—Alexander Walker[1]

He [Kubrick] was a conceptual illustrator of the human condition.

—Steven Spielberg[2]

In the previous chapter we demonstrated how film is capable of eliciting the same kind of image-schematic structures of sensory-motor experience that were responsible for fleshing out the literal meaning structure of mental causation in language. In this chapter we go a step further by showing how the films of Kubrick similarly make use of these patterns in order to convey the kind of stories of mental causation as they were identified in the first chapter.[3] The chapter is organized in such a way as to reflect the twofoldness of the flow-of-emotion scenario. In the first part we consider the question as to how the films of Kubrick purport to convey the concept of character perception (i.e., as cause of emotion) by resorting to the kind of dynamic patterns of the filmic frame as elaborated in the previous chapter. Here, we will gradually come to construe the embodied metaphors of perception, as discussed earlier in this book. In the second part of this chapter we engage in the same metaphorical undertaking, but with respect to the concepts of emotion (i.e., as cause of physical behaviors) and human relationships. Both aims will be explained and illustrated through a close analysis of various film scenes of Kubrick's work. Analysing these examples from the framework of embodiment, rather than the linguistic framework, will allow us to challenge the paradox of cinema and the question as raised at the beginning of this book: how are films able to structure meaning visually?

1. The art of embodying perception in film

Engaging or identifying with characters is of crucial importance in our reaction to any narrative work. Kubrick's work poses no exception in this regard. It is said that character perception contributes significantly, albeit not exclusively, to the degree in which we are engaged with characters.[4] This ought not to come as a surprise as character perception is essential to our understanding of the kind of stories of mental causation as we have identified them in the films of Kubrick. As chapter 1 made clear to us, perception lies at the heart of our Western folk theory of emotions according to which a person's change from a nonemotional to an emotional state is caused by a person's perception of an entity or an event. While many scholars have acknowledged the role of perception in our engagement with characters, few, however, have addressed the various creative ways in which this target domain may be given form in film. In the literature, the discussion of perceptual alignment with characters is often restricted to a discussion of the POV structure. However, as Kubrick's films are soon to reveal, this strategy is just one of many ways in which the bare scheme of perception, as diagrammed in figure 1.4, might be fleshed out in film. Indeed, one might even go as far to say that it is one of the definable features of Kubrick's art of filmmaking that it exploits all of the creative possibilities at hand to express the narrative concept in cinematic terms. Revealing this aspect, will be the primary goal of this section. Using various examples from Kubrick's work, we will show how his films resort precisely to the dynamic patterns of containment, as elaborated in the previous chapter, in order to shape the relationship between the PR and the OP. More specifically, the section is structured in such a way as to reflect some of the most significant ways in which perception is fleshed out by the patterns of fixed-frame movement and camera movement.

Entry of the OP in the PR's visual field

In chapter 2 of this book we already became acquainted with the metaphor PERCEPTION IS A FORCED INTERACTION BETWEEN PERCEIVER AND OBJECT PERCEIVED. One way to conceive of this metaphor was by retrieving the VISUAL FIELD AS A CONTAINER metaphor and relating it to the dynamic pattern of ENTRY (e.g., "He *came into* my visual field"). Let us now try to see, with the help of the insights on film style and performance, as offered in the previous chapter, how this embodied conceptual structure might be given form in cinema. To start off our analysis, consider, for example, a fragment of the "stalker" scene from *Eyes Wide Shut* as illustrated in figure 4.1. It shows the character of Bill walking down the street while he is being shadowed by a stalker. In the screenplay, the scene is described as follows (own emphasis): "Bill tries to see if the stalker is still following him and then decides to continue walking. As he reaches a newspaper kiosk, he *sees* the stalker come round the corner and stops. Bill stops too and *looks at* him for some time while wondering what will happen next."[5]

As figure 4.1 illustrates, the target domain of character perception is given form by mapping the back inside of the container of the frame onto the protagonist's visual field. The front inside of the image is mapped onto the location of the perceiver. In this way, by including the PR's visual field as well as the PR in the same container of the frame, Kubrick manages to visualize in one scene what otherwise would take two separate shots to express (i.e., the POV structure). Moreover, it is also not required that we first conceptualize the metonymy EYES FOR SEEING in order to access the target domain. The way Cruise's body language is framed, tells us enough. It is only once the visual field is spatialized that the dynamic pattern of ENTRY can realize itself. The stalker *enters* the inside back of the frame, not by crossing any boundaries of the frame, but by coming from behind the setting. It is precisely this transition from emptiness to fullness, aggressively announced by a sharp piano pitch of György Ligeti's second movement of his piano cycle *Musica Ricercata*, that contributes a great deal to the effect of suspense.[6] As Coëgnarts and Kiss have argued, it is the same kind of strategy that one often encounters in slasher films with the villain suddenly and unexpectedly entering the victim's visual field.[7]

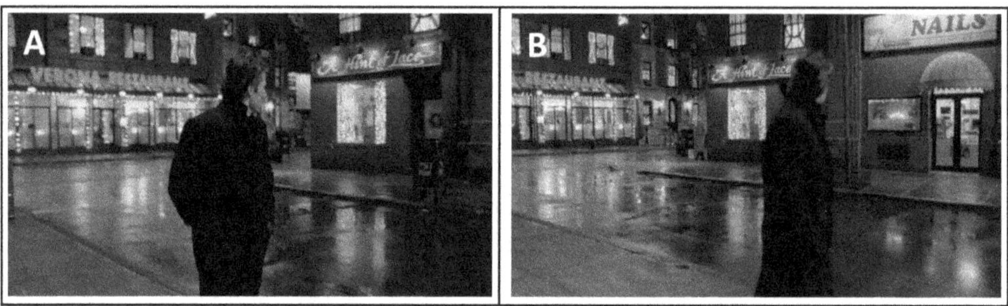

Figure 4.1. The "stalker" scene from *Eyes Wide Shut*.

That the same embodied strategy can also be retrieved for the purpose of creating a more ambiguous and unclear effect, can be illustrated with *The Shining*. Consider, for example, the scene where Jack enters Room 237 and sees a naked young lady stepping out of a bath (see figure 4.2). The music that underscores this scene is Krzystof Penderecki's *The Awakening of Jacob* layered with Wendy Carlos's "Shining/Heartbeat" cue which might be taken to represent, as Gengaro pointed out, "Jack's nervously beating heart."[8] As the camera reaches the door of the bathroom, we see the hand of Jack entering the frame and pushing the door open (*A*). Contrary to the example above, the viewer is thus prompted to map the full inside of the frame onto the protagonist's visual field (VISUAL FIELD IS A CONTAINER). As Jack removes the visual restraint of the door, the bathroom appears to his eyes as well as ours (*B-C*). From behind the curtain a young lady reveals herself as she draws the curtain aside with her right hand. As with the revelation of the bathroom, the appearance of the lady is elicited by the removal of a visual restraint, this time within the boundary of the room itself. Jack is standing stationary while he gazes at the young lady who now steps out of the bath in order to come closer to Jack (*E* and *G*). Through a series of medium close shots of Jack's facial expression, we are able to see his reaction (e.g., *D* and *F*). As Jack's eyes are fixed on the lady, so does the camera stay motionless. As a result, the dynamic pattern unfolding itself is that of APPROACHING.

Then the roles are reversed. The woman calls a halt to the pattern of APPROACHING as she stops in his visual field (*G*). There is something peculiar, however, about the way she directs her gaze toward the left edge of the frame, which suggests that Jack is not standing perpendicular to the lady. In this way, we are forced to question our metaphorical conceptualization of the frame as a container for Jack's visual field (are we still seeing things from his point of view?). This confusion is confirmed by the cut on action that follows as Jack approaches the lady by entering the frame from the left edge (*H-I*). However, because the content of this frame was previously attributed to his visual field, the effect is cognitively disorienting, as if Jack is seemingly entering the space that was earlier mapped on his own visual field. Diagrammatically, this cognitive paradox (how does one enter one's own visual field?) might be represented as in figure 4.3*B*. Figure 4.3*A* shows the pattern of ENTRY from a naturalistic perspective. OP and PR are both mapped on two different locations (object and container, respectively). In the previous figure 4.1, the bounded region was manifested in the back inside of the filmic frame. In a POV shot, this boundary would overlap with the total inside content of the frame. By contrast, figure 4.3*B* shows the conceptual implausibility that comes to the surface once the PR is also treated as the entering object in the PR's visual field. As such, character perception adds much to the overall theme of Jack's duality that runs as a red thread throughout the whole film.

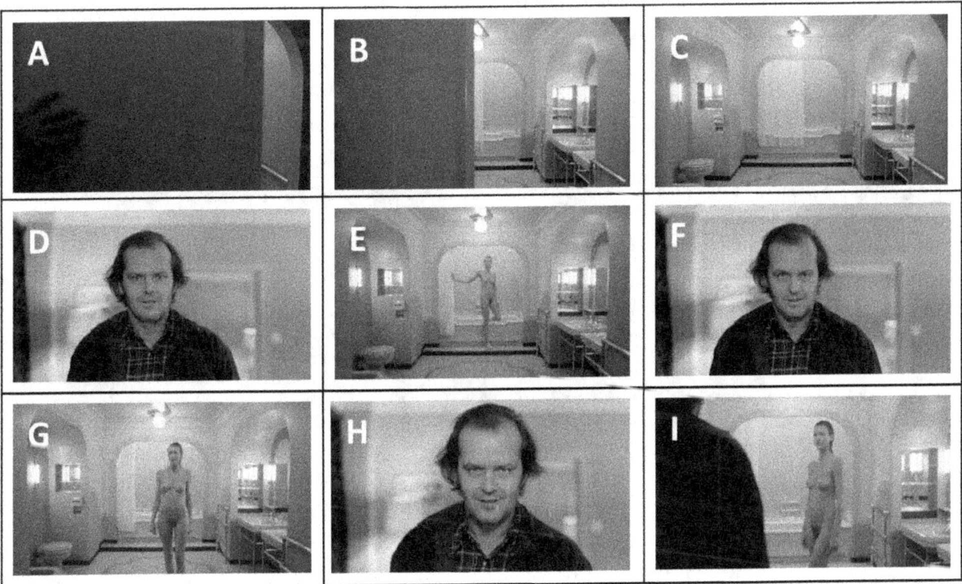

Figure 4.2. Jack enters Room 237 in *The Shining*.

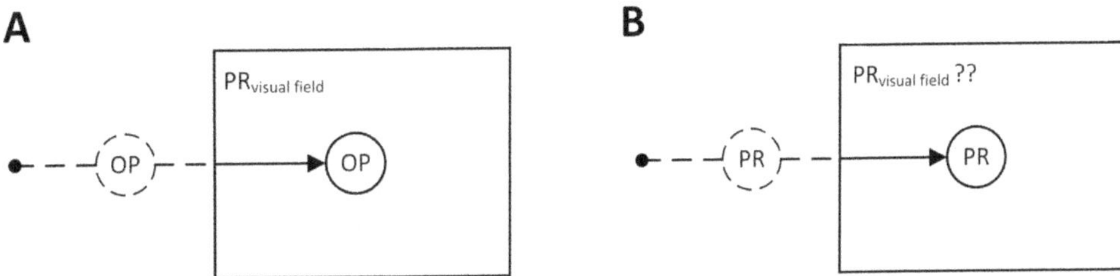

Figure 4.3. *A*, mapping the OP and the PR naturally versus *B*, mapping the OP and the PR unnaturally.

Inclusion of the OP in the PR's visual field

Let us now consider the opposite way in which the PERCEPTION IS A FORCED INTERACTION BETWEEN PERCEIVER AND OBJECT PERCEIVED metaphor is not elicited by the dynamic pattern of ENTRY, but by the dynamic pattern of INCLUSION. As we have seen in the previous chapter, this pattern may be elicited by camera movement in which the camera includes an object into its frame. One may establish the above metaphor then by simply attributing the mobile frame to the protagonist's visual field. To illustrate this, let us consider, for example, the scene at the end of *2001* which shows the aging of David Bowman and his gradual transformation into the Star Child. This transition is given form through a continuous flow of David's visual perceptions, one of which is shown in figure 4.4.

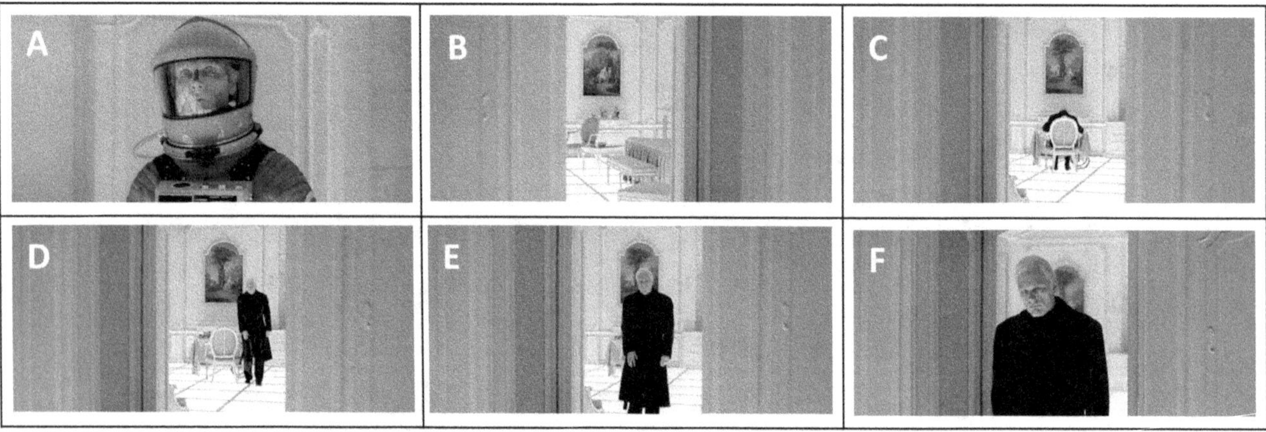

Figure 4.4. The "younger" Bowman includes the "older" Bowman in his visual field (*2001: A Space Odyssey*).

It shows David, already visibly aged, as he looks toward the entrance of a room (*A*). In contrast to *The Shining*, visualisation of the inside content of this room is not achieved by removing the door—the door is already open—but by moving the camera in such a way as to include the inside of the room into Bowman's visual field (and that of the viewer) (*B*). Bowman's point of view (i.e., the camera) halts as soon as the inside is clearly visible (*C*). In the background of the image we see a man sitting at a table. Hearing the echoes of cutlery clanking, we assume that he is eating. He seems to have sensed the appearance of Bowman as he stands up. He turns himself and, like the naked lady in our example of *The Shining* above, he APPROACHES the viewer (*D-E*). As the frame is gradually filled by his presence, his facial expression becomes more visible (*F*). We recognize him as an older version of Bowman. From his body language we infer that the younger version of himself is no longer there. As such and similar to our observation in *The Shining* above, the viewer can no longer maintain (at least from a realistic perspective) his or her previous conceptualization of the frame as Bowman's visual field. At the same time, the POV structure serves as a means to convey a leap forward in time. Following the Time-Orientation metaphor, the space in front of the perceiver (the younger Bowman in the present) is mapped onto the future (i.e., Bowman sees himself in the future).[9] Schematically, we might diagram the underlying dynamic structure of figure 4.4 (INCLUSION + APPROACHING) as in figure 4.5.

A comparable example of ambiguous character perception that involves the pattern of INCLUSION can be found, once more, in *The Shining*. Consider, for example, the scene, as illustrated in figure 4.6, which shows Jack quietly approaching Wendy from behind, thus scaring her. Wendy has just found out that Jack has done nothing more than type the same line "All work and no play makes Jack a dull boy" over and over again on what seems to be more than hundreds sheets of paper; a discovery which is aroused musically by a "a long-held high note in a dozen violins" from Penderecki's *Polymorphia*.[10] In contrast to the example of *2001*, the shot starts *in medias res* without first showing the perceiving character's face in the act of looking. In other words, the viewer is prevented from conceptualizing the metonymy EYES FOR SEEING. As with *2001*, the camera slowly moves away from a visual obstacle (a wall) in order to include a new character (*A-B*). As the camera pans to the left, the frantic and uncoordinated glissandi of the violas decrease in volume and intensity. We now hear the nervous tapping of fingertips on the strings behind the bridge, and the hitting of the strings with the wood of the bow rather than the hair.[11] Although we do not see Jack, we infer, on the basis of the frightful music and our general knowledge about horror films and its conventions, that it must be the villain's eyes that we are looking through. As with *2001* and our earlier example from *The Shining*, however, this convention is once more tested. As soon as Wendy is captured in the centre of the frame (*C*), which coincides with the camera's halting, Jack enters the frame from its right side (*D*), thus turning the subjective (i.e., our conceptualization of the metaphor VISUAL FIELD IS A CONTAINER) into the semi-subjective. The shot thus becomes reminiscent of the over-the-shoulder shot from *Eyes Wide Shut*, as seen in figure 4.1*B*. The initial camera movement before Jack's appearance thus created, to quote Kolker, "a curious sense of false comfort. . . . Jack's appearance . . . is a surprise and suggests that the moving camera signified another point of view altogether (a suspicion confirmed by the suggestion that the hotel has some strange life of its own that controls Jack himself)."[12] Because Wendy's back is turned toward the camera, the viewer knows something that she is not aware of. Paradoxically, we cannot use this knowledge in order to warn her. As it has been stressed in the literature, this experiential mode of cognitive frustration, grounded in our inability to satisfy our strong desire for knowledge-use, is central to the viewers' experience of suspense.[13]

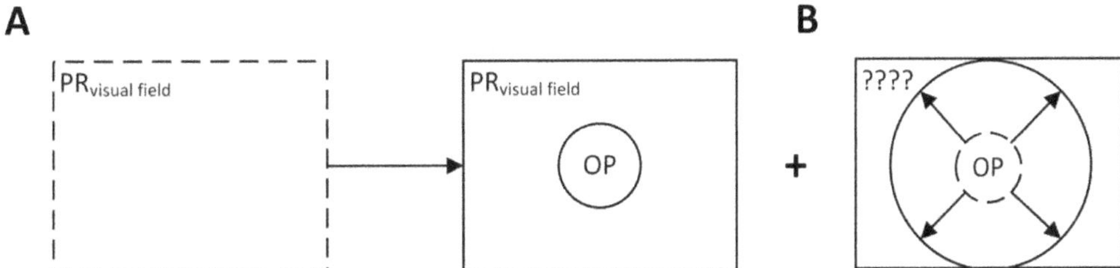

Figure 4.5. *A*, INCLUSION of the OP, followed by *B*, APPROACHING of the OP.

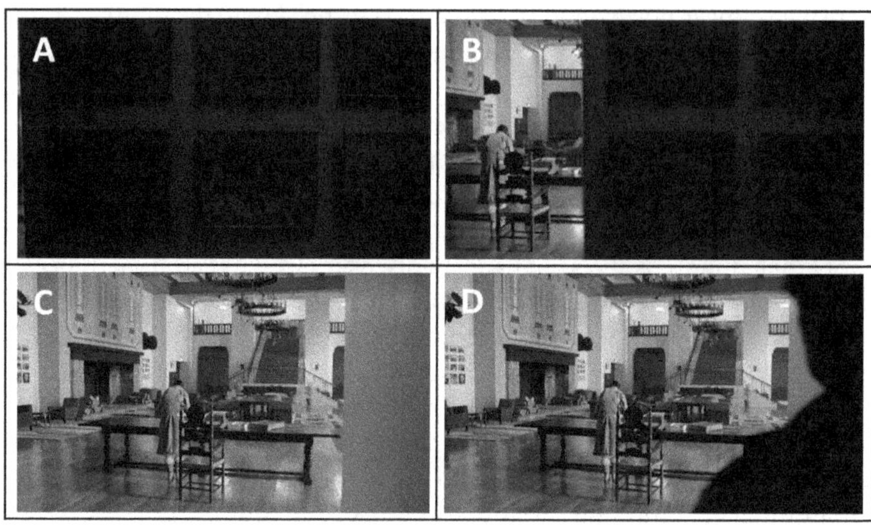

Figure 4.6. Inclusion of Wendy in Jack's visual field (?) (*The Shining*).

In the two examples discussed so far, the pattern of INCLUSION unfolded itself without the visible presence of the moving PR on-screen. This is a logical consequence of the POV structure which allocates the two entities of perception over two separate shots. For our last example, let us consider an instance of INCLUSION in which the pattern is intrinsically tied to the perceiver's bodily movement as articulated visually on-screen. There is perhaps no better way to illustrate this than through an exploration of the iconic tricycle scene from *The Shining*, as illustrated in figure 4.7. It shows Danny riding his tricycle. As he turns a corner, the Grady sisters are included in his (and the viewer's) visual field. The surprise of it is articulated musically by a "percussive crash" in Penderecki's *De Natura Sonoris No.1.*[14] The scene regards a following shot in the sense that there is no ENTRY or EXIT pattern elicited by Danny. This is achieved by the fact that the camera, through its movement, prevents him from leaving the frame. At first, the viewer is withheld to see what lies beyond the corner of the hallway (figure 4.7*A*). Here, suspense is not so much triggered by the presence of knowledge, but by the absence of it. We only know what the character is seeing. As with figures 4.1*B* and 4.6*D*, the back inside of the container is mapped onto the protagonist's visual field. Visualisation of the space beyond the corner, then, is achieved by having the "container" follow Danny's forceful movement. As with our example from *Eyes Wide Shut*, the power of the scene owes a great deal to the sudden image-schematic change from EMPTINESS (an empty visual field) to FULLNESS (a full visual field). In a way the scene can be seen as a gratification of our own desire to know. We expect there to be something behind the corner. When the interaction between the PR and the OP finally occurs and our desire to know is satisfied, it hits us in the same frightful way as it hits little Danny.

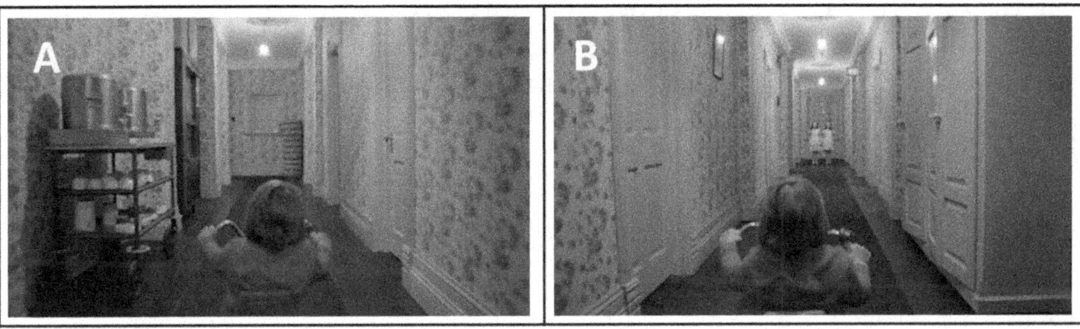

Figure 4.7. Inclusion of the Grady twins in Danny's visual field (*The Shining*).

Inclusion of the PR through movement of the OP

Interaction between the PR and the OP can not only be achieved by way of including the OP, but also by virtue of including the PR. To illustrate this, let us consider the scene in *Lolita*, as shown in figure 4.8, where Humbert goes down to the lobby of a hotel to enquire about a rollaway cot to place in Lolita's room.

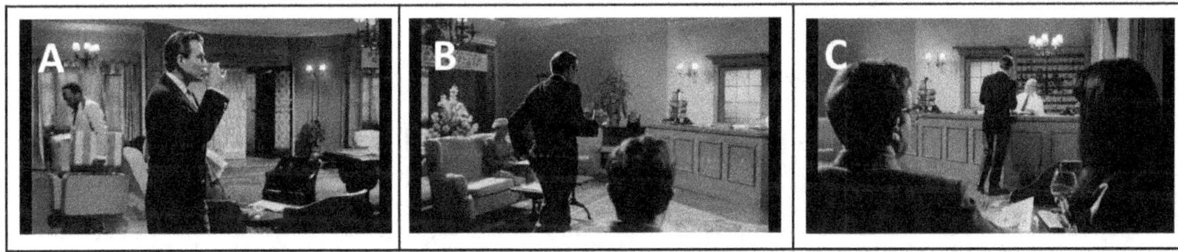

Figure 4.8. Humbert becomes the OP of Clare Quilty's visual field in *Lolita*.

The scene shows Humbert as he walks down the lobby while drinking at the same time (*A*). As with the tricycle scene, the protagonist is withheld to leave the frame by the following camera. However, in contrast to this scene, we are not able to map any bounded region (any part of the inside space of the frame) onto the protagonist's visual field. This is due to the lateral way in which the character is framed which prevents us from seeing the space in front of the character's eyes. As he approaches the front desk from the left, the silhouette of a male head is included in the lower right corner of the frame (*B*). The viewer recognizes it as the head of Clare Quilty (Peter Sellers). As Humbert reaches the desk, Clare gains the company of his female writing partner. Humbert is now positioned in the centre background of the frame in the middle of the couple in the foreground (*C*). By walking toward the desk, Humbert has placed himself within the visual field of the couple, thus becoming the object of their gazes. In one single camera movement the film moves from objective to semi-subjective. Diagrammatically, this might be presented as in figure 4.9. At first, the inside content of the container (i.e., the frame) cannot yet be mapped onto the perceiver's visual field. The frame is merely an objective trajector that follows the protagonist's movement. This changes, however, when the camera halts and the two perceivers are included in the frame. As such the background of the frame, a bounded region in its own right, is transformed into the perceivers' visual field (see also figures 4.1*B*, 4.6*D* and 4.7*B*).

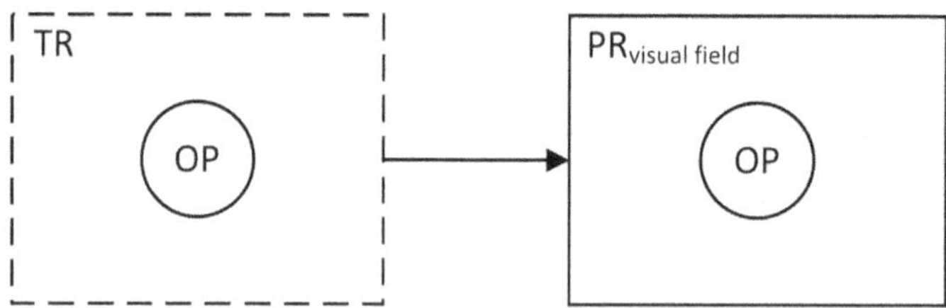

Figure 4.9. Becoming the OP in one's visual field through the inclusion of the PR.

Inclusion of the OP through exclusion of the PR

In the examples discussed so far inclusion of the OP was motivated by the visual field of the protagonist, either subjectively through the POV shot or semi-subjectively through the over-the-shoulder shot. Film, however, provides us with the means to elicit the same effect objectively while at the same time preserving the interaction between the PR and the OP. To conceive of this strategy, let us consider the visual way in which the narrative sentence, "Bill sees the mask on the pillow next to his wife Alice," is given form in *Eyes Wide Shut*, as illustrated in figure 4.10.

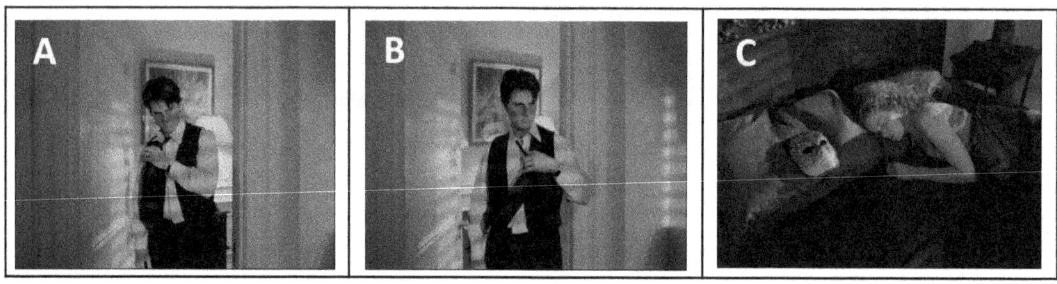

Figure 4.10. Bill perceives the mask in *Eyes Wide Shut*.

What this example shows, is cinema's own way for prompting the conceptual metaphor PERCEPTION IS TOUCHING. As we have seen in chapter 2, this metaphor was licensed by such expressions as "My eyes *picked out* every detail of the pattern" or "My gaze *is out over* the bay." It would be hard, however, to render such expressions pictorially because of the iconicity of the film image. One way to overcome this problem, as our example indicates, is to move the camera away from the PR's eyes (*B*) and toward the object of his perception (*C*). When the camera moves very fast from a fixed position, as it is the case in figure 4.10, we might refer to this as a "whip" or "swish pan." Diagrammatically, this inclusion of the OP via the exclusion of the PR, might be represented as in figure 4.11.

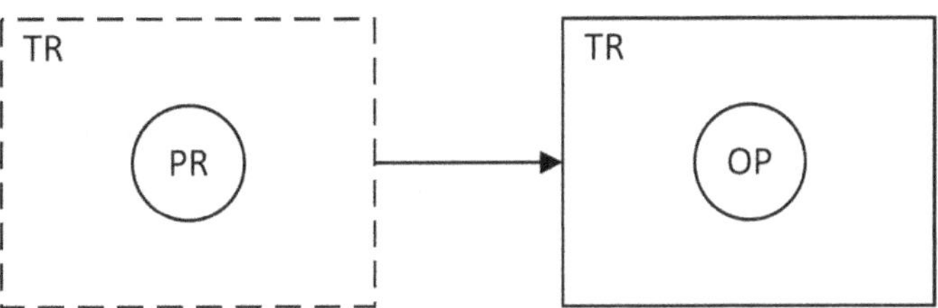

Figure 4.11. Excluding the PR and including the OP.

As this example indicates, the non-verbal behavior of the actor is of crucial importance for eliciting this dynamic pattern. Without the turning of the actor's head in the direction of the object perceived (i.e., the transition from *A* to *B*), it would be impossible for the viewer to extend the two dynamic patterns of containment toward the target domain of perception. The actor's body language allows for a preservation of the link between the PR and the OP, despite the visual exclusion of the PR. Other filmic manifestations of the above diagram can be found in various of Kubrick's films, some of which are illustrated in figure 4.12. In each of the three examples, the same principles are discernible. There is the turning of the PR's head toward the off-screen location where the object of perception is residing, followed by the exclusion of the PR and the inclusion of the OP.

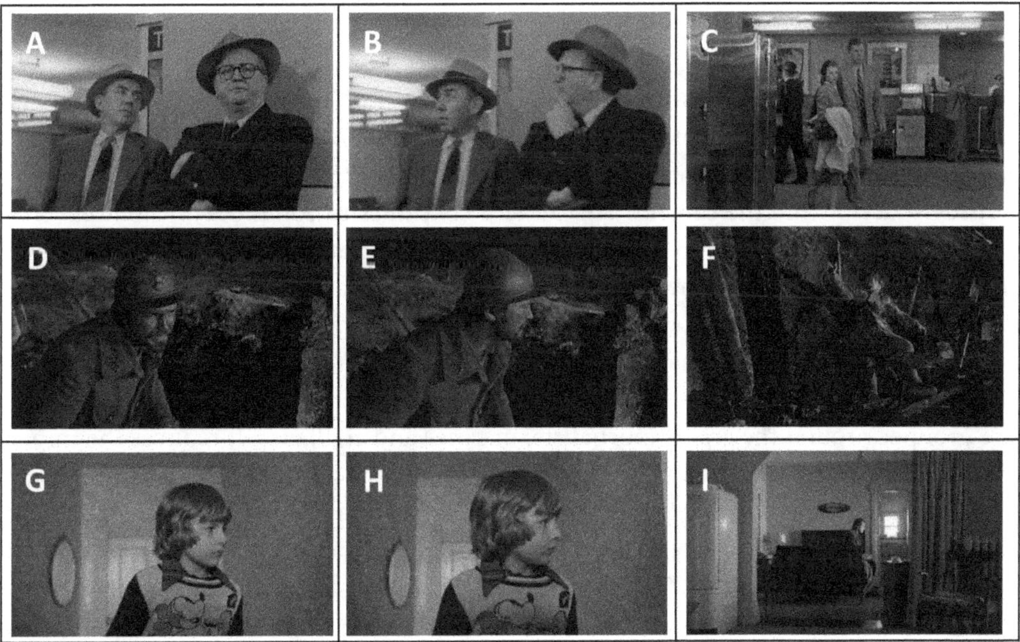

Figure 4.12. Inclusion of the OP through exclusion of the PR in *A-C*, *The Killing*, *D-F*, *Paths of Glory*, and *G-I*, *The Shining*.

Exposing the OP without exclusion of the PR

The visual strategy above begs the question as to how the same interaction between the PR and the OP might be elicited without excluding the PR. It is in search for an answer to this question that we may turn to the dynamic pattern of EXPOSURE. As we have seen in the previous chapter, this pattern might be provoked stylistically by the zoom-out camera movement. Consequently, a filmmaker might be able to establish the interaction with the preservation of the PR on-screen by zooming out from the perceiver's facial expression so as to gradually include the object that the character is looking at (i.e., the object in front of the perceiver's eyes). One such example, can be found, for instance, in *Full Metal Jacket* as when Private Joker stands "looking down into" a large open grave at a row of white, lime-covered corpses (see figure 4.13).

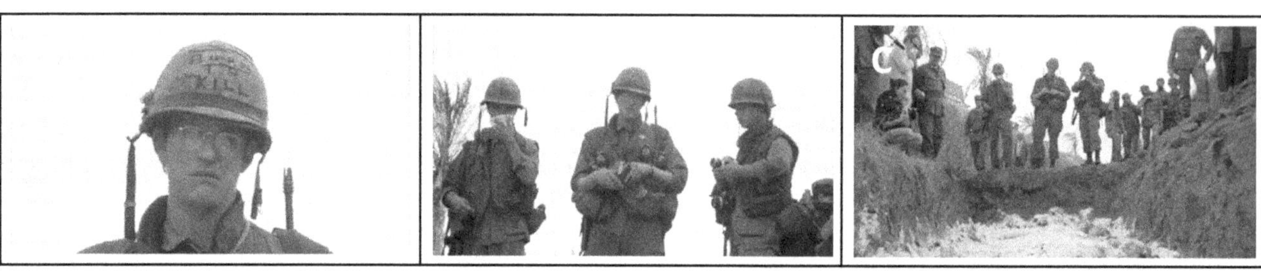

Figure 4.13. Private Joker looks down into a grave in *Full Metal Jacket.*

It is interesting to contrast this example with the glare of Alex during the opening zoom-out from *A Clockwork Orange*, as discussed in the previous chapter (see figure 3.45*A-C*). In the former case Modine's face clearly points toward the outside space beneath the lower edge of the frame. In the latter case, however, McDowell's face points toward the outside space behind the camera. The camera continues to zoom out without never revealing the object of his perception to the viewer. So despite the movement, the attention is never fully drawn away from the perceiver himself. By contrast, in the example of *Full Metal Jacket*, the zoom-out movement has a clear destination. It stops once it has revealed what lies in front of the character's eyes, namely the object perceived by the protagonist. It must be stressed that there is also something paradoxical about the pattern of EXPOSURE that manifests itself on-screen. By distancing itself from the perceiver, the camera also includes all of the other people that are grouped around the grave (journalists, marines and civilians). It reduces the importance of the individual by placing him, to quote Kolker, "within a greater natural design. . . . The individual becomes part of a much larger composition, engulfed by the natural world that surrounds him."[15] As such, the object perceived becomes no longer the exclusive property of Joker's perception. Diagrammatically, we might represent the difference between the non-exposure of the OP (e.g., *A Clockwork Orange*), and the exposure of the OP (e.g., *Full Metal Jacket*), as in figure 4.14.

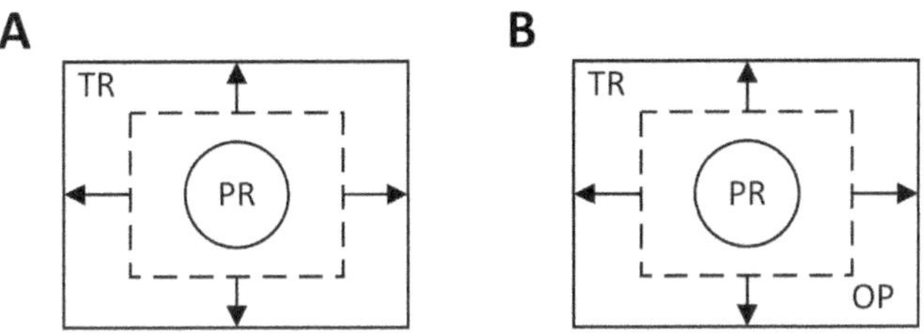

Figure 4.14. *A*, non-exposure of OP versus *B*, exposure of OP.

Exposing the PR without exclusion of the OP

The same question can now also be addressed in opposite terms: is there a way to elicit the interaction between the PR and the OP by exposing the PR without excluding the OP? Likewise, it is not difficult to see how this might be externalized in cinematic terms by means of the zoom-out movement. Consider, for example, figure 4.15*A-C* which shows the moment in *Dr. Strangelove* when Group Capt. Lionel Mandrake, in an attempt to figure out the three-letter code prefix, is looking at crosswords written by General Ripper. At first, the viewer is provided with a detail of the visual scene as the camera shows us a close shot of the written words "Peace On Earth" and "Purity of Essence." Then, the camera zooms out, thus exposing the whole page and a part of Mandrake's hands. We now assume the VISUAL FIELD IS A CONTAINER metaphor. In the next shot, we see the head and body of the character to which the previous POV shot can be linked.

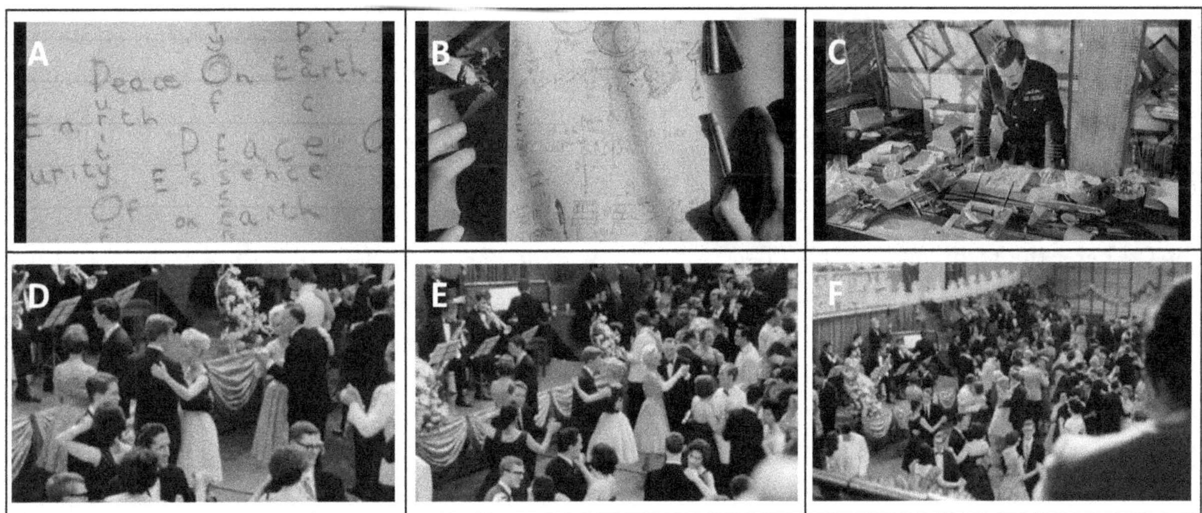

Figure 4.15. Exposing the PR without excluding the OP in *A-C*, *Dr. Strangelove*, and *D-F*, *Lolita*.

In this example the movement from the OP to the PR is embedded in the conventional POV structure. As such, it delineates two shots. Additionally, one might well arrive at the same interaction by including the PR's head straightaway in the same shot. One example of this can be found, for instance, in *Lolita* as when Humbert is spying on Dolores while she is dancing. As figure 4.15*D-F* shows, the container of the frame gradually turns into semi-subjective mode with the location of the OP being mapped onto the background of the image, and the location of the PR onto the foreground. When the zoom-out eventually halts, the framing is reminiscent of the framing of figures 4.1*B* and 4.6*D*.

Enclosing the OP in the PR's visual field

Having discussed how the dynamic pattern of EXPOSURE may shape the relationship between the PR and the OP in both ways (from the PR to the OP and vice versa), let us now move toward its counterpart, the pattern of ENCLOSURE. To see which aspect of perception this pattern might serve, let us consider again briefly the pattern of INCLUSION as it was shown above to underlie the moving POV shot. One might argue that this technique gave form to the change of visual scene that occurs when one moves one's head. In the POV shot the attention is distributed uniformly over the whole that constitutes the external visual scene. Following cognitive psychology, one may argue that this stage is only the first one of a two-staged process through which visual attention operates.[16] In the second stage, attention is concentrated to a specific part of that visual whole (i.e., the focus). It is precisely this second stage that may be externalized by the pattern of ENCLOSURE. We have already seen how this pattern may be elicited through the zoom-in camera movement. It does not have to come as a surprise then, that Kubrick, as many other filmmakers, makes use of this technique in order to shape the "focusing" aspect of visual attention. Figure 4.16 shows three various ways in which the technique can be applied. The first variation (*A-C*) from *Barry Lyndon* can be seen as the opposite of figure 4.15*D-F*. It depicts the zoom-in movement that immediately follows the lateral camera movement as analysed in chapter 3 (see figure 3.23). This time, the camera starts to move from behind the characters after which it gradually focuses on the object of their perception. Although Barry and the Chevalier are excluded by this movement (*B-C*), we continue to map the full inside of the frame onto the characters' visual field on the basis of the connection already established at the beginning of the shot (*A*). The zoom-in serves the same purpose in the second variation (*D-F*), as taken from *The Shining*, except for here, the technique is embedded in the POV structure. Both elements (PR + visual focusing) are shown in two separate shots. In this way the viewer is also allowed to infer the emotion concept (i.e., fear) metonymically on the basis of the perceiver's facial expression. A more restricted variation can be found in *Full Metal Jacket* as when the sniper locates its target (*G-I*). Here, the identity of the PR is deliberately withheld from the viewer. Again, this is motivated by the narrative context (i.e., soldiers in search of the sniper who killed their comrades).

Diagrammatically, one may put the extension of both patterns (ENCLOSURE as well as EXPOSURE) to the domain of character perception as in figure 4.17.

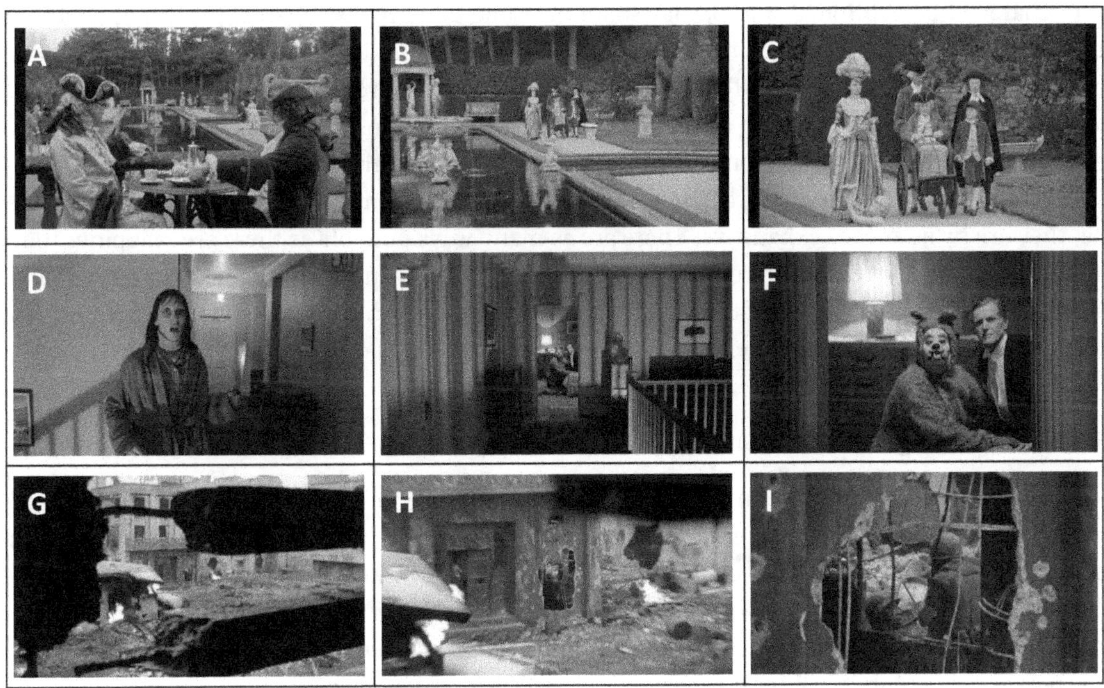

Figure 4.16. Enclosing the OP in the PR's visual field in, *A-C*, *Barry Lyndon*, *D-F*, *The Shining* and, *G-I*, *Full Metal Jacket*.

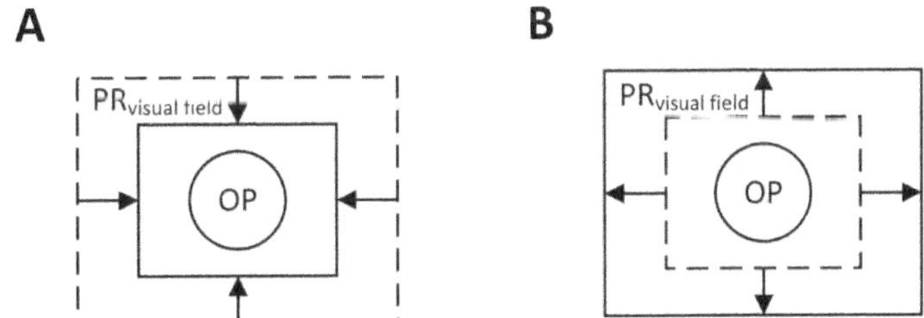

Figure 4.17. *A*, ENCLOSURE of the OP versus *B*, EXPOSURE of the PR.

Summarizing this section, we can say that Kubrick's films provide us with various artistic ways to express the perception of a character non-verbally in film. They differ from each other with respect to the way the structural and spatial features of the dynamic pattern of containment are mapped onto the conceptual features of perception. Two instances of character perception, A and B, may share the same underlying dynamic pattern of containment, but if the mapping of its structural features into A is radically different from its mapping into B, the result will be two different ways of expressing perception. To illustrate this, let us recall figure 4.14*B* and compare it with figure 4.17*B*. The pattern of EXPOSURE underlies both cases, yet, in the first case, the inside of the container is mapped onto the location of the PR, whereas this is the opposite in the second case where the inside is projected onto the PR's visual field. Although the variations presented here cover some of the most conventional ways of expressing perception in cinema, they are by no means exhaustive. There are as many ways possible as there are mappings to make, and not all of them are in tune with man's intuitive notion of perception. As our analyses of *2001* and *The Shining* above indicated, film, as any other artistic product of human imagination, has the unique power to go beyond the spatial, causal and temporal laws of human experience.[17]

2. The art of embodying emotions and human relationships in film

Having considered some of the ways in which the dynamic patterns of containment are extended in Kubrick's films for the purpose of structuring the concept of character perception cinematically, we may now attempt to do the same with regard to the concepts of emotion and (human) relationship. In which ways does Kubrick's cinema appropriate these patterns in order to convey both concepts non-verbally? Similarly, let us investigate this question by analysing some significant film scenes taken from the filmmaker's oeuvre. In what follows, we will treat both concepts separately, although it will soon become clear that they are closely related.

2.1 The art of embodying emotions

How do the films of Kubrick prompt us to conceptualize the emotion that is brought about by the force of perception and that at the same time can be regarded as a cause/force in its own right that brings about a bodily response? To see how this second part of the flow-of-emotion scenario might be fleshed out at the cinematic level, let us recall chapter 1 and consider three stories of mental causation as they are expressed in Kubrick's work. The first one picks up where we left off above and considers the iconic scene from *The Shining* where the Grady twins invite little Danny to "come and play with [them] forever and ever." The second one involves the astonishing scene in *Barry Lyndon* where Lady Lyndon falls in love with Barry at the gaming table. The third and last instance occurs at the end of *Eyes Wide Shut* and considers the scene where Bill emotionally collapses after seeing the mask lying next to his wife (see also the thirteenth narrative as described in chapter 1). These three instances are bounded by the same conceptual structure of mental causation: the protagonist perceives an event which causes the state of the character to change from a nonemotional state to an emotional one, which, in turn, brings about a behavioral response in the character. Inspired by Kövecses, we might rephrase this more schematically by making use of the following three-stage model (where the double-lined arrow indicates "causes, leads to"):[18] Perception [Entity/event] => Emotion => Behavioral Response. Applying this general model to the three instances above, we may formulate the following emotional trajectories:

- *The Shining*: Danny's Perception [Grady Twins] => Emotion [Fear] => Behavioral Response [Closing Eyes]
- *Barry Lyndon*: Lady Lyndon's Perception [Redmond] => Emotion [Love] => Behavioral Response [Going Outside]
- *Eyes Wide Shut*: Bill's Perception [Mask] => Emotion [Sadness] => Behavioral Response [Crying, Lying Down Next to Alice]

As our analysis below will show, all three scenarios make use of the same specific-level metaphor in order to flesh out the "emotion as force" part of the flow-of-emotion scenario, namely the EMOTION IS INTERNAL PRESSURE INSIDE A CONTAINER metaphor. As we have seen in chapter 2, this metaphor presumes the conceptualization of a person as a container with the substance inside corresponding to the emotion. If the substance increases, so will the pressure become higher, and by metaphorical consequence also the intensity of the emotion. To see how this metaphorical logic is at work in the three scenarios above and to see which role the dynamic patterns of containment play in fleshing out this logic, we will now analyse each scene in turn.

The Shining

After little Danny has made visually contact with the twin sisters, the scene continues with a juxtaposition of images, most of which are shown in successive order in figure 4.18. Considering them all together, one may discriminate between three observations. The first one is the observation of a pattern that is reminiscent of ENCLOSURE and that concurs with the gradual enlargement of the two little Grady girls holding hands at the back of the corridor (*E-H-J*). This pattern, the exclusion of space surrounding the girls, is not elicited through camera movement, as was the case with respect to some of the examples of perception above, but through editing. The pattern is holding the various shots together rather than the shot holding the pattern. As such, the film seems to express something different than merely Danny's perception of the girls which was already established prior to the enclosure of the Grady twins. In conjunction with this, there is the observation of a behavioral change with respect to Danny. His facial expression signals an increase of anxiety and fear (*B-G*). We are allowed to share this negative emotion because we are allowed to conceptualize it as such through the metonymy FACIAL EXPRESSION FOR EMOTION. Third and last, there is the observation of a fixed, almost subliminal image of a horrifying event that is intersected throughout the scene and that shows the two Grady girls laying on the floor covered with bloodstains (*D-F-I-K*). The recurrence of this image is also echoed at the level of speech as the second part of their line "for ever" is repeated twice more with each increase in visual size. Through editing, these observations are correlated to each other. As the girls (i.e., the visual substance) take more space inside the container (i.e., Danny's visual field) and the substance-pressure on the container (the frame) increases, Danny becomes increasingly more frightful. Eventually, the pressure becomes too high to the extent that Danny can no longer control his emotional response. The emotion causes him to put his hands over his eyes (*L*). When the girls finally disappear from his visual field (*N*), the substance-pressure on the container dissolves (and so do the high notes in Penderecki's *De Natura Sonoris No. 1* fade away), and Danny has the courage again to uncover his eyes (*O*).

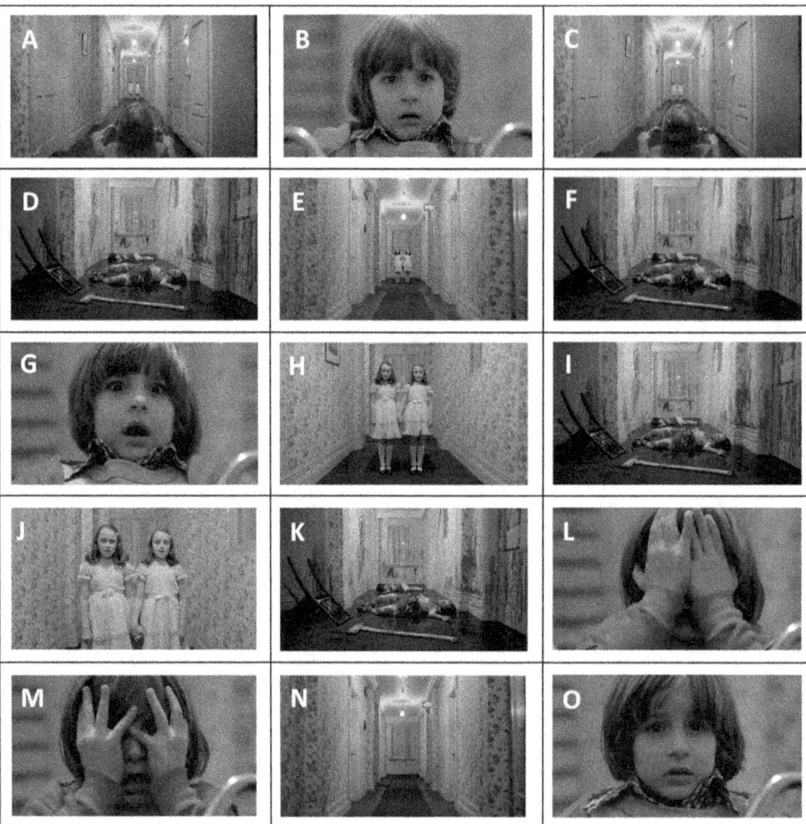

Figure 4.18. Danny experiences an intense negative emotion after seeing the Grady twins (*The Shining*).

In this example, the pattern of ENCLOSURE, as elicited through editing, is directed to the object of perception and not to the emotional self. The container of the frame closes in on the Grady twins rather than on Danny. They are the visual content of the container that is increasing in substance. However, because the boundary of the frame, by virtue of the POV shot, also represents the visual field of Danny, the dynamic pattern of containment is intrinsically related to Danny's subjective self. This is the reason, for instance, why we, as viewers, do not extend the pattern toward the emotional state of the Grady twins. Their enlargement on-screen has to be seen exclusively in relation to Danny's intense negative emotional experience. Examples of the opposite case in which the pattern of ENCLOSURE is not primarily directed to the object of perception, but to the emotional self itself are perhaps more common and can be found on many occasions throughout Kubrick's work. To discuss one such instance, let us consider the famous scene at the card table from *Barry Lyndon*, as illustrated in figure 4.19.

Barry Lyndon

The scene comes right after the scene outdoors in which Barry, for the first time, lays his eyes on Lady Lyndon (see figure 3.23). The transition is smoothed by Franz Schubert's *Piano Trio in E-flat, op 100* which continues uninterrupted.[19] Redmond Barry and Lady Lyndon are silently sitting at a table opposite each other while playing cards. As with *The Shining*, the scene is entirely composed of a juxtaposition of static shots. The first shot, *A*, establishes the spatial whole of the location and the positions of Barry and Lady Lyndon inside of it. This shot is followed by two shots which are both part of that space and which now render both characters separately (*B-C*). Each character is thus given its own bounded region of space. Both containers are, in turn, linked to each other through editing and the shot-reverse-shot technique. The film then closes in on Barry's face. As with little Danny in *The Shining*, Barry's face is rendered in the same shot size during the whole time of the intersection of their gazes, yet, with this crucial difference that Barry's facial expression remains unchanged in each of the separate shots (*D-F-H-J*). His face almost fully occupies the space he is residing in, giving him an intense and domineering presence. His "container" is not being interfered by the appearance of other characters. The contrast could not be greater with the way Lady Lyndon is portrayed. The camera does not capture her in medium shot, but in long shot (*C*). She resides in the background, right side of the frame. In the left foreground we can see the back of Barry interfering with "her space." By eliciting this formal contrast, the film manages to realize two things. Firstly, it succeeds in giving Lady Lyndon the impression that she is less in control of her container (her own self) as opposed to Barry (LOSS OF CONTROL IS LOSS OF POSSESSION OF SPACE). Reverent Runt is still keeping an eye on her as he sits in between them. Secondly, by keeping a distance between the camera and Lady Lyndon, the film elicits the idea that Barry has not yet fully taken control over her. The film upholds this strategy for the duration of two connections (*E-G*). As we enter the third connection, however, the situation changes as Lady Lyndon is now also portrayed in the same way as Barry (*I-K*). Lady Lyndon now occupies more space in the frame (INCREASE OF EMOTIONAL INTENSITY IS INCREASE OF AMOUNT OF SUBSTANCE IN A CONTAINER), while at the same time the distance is seemingly reduced (INTIMACY IS CLOSENESS). Simultaneously, as a result of the change of shot size, Reverent Runt is excluded from the on-screen space. He has no longer control over Lady Lyndon. In the last shot we have Lady Lyndon announcing that she is going outside "for a breath of fresh air." She exits the frame not by crossing the boundary of the frame, but by disappearing behind the set (*L*). As with little Danny, the emotion has taken control over her to the extent that she is drawn toward a behavioral response. In the upcoming balcony scene Barry consolidates his conquest by approaching her and kissing her, an act which is grasped cinematically by having the camera following Redmond until Lady Lyndon is included ("captured") in "his" frame. At the musical level, "their kiss coincides with a move from the sorrowful, pensive-sounding C minor to a splendid E-flat major" in which Schubert's piano arpeggios "bring a feeling of abundance and happiness, and the violin and cello carry on their dialogue."[20]

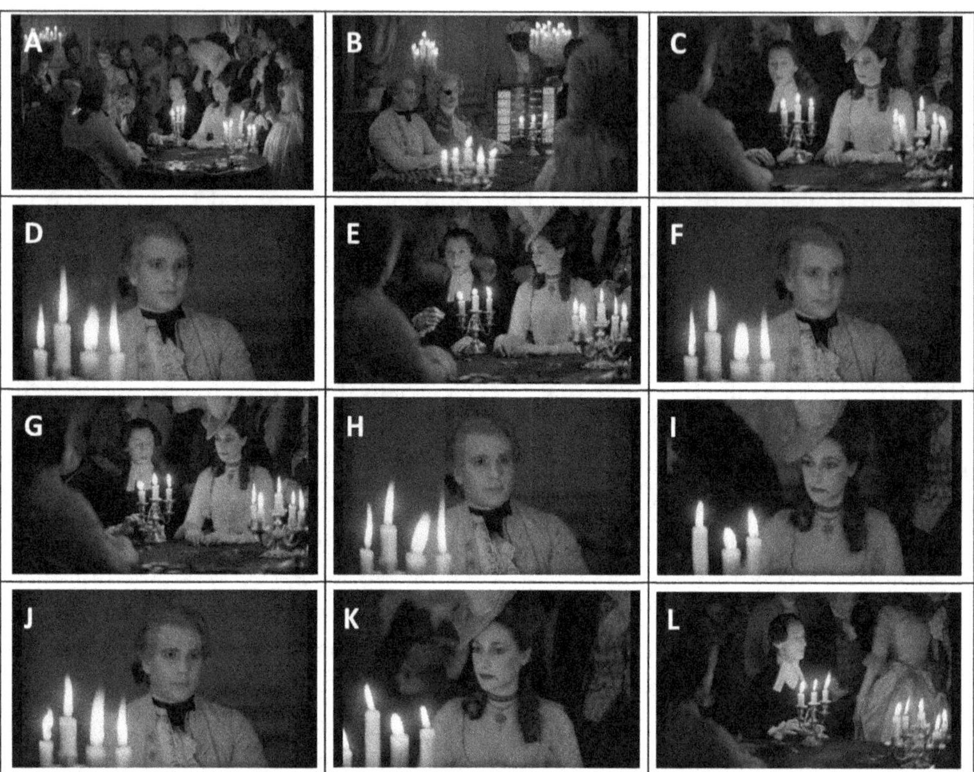

Figure 4.19. Barry seduces Lady Lyndon in *Barry Lyndon.*

Eyes Wide Shut

To conclude this section, let us consider the flow-of-emotion scenario of *Eyes Wide Shut* as described in chapter 1 (thirteenth narrative), and as illustrated here in figure 4.20. As was shown in figure 4.10, the perception part of this scenario is rendered through a single camera movement: as Bill enters the bedroom and his head turns to the bed, the camera quickly moves to the right connecting his facial expression to the mask, the object of his perception (*A-B*). The speed of this swipe pan is fast as a way to evoke Bill's shock of seeing the object. In chapter 5, we will also see how Ligeti's *Musica ricercata* plays an equally important role in fleshing out this panic, and the rest of the emotional texture of the scene, in musical terms. The film, then, cuts to a medium shot of his reaction (*C*). This is where the second part begins. The intensity of the emotion increases, as he now occupies more space inside the frame. The film then cuts to a closer shot of his wife (*D*). This back and forth change of location is repeated once more. Despite these connections between the PR and the OP, each character resides in his/her private space. Then the scene reaches its emotional climax. The stationary camera shows an empty blue colored space. From above right side of the frame, Bill enters the frame with his body (mid-level) (*E*). As he keeps staring at his wife, he falls lower and lower into the frame until his face fully occupies the centre of the frame (*F-G*). He can restrain himself no longer, and breaks down into uncontrollable sobbing (*I*). The location of the camera is remarkable. By placing the camera at a level closer to the marital bed (to his wife) and lower than Bill's eye level (at standing position), the film manages to express even more intensely the effect of falling down (SADNESS IS DOWN). In the next shot, Alice wakes to see Bill's complete helplessness (*J*). The film cuts back to Bill who continues to lower his face closer toward Alice (*K*). There is no exit as the camera follows the entire movement of Bill as he collapses and lays his head on her breasts (*L*). It is through this following shot that Alice is gradually included in the frame of Bill. As such, he allows her to become part of his container (his own true self). As Alice is caressing him, Bill utters the words: "I'll tell you everything." The mask has finally fallen off.

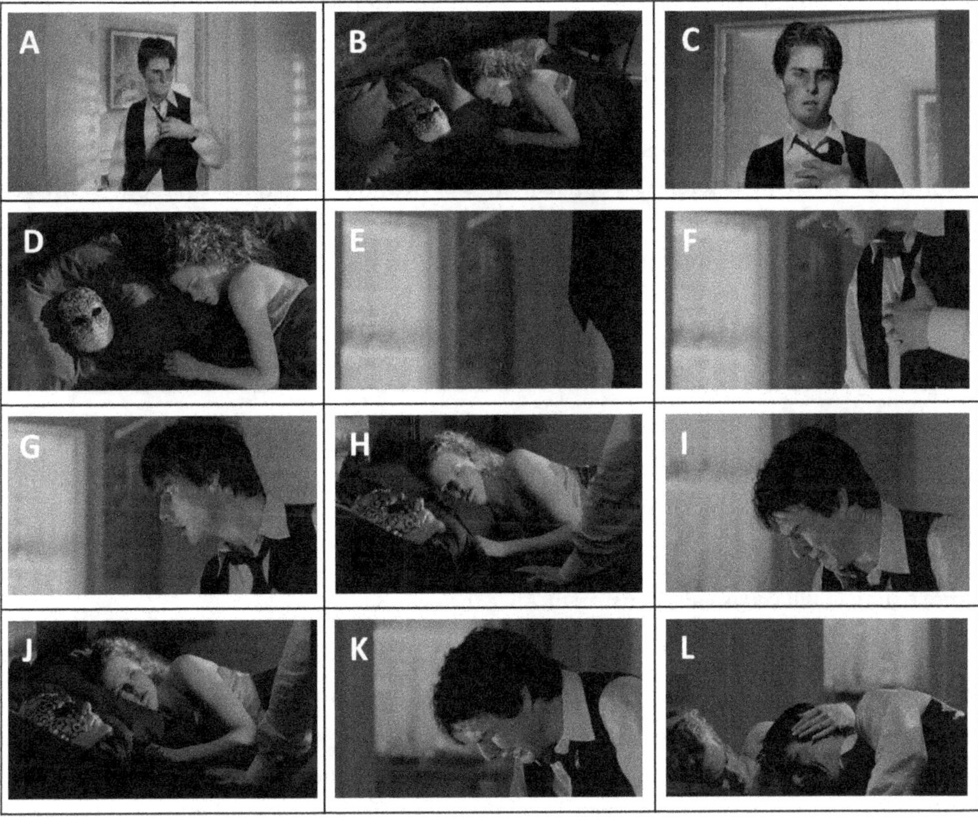

Figure 4.20. Bill opens himself up to Alice in *Eyes Wide Shut.*

2.2. The art of embodying relationships in film

Having demonstrated how Kubrick's films provide us with some vivid ways for expressing the FORCE OF EMOTION metaphor cinematically, let us now turn toward a consideration of that other concept that is closely connected to emotions, namely relationships. As we have seen in chapter 2, interpersonal relationships such as friendship depend significantly upon the logic of the CONTAINER image schema for their conceptualization. This was evident in the metaphor A PERSON IS A CONTAINER which conceptualizes a person as a bounded region in whom one can confide in. Hence, given that the frame corresponds to a container and given the potentiality for many, albeit restricted dynamic patterns of containment, it is possible to distinguish between various creative ways of expressing the interaction between two characters. In the "emotion" examples discussed so far there was little to no interference of one bounded region with another. Danny and the two girls, Lady Lyndon and Redmond, Bill and Alice, they were all predominantly confined to their own static frames. The dynamic pattern of ENCLOSURE that was elicited through editing was unidirectional in the sense that it only unfolded in relation to the content of one bounded region (e.g., a character). Their main purpose was to convey the increase of emotional intensity of the scene. The last part of the fragment from *Eyes Wide Shut* might be seen as an exception in this regard in that the pattern of INCLUSION involved two entities, Bill and Alice, which were, prior to the manifestation of the pattern, confined to their own private containers. As a consequence of this, they excluded each other. Inclusion put an end to this separation as the camera, motivated by Bill's movement, actively allowed Alice into "his" frame (i.e., his emotional self). The difference with the emotion examples above becomes particularly evident when we make a comparison at the diagrammatical level as shown in figure 4.21.

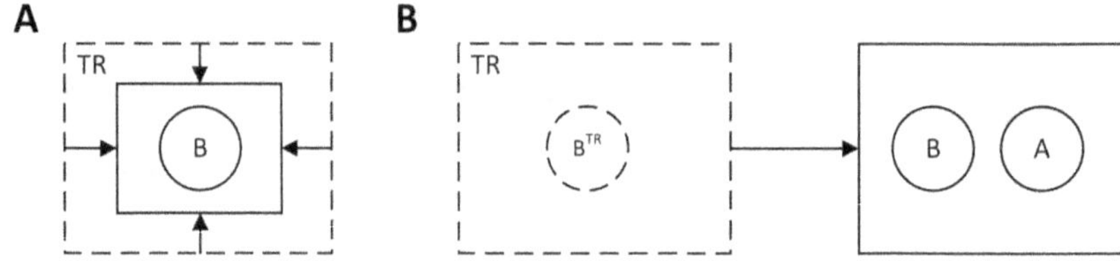

Figure 4.21. *A*, ENCLOSURE of Bill versus *B*, INCLUSION of Alice through Bill.

Both figures are representations of dynamic patterns of containment (ENCLOSURE and INCLUSION, respectively), notwithstanding that in figure *A* only one character (Bill) is diagrammed in the schema as opposed to two in figure *B* (Bill and Alice). With respect to the latter, it is interesting to consider its degree of overlap with perception. As we have seen in the first section of this chapter, the dynamic patterns underlying the cinematic representations of character perception also involved the presence of two entities, the PR and the OP, the latter which might well be another person. What, then, is it that makes a pattern to be an expression of a human (emotional) relationship rather than an expression of a perceptual one? To answer this question, one has to consider the metonymical cues of the scene at the level of acting, the phenomenological qualities of the cinematic expression, and the point in time at which the pattern is manifested in the scene. Compare, for example, the pattern of INCLUSION as expressed in figure 4.10 (Bill perceives the mask/Alice) with the pattern of INCLUSION as expressed in figure 4.20*K-L*. In the former case, the pattern was clearly cued metonymically by Bill's movement of the head. There was a clear correspondence between the direction of Bill's eyes and the direction of the camera movement. In the latter case, by contrast, Bill's head is facing downwards. In other words, the camera movement is not in tune with the direction of the character's eyes. Moreover, in the first case, the camera moves very fast to its object, whereas in the second case, the tempo is held deliberately slow and contemplative. Lastly, there is the causal order in which the patterns unfold. The inclusion of Alice at the end of the scene comes only after the perceptual relationship and the increase of emotional intensity have been established. Given all this, there is no reason to assume that the latter pattern of inclusion gave expression to the perception of the character. By this, however, we do not want to imply that character perception cannot tell anything about the kind of (emotional) relationship that the PR upholds with the OP. Character perception can be highly revealing especially when the cinematic rendering of the perception of one character distinguishes fundamentally from the cinematic rendering of the perception of another character. To illustrate this, let us compare two scenes as taken from *Paths of Glory*. In both cases a similar action is depicted, yet the visual way in which it is rendered is significantly dissimilar. In the first case, as illustrated in figure 4.22*A-B*, we see General Mireau as he strolls through the trenches while inspecting several soldiers. The scene is characterized by a perceptual distance. The camera tracks backward as the general moves forward without revealing, in separate shots, what the character is looking at. "The camera flees in front of him," as Kolker put it, "making dynamic the viewer's revulsion at his mechanical 'Hello there, soldier, ready to kill more Germans?'"[21] The contrast could not be more stark with the second scene which shows a similar action from the perspective of Colonel Dax (see figure 4.22*C-D*). Likewise, the camera tracks backward, but this time the walk is intersected with POV shots, such as the one illustrated in figure 4.22*D*, which allow the viewer to map the inside of the second shot onto the character's visual field. The men are confined *in* his visual field. As such, the logic of containment is extended in order to express Dax's engaging relationship with his soldiers (and hence, to sharpen the contrast with General Mireau).[22]

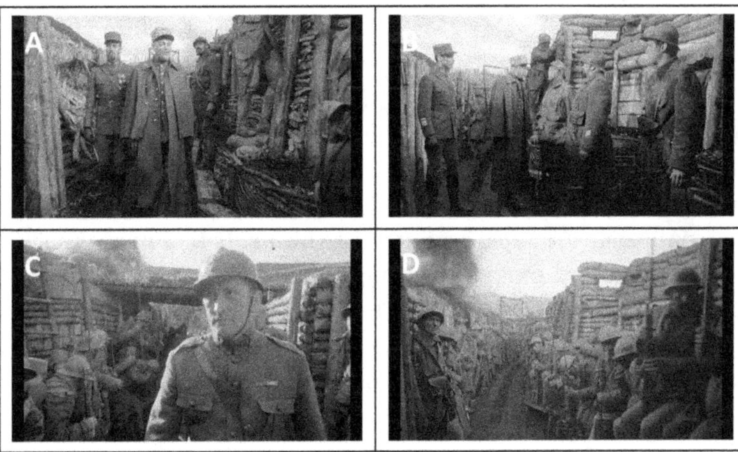

Figure 4.22. Different relationships: *A*, General Mireau versus *B*, Colonel Dax.

In what follows, we will not so much elaborate further on the implications of character perception for our understanding of relationships, but we will provide some more examples akin to the one from *Eyes Wide Shut* in which a dynamic pattern of containment serves the purpose of conveying meaning about the relationship between characters. To gain a sense of the range of possibilities and the complex interplay of patterns and meaning, examples will be drawn from *Paths of Glory* (the relationship between General Mireau and General Broulard), *The Shining* (the relationship between Jack Torrance and his wife and son) and *Eyes Wide Shut* (the relationship between Alice and Bill), respectively.

Paths of Glory

As a first example, let us consider the visually complex opening scene from *Paths of Glory* as already verbally described in the first chapter and as here illustrated over three figures (4.23, 4.24 and 4.25). General Mireau is promised a promotion by his superior General Broulard on the condition that he launches a "suicidal" attack on the heavily defended "anthill." During the scene the state of their relationship repetitiously alters between "cold" and "warm," eventually ending up in friendship as soon as Mireau accepts Broulard's offer. As can be seen in figure 4.23*A-B*, the scene starts in affection: General Broulard (on the right) enters the room and complements General Mireau (on the left) admiringly on the interior of the room. Both men are captured together in one shot (INTIMACY IS CLOSENESS). But as soon as they are seated, and Broulard starts to outline his plans to attack the anthill, fragmentation takes over as each character is now reduced to its own bounded region (PEOPLE ARE CONTAINERS). The camera alternatively cuts between the two generals (*C* to *L*). When Broulard mentions his plans to Mireau, he is no longer filmed in long shot, but in medium shot (*I*). By shortening the distance between the camera and the character, the film visually announces the increase in intensity of their talk and the importance of its subject (IMPORTANCE IS SIZE).

As with the emotion examples discussed above, both characters remain stationary in their own private containers. This, however, changes as soon as Broulard stands up out of disappointment of Mireau's lack of excitement toward his plans (see figure 4.24*M*)). Matching this action, the film cuts to a long shot uniting both generals again in the same frame (*N*). This unity, however, is short lived as Broulard walks away and the camera simultaneously pans to the right, thereby abandoning Mireau to the off-screen space (*O-P*). In other words, the pattern of EXCLUSION is extended in order to emphasize the fact that Mireau is of no use for Broulard if he does not comply. To regain his favour, Mireau reclaims his space on-screen by walking into Broulard's frame as they encounter each other near the whisky table (*Q-S*). EXCLUSION is counterbalanced by the pattern of ENTRY. This spatial unity however, only lasts for a few seconds. The film cuts to a medium shot of Mireau showing the viewer his facial expression as Broulard EXITS the frame while returning to his chair (*T*). Fragmentation takes over again. As Broulard stays seated (*U*), Mireau walks toward a desk (*V*). He starts to talk about how important the lives of his men are. The camera, however, does not follow him which results in a pattern of DISTANCING. Because Mireau is left standing in the background, he loses his dominance within the frame. As such his words are ripped from any credibility. At the same time, the film manages to preserve the distance with General Broulard.

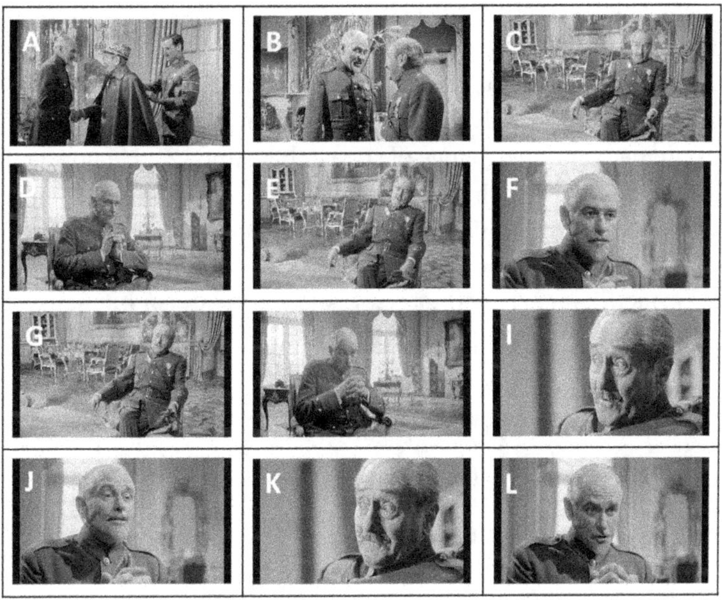

Figure 4.23. The cat and mouse game between General Mireau and General Broulard from *Paths of Glory* (part one).

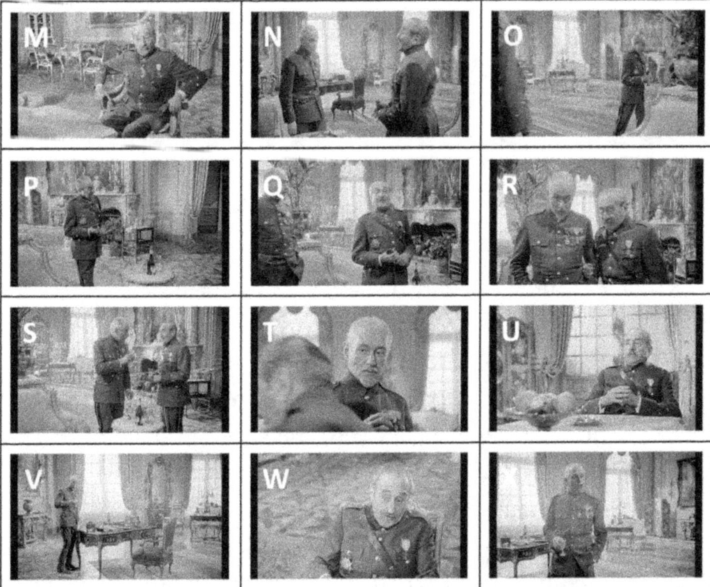

Figure 4.24. The cat and mouse game between General Mireau and General Broulard from *Paths of Glory* (part two).

Mireau approaches the table again (*X*), yet now it is Broulard who is distancing himself by leaving the table and moving to a location further behind him (figure 4.25*Y*). The camera renders them together as a perceptual relationship in one shot by extending the FRONT-BACK schema. Then, General Broulard starts to lure him with the possibility of a promotion. The film cuts hastily to a medium shot of Mireau's facial expression in profile, thus metonymically revealing his excitement and the change of state in his mind (*Z*). He now approaches General Broulard who now, as a result of this movement, is included into the bounded region of Mireau. He takes him by the arm, and together they start to walk twice around the round shaped interior plant in the middle of the room (*AA-AF*). Their bond is ratified by way of circularity (FRIENDSHIP IS A STRONG SPATIAL BOND). Their movement ends up with a handshake in the corner of the room (*AG*). The camera, however, stopped following the two generals as soon as they left the center of the room, detaching itself from their immoral agreement.

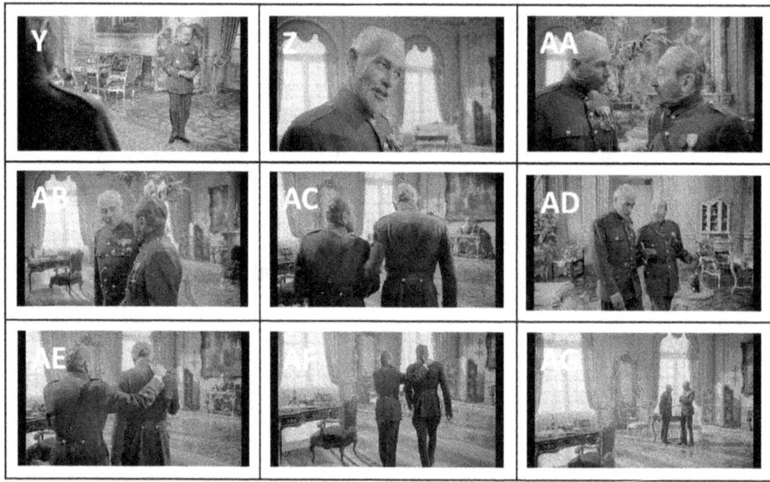

Figure 4.25. The cat and mouse game between General Mireau and General Broulard from *Paths of Glory* (part three).

Putting all these patterns together, a complex structural schema unfolds itself, a conceptual blueprint of the cat and mouse game that is taking place between the two generals. The two characters shift into new positions as if they were pieces on a chess board.[23] The state of their relationship ends as it started (i.e., in friendship), but in between there was a complicated series of moves that the two generals were making against each other, the dynamics of which might be captured as in figure 4.26. As can be seen, the scene is structured in terms of a set of four patterns of containment which were all extended in order to convey the relationship between Mireau and Broulard non-verbally: EXCLUSION, ENTRY, EXIT and INCLUSION. Moreover, as the viewer already may have noticed, we may see in the configuration of ENTRY followed by EXIT (*B-C*) a remarkable (albeit not absolute) resemblance to what Michotte famously labeled the "launching effect."[24] With this effect Michotte attempted to show how some configurations of moving objects can give rise to a mentally represented concept of causation. For example, in one of his experiments, a naïve observer is shown a simple film of two small triangles that are drawn on a line, separated by several inches. The first triangle A moves in a straight line until it approaches the second triangle B, whereupon A stays in its place and B starts moving away in the same direction. Objectively speaking, the film has nothing to do with causation. All that is happening are the events described above. Perceptually, however, something remarkable occurs as the viewer tends to perceive the motion of triangle A as *causing* the motion of triangle B.[25] Although the visual scene of *Paths of Glory* is much more complex than Michotte's experiment and the conditions of both are significantly dissimilar, one may nevertheless understand the succession of the dynamic patterns as unfolding in the former likewise as not random, but as causally ordered. As the motion of triangle B could not have occurred without the motion of triangle A, so one might argue in similar terms that the pattern of *B* could not have taken place without the end stage of pattern *A*, the pattern of *C* could not have taken place without the end stage of pattern *B*, and so on.

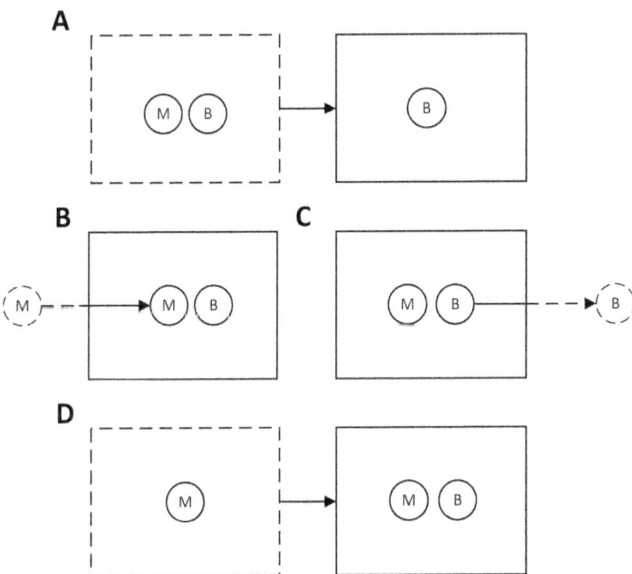

Figure 4.26. *A*, EXCLUSION of Mireau, *B*, ENTRY of Mireau, *C*, EXIT of Broulard, and *D*, INCLUSION of Broulard.

The Shining

For our second case, let us consider the relationship between Jack, on the one hand, and Wendy and Danny, on the other hand, which might be conceived of as an opposite relationship between the murderer and his victims. Many scholars already have pointed toward the twofold nature of Jack's personality. His behavior leads many to believe that he is a schizophrenic with a history of violence and alcoholism. Given the PERSON IS A CONTAINER metaphor, one might therefore assume that Jack's split personality might be expressed non-verbally by attributing two bounded regions or locations to the person Jack. One visual strategy that directly comes to mind in this regard is the use of mirrors inside the filmic frame. Here it is useful to borrow Julian Hanich's distinction between what he calls "complex mirror shots" and "the more widespread and less demanding mirror scenes."[26] In the former case "characters and other salient sources of attention are reflected in the mirror but remain beyond the screen frame (and hence were not placed between the mirror and the camera during shooting)." In the latter case, by contrast, the source of attention is placed "between the mirror and the camera during shooting and which thus allows a character or an object to be glimpsed from different angles simultaneously." With this conceptual distinction in mind, let us now consider the complex mirror shot as illustrated in figure 4.27.[27] We see Jack asleep (*A*). As the camera slowly zooms out, his wife Wendy is included into the frame while she enters the bedroom with a tray and wakes up Jack (*B-C*). During this process, the viewer is challenged to question the status of the previous image. The image we initially saw was not the image of the "real" Jack, but that of his reflection in the mirror. The size of the mirror thus serves as what Hanich calls a "strategy of mirror disorientation."[28] The camera was deliberately placed so close to the mirror surface that the edges of the mirror (container A) stretched beyond the four edges of the screen (container B). As a result, the viewer was not able to distinguish the mirror image from the "real" image. When the camera zooms out, the mirror frame is revealed and the audience is again provided with the guiding frame within the frame composition. This time, however, a new contrast comes to the surface as Wendy is included as a "real" self between the mirror and the camera, and not exclusively as a reflected one. Thus, although the pattern of EXPOSURE includes husband and wife *together* in the same frame, thus suggesting a sense of unity between the two persons, this effect is counterbalanced by the contrast of their appearances inside of the frame. This assumption of a divide between the couple is carried out subsequently as the zoom, almost unnoticeable, reverses to a medium close-up of Jack, who is now sitting semi-upright in bed talking to Wendy (*D* to *F*). The pattern of ENCLOSURE now excludes Wendy's face from the inside content of the frame (and hence, from Jack). It is now clear from the writing that appears in inverted form on his T-shirt that we are dealing with a reflected image.

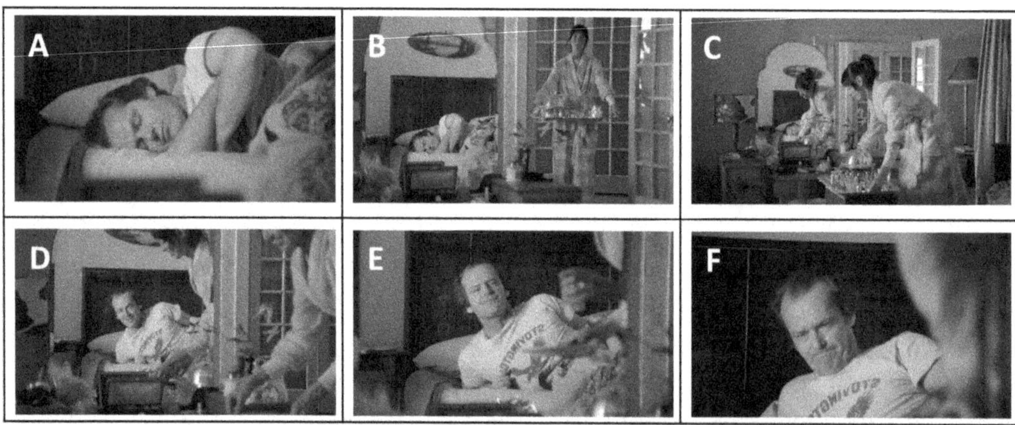

Figure 4.27. A complex mirror shot in *The Shining.*

Let us now shift our attention from Jack's relationship with his wife to his relationship with his son, Danny, by taking a closer look at a scene that interestingly makes use of the same setting as the scene above and that comes after the shot in which little Danny is shown entering the room and seeing Jack sitting on the bed, as already illustrated in figure 4.12*G-I*.

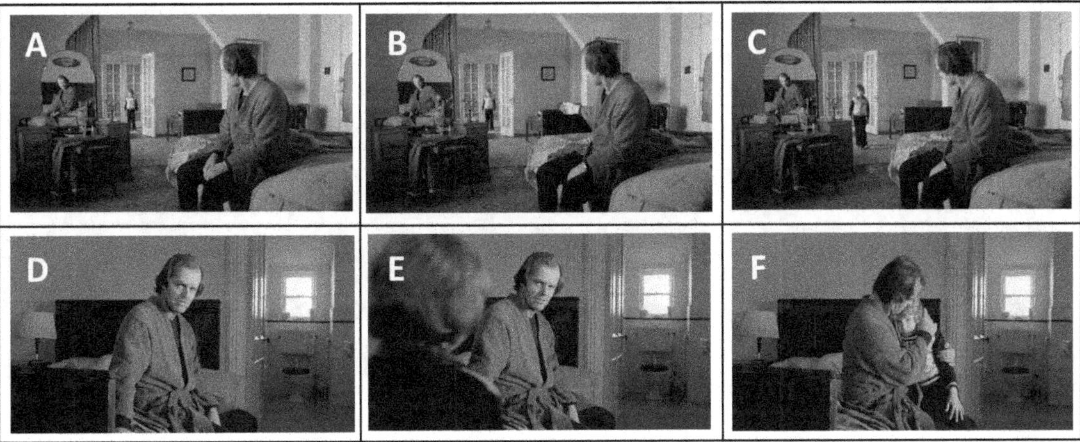

Figure 4.28. Danny "enters the lion's den" in *The Shining*.

As with the scene with Wendy, the shot starts off with a reflection of Jack in the mirror, only this time Jack is placed between the camera and the mirror during the shooting (see figure 4.28*A*). Thus, both selves are shown in one and the same frame, making this shot not a complex mirror shot. However, what makes this shot intimidating apart from the menacing third movement from Bartók's *Music for Strings, Percussion and Celesta*, which we shall address more in detail in chapter 5, is the way in which Danny, in the centre background of the frame, is caught in between those two selves.[29] As Mullen observes: "Danny is easily the smallest figure in the frame as he asks for permission to get his fire engine."[30] When Jack reaches out his hand, which is doubled in the mirror, and asks him "to come here for a minute" (*B*), he approaches carefully the scene of his father (*C*). This movement, however, is not shown uninterruptedly as the film now cuts to a medium shot of the front side of Jack that in the previous shot was reflected in the mirror (*D*). It is not a cut on action as there are still a couple of seconds before Danny enters Jack's territory from the left side of the frame into his father's arms (*E-F*). As if the film deliberately wants to draw our attention to the pattern of ENTRY by making it as visible and intelligible as possible (i.e., "Danny is *entering* the lion's den").

As a way of consolidating our discussion of *The Shining*, let us consider the scene, as illustrated in figure 4.29, in which all three members of the family are involved. While Wendy and Danny stroll through the maze in the daytime, Jack is at the same time looking over an architectural model of the same maze in the Colorado Room at the Overlook Hotel (*A-B*). However, by virtue of the POV structure, it seems as if the discontinuity between the two spatial locations is transcended and Jack, as a God like figure, is overseeing his family in the middle of the maze. The camera starts on a hedge maze of vast proportions and slowly zooms in to allow us to see that Wendy and Danny are actually enclosed in the centre of it (C). Accompanying this pattern of ENCLOSURE is the part of Bartók's *Music for Strings, Percussion and Celesta* that features "flowing arpeggios in the piano, harp, and celesta, with an underpinning of tremolos in the strings."[31] The music grows in intensity as the camera (i.e., Jack's POV) comes closer to the centre of the maze. As in our example of *Paths of Glory*, the VISUAL OF FIELD IS A CONTAINER metaphor is thus extended in order to express the nature of their relationship, except here the extension serves a negative and imprisoning purpose rather than a positive and confiding one. Wendy and Danny are caught and can only escape the confinement of Jack's mind by escaping the maze. As such the film already foreshadows the end sequence of the film. Ironically, it will be Jack himself who will end up dying in the middle of the maze, unable to find his way out.

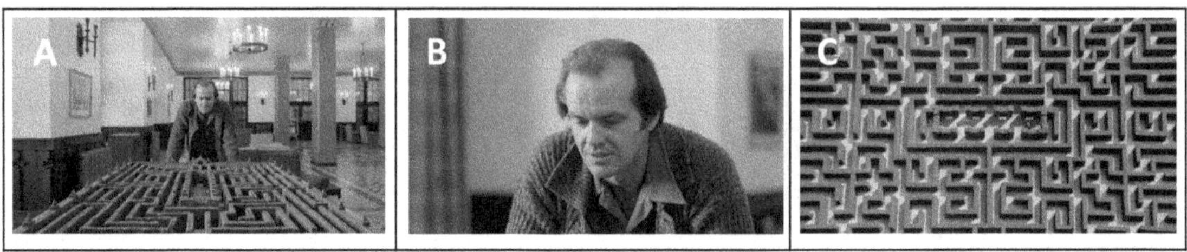

Figure 4.29. Wendy and Danny are caught in the "labyrinth" of Jack's mind (*The Shining*).

Eyes Wide Shut

There is a moment in *Eyes Wide Shut*, as Bill Harford gets of the bed of a prostitute to switch off the music and take up the call from his wife Alice, when we see, on a bookshelf, a glimpse of a textbook in the foreground entitled *Introducing Sociology*. In his review of the film, Kreider has argued that this book reference is not incidental.[32] In his opinion it is a "key to understanding the film, suggesting that we ought to interpret it sociologically." Although such a claim may sound too strong to some readers, it seems less far-fetched when one considers the role of the mask in the film. According to Erving Goffman, one of America's most influential sociologists of the twentieth century, Shakespeare was right when he said that "All the world's a stage, and all the men and women merely players. They have their exits and their entrances."[33] Considering the LIFE IS A PLAY metaphor, as discussed in chapter 2 of this book, he compared social interaction to a theater and people in everyday life to actors on a stage who perform and hide their true selves behind a variety of roles (i.e., masks). We already saw above how Bill's mask fell off at the end of the film. What caused him to wear this mask in the first place (and hence, to hide his true self), was the fantasy inflicted upon his mind by the revelation of his wife that she once was so attracted to a naval officer that she was "ready to give up everything." Similarly, one might argue that Bill's fantasy embodies a dream-like version of Alice (the one who has sex with other men), as distinguishable from the "real" Alice who confesses to her husband her private dreams in all honesty. It is precisely Bill's obsession with the former one that will haunt him and that sets the events of the rest of the movie in motion, a sexual odyssey through the streets of New York that resolves around Bill's failed attempts to experience in real-life what his wife is only experiencing in her dreams. To see how Bill's obsession with the "imaginary" Alice rather than the "real" one is already foreshadowed at the start of the film, let us have a closer look at what is perhaps the most iconic scene of the film: the brief and wordless scene in which Alice and Bill are making love in front of a mirror (see figure 4.30). The scene, renowned by its inclusion of Chris Isaak's song "Baby Did a Bad Bad Thing," begins as Alice, framed in medium long shot, stands naked in front of the mirror (*A*). Similar to *The Shining*, the film thus gives rise to two versions of Alice: the "real" one and her reflection. As the film slowly zooms in, Bill, also naked, enters the inside content of the frame, not by crossing any edges of the frame, but by crossing the right edge of the mirror inside of the frame, thus suggesting that Bill's attention is not drawn toward the "real" Alice, but as we later shall see, her "dream" version (*B*). When the "real" Bill finally enters the frame from the right edge (*C*), thus contesting the previous assertion somehow, his appearance (and that of the "real" Alice) is yet again excluded by the camera as it continues to close in on the mirror image (*D*). This exclusion of "the real" in favor of the inclusion of "the unreal" is fortified with an almost unnoticeable cut to their reflection in the mirror (*E*). The camera keeps zooming in until it rests on the reflection of Alice's facial expression while Bill is further taking hold of her body (*F*).

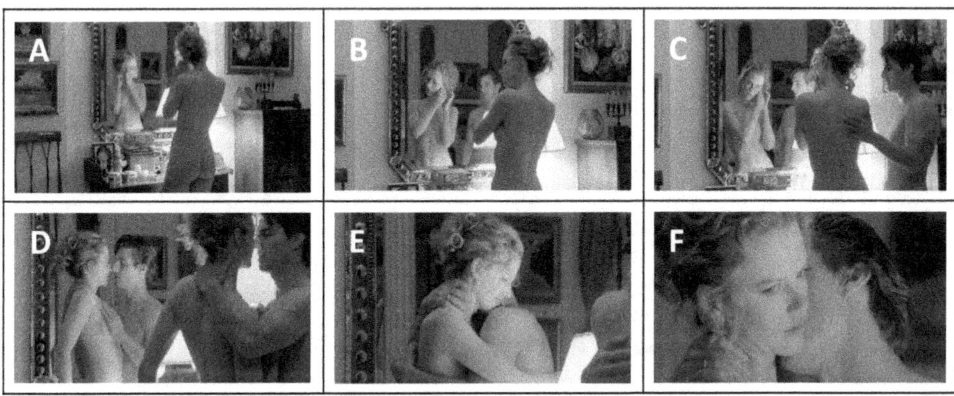

Figure 4.30. Enclosing of the mirror image of Alice in *Eyes Wide Shut*.

Once more, this example demonstrates how dynamic patterns of containment play a fundamental role in fleshing out the meanings of the film visually. Let us further provide evidence for this statement by considering the moment in the film that appears closely after the mirror scene and that prompts Alice to make her confession about the naval officer (see figure 4.31). Likewise this scene, the first of three bedroom scenes with Bill and Alice, the third and last of which was already described above, can be conceived of as an instance of the flow-of-emotion scenario in the sense that Alice's hearing of a statement of Bill prompts an emotional reaction in Alice which, in turn, causes her to make the confession. The film shows the couple lying on their bed (*A*). They are smoking marihuana together. Alice is questioning Bill about a couple of models that he was "hitting on" last night at Ziegler's Christmas Party. When Bill bluntly states that it is understandable for guys to want to have sex with his wife for the only reason that she is beautiful, Alice hastily stands up (*B*). Irritated by his remark, she repositions herself in the opening of the bathroom door, thus leaving her husband behind on the bed. This concrete bodily gesture is accentuated at the filmic level. As Alice is relocating herself in the opening of the door, the camera slowly closes in on her, thus abandoning Bill to the off-screen space (*C*). As such the film manages to achieve two things at the same time: firstly, to cue the increase of emotional intensity inside the character of Alice which resulted from her hearing Bill's reaction, and secondly, to settle the divide between Bill and Alice caused by his remark. As with many of our previous examples, this divide is established by the zoom-in camera movement and the pattern of ENCLOSURE which is inherent to it. The structural features of inside and outside are mapped onto the locations of Alice and Bill, respectively, thus allowing the filmmaker to highlight the emotional shift of balance between the two characters that goes together with the flow-of-emotion scenario that is unfolding on-screen. While the couple was at first repeatedly shown together, they are from that moment on, until the end of the scene, separated through editing. Similarly, when Alice tells Bill about the first time she saw the naval officer in Cape God, and the rich and mysterious sounds of Jocelyn Pook's strings start to underpin the surface of the monologue, moving in and out of dissonance, the visual form adjusts itself once more to the content.[34] In order to evoke the increase of emotional intensity caused by Alice's confession, the film shows Bill no longer in a medium shot, but in a close-up (the transition from *D* to *F*). This time the pattern of ENCLOSURE, here elicited through editing, is solely directed toward Bill's emotional experience. The heightening of the psychological tension, caused by the content of the confession, is rendered visually by narrowing the edges of the film frame in relationship to the front side of Bill's face. His face is "hooked" in the frame. When her confession is interrupted by a telephone call, the pressure is temporally released, and Bill is shown again in a medium shot.

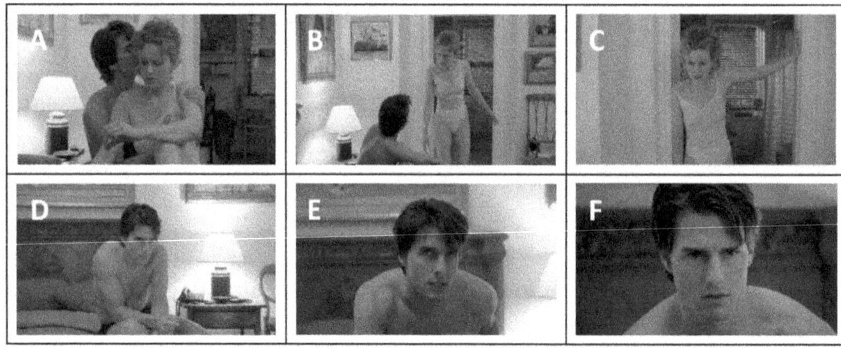

Figure 4.31. Alice tells Bill about the naval officer in *Eyes Wide Shut*.

As a last example, let us turn to a discussion of the second and middle bedroom scene, somewhere past the first half of the film, where Alice tells Bill about the dream she was having while she was asleep (see figure 4.32). In the screenplay the first actions are described as follows: "Bill walks into the bedroom to find Alice asleep but murmuring in a dream. He sits on the side of the bed, and Alice's noises turn to laughing. As the laugh becomes almost hysterical, Bill gently touches her. She awakes with a 'start' and is a little distressed. . . . Bill starts to take off his shoes as Alice tries to calm down. . . . Alice, slightly upset, reaches out to him and pulls Bill down next to her (*A*)."[35] As the mirror scene from above already made clear to us, Bill is obsessed with the dream version of Alice, so he inquires about it, asking her to tell the dream. "Alice sits up trying to recapture her dream." As she moves upward, the camera follows her, thus excluding Bill from the space on-screen (*B*). As such, a divide is manifesting itself visually between speaker/storyteller and listener/observer. As with the naval officer scene, a monologue serves as a cue for Pook's foreboding music: "We were in a deserted city and . . . and our clothes were gone. We were naked, and . . . and I was terrified, and I . . ." The film cuts to Bill's frozen reaction (*C*) at the same time when Alice's voice continues to utter the words "and I felt ashamed" off-screen. Then an interlude takes place as Alice lies down again, burying her face in her pillow (*D*). Through this movement, Bill is back again included into the frame. Now it is Bill who sits up and looks at her crying into the pillow. In contrast to above, however, the camera is not following Bill in one movement, thus excluding Alice. The film turns to a cut on action which allows to preserve Alice into the frame (*E*). However, this time editing does the job as the film cuts to a frontal close-up of Bill's face who now compulsively asks further about the rest of the dream (*F*). The film, then, cuts back again to Alice who now sits up for a second time. However, because the "empty" space is now occupied by Bill who was already seated up, her husband is now also included into "her" frame (*G-H*). "Alice gets close to Bill and envelops him in her arms, while summoning the courage to continue to story."[36] Through the dynamic pattern of INCLUSION, he is thus allowed as a witness to her most private dreams. In this way, the pattern can be seen as mirroring the pattern of INCLUSION that unfolded in the third and last bedroom scene, as described above, with this crucial exception that it is now Alice who is including Bill and not the other way around. At the same time, the music reaches its climax as Alice says, "I was fucking other men." "The music swells in the higher strings, and a sinuous melody emerges in the solo cello before the cue fades down into underscore again."[37] However, in contrast to the third bedroom scene in which Bill's sobbing was met by a comforting gesture of Alice (see figure 4.20*L*), the weeping of Alice is not answered at all by Bill. His bewildering impassiveness is captured by a frontal reaction close-up of his frozen face (*I*). His focus is still not upon the "authentic" Alice sitting next to him, but upon the Alice from her dreams and his imagination.

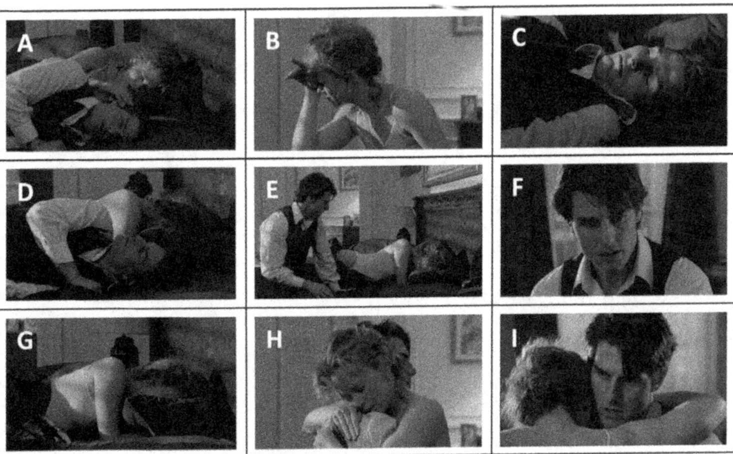

Figure 4.32. Alice tells Bill her dream in *Eyes Wide Shut*.

3. Conclusion

The goal of this chapter was to consolidate all of the insights of the previous chapters by showing how the dynamic patterns of the filmic frame, as described in the previous chapter, can be extended metaphorically for the purpose of fleshing out the abstract conceptual structure of mental causation as it was identified, in chapter 1, to underlie the narratives of Kubrick's work. Through an analysis of various film scenes, we have demonstrated how all of the most important conceptual metaphors of mental causation, in which these patterns serve as important source domains (see chapter 2), can be structured cinematically by such resources of cinema as camera movement and editing. Contesting the paradox of meaning in cinema, we have shown how film, despite its iconic nature, is able to structure the reality in front of the camera in such a way as to give rise to complex meanings. However, it should be stressed that viewers are only able to understand these patterns in a metaphorical way, only because there are abstract target domains for which their inferential logic can be appropriated. In order to grasp these concepts adequately, one has to consider all of the cues that help to convey the concepts of the stories of mental causation to the viewer, including not only the dialogues of the actors, but also and above all their non-verbal, bodily behavior which operates at the metonymical level of meaning-making.

Notes

1. Walker, *Stanley Kubrick Directs*, 7.
2. Spielberg as quoted in Harlan, *Stanley Kubrick: A Life in Pictures*, 2:13:45.
3. Portions of this chapter have appeared previously, albeit in less extended form, in Coëgnarts, "Stanley Kubrick."
4. See, for instance, Choi, "Leaving It Up to the Imagination," 17–25; Smith, *Engaging Characters*; and Vaage, "Varieties of Empathic Engagement," 158–179.
5. Kubrick and Raphael, *Eyes Wide Shut*, 84.
6. For a good discussion of the music of the same scene from the perspective of CMT, see Chattah, "Film Music as Embodiment," 108–109.
7. Coëgnarts and Kiss, "'Look Out Behind You!'," 364–367.
8. Gengaro, *Listening to Stanley Kubrick*, 207
9. Flashback scenes in film, by contrast, systematically provide evidence for an opposite mapping according to which the space in front of the perceiver is mapped onto the past. For a lengthy discussion, see Coëgnarts and Kravanja, "With the Past in Front of the Character," 218–239.
10. Gengaro, *Listening to Stanley Kubrick*, 209.
11. Ibid., 209.
12. Kolker, *A Cinema of Loneliness*, 114.
13. Coëgnarts and Kiss, "Look Out Behind You!," 348–349.
14. Gengaro, *Listening to Stanley Kubrick*, 207.
15. Kolker, *A Cinema of Loneliness*, 164.
16. See, for instance, Jonides, "Mind's Eye's Movement," 247–250.
17. For a discussion of the role of character perception in complex cinema or puzzle films, see Coëgnarts et al., "Seeing Yourself in the Future," 114–138.
18. Kövecses, *Metaphor and* Emotion, 55.

19. For a good discussion of the music in this scene, see McQuiston, *We'll Meet Again*, 102–105.
20. Ibid., 102.
21. Kolker, *A Cinema of Loneliness*, 124.
22. For Kolker this contrast raises a very fascinating question: Does the fact that Dax is comfortable with his men also mean that "his is the mediating and ameliorating voice of the film, speaking of humanity in the midst of the terrifying brutality that occurs around him?" Backed by other formal cues in the film, the author answers this question negatively, claiming that Dax's comfort with his men is merely "an illusion." Ibid., 124.
23. As is well known, Kubrick himself was captivated by the game of chess ever since childhood. To quote LoBrutto: "Chess was more than a game to Stanley—it represented order, logic, perseverance, and self-discipline. The game embraced the young man's fascination with war and the military." See LoBrutto, *Kubrick*, 19. See also Ciment, *Kubrick*, 196.
24. Michotte, *La perception de la causalité*. For a more recent discussion, see Scholl and Tremoulet, "Perceptual Causality and Animacy," 299–309.
25. For a discussion, see also Coëgnarts and Kravanja, "Perceiving Emotional Causality," 450–451.
26. Hanich, "Reflecting on Reflections," 131.
27. For a good description of the same scene, see also Appelt, "The Craft of Seeing," 260.
28. Hanich, "Reflecting on Reflections," 149.
29. For a discussion of Barók's music in this scene, see Gengaro, *Listening to Stanley Kubrick*, 200–201; and McQuiston, *We'll Meet Again*, 78–80
30. Mullen, "Do You Speak Kubrick?," 102.
31. Gengaro, *Listening to Stanley Kubrick*, 200.
32. Kreider, "Introducing Sociology," 281.
33. Goffman, *The Presentation of Self in Everyday Life*.
34. Gengaro, *Listening to Stanley Kubrick*, 234–235
35. Kubrick and Raphael, *Eyes Wide Shut*, 65–66.
36. Ibid., 67.
37. Gengaro, *Listening to Stanley Kubrick*, 236.

Chapter 5

Seeing and Listening to Kubrick's Films: The Embodied Film Viewer

The ideas have to be discovered by the audience, and their thrill in making the discovery makes those ideas all the more powerful.

—Stanley Kubrick[1]

In this concluding chapter, we shift the focus from a discussion of embodied visual meaning in the cinema of Kubrick to the film-goer who attends it with its senses. We will assess the film viewer through an examination of two theoretical dilemmas. The first dilemma is inherent to the experience of seeing films and involves the question as to how viewers are able to discover the situational meaning of a film (e.g., mental causation), and thus are potentially susceptible to the experiential states of narrative absorption and suspense, notwithstanding the fact that they in a strict sense reside outside the narrated events. In proposing an answer to this question, we will take into account the neuroscientific notion of embodied simulation as it recently has been argued to mediate our capacity to share the meaning of actions, intentions, feelings, and emotions with others. The second dilemma has already been mentioned in the introduction to this book and arises from the relationship between meaning and music. It involves the question as to how musical sounds, as they abundantly accompany Kubrick's images, can convey meaning notwithstanding the fact that they lack a reference model. In contrast to the previous dilemma, this question does not explicitly mention the viewer. Nevertheless, as this chapter will argue, it will be precisely the embodied viewer to which we will have to turn to in order to come to terms with the paradox of musical meaning.

1. Discovering the meaning: The role of embodied simulation

We started this book with a discussion of the paradox of cinematic meaning. This paradox was directed at the relationship between meaning and film. How are films such as those of Kubrick able to convey concepts despite the fact that film essentially is an iconic and visual medium? Subsequently, in the next four chapters we attempted to approach this question systematically from the perspective of embodied cognition, rather than the film-as-language view. Now that we have arrived at the end of this book, we can raise a somewhat similar paradox, this time not with respect to the above mentioned relationship, but with respect to the relationship between the film and the film viewer to whom the embodied visual meaning of the film relates to. This paradox is rooted in the question as to how viewers are able to discover the situational meanings of a film, given the fact that they, as observers, reside outside the events that define these meanings. Resolving this dilemma is important, for the answer to it could well explain why the films of Kubrick are overall perceived as highly engaging. Indeed, as many cognitive film scholars have stressed, there is an intrinsic link between the film audience's strong attentional focus on the events of the story-world, on the one hand, and the film audience's enjoyment of watching films, on the other hand.[2] Ed Tan and his colleagues have proposed to refer to this intense engagement with the story-world, which is said to go hand in hand with a decreased awareness of the self and one's immediate surrounding, as "narrative absorption."[3] As Garreth Brown's quotation in chapter 2 already made clear to us, a good way of making sense of this experience is by observing the language that film viewers use to describe it. An interview study conducted by Bálint and Tan has revealed, for instance, that film viewers have a natural tendency to describe the content of their experience of absorption by resorting to the dynamics of the CONTAINMENT schema (e.g., "To be lost *in* a film," "To be *pulled out* of the story," "To be drawn *into* the film").[4] This may be rendered in a most efficient manner, as the authors have done, by resorting to a superimposition of two of the dynamic patterns of containment as discussed in this book, namely ENTRY and ENCLOSURE.[5] The authors coin this embodied mental model for absorption the "Into Film" model and can be represented as in figure 5.1.[6] In contrast to the figure proposed by Bálint and Tan, we opt to show both patterns separately. In the first, the motion is attributed to the viewer's self. The viewer's self "travels" into the film's story-world. Once inside, the portrayed story can execute more "force" on the viewer's self. This is where the pattern of ENCLOSURE takes over. Likewise, one might represent the opposite, the decreased awareness of a fictional narrative, by the patterns of EXIT and ENCLOSURE, respectively.

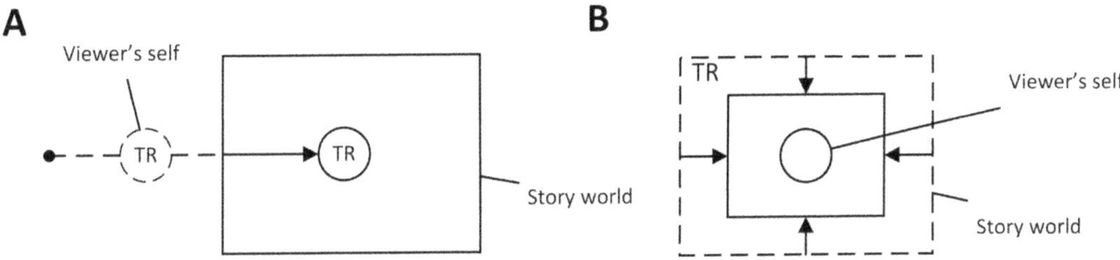

Figure. 5.1. Representing narrative absorption through *A*, ENTRY, and *B*, ENCLOSURE.

The concept of narrative absorption has also been closely associated with that other strong felt aspect of cinematic experience, namely suspense.[7] In its most general sense, suspense has been defined as an "emotional response to narrative fictions."[8] Although suspense has been sometimes argued to be more emotional than cognitive, as compared to narrative absorption, it has also been argued to share with the latter a strong dependence on the viewer's or reader's knowledge of the events. In the literature this relationship is often further explicated in terms of a delay of the "outcome event."[9] The outcome event is "an event of high importance that usually represents the resolution of a conflict (e.g., the car of the protagonist explodes when he steps in)."[10] The event that "announces the occurrence of the outcome event in the immediate proximity" is called the "initiating event" (e.g., "the villain places a bomb in the protagonist's car").[11] Upon perceiving the latter, so the argument goes, the audience desires to see the outcome event, and the longer the expectations are held without fulfilling them by an outcome event, the more uncertainty, and hence suspense, will be experienced.[12] There is probably no better way to illustrate this principle than with the final duel scene between Barry Lyndon and his step-son Lord Bullingdon. This duel distinguishes itself from the ones shown earlier in the film in that the two men are not shooting each other at the same time, but take turns with each turn marking an initiating event in its own right. Tension is built as the outcome event is postponed twice, first by Bullingdon whose first shot is a misfire, and second, by Barry who chooses to spare his step-son's life, in an effort to heal their relationship, by firing his pistol into the ground. Eventually, the duel ends in a decisive outcome as Bullingdon decides to continue the gunfight and wounds Barry's leg.[13]

In sum, if our enjoyment of watching films, as articulated through the experiential states of narrative absorption and suspense, is closely tied to an understanding of the situational meanings, but the viewer is only an observer, and not a performer of the events that constitute those meanings, how, then, can such an understanding be achieved? For instance, how are we able to understand the acts of camera devices in terms of the psychology of characters, while we are not performing those acts ourselves when sitting stationary in the film theatre? It is in the search for an answer to this paradox that we may turn to the field of neuroscience, and in particular to Vittorio Gallese's theory of Embodied Simulation (henceforth, ES theory).[14] Central to this theory is the idea that individuals "reuse their own mental states or processes in functionally attributing them to others, where the extent and reliability of such reuse and functional attribution depend on the simulator's bodily resources and their being shared with the target's bodily resources."[15] Neurological evidence for this connection can be found in the discovery of so called "mirror neurons" in the macaque monkey brain and the discovery of a similar mirror mechanism in the human brain.[16] Mirror neurons are claimed to map the sensory description of others' expressive acts (for example, actions, emotions and sensations) onto the perceiver's own motor, visceromotor and somatosensory representations of those acts.[17] This mapping enables one to perceive the action, emotion or sensation of another as if she were performing that action or experiencing that emotion or sensation herself. Because they discharge both during the execution and the observation of a given behavior, mirror neurons have been argued to provide a neural basis for social identification and a variety of related concepts such as mind-reading, intersubjectivity, empathy and theory of mind.[18] Hence, since film, like all other arts, exemplifies a form of intersubjectivity that mediates between the filmmaker and the film viewer, it can be assumed that ES also plays a significant role in the way audiences get hold on the events of films and hence, their situational meanings.

Since these meanings are foremost represented visually in the cinema of Kubrick with the aid of such embodied principles as metaphor and metonymy, we have to ask ourselves as to what degree ES can be linked to the notion of embodied visual meaning.[19] Gallese's own collaborative work with film scholar Michele Guerra provides a promising start to explore this issue further.[20] Extending ES theory to film spectatorship, both authors have stressed that viewers are not only bodily engaged (in terms of sensory-motor cortex activation) with the actions and emotions of actors and actresses (the most obvious level of embodiment), but also with cinematic devices (e.g., camera movements, changes of shot scale, different editing techniques).[21] Since these cinematic devises are the tools by virtue of which the embodied meaning is fleshed out visually, as the previous chapter revealed to us, we can well assume that ES theory offers us some valuable insight into the question as to how viewers are able to discover the situational meanings (and hence, are potentially capable of reaching the states of narrative absorption and suspense).

As a way of illustrating this assumption, let us consider Gallese's and Guerra's own analysis of a scene from Hitchcock's *Notorious* (1946), which, by extension, might give us a better understanding of how viewers are able to connect to the situational meaning structure of mental causation, as discerned in the cinema of Kubrick.[22] It concerns the scene in which the lead heroine Alicia (Ingrid Bergman) is going to enter Sebastian's room to steal the key of the wine cellar. The scene is rendered as follows: first, we see Alicia as she approaches the camera until she is captured in medium-shot. Her eyes are directed toward the left space off-screen. From the metonymy EYES FOR SEEING, the film subsequently cuts to her visual field, showing us in the background of the frame, Sebastian's shadow as reflected on his bathroom door, and in the foreground, outside the bathroom, his desk. Next, the film cuts away from this static point-of-view shot, and back again to Alice who now lowers her gaze. The film repeats the same point-of-view, albeit this time the static shot becomes a moving one as the camera tracks closer to the desk so as to enclose the keys which are left unguarded on the desk. From this the viewer might infer that Alicia has left her initial place for the purpose of grasping the keys. Yet, this assumption is inconsistent with the following shot which shows Alice still standing on the same threshold, thus suggesting to the viewer that she has never left her location.

Gallese and Guerra consider this scene to be a striking example of how a cinematic technique prompts ES. As they write, "the tracking shot mimicks not only Alicia's potential approach to the keys, but also, by means of ES, the viewer's own potential approach, which turns into a grasping simulation the more the keys are made ready-to-hand, thus evoking the activation of the viewer's canonical neurons."[23] Thereby the authors emphasize the workings of two distinct simulation processes. There is the simulation process of approaching the desk which brings the keys on the table within the viewer's simulated peri-personal space. The keys are turned into potentially graspable objects. This, in turn, allows for the simulation process of grasping the keys which is triggered by the activation of the viewer's canonical neurons. Consequently, because the simulated actions of approaching and grasping constitute important source domains for our understanding of the abstract concept of desire, it may be assumed that the viewer is perfectly capable of understanding the tracking shot, and the pattern of INCLUSION which it embodies, in terms of Alice's desire for the keys. The viewer is further encouraged in this hypothesis by the upcoming shot which shows Alice actually fulfilling her desire by taking hold of the keys.

If the observation of an action of the camera activates in the film viewer the same neural mechanism that is triggered by executing the action oneself (e.g., approaching), then we might well assume that the film viewer also simulates all of the other actions that accompany the dynamic patterns of the filmic frame (e.g., entering, distancing, exiting, excluding, including). Since these dynamic patterns are the tools by virtue of which the viewer makes sense of the conceptual structure of mental causation, as this book has demonstrated, we might well conclude that ES plays an equally important role in making the viewer aware of the embodied visual meanings of Kubrick's cinema. In other words, the viewer is able to understand the dynamic patterns of containment, as manifested in the work of Kubrick, in terms of various concepts of mental causation, because ES allows us to simulate the experiences that lie at the heart of these patterns and that are central to our own everyday embodied understanding of these concepts.

From the above consideration we may now infer the following hypothesis: by employing cinematic devices, and thus imposing image schematic structures on the visual content, the film director is able to exert more control on the viewers' responses or brain states. Since these states are widely believed by most neuroscientists and many philosophers to be tightly related to the viewers' mental states, controlling viewers' brain states, for our purpose, is the same as directing the viewers' attention toward the situational meanings of the film (e.g., mental causation in the case of Kubrick).[24] Naturally, this begs the question of evidence: are there any notable neurological differences to discern across viewers of structured movies and viewers of arbitrary and unstructured segments of reality? An answer to this question has been proposed by neuroscientist Uri Hasson.[25] Together with his colleagues he proposed a method for assessing the effect of a given film on the brain activity of viewers. They dubbed this method the "inter-subject correlation analysis (ISC)." What is significant about this analysis is that it allows one to measure similarities in brain activity across viewers of a same film by comparing "the response time course in each brain region (e.g., in a small region of the visual system of the brain) from one viewer to the response time courses obtained in the same brain region from other viewers."[26] With this definition in mind, they compared the ISC for an unstructured real life event (i.e., filmed without the employment of cinematic devices), with the ISC for a tightly edited and structured film (i.e., a segment from Sergio Leone's *The Good, The Bad and the Ugly*). Subsequently, it was revealed that the former evoked far less ISC across viewers than the latter, thus suggesting that "a mere mechanical reproduction of reality, with no directorial intention or intervention, is not sufficient by itself for controlling viewer's brain activity."[27] In other words, the more a filmmaker imposes image-schematic structure on the visual content with the aid of cinematic devices, the more control the filmmaker will exert on the viewer's responses, and the more he or she will be able to direct the viewer's attention toward the film's referential meanings. It is precisely in this sense that filmmakers such as Leone, Hitchcock and Kubrick can be seen to assert a considerable degree of control over the viewer's mind.

Coming to the end of our discussion of the first dilemma, a critical reader may wonder where emotions and top-down processes, these two other important components of the film experience, fit in the picture? What role do they play in the viewers' discovery of the situational meanings of a film? Here, we may turn to Torben Grodal's general model of visual aesthetics, which he labels the PECMA flow (short for perception, emotion, cognition and motor action).[28] We have already seen above how the discovery of the situational meanings is made possible by the activation of embodied simulation processes inside the film viewer. These processes allow the viewer to connect to the image schemas upon which the situational meanings, as visually manifested in the films, are grounded. In the light of this claim, Grodal has argued that the viewer's connection to these significant patterns, which he situates within the first stage of the flow, works in tandem with positive emotional responses from the limbic system. As he argues, "the function of the visual cortex is finding salient forms in the chaos of information that arrives through the eyes and the brain receives a small emotional reward every time it discovers a significant form."[29] He finds support for this in Ramachandran's and Hirstein's neurological theory of aesthetic experience.[30] This theory proposes a list of "eight laws of artistic experience"—"a set of heuristics that artists either consciously or unconsciously deploy to optimally titillate the visual areas of the brain."[31] One of these laws is based on a psychological phenomenon called the "peak shift effect": "If a rat is taught to discriminate a square from a rectangle (of say, 3:2 aspect ratio) and rewarded for the rectangle, it will soon learn to respond more frequently to the rectangle."[32] What is remarkable, however, is that the rat's response to a rectangle that is even longer and skinnier (say, of aspect ratio 4:1) is even greater than it was to the initial prototype on which it was trained. As the authors point out, what this neurological finding tells us, is that the rat "is not learning a prototype but a rule," an image schematic one at that, of "rectangularity."[33] It is precisely this principle that is said by the authors to provide a key to our understanding of the evocativeness of much of visual art. As they explain, what artists essentially try to do (either consciously or unconsciously) "is not only capture the 'very essence' of something" (what Hindu artists call "the rasa"), but also to "amplify" it, much in the same way as caricaturists do when they simplify or exaggerate the features of their subjects, "in order to more powerfully activate the same neural mechanisms that would be activated by the original object."[34] Something similar might now also be said of Kubrick's films in which the psychological essence of the conveyed stories is significantly amplified in visual terms, and, as we shall see in the second part of this chapter, also in musical terms. Since this audio-visual amplification goes together with a recognition of image schematic patterns, and hence, pleasurable "rewarding" sensations, it could well explain why the discovery of the situational meanings in Kubrick's film (which rests on this pattern recognition), is overall experienced as exceptionally pleasurable and gratifying (in contrast to the more word-driven films).

Furthermore, Grodal has claimed that emotions also have a significant role in the second stage of the PECMA flow, the process of associating or matching the significant input to stored memories and schemata.[35] As he writes, these memories are stored with an "emotional tag or marker" that indicates how to relate to these significant forms. This stage can be seen as a top-down procedure insofar as this matching or reconstruction requires the "reconstruction of the past without much help from your senses."[36] Another top-down flow which is worth mentioning here is what Grodal refers to as "cueing attention."[37] Underlying this process is the neurological notion that only a fraction of the information will get focal attention. This priming and cueing of the viewer's attention can be considered as a top-down process in that this selection process is influenced by forms of implicit knowledge that occur "unconsciously and with seemingly little effort."[38] Thus, one can assume that the viewers' discovery of the situational meanings is not only mediated by patterns that are emotionally gratifying, but also by patterns that already have been selected for attention.

Having provided a general and tentative answer to the first dilemma, let us now turn toward a consideration of the role of music in Kubrick's films.

2. The bodily grounding of meaning in the film music of Kubrick's films

Although the films of Kubrick are widely acknowledged for their visual sense, they are equally well known for their use of music.[39] This has not to come as a surprise as music, in addition to pictures and acting, provides Kubrick with an additional means, and a powerful one at that, to confront the FILM AS LANGUAGE metaphor. From the powerful effects of Strauss's *Also sprach Zarathustra* in *2001*, and the beauteous "Ode an die Freude" from Beethoven's *9th Symphony* in *A Clockwork Orange* to Ligeti's piercing *Musica ricercata*, each excerpt was carefully chosen by the director himself to match the meanings of his films. As McQuiston has argued: "For Kubrick, a director who habitually compared filmmaking with music and devoted his characteristic scrutiny to music in his work, music is primary and generative to the films' themes."[40] This, in turn, begs the following question: if the music in his films is neither to be conceived of as postproduction afterthought nor as background music, but as the core to the films' meanings, as McQuiston argues, and these meanings can be to a significant extent understood in terms of mental causation, as this book shows, how then does this relationship actually come about? For instance, how is music capable of expressing mental states of characters non-verbally? As we have demonstrated in this book, images were able to convey meaning visually because they are capable of expressing the same kind of tools of embodied meaning-making (i.e., metaphor and metonymy) which in language were responsible for fleshing out the conceptual structure of mental causation. When we consider these tools with respect to music, however, we seem to be confronted with a dilemma that, at least from a theoretical perspective, seems to be more problematic and puzzling. If we say that the music in the films of Kubrick is an expression of the underlying themes, we silently take for granted that some external reference is the source of the music's expression (e.g., a character's emotion). This assumption, however, is problematic because it assumes, as Leman has pointed out, that music just like words or iconic images "relies on a reference model." [41] Music, however, is abstract and non-representational. In what sense, then, can we say that music expresses, or is expressive of a certain state of mind? As Baker, Paddison and Scruton write, this question is a philosophical one, and "reflects the profound uncertainty in contemporary aesthetics over the most important concept bequeathed to it by the Romantic movement."[42] The same uncertainty also arises when we extend the embodied view of meaning to music. If our understanding of abstract meaning is bodily grounded in such spatial patterns of sensory-motor experience as containment and motion, and music is not capable of expressing these spatial patterns due to its abstract nature, how then can we say of a piece of music that it is equally capable of expressing abstract meaning? In language as well as in moving pictures there is a reference model in which these patterns are signalled, the symbolic model and the iconic model, respectively. Music, however, lacks such a reference model, and therefore its status as a meaningful art form becomes questionable.

Before taking into consideration the embodied cognitive view on this issue, let us first say a few words about what has been for long time considered the dominant approach to the problem of meaning in music. It should not come as a surprise for the reader that this approach is informed by the same linguistic view of meaning that, as we have seen in the introduction, dominated the discussion of meaning in film. From the widespread preconception that only language can be meaningful, it follows that music like any other art form that is not substantially linguistic in nature, can only be meaningful if it is structured like a kind of language, "where passages in music are conceived as sentences, with individual notes or clusters of notes taken to be the equivalent of words."[43] In accordance with the FILM AS LANGUAGE metaphor, as outlined in the introduction to this book, we can call this projection of language onto music, the MUSIC AS LANGUAGE metaphor.[44] References to language in our theorizing about music are abundant as evidenced by such terms as "musical ideas, music sentences, propositions, punctuation, musical questions, and other quasi-linguistic phrases."[45] One merely has to cast a glance at the vast amount of literature on meaning in music to see how widespread this metaphor actually is. As Johnson observes: "One always has the sense that the key terms of linguistic theory gets twisted and stretched, sometimes to the point of breaking, as theorists try to make the MUSIC AS LANGUAGE metaphor work." [46]

We have already spent a considerable amount of time arguing why linguistic or grammatical approaches to meaning are no longer sustainable in the light of the embodied turn in cognitive science. Therefore, we will not elaborate further on this issue. Instead, we will immediately pick up where we left off above and try to explain, albeit from an embodied perspective this time, what music makes meaningful in view of the absence of any referential content. As we already have pointed out above, addressing this question entails, foremost, that we find a solution to the question as to how music can be meaningful if the bodily patterns that are responsible for structuring this meaning cannot be regarded as intrinsic properties of musical sounds. A possible resolution to this problem has been proposed by Johnson and other followers of the embodied (cognitive) theory of meaning such as Aksnes, Brower, Larson, McKee, Saslaw and Zbikowski, who all have argued that the answer is not to be found in the music itself, but within the embodied hearer who conceives and makes sense of the music.[47] As the argument goes, physical properties such as motion, gravity and containment may well not be properties of music, they nonetheless play a crucial role in our *understanding* and *conceptualization* of music. As Mckee put it, "not only do we perform music with and through our bodies but we also conceive of and analyse music, whether we realize it or not, with and through our bodies."[48] This reference to spatial phenomena becomes especially clear in our discourse about music which speaks of such terms (as quoted from Walton): "'ascending' and 'descending' motives, 'thick' and 'thin' textures, 'strain' and 'repose,' 'conflict' and 'concord,' 'movement,' 'return,' 'destinations,' 'renewal,' 'soaring' and 'whispering' melodies, 'throbbing' rhythms, etc."[49] These verbal metaphors are not merely colorful ways of describing music's formal or acoustic properties. Rather, they are verbal manifestations of conceptual metaphors that result from cross-domain mappings of image schemas onto music. Following McKee we may list four such metaphors as in table 5.1.[50]

Table 5.1. Elaborations of four conceptual metaphors based on musical descriptive practices (after McKee).

Conceptual metaphor	*Entailments*
MUSIC IS MOTION	Music is purposeful motion operating within a field of musical forces, gravity being the most important. Music moves at different speeds. Motion follows a path or trajectory with beginning points and goals.
PITCH RELATIONSHIPS ARE RELATIONSHIPS IN VERTICAL SPACE	Musical pitches, events, and motions are plotted on a vertical axis. Scale-degree 1 is the *Grundton* (ground tone), the bottom floor of diatonic pitch space.
MUSIC IS CONTAINED WITHIN BOUNDARIES	Motion occurs within bounded spaces with beginnings, middles, and ends. Gestures, motives, phrases, sections, and pieces contain musical content. Typically, a tonal work will begin in one key and, at some point, modulate out of that key and into another key. Triads may be prolonged resulting in a prolongational area. Music and instruments have registral boundaries.
MUSIC HAS WEIGHT	Tonic is a gravitational field to which other pitches/chords are attracted. Ascending motion requires more effort than descending motion. Cadences (from the latin cadere, "to fall") tend to fall into a point of repose. Lower pitches are heavier than higher pitches. Meter is a gravitational field in which downbeats attract contextually stable events. Downbeats are heavier than upbeats.

While it lies beyond the scope of this book to discuss the entailments of each metaphor in detail, which would require knowledge about such complex notions as pitch, chord, scale, and so on, it nevertheless gives the reader a general sense of the pervasive role of metaphor in our thinking about music. Not surprisingly, the primary source domain that people use to make sense of music is also the source domain that we resort to when making sense of other target domains (including mental causation), namely motion. This gives rise to what is perhaps the principle metaphor for conceptualizing music, the MUSIC IS MOTION metaphor.[51] According to this metaphor, changes of states are understood in terms of a motion schema; musical states in terms of bounded regions or locations, and difference between states in terms of a distance between locations. Another important source domain is that of gravity. We already encountered in chapter 3 how Arnheim applied the notion of physical weight to visual perception. In one of his later, lesser known works, he extended this idea also to music. As he writes, "moving upward on the pitch scale carries the connotation of a victorious liberation from weight, whereas descent is experienced as a passive giving in to weight."[52] Inspired by Arnheim, among others, the musical theorist Steve Larson developed this idea of musical forces more elaborately in his book *Musical Forces: Motion, Metaphor, and Meaning in Music*. The author claims that musical forces "affect our perception of both melody and rhythm, by analogy to our embodied (and cultural) understanding of physical forces."[53] Through the unconscious mappings of these and other image schemas, we are able to create, as McKee writes "an imaginary world in which we hear music as a transmutation of physiological impulses, as gesture."[54] Although these image schemas are strictly speaking not to be found in the music itself, they are nonetheless "experientially real and essential properties of our understanding of music."[55]

It is here that one begins to see how the problem of expressiveness might be resolved with respect to music. As Walton already foreshadowed in his article on music and meaning, if our language about music necessary involves reference to spatial phenomena, then this fact will be "welcomed by those who hope to find a subject matter for music."[56] Music is able to express meaning about something other than itself because our embodied understanding of the music is structurally similar to our embodied understanding of the meaning. For instance, in his own analysis of the hymn topic in classical music, McKee has demonstrated convincingly how music is capable of depicting spiritual states ("a sense of walking in the spirit") through the use of the popular chord progression known as I-V7-I. As he writes, this progression, when used with other attributes of the hymn topic, is apt to depict spiritual states, because "its conceptual structure closely correlates to our embodied understanding of exalted states of consciousness."[57] He refers in this regard to such image schemas as VERTICALITY, GRAVITY, and LIGHT (brightness/darkness) which are all central to our understanding of spiritual states. These states, he writes, are commonly conceptualized as "weightless, unaffected by the force of gravity, and bright, radiant and illuminated."[58] The structural similarities between the two domains thus allow one to easily map the domain of meaning (i.e., spirituality) onto the domain of music.

Something similar can now be said about the music used in Kubrick's films. The viewer experiences the latter as meaningful (e.g., as capable of expressing the concepts of mental causation), because the bodily means that he or she draws upon to make sense of this music are structurally similar to the bodily means that he or she uses in ordinary life to make sense of the meaning, the same bodily means that were also used to flesh out the referential meanings visually.

As to the question how this attribution of expressiveness to music is achieved, we may turn once more to the importance of mirror mechanisms inside of the perceiver. Marc Leman in this regard speaks of a process of "corporeal imitation." As he writes, "in corporeal imitation, moving sonic forms (the changing physical energy) are fully taken into the body, and via the body they are turned into action-oriented precepts that associate with expressions."[59] The author regards this process as a sufficient source for the induction of expression. In other words, for Leman the search for a possible source of this expression or the possible intended meaning (e.g., an emotion) is only optional, not necessary. He backs his claim by inviting us to think about a suite by J.S. Bach, which, despite its relation to dance, might be characterized as abstract. As such, it does not express nor imitate something specific. Nevertheless, many listeners attribute a very concrete expressiveness to the music when articulating it. As he concludes, "listeners can engage in different degrees of involvement with music without having to draw upon a reference or to know what this music expresses."[60]

In this book, however, we are not dealing with music as such, but with *film music* or *musical soundtracks*, that is, music that was carefully selected by the director to "influence the interpretation of images that they accompany."[61] Since these visuals provide the viewer with the cues from which he or she construes the films' narratives, it might be assumed that the image schemas that we use to make sense of the musical sounds, are not there for their own sake, but there to be linked to our understanding of the situational meanings of the films. Since the latter depends considerably on the structure of mental causation, as demonstrated in this book, we may well ask ourselves to what degree music contributes to the expression of such concepts as feelings and emotions.[62] Burt suggested something similar when he wrote that film music has "the power to open the frame of reference to a story and to reveal its inner life in a way that could not have been as fully articulated in any other way."[63]

Moreover, the visuals that go together with the music are also referential. This entails that the image schemas that we map onto the music (e.g., musical movement), when hearing it, may well correlate with the image schemas, as physically instantiated in the visuals (e.g., visual movement). Juan Chattah in similar terms calls this correlation, "structural congruence."[64] This gives rise to such conceptual metaphors as PITCH FREQUENCY IS MOTION IN VERTICAL SPACE according to which "upward motion correlates with increasing pitch frequency, and downward motion correlates with decreasing pitch frequency."[65] There is probably no better way to illustrate this "musico-visual alliance," as McQuiston coins it, than with the famous *Blue Danube* sequence from *2001* in which the sonic qualities of a Viennese dance waltz are carefully aligned with breathtaking images of spinning satellites and moving spacecrafts.[66] As McQuiston observes, "among the first clues as to this alliance is the strong suggestion of ascent; the effortless, ascending arpeggios of the melody in the introduction each conclude with one note that remains afloat, almost always the highest pitch of each phrase. These high, held notes create an open feeling and keep the melody suspended with respect to its key (the ground)."[67] A point of harmonization, then, can be created when the VERTICALITY schema, as mapped onto these high notes, accompanies visual images in which the same feeling of ascent is suggested. As we have seen in chapter 3, a strong sense of rising might be provoked on-screen by visual compositions that instantiate the HIGH-LOW schema in such dynamic patterns of containment as ENTRY and INCLUSION. A powerful visual manifestation of the latter is shown in figure 5.2. While the highest pitch carried by cellos and horns is hearable, the camera slowly moves upward, away from earth (O1) and toward the long spacecraft that is entering the frame overhead (O2).

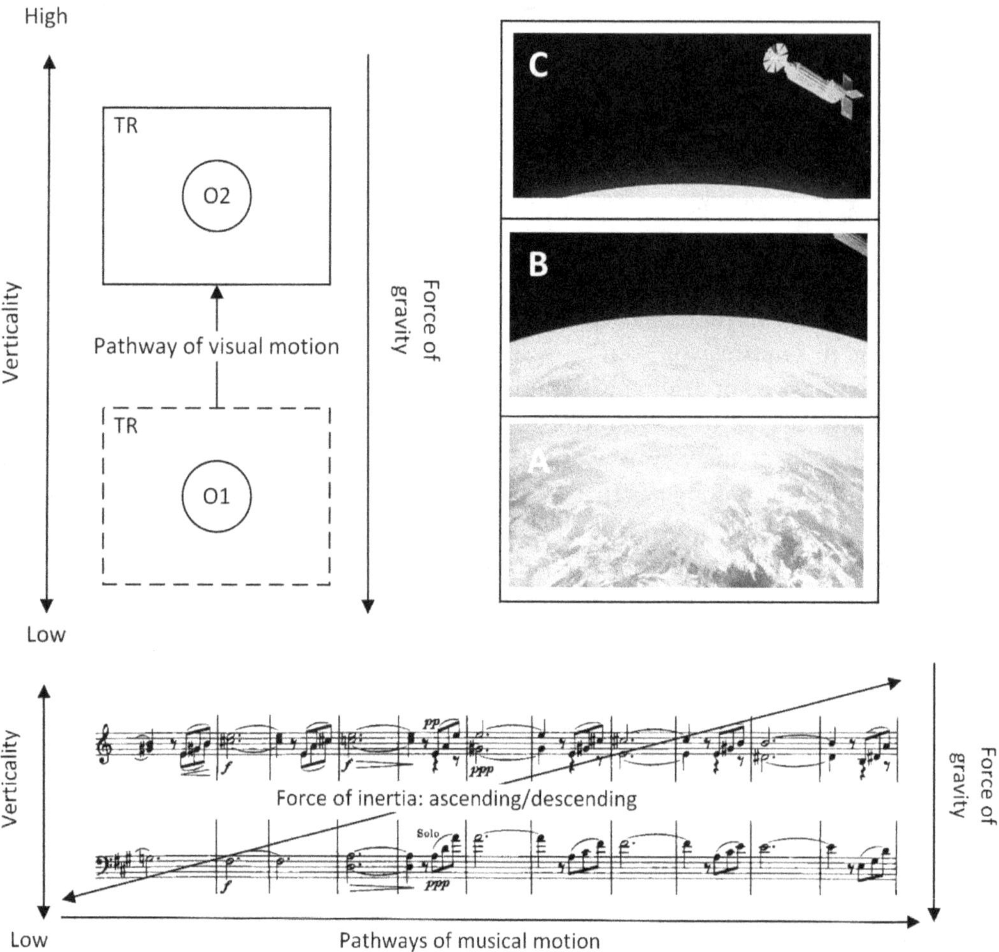

Figure 5.2. Musico-visual alliance in *2001*: ascending INCLUSION as accompanied by Johan Strauss's *The Blue Danube* (sheet music excerpts for horns and cello, respectively).

The function of film music, however, is not limited to enhancing on-screen visual movement. As stated, Kubrick, like many other narrative filmmakers of narrative cinema, carefully selects the music on the basis of whether or not our embodying understanding of it mirrors our embodied understanding of the inner psychological states of characters. Chattah refers to this as "semantic congruence" to contrast it with the earlier notion of "structural congruence."[68] In what follows, we will examine the relationship between film music and the conceptual structure of mental causation more closely by considering the expressive role of music in three scenes as they were already analysed in visual terms in the previous chapters. They concern Moon-Watcher's epiphany scene from *2001* (Richard Strauss's *Also sprach Zarathustra*), the scene from *The Shining* in which Danny enters Jack's bedroom, approaches and talks to his destabilizing father on the bed (Béla Bartók's *Music for Strings, Percussion and Celesta*), and lastly, Bill's emotional breakdown at the end of *Eyes Wide Shut* (György Ligeti's *Musica ricercata*).

2001: A Space Odyssey

It is not difficult to see how the opening melody to Richard Strauss's tone poem *Also sprach Zarathustra*, a slow giant of a fanfare, fits well with Moon-Watcher's moment of epiphany as well as with the later transformation of Bowman into the Starchild at the end of the film. The title refers to Friedrich Nietzsche's eponymous work by the same name in which the German philosopher put forward the idea that man, as evolved from apes, has the potential to surpass himself and thus become what he calls an "Übermensch" or "Superman." It is precisely this idea of evolution that Strauss was inspired by when he wrote the music. As the composer himself put it:

> I did not intend to write philosophical music or portray Nietzsche's great work musically. I meant rather to convey in music an idea of the evolution of the human race from its origin, through the various phases of development, religious as well as scientific, up to Nietzsche's idea of the Übermensch.[69]

What is it about Strauss's music, then, that allows one to hear it as an expression of intellectual evolution? Likewise, we may argue that the opening melody is appropriate because our embodied metaphorical understanding of it is similarly structured to our embodied metaphoric conceptualization of evolution, as also manifested visually in the film. To clarify this point, let us have a look at the structure that is responsible for conveying this idea.[70] This structure consists of three identical, ascending statements of a brass melody with each statement containing three elemental pitches, coming in intervals of a fifth and octave, as C–G–C (also known as the "Nature" motif or the "Dawn" motif).[71] The first statement, as shown in figure 5.3, comes right after the appearance of the celestial alignment with the monolith and conjures with the image of Moon-Watcher as he suspends his instinctive search for food (see figure 3.39*D*). The mapping of the VERTICALITY schema onto the music resonates in the image of Moon-Watcher lifting up his head and directing his gaze toward the bones in front of him (cfr. THE HEAD FOR THINKING metonymy). This suggestion of ascending motion, however, is counterbalanced at the end when the phrase lands on a minor chord, as if the music, through this downward gesture wants to suggest that Moon-Watcher has not yet "arrived" at the idea, or solved the "riddle" as McQuiston describes it, thereby referring to "The World Riddle," a label that Arthur Hann ascribed to the opening theme in a guide that Strauss himself agreed on.[72] There is still the force of gravity holding him down, preventing him from capturing the idea in the fullest. As McQuiston writes, "the major chord, by virtue of associations accorded to it in Western music, may sound like an optimistic revision of the answer to the first phrase, yet the riddle remains unsolved."[73]

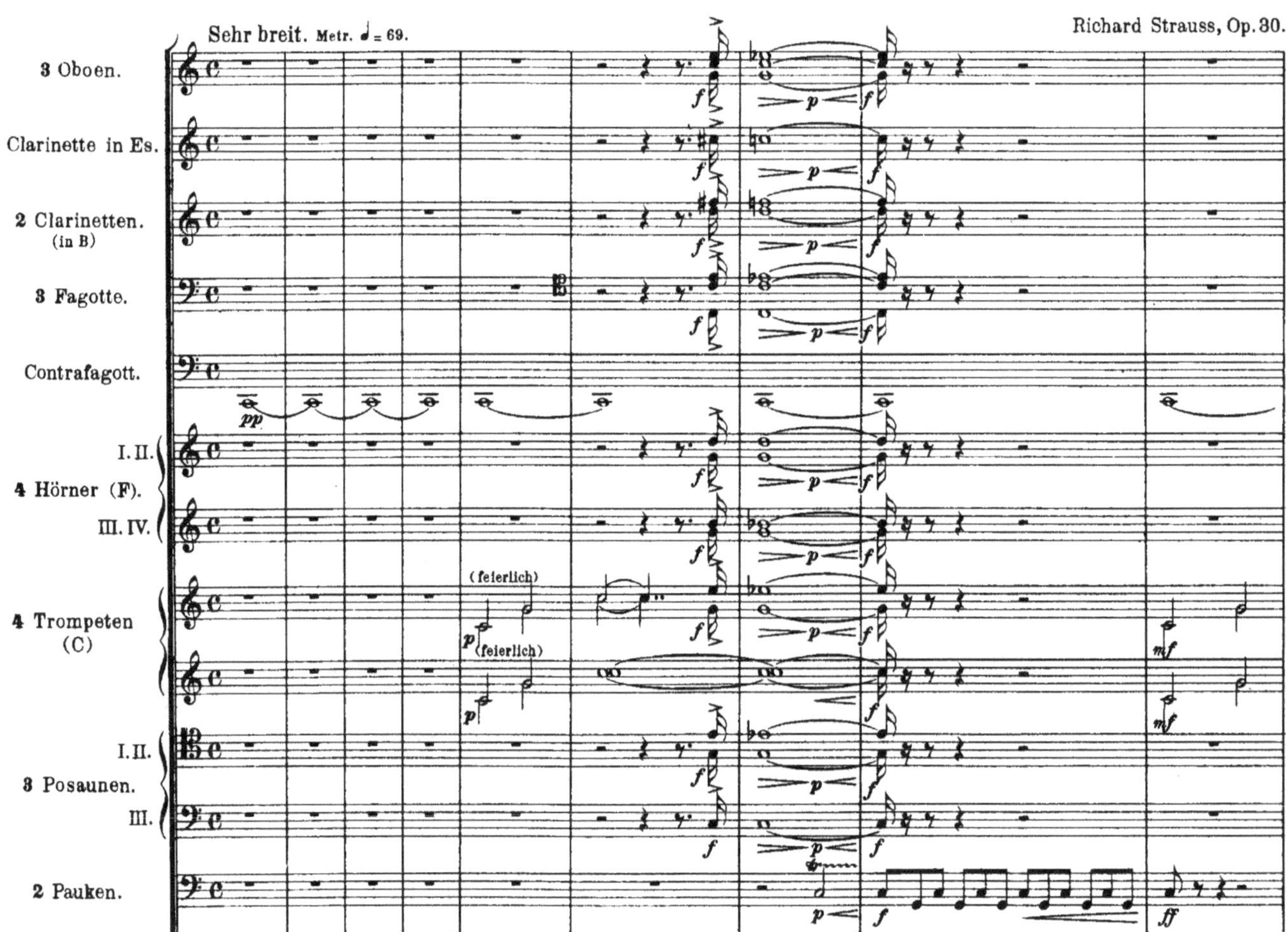

Figure 5.3. First statement and beginning of second statement of Richard Strauss's *Also sprach Zarathustra* as in Moon-Watcher's epiphany scene from *2001*: the riddle remains unsolved.

The second entrance of the theme, as shown separately over figures 5.3 and 5.4, conjures with the image of Moon-Watcher as he picks up and inspects one of the bones (see figure 3.39*F*). The melody continues to convey the sense of rising as echoed in the first statement, yet, this time, the phrase does not land on a minor chord, but on a major chord. The cadence pushes upward rather than downward, thus fostering the idea that something momentous is about to happen.[74]

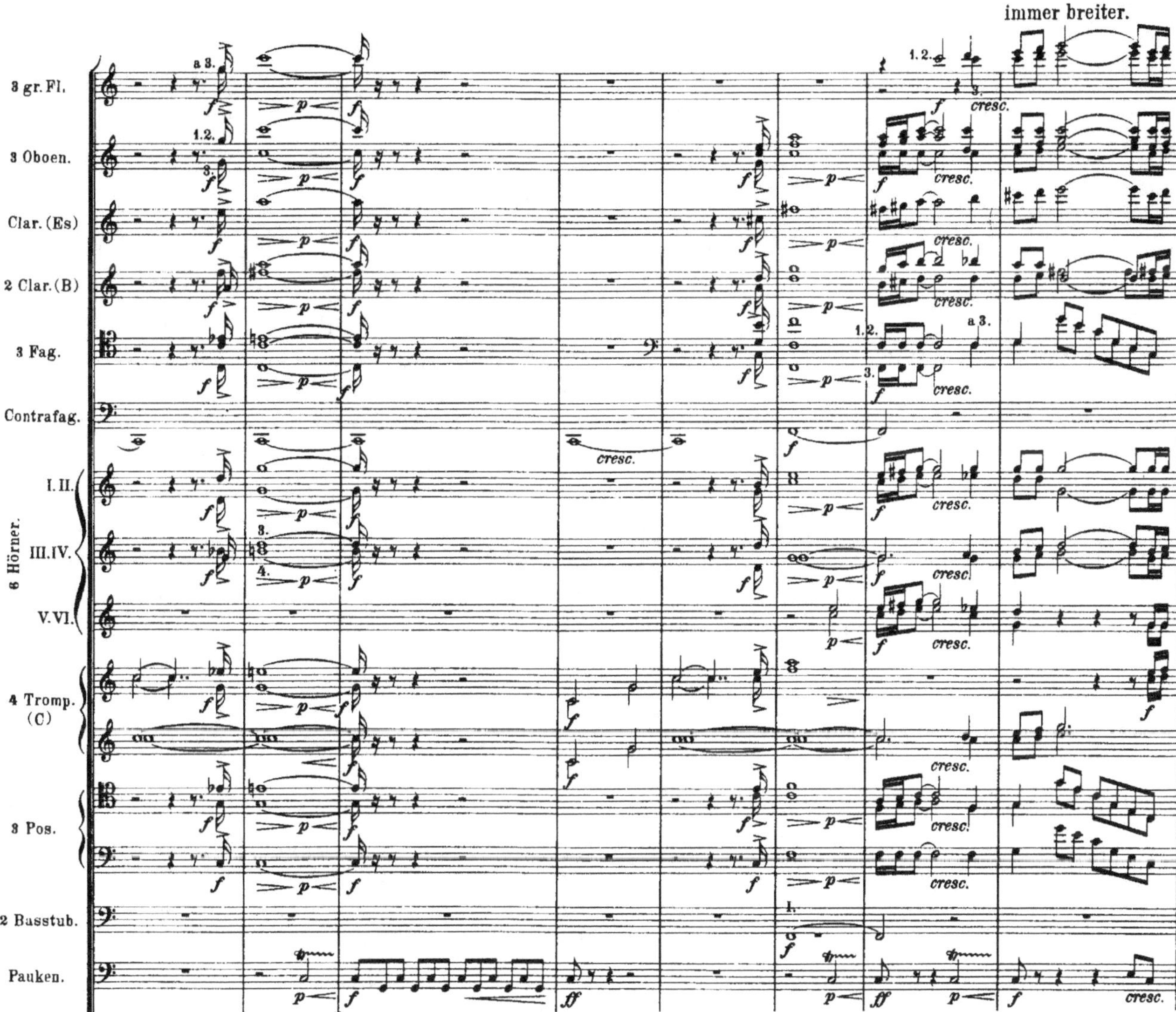

Figure 5.4. Continuation of second statement and unfoldment of the third statement of Richard Strauss's *Also sprach Zarathustra* as used in Moon-Watcher's epiphany scene from *2001*: the riddle is solved.

When, finally, Moon-Watcher stands nearly erect, using both hands to wield his club against the pile of bones, the melody reaches its final resolution. The third statement culminates in a grand musical gesture that "sticks the landing" and triumphantly shouts, "Ta-daaaa!," at the same time as the viewer sees Moon-Watcher crashing the bone onto the head of the skeleton (see figure 3.40).[75] As McQuiston writes, this last cadence "seems to be 'right' way to end," because it "allows the music to move not only to a new key (from C to F) but also into a more fully developed and grand cadence that seems to energize the entire orchestra. As the last and most grandiose, this third statement carries connotations of progress or breakthrough by virtue of the musical topics it employs."[76]

The Shining

The wordless scene from *2001* was dominated by an intimate liaison between music and image. Our second scene under investigation, by contrast, provides us with an example in which the music does not so much interact with the visual action, as there is almost none to observe with exception of Nicholson's facial performance inside the predominantly visually static scene, but with the dialogue. It involves the moment in *The Shining* when Danny enters the frame from behind the set by opening the door that gives entrance to the bedroom where Jack is residing, as shown in figure 4.28, whereupon he approaches and talks with his destabilizing father. Although Kubrick initially did not want any music to this scene, he ultimately agreed on using the first forty-five bars of the third movement of Béla Bartok's music for *Strings, Percussion and Celesta* (1936), an idea that was suggested to him by his music editor Gordon Stainforth. McQuiston sees this as comparable to the music editing history of the iconic shower scene from *Psycho* (1960) where Alfred Hitchcock similarly (and wisely) dropped his initial plan of using no music at all in favour of Bernard Hermann's screeching string music.[77] John McCabe has described the effect of Bartók's third movement aptly in terms of a sense of "remote feeling" and "inhuman iciness," and the "touches of frozen humanity."[78] Undoubtedly, Kubrick must have regarded these musical features as particularly suitable for expressing the abstract psychological level of the scene where the narrative demands for an embodiment of the omnipresent but unseen evil that is lurking behind the banality of the conversation. Indeed, taken the dialogue in isolation the scene might even look as seemingly normal. It is only when we add Bartók's music to it, in conjunction with Nicholson's "worn-out" performance, that the scene reaches a level of psychological uncanniness rarely unequalled in cinematic history. As Mullen writes: "Were it not for the eerie music, what follows would seem tender at first. The camera cuts to a two-shot of Danny and Jack, who continues to caress his hair. Imperceptibly the dialogue . . . becomes more strained, each phrase becoming more charged with menace as Jack's expression becomes more and more calculating and his tone more alarming."[79] Barham already did a very good job in diagramming the interaction between the music, the visuals, and the dialogue. With his permission we are reproducing it here in figures 5.6 and 5.7.[80] The first three shots of a total of six shots have already been discussed in the previous chapter (see figure 4.12*G-I* for the first shot, figure 4.28*A-C* for the second shot and figure 4.28*D-F* for the third shot which is identical to the fifth shot). The longest shot and hence the largest part of Bartok's music, however, is reserved, as Barham's diagrams show, for the fourth shot which is also identical to the last shot, and which centres on a medium shot of Jack and Danny on the bed (see figure 5.5).

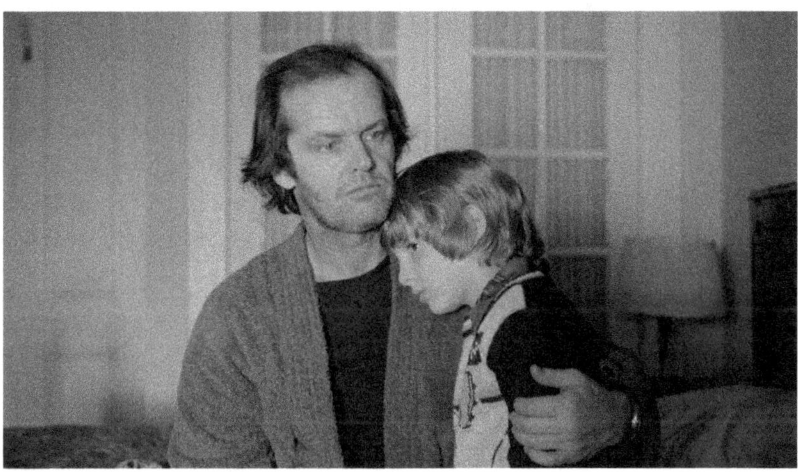

Figure 5.5. Aligning dialogue and music in *The Shining*: Danny and Jack are having a talk on the bed as we hear the third movement from Bartók's *Music for Strings, Percussion and Celesta*.

As with many other scenes of the film, one would expect that the images were predominantly choreographed to the music, that for instance, Bartók's music was dictating Nicholson's performance. This myth, however, which is still pervasive among many film scholars, as Barham has pointed out, has been undermined by Stainforth himself, who in a personal communication with Barham, has stated that "it was all done completely the other way round."[81]

The following significant observations can now be made with reference to Barham's diagrams. First, there is the swish-pan that embodies Danny's perception of Jack through an exclusion of the PR in favour of an inclusion of the OP (see figure 4.12*G-I*), which concurs almost precisely with the "first viola demisemiquaver" or "thirty second note." A brief moment, but a noteworthy one for it is the only movement to discern in the total duration of four minutes and thirteen seconds that the scene lasts. Second, there is the lack of energy and vitality in which the scene is immersed. According to Barham this lack of movement, which is also echoed in Jack's monotone voice that speaks in a manner as if he is mentally drained and "empty," is matched at the musical level by "the pace, volume and relative inertness of the score's kinetic content, often underpinned by extended pedals, and later by ostinato."[82] Third, despite this lack of liveliness, there is nevertheless a clear trajectory to discern within the dialogue and Jack's performance that runs from "seeming inanity towards the suggestion of violence." Fascinatingly, this emotional trajectory follows a succession of upwardly and downwardly inflected and repeated questions and answers that are all aligned, as Barham observes, "with changes in the music's texture, degree of linearity and intermediate moments of climax."[83] For instance, when Danny first inquires "Dad?," the balance is distorted by "an upward glissando that breaks the pattern in the strings and upsets the atmosphere."[84] Similarly, the pivotal scene-altering question, "You would never hurt mummy and me, would you?," is echoed by string glissandi suggesting parallel directed motion. Subsequent questions such as "What do you mean?"

and "Did your mother say that to you?" are all aligned with, to quote Barham, "piano and celeste chords at the beginnings of bars 31, 21, and 33, which interrupt the prevailing linearity of the musical activity and pulse."[85] The tenderness of what should be an emotionally positive and reassuring linguistic token of a father's love for his child (the linguistic meaning, "I love you more than anything else in the whole world and I'd never do anything to hurt you" as uttered by Jack at the end of the scene), is even completely altered and reconceptualized by our embodied (negative) understanding of the music, which Barham, in more technical terms, describes as a "passage from bar 35 of alternating 'black-note/white-note' pentatonic ostinato (rapidly covering ten of the twelve notes of the chromatic pitch spectrum) on celeste, together with piano and harp glissandi and intensifying string tremolandi."[86]

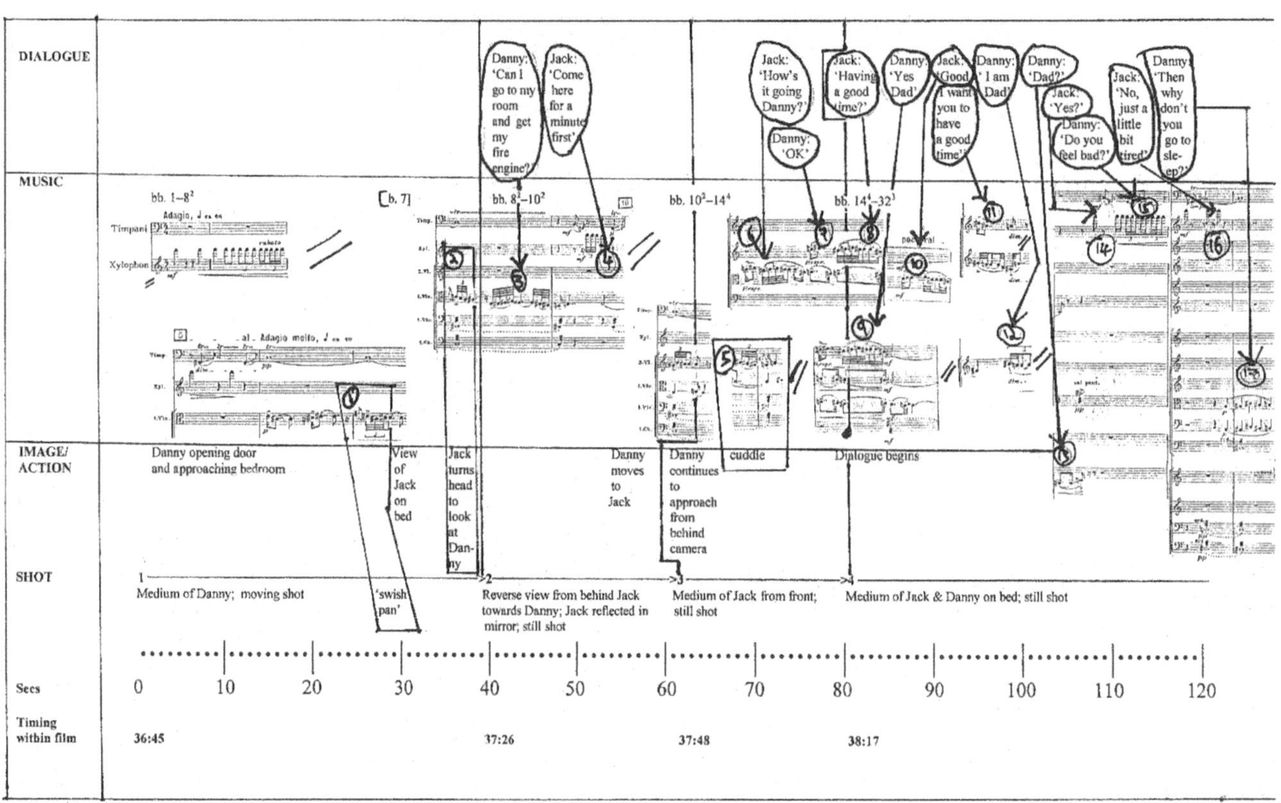

Figure 5.6. The use of the third movement from Bartók's *Music for Strings, Percussion and Celesta* in *The Shining* (part one). Used by permission of Jeremy Barham.

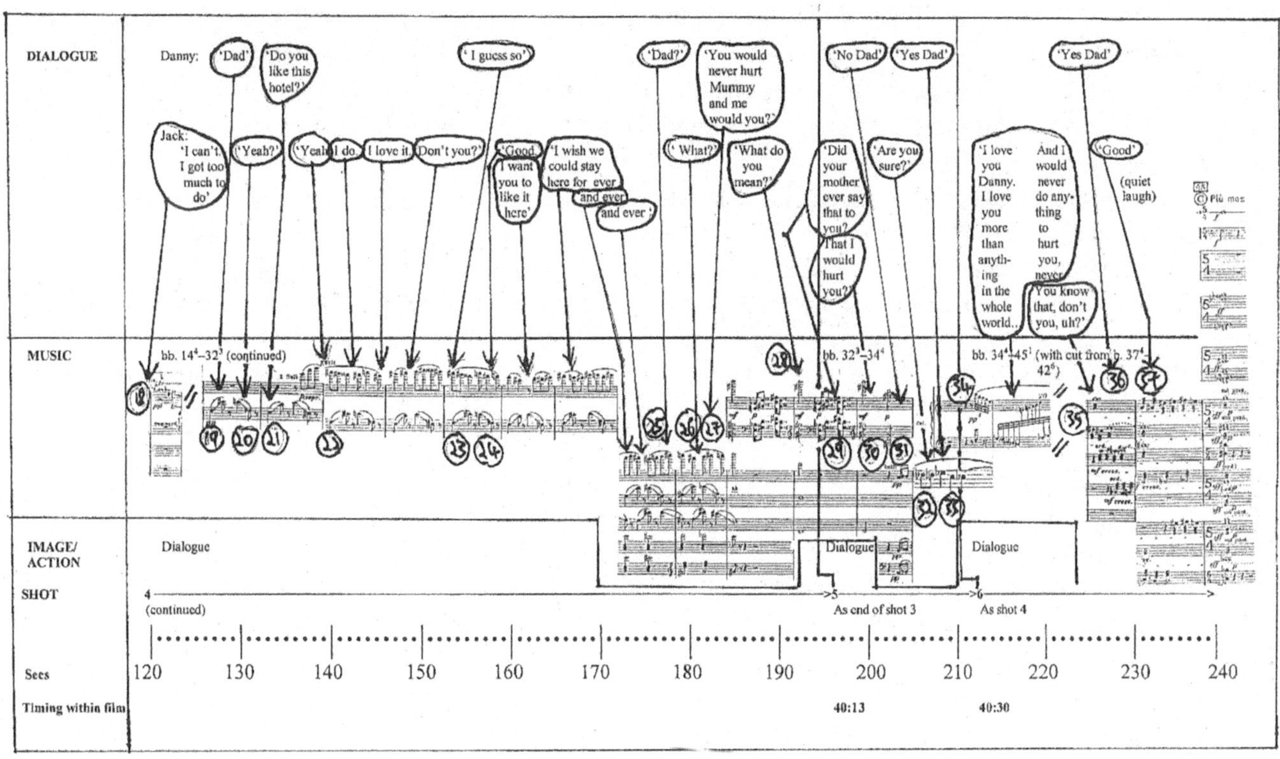

Figure 5.7. The use of the third movement from Bartók's *Music for Strings, Percussion and Celesta* in *The Shining* (part two). Used by permission of Jeremy Barham.

Eyes Wide Shut

Let us end this book appropriately by analysing the music to a scene which is not only one of the very last scenes of the filmmaker's oeuvre, but also one of the finest cinematic renderings of mental causation ever put on screen. It concerns Bill's confession scene as already discussed in visual terms in the previous chapter (see figure 4.20). As a musical accompaniment to this scene, Kubrick decided to use Ligeti's second movement of the eleven movements that together constitute his *Musica ricercata*.[87] This work, which the Hungarian composer composed in the 1950s under Stalinist oppression, is intriguing from a musical point of view in that each movement is limited to only a number of pitch classes, with each subsequent movement containing exactly one more pitch class than the last. The three pitches out of which the second movement is formed are E-sharp, F-sharp, and G. The first half of the piece is dominated by a heavy alternation between the first two pitches as they appear in the low register. This semitone is the main theme of the piece. After a pause, near the middle of the piece, the G appears as a stark high pitch. The pianist is instructed to play this note with both fingers at once. Once the G is introduced, the pianist is ordered to gradually increase the tempo of the pitch until he or she repeats it as dense as possible (the "knife in Stalin's heart," as Ligeti called it). The weight of the music is pushed down again as the main theme returns in the low register, this time louder. There is a menacing quality to it. Ligeti marks this section intense. The main theme and the high Gs are heard together in an unmetered tremolo. The repeated Gs fade away and the main theme eventually resolves into silence as the movement ends.

A close look at the interplay between these distinctive compositional features and the story of mental causation as narrated visually in the last bedroom scene (see figure 4.20), reveals rich and consistent connections. As we have seen in the previous chapter, this story consists of a causal succession of three key events: a perceptual one (Bill sees the mask), an emotional one (the mounting increase of emotional intensity inside Bill as a result of seeing the mask), and a behavioral one (Bill starts to cry and vows to his wife to tell everything).

The first G, as shown in figure 5.8, occurs right after a pause in the texture of the music and is perfectly synchronized with the image of Bill turning his head toward the mask on the pillow off-screen (see figure 4.20*A*), a swish-pan that bears a striking resemblance to the one from *The Shining* as analysed above. The alarming sound corresponds to Bill's panic of seeing it. Chattah refers to this as the PSYCHOLOGICAL TENSION IS LOUDNESS metaphor according to which "soft sounds correspond to a relaxed state and loud sounds correspond to a tense state."[88] The high G is immediately followed by the whip pan that excludes Bill in exchange for an inclusion of the mask (see figure 4.20*B*). The camera moves as fast as the G sounded loud.

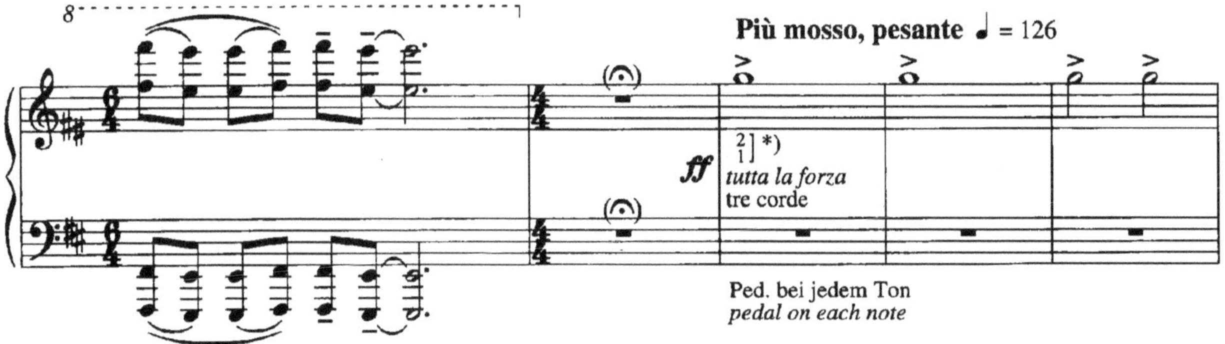

Figure 5.8. The appearance of the high note G in Ligeti's *Musica ricercata*, as aligned with the image of Bill seeing the mask on the pillow (*Eyes Wide Shut*).

The accelerated repetition of this note that immediately comes after the alarming signal of the G, voices the increase of emotional intensity that is taking place inside of Bill as a result of him seeing the mask (see figure 5.9). This increase of intensity is echoed at the visual level as Bill is no longer filmed in long shot, but in medium shot, a visual manifestation of a conceptual metaphor that we have identified earlier as the INCREASE OF EMOTIONAL INTENSITY IS INCREASE OF SUBSTANCE IN A CONTAINER metaphor (see figure 4.20*C*).

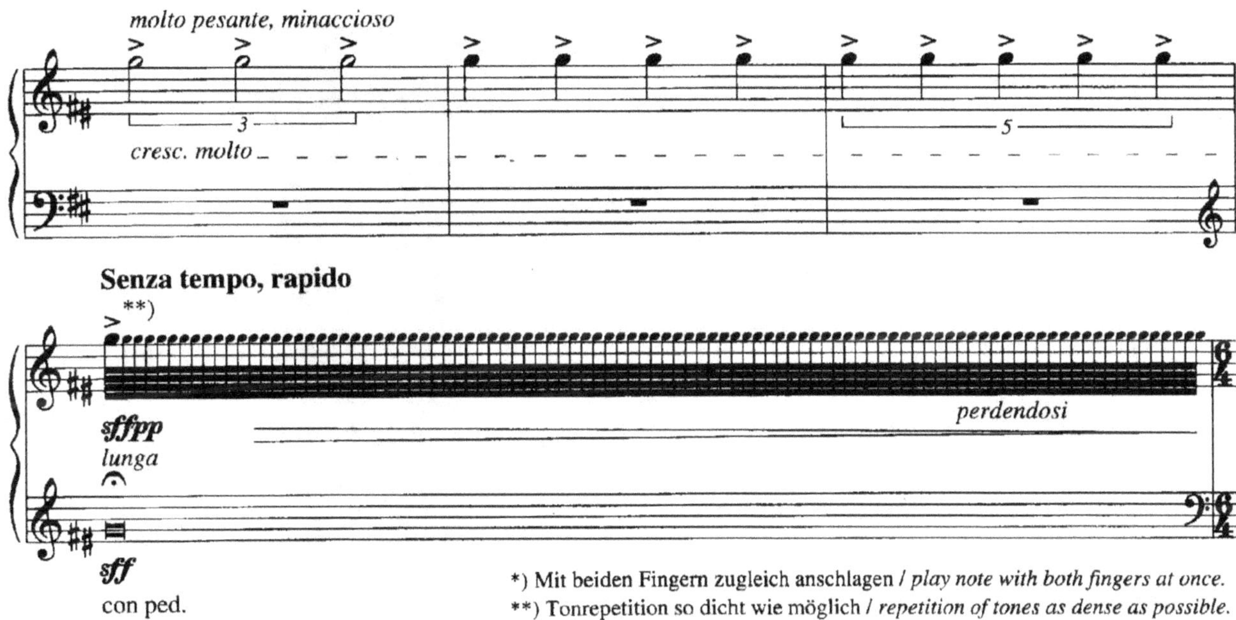

Figure 5.9. The repetition of the G note in Ligeti's *Musica ricercata*, as aligned with the increase of emotional intensity inside Bill as inflicted upon him by his perception of the mask (*Eyes Wide Shut*).

The return of the lower main theme can be heard precisely as Bill lowers himself into the frame from the top edge (see figure 4.20*E-F-G*). The direction of the ENTRY path into the frame is congruent with the downward pull of the force of gravity. In a way this can be seen as standing opposite to *The Blue Danube* example as discussed above, or the *Utrenja* example from chapter 3 (see figure 3.12), where the dynamic patterns of INCLUSION and ENTRY, respectively, were contesting the pull of gravity, thus evoking a sense of "floating in space" and a sense of "triumph," respectively. The visuals as well as the music are in perfect alignment with our embodied understanding of intense negative emotions. They both suggest a heightened sense of weight and heaviness that is strongly correlated with feelings of sadness. The feeling of guilt is pulling Bill down to the ground (see figure 5.10).

When, subsequently, the high Gs continue to pierce through the main theme (figure 5.11), the tension builds up and the increase of emotionality reaches its culmination point. Bill loses his control over his emotions and he starts to cry (see figure 4.20*I*).

When Bill finally vows to tell everything and decides to keep no secrets from his wife the piercing Gs are gone and we can only hear the semitone music which now fulfils, as McQuiston pointed out, the "role of releasing tension" (see figure 5.12).[89] The scene reaches its moment of truth and resolution, not of "the unsolved mysteries in the plot, but of Bill's solitariness in his bizarre adventures."[90] As discussed in the previous chapter, this openness from Bill toward his wife is expressed at the visual level by the camera including Alice into the frame (of Bill) (see figure 4.20*L*).

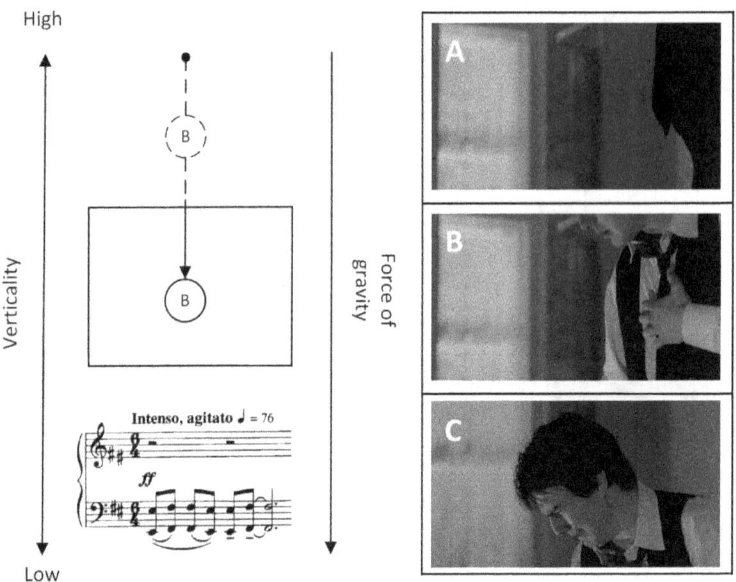

Figure 5.10. The return of the lower main theme in Ligeti's *Musica ricercata*, as aligned with Bill's downward entry into the frame (*Eyes Wide Shut*).

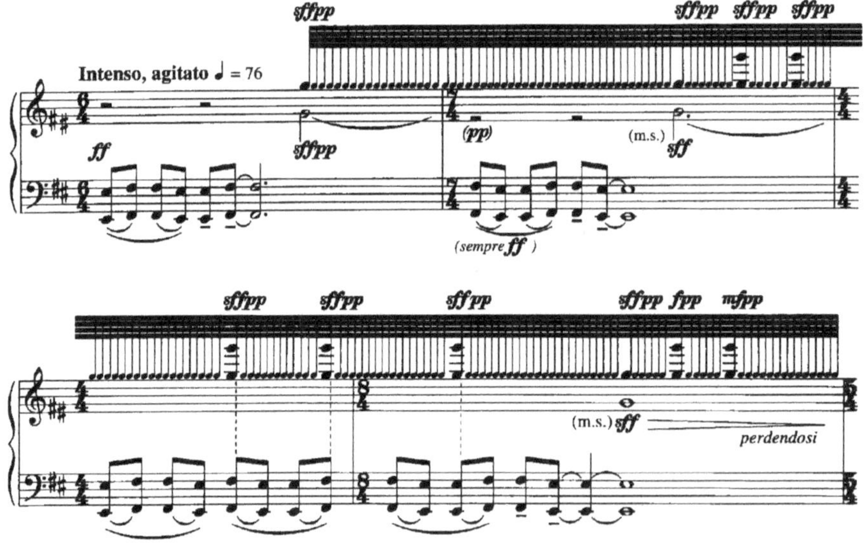

Figure 5.11. The high Gs pierce through the semitones in Ligeti's *Musica ricercata*, as aligned with Bill's emotional collapse (*Eyes Wide Shut*).

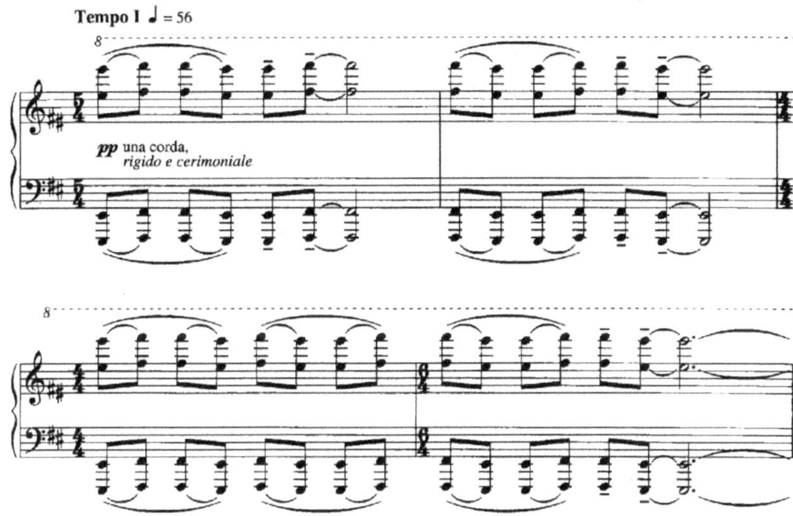

Figure 5.12. The disappearance of the high Gs and the release of tension in Ligeti's *Musica ricercata*, as aligned with Bill's vow to confess everything to Alice (*Eyes Wide Shut*).

Conclusion

In this concluding chapter, we set ourselves the task of addressing two theoretical problems. The first one had its roots in the distance between the film and the film viewer. How is the audience able to discover the meanings of a film given the fact that they are not performing the bodily actions that lie at the heart of the conveyance of those meanings? Resolving this issue is important, for an understanding of the situations of a film contributes considerably to our experiences of narrative absorption and suspense, and hence our enjoyment of watching films. A scientific argument for overcoming this problem was found in the neurological concept of embodied simulation which allowed one to transcend the distance between "doing" and "observing." Viewers are capable of grasping the concepts of Kubrick's films because simulation processes inside the viewer allow them to activate the bodily sources that were used to flesh out those concepts visually, and that are the same ones that viewers resort to when reasoning about them in their day-to-day verbal interactions. Although embodied simulation provides a promising lens to examine this issue, it should be stressed, however, that the viewer's discovery of the meanings is most likely to be influenced by other factors as well, notably emotions and top-down processes. All these aspects (and their relations) should be taken into consideration in order to come to a fuller picture of the problem of how viewers are able to become aware of the films' intended referential meanings. The second problem originated from the distance between meaning and music. How is music able to express something given the fact that music does not refer to anything unlike words and images? Following an embodied cognitive approach to music, we located the answer not so much in the music itself, but in the embodied listener who makes sense of the music. Physical properties such as motion, gravity and containment may well not be signalled in music, they nonetheless play a crucial role in our understanding and conceptualization of music. It is precisely in this sense that it can be said that music expresses meaning because our embodied understanding of the former correlates to our embodied understanding of the latter. Moreover, if this music accompanies images in which the same embodied meaning is fleshed out in visual terms, the result is a *gesamtkunstwerk* in which both levels of expression interact for the purpose of conveying the meaning non-verbally. This was shown to be brought into perfection in Kubrick's films where the music, like the images they accompany, serve the concepts of the overall narrative form.

Notes

1. Kubrick, "Words and Movies," 14.
2. Tan, "A Psychology of the Film," 10.
3. Hakemulder et al., *Narrative Absorption.*
4. Bálint and Tan, "'It Feels Like There are Hooks Inside My Chest,'" 63–88.
5. Ibid., 76–77.
6. Ibid., 65. For a discussion, see also Tan, et al., "Into Film," 97–118.
7. Bálint, Kuijpers and Doicaru, "The Effect of Suspense Structure," 177–198.
8. Carroll, "Paradox of Suspense," 74.
9. Doicaru, "Gripped by Movies," 34–71.
10. Ibid., 37.
11. Ibid., 37.
12. Theoretical accounts which treat uncertainty as conditional for suspense include, among others, Carroll, "Towards a Theory of Film Suspense," 94–117; Gerrig, *Experiencing Narrative Worlds*; Ortony, Clore and Collins, *The Cognitive Structure of Emotions*; and Walton, *Mimesis as Make-believe.*
13. The condition of uncertainty, in turn, has led many scholars to raise the "paradox of suspense" or the phenomenon of "anomalous suspense." This paradox is based on the contention that viewers can still experience suspense even after repeated viewings of the same film. In that case the uncertainty principle would no longer hold as the viewer is already familiar with the story's outcome. For discussions of this paradox, see among others, Carroll, "The Paradox of Suspense," 254–270; Gerrig, "Is There a PARADOX of Suspense?," 168–174; Mag Uidhir, "The Paradox of Suspense Realism," 161–171; Smuts, "The Desire-frustration Theory of Suspense," 282; and Yanal, "The Paradox of Suspense," 146–158.
14. This part is a recapitulation of the argument as elaborated in Coëgnarts, "Cinema and the Embodied Mind."
15. Gallese and Sinigaglia, "What Is So Special About Embodied Simulation?," 518.
16. Gallese, Fadiga, Fogassi and Rizzolatti, "Action Recognition in the Premotor Cortex," 593–609; Rizzolatti, Fadiga, Gallese and Fogassi, "Premotor Cortex and the Recognition of Motor Actions," 131–141.
17. Gallese and Sinigaglia, "What Is So Special," 512.
18. Gallese, "The 'Shared Manifold' Hypothesis," 33–50; Gallese, "The Roots of Empathy," 171–180; and Gallese, "Mirror Neurons," 519–536.
19. For a discussion of this question, see also Coëgnarts, "Cinema and the Embodied Mind."
20. Gallese and Guerra, "Embodying Movies," 183–210.
21. For empirical support of their claim, see among others, Heimann et al., "'Cuts in Action'"; Heimann et al., "Embodying the Camera"; and Heimann, Umiltà, Guerra and Gallese, "Moving Mirrors." These studies show, among others, that the indicator of sensory-motor

activity (the so called "central mu rhythm ERD") varies depending on the kind of editing system (for example, continuity editing versus violations of the 180 degrees rule) and the type of camera movement (for example, zoom, Steadicam, dolly). For instance, with regard to the latter, the sensory-motor areas of the brain were found to be more active in cases for videos that were filmed while approaching the scene with a Steadicam.

22. Gallese and Guerra, "Embodying Movies," 200–202.
23. Ibid., 201.
24. Hasson et al., "Neurocinematics," 2.
25. Ibid., 1–26.
26. Ibid., 2.
27. Ibid., 8.
28. Grodal, "The PECMA Flow," 1–11. See also Grodal, *Embodied Visions*, 145–157.
29. Ibid., 4.
30. Ramachandran and Hirstein, "The Science of Art," 15–51.
31. Ibid., 15.
32. Ibid., 18.
33. Ibid., 18.
34. Ibid., 17.
35. Grodal, *Embodied Visions*, 148–149.
36. Shimamura, *Experiencing Art*, 133.
37. Grodal, *Embodied Visions*, 152.
38. Shimamura, *Experiencing Art*, 101.
39. For discussions of the music in Kubrick's film, see, among others, Gengaro, *Listening to Stanley Kubrick*; McQuiston, *We'll Meet Again*; Schultheis, "Expanse of Possibilities," and Sperl, *Die Semantisierung*.
40. McQuiston, *We'll Meet Again*, i.
41. Leman, *Embodied Music Cognition*, 130.
42. Baker, Paddison and Roger Scruton, "Expression," 463.
43. Johnson, *The Meaning of the* Body, 235. See also Johnson and Larson, "'Something in the Way She Moves,'" 63–84.
44. Ibid., 235.
45. Ibid., 235.
46. Ibid., 235.
47. Ibid., 235–262; Brower, "A Cognitive Theory of Musical Meaning," 323–379; Larson, "Musical Forces," 55–72; Larson, *Musical Forces*; Mckee, "The Topic of the Sacred Hymn," 23–52; Saslaw, "Forces, Containers, and Paths," 217–243; and Zbikowski, "Metaphor and Music," 502–524.
48. McKee, "The Topic of the Sacred Hymn," 23.
49. Walton, "What Is Abstract About the Art of Music?," 354–355.
50. McKee, "The Topic of the Sacred Hymn," 31.
51. For discussions of this metaphor, see also Cox, "The Metaphorical Logic of Musical Motion and Space," Johnson, *The Meaning of the Body*, 243–256; and Lockhead, "The Metaphor of Musical Motion," 83–103.
52. Arnheim, "Perceptual Dynamics in Musical Expression," 298–299.
53. Larson, *Musical Forces*, ix.
54. McKee, "The Topic of the Sacred Hymn," 30.
55. Ibid., 30.
56. Walton, "What is Abstract," 355.

57. McKee, "The Topic of the Sacred Hymn," 34.
58. Ibid., 34.
59. Leman, *Embodied Music Cognition*, 130.
60. Ibid., 131.
61. Cohen, "Perspectives from Cognitive Psychology," 362.
62. See, for instance, Cohen, "Music as a Source of Emotion in Film," 249.
63. Burt, *The Art of Film Music*, 4.
64. Chattah, "Film Music as Embodiment," 83.
65. Ibid., 84.
66. McQuiston, *We'll Meet Again*, 137.
67. Ibid., 137.
68. Chattah, "Film Music as Embodiment," 86.
69. Williamson, *Strauss*, 28.
70. For a discussion, see also McQuiston, *We'll Meet Again*, 157–159; and Gengaro, *Listening to Stanley Kubrick*, 87–89.
71. Gengaro, *Listening to Stanley Kubrick*, 88.
72. Ibid., McQuiston, *We'll Meet Again*, 158.
73. Ibid., 158.
74. Ibid., 158.
75. Ibid, 158–159.
76. Ibid., 158.
77. Ibid., 79.
78. McCabe, *Bartók Orchestral Music*, 49, 52. See also Barham, "Incorporating Monsters," 153.
79. Mullen, "Do You Speak Kubrick?," 102.
80. Barham provides the following explanatory note: "The encircled numbers and the arrows extending to them in the example represent in order and as accurately as possible, the placement of either dialogue or action in relation to musical events." See Barham, "Incorporating Monsters," 159.
81. Ibid., 143.
82. Ibid., 153.
83. Ibid., 153.
84. McQuiston, *We'll Meet Again*, 79.
85. In order to bring Bartók's music and the scene to a satisfying end, Stainforth had to cut a few bars at the end of the music. In his personal communication with Barham, he recalls this painstaking editorial process as follows: "At first I first cut [the music] (simply reduced to ABA from an ABABA structure), it was still a bit too long for the scene, and it took all sorts of jiggery-pokery to make it fit really well . . . If my memory is correct . . . I had to cut out about 15–20 frames of the music, maybe more, with two very subtle cuts, and then we had to lengthen at least two of the cuts of Jack and Danny, and I think the very last cut to get the final chord to come right on the title 'Wednesday'. . . Fitting classical music to a scene like this always involves many compromises, but a few cues had to be absolutely right. I remember an absolutely 'key' cue was where Danny says 'You would never hurt me or mommy would you?' and Jack says 'What do you mean?' Even then, to make it all fit, some of the picture cuts had to be changed slightly." Barham, "Incorporating Monsters," 154.
86. Ibid., 153.
87. For a discussion, see also McQuiston, *We'll Meet Again*, 119–127; and Gengaro, *Listening to Stanley Kubrick*, 242–245.
88. Chattah, "Film Music as Embodiment," 86.
89. McQuiston, *We'll Meet Again*, 126.
90. Ibid., 125.

Appendix

List of reference numbers as quoted in this book, and as consulted at The Stanley Kubrick Archive of the University of the Arts London (UAL).

Ref. no.	*Description as provided by the UAL Archives and Special Collections Online Catalogue (http://archives.arts.ac.uk)*
SK/5/2/3	Bound pre-production/production script for *Fear and Desire* entitled "An Untitled Screenplay By Howard O. Sackler and Stanley Kubrick." There are a few handwritten script corrections, they are faded but are not Kubrick's writing. The script was clearly being worked on prior to naming the project.
SK/8/1/3	One bound copy of the third draft screenplay credited to Stanley Kubrick, Jim Thompson and Calder Willingham.
SK/9/1/2/2	The file contains the first draft screenplay by Howard Fast for Bryna Productions and the revised final screenplay, 16 Jan 1959 with Kirk Douglas' name on it. There are no annotations.
SK/10/1/26	The file consists of a completed screenplay for *Lolita*, typed and bound. It contains some scenes not in the final film for example, between Dr Ray and Humbert.
SK/11/1/26	Late version of the *Dr. Strangelove* script which was typed after the Kennedy assassination (November 22, 1963) as one line spoken by Major Kong was changed from mentioning a "good night out in Dallas" to "Vegas" after Kennedy was shot in Dallas, this script has the corrected text. The script also does not include the Pie Fight sequence which was removed from the film at a late date. The text reads like a novel but the dialogue is in narrow columns like a script. It includes handwritten inserts, crossings out and comments by Kubrick.
SK/12/1/2/3	Four copies of a draft screenplay for *2001: A Space Odyssey* by Stanley Kubrick and Arthur C Clarke, with dialogue, details of actions and character movements. The screenplay is divided into 4 sections A, B, C and D, reflecting the chapters of the finished film A) Dawn of Man, B) Journey to the Moon and investigation of the Monolith and C) the voyage of the Discovery to Saturn [in the film the planet was changed to Jupiter] and D) an encounter with another monolith. Each section has its own page numbering. The screenplay includes a narrator describing some of the events in the film.

Continued

SK/12/1/2/4	One bound copy of a screenplay for *2001: A Space Odyssey* by Stanley Kubrick and Arthur C. Clarke, with additions to certain scenes, including dialogue for an "Other HAL" which speaks to Dave Bowman in the computer brain room scene explaining what has gone wrong with the original HAL. The screenplay includes dialogue, details of actions and character movements and a narrator for some sections of the film. It is divided into 4 sections A, B, C and D, reflecting the chapters of the finished film A) Dawn of Man, B) Journey to the Moon and investigation of the Monolith and C) the voyage of the Discovery to Saturn [in the film the planet was changed to Jupiter] and D) the end sequences in the hotel room, fantastic voyage and Star Child. Each section has its own page numbering. The screenplay includes a narrator describing some of the events in the film.
SK/12/1/2/5	A typewritten script supplement to the "A" script for *2001: A Space Odyssey* containing proposed changes to the Dawn of Man sequence of the film with information on the cast, a basic outline of the action and timings. The sheets are stapled together. [It is unknown what constitutes the "A" Script].
SK/14/1/11	Heavily annotated draft of an early, incomplete script, with Barry as narrator. There are several inserted pages, one of which contains sections of Thackeray's *Barry Lyndon* which have been cut out and sellotaped onto paper.
SK/15/1/38	A black ringbinder with a green spine, labelled "The Shining Screenplay." The binder contains a one-line scene synopsis for the whole film (scenes–153), annotated by Stanley Kubrick. Each page of the synopsis is dated 31 Oct [1978], and a note is dated 25 Dec 1978. The binder also contains a screenplay, annotated by Stanley Kubrick and at least one other person [probably Ray Lovejoy], covering the first to last scene (the last scene is now numbered 153A).
SK/16/1/22	Final script of *Full Metal Jacket* as shot.
SK/17/1/11	The file contains a copy of script entitled "Eyes Wide Shut: Stanley Kubrick Project" with stage directions and includes the scene in which Alice Harford relates her dream to Bill Harford, with timings.

Glossary

This selective glossary of theoretical terms is indebted to definitions across various disciplines including philosophy of mind, cognitive linguistics, cognitive psychology, cognitive film studies, neuroscience and theatre studies. Among the primary sources used explicitly in its compilation were David Bordwell's and Kristin Thompson's *Film as Art*, Rudolf Arnheim's *The Power of the Center*, Vyvyan Evans' and Melanie Green's *Cognitive Linguistics: An Introduction*, and Nikolai M. Gorchakov's *Stanislavsky Directs*. For a glossary of musical terms, we refer the reader to *The Harvard Dictionary of Music*.

Absorption: Narratively, an intense engagement with the story-world, which is thought to go hand in hand with a decreased awareness of the self and one's immediate surrounding.

Active analysis: A technique of acting rehearsal with deep roots in the theory of stage performance known as the "Stanislavski system" (after the Russian stage director Konstantin Stanislavski). In this method actors attempt to grasp a play, not in the first place by memorising their lines, but by grasping the play's psychological structure or anatomy. See also *scheme*.

Approaching: A dynamic pattern of *containment*, the opposite of *DISTANCING*, that unfolds on-screen when an entity moves toward the camera. See also *fixed-frame movement*.

Balance: An image schema that involves a symmetrical (or proportional) arrangement of *forces* around a point or axis. Visually, the dynamic state in which the forces constituting a visual configuration compensate for one another. Although visual balance is closely tied to *symmetry*, it cannot be reduced to it. The mutual neutralization of directed tensions produces an effect of immobility. Musically, the interrelationship of the dynamic levels of each sound source or instrument, to one another in the overall musical texture.

Conceptual structure: The nature and organization of mental representations in all its richness and diversity. Second-generation cognitive science holds that this structure is fundamentally embodied, meaning that it arises from bodily experiences and interactions with the environment. See also *embodied cognition thesis*, *image schema*.

Containment: An *image schema* that is characterized by the structural features of an inside, an outside and a boundary. Superimposed with the SOURCE-PATH-GOAL image schema, it gives rise to a series of dynamic patterns of containment such as *APPROACHING*, *DISTANCING*, *ENCLOSURE*, *ENTRY*, *EXCLUSION*, *EXIT*, *EXPOSURE* and *INCLUSION*. These patterns are fundamentally important in metaphorically structuring abstract target domains such as those that pertain to the conceptual structure of *mental causation* (e.g., emotions, perception, cognition). The boundary of a CONTAINER schema is physically instantiated in a *frame*.

Distancing: A dynamic pattern of *containment*, the opposite of *APPROACHING*, that unfolds on-screen when an entity moves away from a relatively stationary camera. See also *fixed-frame movement.*

Embodied cognition thesis: The thesis which holds that *conceptual structure* arises from our sensory-motor, bodily experience and the neural structures that give rise to it. It stands in contrast to first-generation cognitive science or the cognitive science of the disembodied mind. Also known as second-generation cognitive science or the cognitive science of the embodied mind.

Embodied simulation: A functional neural mechanism of the brain that allows a third-person observer, such as a film viewer, to experience the observed behaviors and actions of others as if he or she were experiencing those social stimuli oneself in first-person. See also *mirror neurons.*

Enclosure: A dynamic pattern of *containment*, the opposite of *EXPOSURE* and a specific sub-variant of *EXCLUSION*, that unfolds on-screen when a camera moves, apparently or literally, toward an entity so as to exclude the space surrounding the entity. See also *mobile frame*, *zoom-lens.*

Entry: A dynamic pattern of *containment*, the opposite of *EXIT*, that unfolds on-screen when an entity moves along a pathway starting off-screen an ending on-screen. See also *fixed-frame movement*, *off-screen space.*

Event-Indexing model: A theoretical model of narrative comprehension that accounts for the way that readers and viewers relate the basic units of *situation models* to one another. When comprehending stories, these basic units or events are thought to be monitored and continually updated on at least five dimensions including time, space, entity, causation, and intentionality.

Exclusion: A dynamic pattern of *containment*, the opposite of *INCLUSION*, that unfolds on-screen when a moving camera excludes an entity from the inside space of the frame. See also *mobile frame.*

Exit: A dynamic pattern of *containment*, the opposite of *ENTRY*, that unfolds on-screen when an entity moves along a pathway starting on-screen and ending off-screen. Its instantiation can be prevented by the employment of the *following shot*. See also *fixed-frame movement*, *off-screen space.*

Exposure: A dynamic pattern of *containment*, the opposite of *ENCLOSURE* and specific sub-variant of *INCLUSION*, that unfolds on-screen when a camera moves away, apparently or literally, from an entity on-screen so as to include "new" space into the frame. See also *mobile frame*, *zoom-lens.*

External action: The physical activity capped forth by the inner action of the characters, their desires, and their motivations. It plays an important role in signalling mental events such as cognition, perception and emotion *metonymically*. Also known as outer action.

Fixed-frame movement: Movement of an entity within a static frame established by a camera that remains in the same or fixed position. This movement can be either lateral (from the left to the right of the frame), in-depth (toward or away from the camera) or diagonal (a combination of lateral and in-depth-movement). Dynamic patterns of containment that are intrinsically connected to this cinematic technique are *APPROACHING*, *DISTANCING*, *ENTRY* and *EXIT*. See also *containment.*

Flow-of-emotion scenario: A folk theory of emotions according to which emotions are thought to be embedded in a causal chain of three events: an emotion-arousing event (the cause of emotion), an emotional state, and a behavioural response (the effect of emotion). Also known as the Western folk theory of emotions. See also *folk theory*, *mental causation.*

Following shot: A shot with framing that prevents the dynamic pattern of *EXIT* from unfolding on-screen.

Folk theory: An intuitive and common-sense causal explanatory "theory" that people construct to make sense of the world around them. Folk theories stand in contrast to scientific or expert theories. See also *flow-of-emotion scenario.*

Force dynamics: A semantic category that accounts for the way in which *force* interactions between entities might be conceptualized. Force dynamic expressions such as "The ball kept rolling because of the wind blowing on it" typically involve a role difference between two force entities with each entity having its own intrinsic force tendency, either toward action or toward rest. The entity that is in focus is called the agonist (i.e., the ball with a tendency toward rest). The entity that is opposing it, is called the antagonist (i.e., the wind with a tendency toward action). The outcome, either toward action or inaction (or rest), that results from both the balance between the forces and the intrinsic force tendencies of the entities, is called the resultant (i.e., the ball moves).

Force: Physically, that what imparts a directionality or vector quality on a moving entity. It is typically experienced through interaction, it has a direction, a path of motion, an origin, and a degree of power. It always involves a structure or sequence of causality, a consequence of having all the other properties. Visual objects and musical sounds are thought to generate forces through their intrinsic properties.

Frame: The rectangle shaped image that is projected onto a screen. When a series of such images is projected quickly and in succession, the illusion of movement is created. By its definition, the frame can be held to exhibit all of the properties of the CONTAINER schema. See also *containment.*

Image schema: A recurring dynamic pattern of perceptual interactions and motor programs that is thought to give coherence and structure to human experience. It provides the concrete basis for conceptual *metaphors*. See also *conceptual structure, embodied cognition thesis, source domain.*

Inclusion: A dynamic pattern of *containment*, the opposite of *EXCLUSION*, that unfolds on-screen when a moving camera includes an entity into its frame. See also *containment, mobile frame.*

Long take: A shot that continues for an unusually lengthy time before the transition to the next shot. By its length, long takes have the potential for unfolding many dynamic patterns of *containment*.

Mappings: The set of conceptual correspondences between a *source domain* and a *target domain*. See also *metaphor*.

Mental causation: The principle that asserts that mental events interact causally with other events whether physical or mental. From this we can infer three kinds of causal relations in which mental events are involved: (1) causality that runs from the mental to the physical or mental-to-physical causation, (2) causality that runs from the mental to the mental or mental-to-mental causation, and (3) causality that runs from the physical to the mental or physical-to-mental causation. See also *pairing problem*.

Metaphor: A structure of human understanding that allows one to understand an abstract conceptual domain (the *target domain*) in terms of another more physical and concrete conceptual domain (the *source domain*). It is commonly characterized with the formula "a is b." See also *image schema, mappings.*

Metonymy: A structure of human understanding that allows one to understand one conceptual domain through a part of the same domain. Unlike metaphors, metonymies designate an "a stand for b" relation within a single domain (e.g., a part stands for the whole) rather than an "a is b" relation across different domains.

Mirror neurons: Neurons that are activated not only when an agent is executing a motor action (such as grasping an object), but also when an agent is perceiving another agent executing the same motor action. It has been suggested that mirror neurons are the key to explaining humans' capacity to attribute mental states to others. See also *embodied simulation, Theory of Mind.*

Mobile frame: The effect on the space inside the *frame* as a result of actual or apparent camera movement caused by external *forces* exerted on the camera. It stands in contrast to *fixed-frame movement*. See also *ENCLOSURE, EXCLUSION, EXPOSURE, INCLUSION.*

Narrative: A type of filmic organization that arises, as a final product, from an ongoing process of construction, whereby the spectator actively construes a chain of causally related events taking place in time and space.

Off-screen space: The six areas of space that lie outside the boundary of the projected frame: (1) the space left of the frame, (2) the space right of the frame, (3) the space above the frame, (4) the space below the frame, (5) the space behind the set and (6) the space behind and near the camera. See also *ENTRY, EXIT.*

Other minds problem: A philosophical problem that involves the question as to how we can know that others besides oneself possess minds given that we can only observe the behavior of others.

Pairing problem: A philosophical problem that involves the question as to how minds, as immaterial substances outside space, can participate in the causal relations of the material world. Also known as the problem of interaction. See also *mental causation.*

Paradox of cinematic meaning: Generally, the paradox which is based on a logical inconsistency between the non-conceptual nature of film and the conceptual nature of meaning. Visually, it concerns the question as to how visual images can convey abstract concepts notwithstanding the fact that they are iconic. Musically, it concerns the question as to how musical sounds that are "pure" or "absolute" can convey meaning notwithstanding the fact that they lack a reference model.

Paradox of suspense: The paradox which is based on the contention that viewers can still experience *suspense* even after repeated viewings of the same film. In that case the uncertainty principle, which is thought to guide suspense, would no longer hold as the viewer is already familiar with the story's outcome. Also known as the phenomenon of anomalous suspense.

Point-of-view shot (POV shot): A shot in which the camera assumes the position of a character in order to show us what the character sees. It is based on a metaphorical extension of the CONTAINER schema onto the character's *visual field*. It is usually shown before or after a shot in which the camera prompts us to construe the EYES FOR SEEING metonymy (the character in the act of looking). See also *containment.*

Referential meaning: The sort of meaning that is central to narrative comprehension. It depends on the spectator's ability to construct a mental model of the situation on the basis of the cues presented to him or her by the film's specific formal system. Such a *situation model* is closely tied to a recognition of most of the causal relations between events and scenes, including the relations that involve mental events of characters. Because of its very concreteness and closeness to the film's bare-plot summary it is thought to stand in contrast to symptomatic meanings which are more abstract and general, and which are central to interpretation. Also known as situational meaning. See also *Event-Indexing model, mental causation.*

Scheme: The bone outline, the skeleton which holds all inner and outer actions of the play. See also *external action*.

Situation model: The mental representation of the situations as conveyed by the words and sentences of a text, or the shots of a film. Also known as mental model. See also *Event-Indexing model, referential meaning.*

Source domain: The conceptual domain that we use metaphorically in order to understand the *target domain*. It is commonly based on the inferential logic of *image schemas*. See also *metaphor*.

Source-path-goal: An *image schema* that is grounded in our experience of physically moving from one location to another. It consists of a starting point or source, a destination or goal, and a series of contiguous locations in between them. The inferential logic of this schema is of fundamental importance for our reasoning about *mental causation*. In film, this logic is intrinsically tied to the cinematic techniques of camera movement and fixed-frame movement. Also known as the PATH schema. See also *containment*.

Suspense: An emotional response to narrative fictions which is thought to go hand in hand with an expectant degree of uncertainty concerning the outcome of a situation. See also *paradox of suspense*.

Symmetry: The exact correspondence of form and constituent configuration on opposite sides of a dividing line or plane or about a center or axis. A vertical axis produces more compelling visual symmetry than a horizontal axis. See also *balance*.

Target domain: The conceptual domain that we try to understand metaphorically through the use of the *source domain*. See also *metaphor*.

Theory of Mind: The human ability to attribute mental states such as desires, beliefs, feelings and intentions, to oneself and to others in order to explain and predict behaviors. See also *mirror neurons*.

Trajector (TR): The entity in a scene that undergoes motion. The entity with respect to which the TR moves, is called the landmark (LM).

Visual field: Objectively, all the objects and state of affairs that come into view when you open your eyes in a certain direction. Subjectively, that area of visual consciousness in front of your face that one experiences when closing your eyes. The objective visual field of a character is usually rendered cinematically by the *point-of-view shot*.

Weight: Physically, the effect of gravitational attraction that is experienced either as an eccentric downward pull or as a downward press generated centrically by the object self. Metaphorically, the term is used to structure our understanding of the dynamic power that is inherent in visual objects and musical sounds by virtue of their intrinsic properties.

Zoom-lens: A cinematic device that allows for the effect of the *mobile frame*, not by moving the camera, but by means of changing the focal length during a shot. A shift toward the telephoto range enlarges the image and flattens its place, giving rise to the pattern of ENCLOSURE, while the opposite, a shift toward the *wide-angle* range provokes the pattern of EXPOSURE.

Filmography

Included in the list below are also Kubrick's early short documentaries which are left outside the scope of this book. This list is much indebted to the filmography of the *Stanley Kubrick Catalogue* that accompanied the touring exhibition organized by the Deutsches Filmmuseum, Frankfurt am Main with the Stanley Kubrick Estate (Kinematograph No. 20, 2004).

Day of the Fight (USA 1951)
Director: Stanley Kubrick
Screenplay: Robert Rein
Assistant Director: Alexander Singer
Cinematography: Stanley Kubrick, Alexander Singer
Editor: Julian Bergman
Sound: Stanley Kubrick
Music: Gerald Fried
Cast: Douglas Edwards (narrator), Walter Cartier (himself: boxer), Vincent Cartier (himself: Walter's twin brother), Nate Fleischer (himself: boxing historian), Bobby James (himself: Walter's opponent), Stanley Kubrick (himself: man at ringside with camera), Alexander Singer (himself: man at ringside with camera), Judy Singer (herself: female fan in the crowd)
Length/Running time: 16 min
Gauge: 35mm, b/w, mono
Distributor: RKO-Pathé, Inc.

Flying Padre (USA 1951)
Director: Stanley Kubrick
Screenplay: Stanley Kubrick
Cinematography: Stanley Kubrick
Editor: Isaac Kleinerman
Sound: Harold R. Vivian
Music: Nathaniel Shilkret
Cast: Bob Hite (narrator, voice), Reverend Fred Stadtmueller (himself)
Length/Running time: 9 min.
Gauge: 35mm, b/w, mono
Distributor: RKO-Pathé, Inc.

The Seafarers (USA 1953)
Director: Stanley Kubrick
Screenplay: Will Chasan
Cinematography: Stanley Kubrick
Editor: Stanley Kubrick
Sound: Stanley Kubrick
Cast: Don Hollenbeck (voice narrator) and Members of the Seafarers Guild
Length/Running time: 30 min.
Gauge: 35mm, color, mono

Fear and Desire (USA 1953)
Production Company: Stanley Kubrick Productions
Alternative/Working Titles: *Shape of Fear / The Trap*
Production Company: Stanley Kubrick Productions
Director: Stanley Kubrick
Screenplay: Stanley Kubrick, Howard O. Sackler, based on the script *The Trap* by Sackler
Assistant Director: Steve Hahn
Dialogue Director: Toba Kubrick

Cinematography: Stanley Kubrick
Editor: Stanley Kubrick
Music: Gerald Fried
Cast: David Allen (narrator, voice), Frank Silvera (Mac), Kenneth Harp (Lieutenant Corby/enemy general), Paul Mazursky (Sidney), Stephen Coit (Fletcher/enemy captain), Virginia Leith (girl)
Length/Running time: 68 min.
Gauge: 35mm (1.33:1), b/w, mono
Distributor: Joseph Burstyn

Killer's Kiss (USA 1955)
Alternative/Working Titles: *Kill Me, Kill Me / The Nymph and the Maniac / Along Came a Spider*
Production Company: Minotaur
Director: Stanley Kubrick
Screenplay: Stanley Kubrick, Howard O. Sackler
Assistant Director: Ernest Nukanen
Cinematography: Stanley Kubrick
Sound: Titra Sound Studios, Walter Ruckersberg / Clifford Van Praag (recording)
Music: Gerald Fried.
Cast: Frank Silvera (Vincent Rapallo), Jamie Smith (Davy Gordon), Irene Kane (Gloria Price), Jerry Jarret (Albert, Manager), Ruth Sobotka (Iris Price)
Length/Running time: 67 min.
Gauge: 35mm (1.33:1), b/w, mono
Distributor: United Artists

The Killing (USA 1956)
Production Company: Harris-Kubrick Productions
Alternative/Working titles: *Day of Violence / Clean Break / Bed of Fear*
Director: Stanley Kubrick
Screenplay: Stanley Kubrick, Jim Thompson (dialogues), based on the novel *Clean Break* by Lionel White (1955)
Assistant Directors: Milton Carter, Paul Feiner, Howard Joslin, Alexander Singer (also Director second unit)
Cinematography: Lucien Ballard
Editor: Betty Steinberg
Sound: Early Snyder
Music: Gerald Fried
Cast: Sterling Hayden (Johnny Clay), Coleen Gray (Fay), Vince Edwards (Val Cannon), Jay C. Flippen (Marvin Unger), Marie Windsor (Sherry Peatty), Elisha Cooke (George Peatty), Ted de Corsia (Randy Kennan), Joe Sawyer (Mike O'Reilly), James Edwards (parking lot attendant), Timothy Carey (Nikki), Joseph Turkel (Tiny), Kola Kwariani (Maurice)
Length/Running time: 84 min.
Gauge: 35mm (1.33:1), b/w, mono (RCA Sound System)
Distributor: United Artists

Paths of Glory (USA 1957)
Production Company: Harris-Kubrick Productions
Director: Stanley Kubrick
Screenplay: Stanley Kubrick, Calder Willingham, Jim Thompson, based on the novel *Paths of Glory* by Humphrey Cobb (1935)
Assistant Directors: Dixie Sensburg, Franz-Josef Spieker, Hans Stumpf
Cinematography: Georg Krause
Editor: Eva Kroll
Sound: Martin Müller
Music: Gerald Fried
Cast: Kirk Douglas (Colonel Dax), Ralph Meeker (Corporal Paris), Adolphe Menjou (General Broulard), George Macready (General Mireau), Wayne Morris (Lieutenant Roget), Richard Anderson (Major Saint-Aubain), Joseph Turkel (Private Arnaud), Timothy Carey (Private Ferol), Peter Capell (Judge), Suzanne Christian (German girl), Bert Freed (Sergeant Boulanger), Emile Meyer (priest), John Stein (Captain Rousseau)
Length/Running time: 87 min.
Gauge: 35mm (1.66:1; with an option for 1.85:1), b/w, mono
Distributor: United Artists (presented by Bryna Productions)

Spartacus (USA 1960)
Production Company: Bryna Productions
Director: Stanley Kubrick (during the first 8 shooting days: Anthony Mann)

Screenplay: Dalton Trumbo, based on the novel *Spartacus* by Howard Fast (1951)
Assistant Director: Marshall Green
Cinematography: Russell Metty, Clifford Stine (special photography)
Editor: Robert Lawrence, Robert Schulz, Fred Chulack
Production Designer: Alexander Golitzen
Title Design: Saul Bass
Sound: Waldon O. Watson, Joe Lapis, Murray Spivack, Ronald Pierce
Music: Alex North
Cast: Kirk Douglas (Spartacus), Laurence Olivier (Marcus Crassus), Jean Simmons (Varinia), Charles Laughton (Gracchus), Peter Ustinov (Batiatus), Tony Curtis (Antoninus), John Gavin (Julius Caesar), Nina Foch (Helena), Herbert Lom (Tigranes), John Ireland (Crixus), John Dall (Glabrus), Charles McGraw (Marcellus), Harold J. Stone (David), Woody Strode (Draba)
Length/Running time: 196 min. (original version) / abridged version: 184 min.
Gauge: 35mm (2.35:1; Panavision), 70 mm, Super Technirama 70 (2.21:1), color (Technicolor); 70 mm 6-Track (70 mm print) / Dolby SR (restored version) / mono (Westrex Recording System) (35 mm print, original version)
Distributor: Universal Pictures

Lolita (UK / USA 1962)
Production Company: Seven Arts / Anya / Transworld
Director: Stanley Kubrick
Screenplay: Vladimir Nabokov, Stanley Kubrick (uncredited), based on Nabokov's novel *Lolita* (1955)
Assistant Directors: René Dupont, Roy Millichip, John Danischewski
Cinematography: Oswald Morris, Robert Gaffney (second unit)
Editor: Anthony Harvey
Sound: Len Shilton (recording), H.L. Bird (mixing)
Music: Various Artists (see Discography)
Cast: James Mason (Humbert Humbert), Peter Sellers (Clare Quilty), Shelley Winters (Charlotte Haze), Sue Lyon (Lolita), Marianne Stone (Vivian Darkbloom), Jerry Stovin (John Farlow), Diana Decker (Jean Farlow), Gary Cockrell (Dick Schiller), Suzanne Gibbs (Mona Farlow), William Greene (Mr. Swine), Cec Linder (physician), Lois Maxwell (Nurse Lord), John Harrison (Tom)
Length/Running time: 152 min.
Gauge: 35mm (1.66:1), b/w, mono
Distributor: Metro-Goldwyn-Mayer

Dr. Strangelove or: How I Learned to Stop Worrying and Love the Bomb (UK / USA 1964)
Production Company: Hawk Films
Director: Stanley Kubrick
Screenplay: Stanley Kubrick, Terry Southern, Peter George, based on the novel *Red Alert* by Peter Bryant aka Peter George (published in 1958 as *Two Hours to Doom*)
Cinematography: Gilbert Taylor
Editor: Anthony Harvey
Production Designer: Ken Adam
Sound: John Cox (recording), H.L. Bird (mixing)
Music: Various Artists (see Discography)
Cast: Peter Sellers (Group Captain Mandrake, President Muffley, Dr. Strangelove), George C. Scott (General "Buck" Turgidson), Sterling Hayden (General Jack D. Ripper), Keenan Wynn (Colonel "Bat" Guano), Slim Pickens (Major T.J. "King" Kong), Peter Bull (Ambassador de Sadesky), James Earl Jones (Lieutenant Lothar Zogg), Tracy Reed (Miss Scott), Jack Creley (Mr. Staines), Frank Berry (Lieutenant Dietrich), Glenn Beck (Lieutenant Kivel), Shane Rimmer (Captain Ace Owens), Paul Tamarin (Lieutenant Goldberg)
Length/Running time: 95 min.
Gauge: 35mm (1.66:1), b/w, mono (Westrex)
Distributor: Columbia Pictures

2001: A Space Odyssey (UK / USA 1968)
Alternative/Working titles: *Journey Beyond the Stars*
Production Company: Metro-Goldwyn-Mayer
Director: Stanley Kubrick
Screenplay: Stanley Kubrick, Arthur C. Clarke, based on his short story *The Sentinel* (1951)
Assistant Director: Derek Cracknell
Cinematography: Geoffrey Unsworth, John Alcott (additional photography)
Editor: Ray Lovejoy
Production Designers: Antony Masters, Harry Lange, Ernest Archer

Sound: A.W. Watkins (recording), Ed Winston Ryder (editing), H.L. Bird (mixing)

Music: Various Artists (see Discography)

Cast: Keir Dullea (Dave Bowman), Gary Lockwood (Frank Poole), William Sylvester (Dr. Heywood Floyd), Douglas Rain (voice of HAL), Daniel Richter (Moonwatcher), Leonard Rossiter (Smyslov), Margaret Tyzack (Elena), Robert Beatty (Halvorsen)

Length/Running time: 141 min. abridged from 160 min. after première.

Gauge: 70mm (2.20:1), Super Panavision, color (Technicolor, prints: Metrocolor), 4-Track Stereo (35mm) / 6-Track (70 mm print) / DTS 70 mm (rescreening 2001)

Distributor: Metro-Goldwyn-Mayer

A Clockwork Orange (UK / USA 1971)

Production Company: Warner Brothers / Hawk Films

Director: Stanley Kubrick

Screenplay: Stanley Kubrick, based on the novel *A Clockwork Orange* by Anthony Burgess (1962)

Assistant Directors: Derek Cracknell, Dusty Symonds

Cinematography: John Alcott

Editor: Bill Butler

Production Designer: John Barry

Sound: John Jordan (recording), Brian Blamey (editing), Bill Rowe / Eddie Haben

Music: Various Artists (see Discography)

Cast: Malcolm McDowell (Alex), Patrick Magee (Mr. Alexander), Michael Bates (Chief Guard), Anthony Sharp (Minister of the Interior), Godfrey Quigley (Prison Chaplain), Adrienne Corri (Mrs. Alexander), Warren Clarke (Dim), Miriam Karlin (Cat Lady), Paul Farrell (tramp), Philip Stone (Dad), Sheila Raynor (Mum), Aubrey Morris (Mr. Deltoid), Carl Duering (Dr. Brodsky), John Clive (stage actor), Madge Ryan (Dr. Branom), Pauline Taylor (psychiatrist), Margaret Tyzack (conspirator), John Savident (conspirator), Steven Berkoff (Constable), David Prouse (Julian), Michael Tarn (Pete)

Length/Running time: 137 min.

Gauge: 35 mm (1.66:1), color (Technicolor), mono, Dolby Digital (re-issue)

Distributor: Warner Brothers

Barry Lyndon (UK / USA 1975)

Production Company: Warner Brothers / Hawk Films / Peregrine Productions

Director: Stanley Kubrick

Screenplay: Stanley Kubrick, based on the novel *The Memoirs of Barry Lyndon* by William Makepeace Thackeray (published in 1844 as *The Luck of Barry Lyndon*)

Cinematography: John Alcott, Paddy Carey (second unit)

Editor: Tony Lawson

Production Designer: Ken Adam

Sound: Robin Gregory (recording), Rodney Holland (editing), Bill Rowe (mixing)

Music: Various Artists (see Discography)

Cast: Ryan O'Neal (Redmond Barry/Barry Lyndon), Marisa Berenson (Lady Lyndon), Patrick Magee (Chevalier de Balibari), Hardy Kruger (Captain Potzdorf), Steven Berkoff (Lord Ludd), Gay Hamilton (Nora Brady), Marie Kean (Mrs. Barry), Murray Melvin (Reverend Runt), Godfrey Quigley (Captain Grogan), Leon Vitali (Lord Bullingdon), Diana Koerner (Lischen), Frank Middlemass (Sir Charles Lyndon), André Morell (Lord Wendover), Philip Stone (Graham), Anthony Sharp (Lord Hallum), Michael Hordern (Narrator)

Length/Running time: 187 min.

Gauge: 35 mm (1.66:1), color (Eastmancolor), mono; special lenses for candlelight shootings by Carl Zeiss

Distributor: Warner Brothers

The Shining (UK / USA 1980)

Production Company: Warner Brothers / Hawk Films / Peregrine Productions

Director: Stanley Kubrick

Screenplay: Stanley Kubrick, Diane Johnson, based on the novel *The Shining* by Stephen King (1977)

Assistant Directors: Brian Cook, Terry Needham, Michael Stevenson

Cinematography: John Alcott, Garrett Brown (Steadicam), Greg McGillivray (aerial photography)

Editor: Ray Lovejoy, Gordon Stainforth (assistant editor)

Production Designer: Roy Walker

Sound: Richard Daniel / Ivan Sharrock (recording), Dino DiCampo / Jack T.Knight (editing), Wyn Rider / Bill Rowe (mixing)
Music: Various Artists (see Discography)
Cast: Jack Nicholson (Jack Torrance), Shelley Duvall (Wendy Torrance), Danny Lloyd (Danny Torrance), Scatman Crothers (Halloran), Philip Stone (Delbert Grady), Joe Turkel (Lloyd), Barry Nelson (Ullman), Anne Jackson (Doctor), Lia Beldam (young woman in bath), Billie Gibson (old woman in bath), Lisa and Louise Burns (Grady girls)
Length/Running time: 146 min. / 119 min. (abridged version for Europe)
Gauge: 35 mm (1.66:1), color, mono
Distributor: Warner Brothers

Full Metal Jacket (UK / USA 1987)
Production Company: Warner Brothers / Hawk Films / Harrier Productions
Director: Stanley Kubrick
Screenplay: Stanley Kubrick, Michael Herr, Gustav Hasford, based on the novel *The Short-Timers* by Gustav Hasford (1979)
Assistant Directors: Terry Needham, Christopher Thompson
Cinematography: Douglas Milsome, Ken Alridge (aerial photography), John Ward / Jean-Marc Bringuier (Steadicam)
Editor: Martin Hunter
Production Designer: Anton Furst
Sound: Nigel Galt, Joe Illing, Edward Tise
Music: Various Artists (see Discography)
Cast: Matthew Modine (Private Joker), Lee Ermey (Sergeant Hartman), Vincent D'Onofrio (Private Pyle), Adam Baldwin (Animal Mother), Arliss Howard (Prive Cowboy), Dorian Harewood (Eightball), Kevyn Major Howard (Rafterman), Ed O'Ross (Lt. Touchdown), John Terry (Lt. Lockhart), Ngoc Le (V.C. Sniper)
Length/Running time: 116 min.
Gauge: 35 mm (1.85:1), color, mono
Distributor: Warner Brothers

Eyes Wide Shut (UK / USA 1999)
Production Company: Warner Brothers / Pole Star / Hobby Productions
Alternative/Working Titles: *EWS* / *Rhapsody*
Director: Stanley Kubrick
Screenplay: Stanley Kubrick, Frederic Raphael, based on motives from *Traumnovelle* (*Rhapsody—A Dream Novel*) by Arthur Schnitzler (1926)
Assistant Directors: Brian W. Cook
Cinematography: Larry Smith, Patrick Turley / Malik Sayeed / Arthur Jaffa (second unit)
Editor: Nigel Galt
Production Designers: Les Tomkins, Roy Walker
Sound: Tony Bell, Paul Conway, Eddy Tise
Music: Various Artists (see Discography)
Cast: Tom Cruise (Dr. William Harford), Nicole Kidman (Alice Harford), Sidney Pollack (Victor Ziegler), Marie Richardson (Marion Nathanson), Rade Sherbedgia (Milich), Todd Field (Nick Nightingale), Vinessa Shaw (Domino), Alan Cumming (Hotel Desk Clerk), Sky Dumont (Sandor Szavost), Fay Masterson (Sally), Leelee Sobieski (Milich's Daughter), Thomas Gibson (Carl), Julienne Davis (Mandy), Madison Eginton (Helena Harford), Leon Vitali (Red Cloak), Abigail Good (Mysterious Woman), Togo Igawa (Japanese Man 1), Eiji Kusuhara (Japanese Man 2), Gary Goba (Naval Officer), Phil Davis (Stalker)
Length/Running time: 159 min.
Gauge: 35 mm (1.85:1), color (DeLuxe), DTS / Dolby Digital / SDDS
Distributor: Warner Brothers

Discography

This discography is intended to cover all of the musical cues as heard in Kubrick's films, and that are officially and publicly known regardless of whether the cue is credited in the film. The reference information is based on a critical reading of the existing literature on Kubrick's music and the track listings and liner notes of the official soundtrack recordings as they are commercially available. If a recorded version of a musical cue has been published on an official soundtrack (including compilations), the recording details of the first CD release are included (if available). These recordings may differ from the actual recordings as used in the film. Cues that have not been released on any soundtrack are marked "unreleased on soundtrack." Musical cues are mostly listed alphabetically by composer and do not follow the order of appearance on the soundtracks. Alternative or translated titles are put in brackets. For time markers indicating when the cues are used in the films, we refer the reader to Stephan Sperl's highly useful charts in *Die Semantisierung der Musik im filmischen Werk Stanley Kubrick* (2006).

Day of the Fight (USA 1951)

Fried, Gerald. *March of the Gloved Gladiators.* Released on the soundtrack compilation *Dr. Strangelove: Music From the Films of Stanley Kubrick.* Performed by The City of Prague Philharmonic. Conducted by Paul Bateman. Silva America, 1999. CD. [SSD 1097].

Fear and Desire (USA 1953)

Fried, Gerald. *Madness.* Released on the soundtrack compilation *Dr. Strangelove: Music From the Films of Stanley Kubrick.* Performed by The City of Prague Philharmonic. Conducted by Paul Bateman. Silva America, 1999. CD. [SSD 1097].

______. *Meditation on War.* Released on the soundtrack compilation *Dr. Strangelove: Music From the Films of Stanley Kubrick.* Performed by The City of Prague Philharmonic. Conducted by Paul Bateman. Silva America, 1999. CD. [SSD 1097].

Johnson, Robert, and William Shakespeare. *The Tempest: Full Fathom Five, Ariel's Song Second Stanza.* Performed by Private Sydney (Paul Mazursky). Unreleased on soundtrack.

Killer's Kiss (USA 1955)

Foster, Stephen. *Oh, Susanna.* Performed on the harmonica by one of the Shriners. Unreleased on soundtrack.

Fried, Gerald. *Murder 'Mongst the Mannikins.* Released on the soundtrack compilation *Dr. Strangelove: Music From the Films of Stanley Kubrick.* Performed by The City of Prague Philharmonic. Conducted by Paul Bateman. Silva America, 1999. CD. [SSD 1097]

Gimbel, Norman, and Arden E. Clar. *Once (Love Theme).* Performed by both orchestra and band. Arranged by Gerald Fried. Unreleased on soundtrack.

The Killing (USA 1956)

Fried, Gerald. *Main Title / The Robbery.* Released on the soundtrack compilation *Dr. Strangelove: Music From the Films of Stanley Kubrick.* Performed by The City of Prague Philharmonic. Conducted by Paul Bateman. Silva America, 1999. CD. [SSD 1097]

Paths of Glory (USA 1957)

Fried, Gerald. *The Patrol.* Released on the soundtrack compilation *Dr. Strangelove: Music From the Films of Stanley Kubrick.* Performed by The City of Prague Philharmonic. Conducted by Paul Bateman. Silva America, 1999. CD. [SSD 1097]

Rouget de Lisle, Claude Joseph. *La Marseillaise.* Released on the soundtrack compilation *Kubrick's Music: Selections From the Films of Stanley Kubrick.* Performed by the Detroit Symphony Orchestra. Conducted by Paul Paray. Cherry Red Records, 2018. CD. [B07FTY88S3]

Strauss, Johann Jr. *Künstlerleben* ["Artist's Life"], *Op. 316.* Released on the soundtrack compilation *Kubrick's Music: Selections From the Films of Stanley Kubrick.* Performed by the Vienna Philharmonic Orchestra. Conducted by Clemens Krauss. Cherry Red Records, 2018. CD. [B07FTY88S3]

Traditional. *The Faitful Hussar* ["Der Treue Husar"]. Performed by The German Girl (Susanne Christian). Unreleased on soundtrack.

______. *The Faitful Hussar* ["Der Treue Husar"]. Adapted and arranged for orchestration by Gerald Fried. Unreleased on soundtrack.

Spartacus (USA 1960)

North, Alex. *Blue Shadows and Purple Hills.* Released on the official soundtrack. Conducted by Alex North. MCA Records, 1991. CD. [MCAD 10256]. Originally released on Hi-Fi Decca Records, 1960. LP. [DL 9092]

______. *Brooding.* Released on the official soundtrack. Conducted by Alex North. Varèse Sarabande, 2010. CD. [VCL 0610 1109]. Unreleased on the 1960 original soundtrack.

______. *Caravan.* Released on the official soundtrack. Conducted by Alex North. Varèse Sarabande, 2010. CD. [VCL 0610 1109]. Unreleased on the 1960 original soundtrack.

______. *Expectant Parents.* Released on the official soundtrack. Conducted by Alex North. Varèse Sarabande, 2010. CD. [VCL 0610 1109]. Unreleased on the 1960 original soundtrack.

______. *First Pair.* Released on the official soundtrack. Conducted by Alex North. Varèse Sarabande, 2010. CD. [VCL 0610 1109]. Unreleased on the 1960 original soundtrack.

______. *Formations.* Released on the official soundtrack. Conducted by Alex North. Varèse Sarabande, 2010. CD. [VCL 0610 1109]. Unreleased on the 1960 original soundtrack.

______. *Gladiators Fight to The Death.* Released on the official soundtrack. Conducted by Alex North. MCA Records, 1991. CD. [MCAD 10256]. Originally released on Hi-Fi Decca Records, 1960. LP. [DL 9092]

______. *Goodbye My Life, My Love / End Title.* Released on the official soundtrack. Conducted by Alex North. MCA Records, 1991. CD. [MCAD 10256]. Originally released on Hi-Fi Decca Records, 1960. LP. [DL 9092]

______. *Headed for Freedom.* Released on the official soundtrack. Conducted by Alex North. MCA Records, 1991. CD. [MCAD 10256]. Originally released on Hi-Fi Decca Records, 1960. LP. [DL 9092]

______. *Homeward Bound: On to the Sea / Beside the Pool.* Released on the official soundtrack. Conducted by Alex North. MCA Records, 1991. CD. [MCAD 10256]. Originally released on Hi-Fi Decca Records, 1960. LP. [DL 9092]

______. *Hopeful Preparations / Vesuvius Camp.* Released on the official soundtrack. Conducted by Alex North. MCA Records, 1991. CD. [MCAD 10256]. Originally released on Hi-Fi Decca Records, 1960. LP. [DL 9092]

______. *Main Title.* Released on the official soundtrack. Conducted by Alex North. MCA Records, 1991. CD. [MCAD 10256]. Originally released on Hi-Fi Decca Records, 1960. LP. [DL 9092]

______. *Metapontum Triumph.* Released on the official soundtrack. Conducted by Alex North. Varèse Sarabande, 2010. CD. [VCL 0610 1109]. Unreleased on the 1960 original soundtrack.

______. *The Mines.* Released on the official soundtrack. Conducted by Alex North. Varèse Sarabande, 2010. CD. [VCL 0610 1109]. Unreleased on the 1960 original soundtrack.

______. *On To Vesuvius: Forward, Gladiators / Forest Meeting.* Released on the official soundtrack. Conducted by Alex North. MCA Records, 1991. CD. [MCAD 10256]. Originally released on Hi-Fi Decca Records, 1960. LP. [DL 9092]

______. *Overture.* Released on the official soundtrack. Conducted by Alex North. Varèse Sarabande, 2010. CD. [VCL 0610 1109]. Unreleased on the 1960 original soundtrack.

______. *Oysters and Snails—Festival.* Released on the official soundtrack. Conducted by Alex North. MCA Records, 1991. CD. [MCAD 10256]. Originally released on Hi-Fi Decca Records, 1960. LP. [DL 9092]. Released as longer and separate tracks on Varèse Sarabande, 2010. CD. [VCL 0610 1109]

______. *Prelude to Battle: Quiet Interlude / The Final Conflict.* Released on the official soundtrack. Conducted by Alex North. MCA Records, 1991. CD. [MCAD 10256]. Originally released on Hi-Fi Decca Records, 1960. LP. [DL 9092]

______. *Spartacus Love Theme.* Released on the official soundtrack. Conducted by Alex North. MCA Records, 1991. CD. [MCAD 10256]. Originally released on Hi-Fi Decca Records, 1960. LP. [DL 9092]

______. *Vesuvius Montage.* Released on the official soundtrack. Conducted by Alex North. Varèse Sarabande, 2010. CD. [VCL 0610 1109]. Unreleased on the 1960 original soundtrack.

Lolita (UK / USA 1962)

Chopin, Frédéric. *Polonaise in A-Major, Op. 40, No. 1* ["Military Polonaise"]. Performed on the piano by Clare Quilty (Peter Sellers). Released on the soundtrack compilation *Kubrick's Music: Selections From the Films of Stanley Kubrick.* Performed by Arthur Rubinstein. Cherry Red Records, 2018. CD. [B07FTY88S3]

Harris, Bob. *Love Theme From Lolita* ["Main Title" / "End Title"]. Released on the official soundtrack. Conducted by Nelson Riddle. Orchestrated by Gil Grau. Rhino Movie Music, 1997. CD. [R2 72841]. Originally released on MGM Records, 1962. LP. [SE4050 ST]

Hopper, Hal and Tom Adair. *There's No You.* Released on the official soundtrack. Instrumental version conducted by Nelson Riddle. Rhino Movie Music, 1997. CD. [R2 72841]. Originally released on the album *Sea of Dreams* by Nelson Riddle & His Orchestra. Capitol Records, 1958. LP. [T 915]

Mann, Paul, Stephan Weiss, and Ruth Lowe. *Put Your Dreams Away (for Another Day).* Released on the official soundtrack. Instrumental version conducted by Nelson Riddle. Rhino Movie Music, 1997. CD. [R2 72841]. Originally released on the album *Sea of Dreams* by Nelson Riddle & His Orchestra. Capitol Records, 1958. LP. [T 915]

Riddle, Nelson, and Bob Harris. *Arrival in Town* ["Ramsdale"]. Released on the official soundtrack. Conducted by Nelson Riddle. Rhino Movie Music, 1997. CD. [R2 72841]. Originally released on MGM Records, 1962. LP. [SE4050 ST]

______. *Discovery of Diary* ["The Last Martini"]. Released on the official soundtrack. Conducted by Nelson Riddle. Rhino Movie Music, 1997. CD. [R2 72841]. Originally released on MGM Records, 1962. LP. [SE4050 ST]

______. *Humbert Contemplates Killing Wife.* Released on the official soundtrack. Conducted by Nelson Riddle. Hallmark Music & Entertainment, 2013. CD. [713042]. Originally released on MGM Records, 1962. LP. [SE4050 ST]

______. *Lolita Ya-Ya.* Released on the official soundtrack. Conducted by Nelson Riddle. Rhino Movie Music, 1997. CD. [R2 72841]. Originally released on MGM Records, 1962. LP. [SE4050 ST]

______. *Mother and Humbert At Dinner* ["Music to Eat By"]. Released on the official soundtrack. Conducted by Nelson Riddle. Rhino Movie Music, 1997. CD. [R2 72841]. Originally released on MGM Records, 1962. LP. [SE4050 ST]

______. *Mrs. Schiller*. Released on the official soundtrack. Conducted by Nelson Riddle. Rhino Movie Music, 1997. CD. [R2 72841]. Unreleased on the 1962 original soundtrack.

______. *Quilty's Theme* ["Quilty"]. Released on the official soundtrack. Conducted by Nelson Riddle. Rhino Movie Music, 1997. CD. [R2 72841]. Originally released on MGM Records, 1962. LP. [SE4050 ST]

______. *School Dance* ["Quilty's Caper"]. Released on the official soundtrack. Conducted by Nelson Riddle. Rhino Movie Music, 1997. CD. [R2 72841]. Originally released on MGM Records, 1962. LP. [SE4050 ST]

______. *Shelley Winters Cha Cha*. Released on the official soundtrack. Conducted by Nelson Riddle. Rhino Movie Music, 1997. CD. [R2 72841]. Unreleased on the 1962 original soundtrack.

______. *The Strange Call*. Released on the official soundtrack. Conducted by Nelson Riddle. Rhino Movie Music, 1997. CD. [R2 72841]. Unreleased on the 1962 original soundtrack.

______. *Thoughts of Lolita* ["Charlotte Is Dead"]. Released on the official soundtrack. Conducted by Nelson Riddle. Rhino Movie Music, 1997. CD. [R2 72841]. Originally released on MGM Records, 1962. LP. [SE4050 ST]

______. *Two Beat Society* ["Instant Music"]. Released on the official soundtrack. Conducted by Nelson Riddle. Rhino Movie Music, 1997. CD. [R2 72841]. Originally released on MGM Records, 1962. LP. [SE4050 ST]

Silvers, Dolores Vicki. *Learnin' the Blues*. Performed by Unknown Artist. Released on the soundtrack compilation *Kubrick's Music: Selections From the Films of Stanley Kubrick*. Performed by the Oscar Peterson Trio. Cherry Red Records, 2018. CD. [B07FTY88S3]. Originally released on the album *Session With Sinatra* by Frank Sinatra with orchestra and chorus conducted by Nelson Riddle. Capital Records, 1955. 7." [EAP 1–629].

Dr. Strangelove or: How I Learned to Stop Worrying and Love the Bomb (UK / USA 1964)

Carter, Benny. *Stick or Twist*. Performed by The Laurie Johnson Orchestra. Unreleased on soundtrack. Originally released on Pye Records, 1962. 7." [7N.15426].

Johnson, Laurie. *The Bomb Run* ["Theme From Dr. Strangelove"]. Based on *When Johnny Comes Marching Home* by Gilmore Patrick Sarsfield. Released on the soundtrack compilation *Dr. Strangelove: Music From the Films of Stanley Kubrick*. Performed by The City of Prague Philharmonic with the Crouch End Festival Chorus. Conducted by Paul Bateman. Silva America, 1999. CD. [SSD 1097]. Originally released on Colpix Records, 1964. LP. [CP 464]

______. *Bossa Nova*. Performed on the radio. Unreleased on soundtrack.

Parker, Ross, and Hughie Charles. *We'll Meet Again*. Released on the soundtrack compilation *Dr. Strangelove: Music From the Films of Stanley Kubrick*. Performed by Vera Lynn. Silva America, 1999. CD. [SSD 1097]. Originally released on Decca Records, 1939. 10". [F. 7268]

Traditional. *Greensleeves*. Performed on the radio. Released on the soundtrack compilation *Kubrick's Music: Selections From the Films of Stanley Kubrick*. Performed by the John Coltrane Quartet. Cherry Red Records, 2018. CD. [B07FTY88S3]

Woods, Harry M., Jimmy Campbell, and Reginald Connelly. *Try a Little Tenderness*. Arranged by Laurie Johnson. Performed by Studio Orchestra. Released on the soundtrack compilation *Kubrick's Music: Selections From the Films of Stanley Kubrick*. Performed by Toots Thielemans. Cherry Red Records, 2018. CD. [B07FTY88S3]

2001: A Space Odyssey (UK / USA 1968)

Dacre, Harry. *Daisy Bell (Bicycle Built for Two)*. Released on the official soundtrack as part of "Hal 9000 Dialog Montage." Performed by HAL 9000 (Douglas Rain). EMI / TCM Turner Classic Movies Music, 1996. CD. [7243 8 55322 2 1]

Khachaturyan, Aram. *Gayane Ballet Suite No. 3, Fourth Movement: Gayane's Adagio.* Released on the official soundtrack. Performed by the Leningrad Philharmonic Orchestra. Conducted by Gennadi Rozhdestvensky. EMI / TCM Turner Classic Movies Music, 1996. CD. [7243 8 55322 2 1]. Originally released on MGM Records, 1968. LP. [MGM CS 8078]

Hill, Mildred Jane, and Patty Smith Hill. *Happy Birthday to You.* Performed by Poole's Parents (Alan Gifford and Ann Gillis). Unreleased on soundtrack.

Ligeti, György. *Atmosphères* ["Overture" / "Jupiter and Beyond: b"]. Released on the official soundtrack. Performed by the Southwest German Radio Orchestra. Conducted by Ernest Bour. EMI / TCM Turner Classic Movies Music, 1996. CD. [7243 8 55322 2 1]. Originally released on MGM Records, 1968. LP. [MGM CS 8078]

______. *Aventures* ["Jupiter and Beyond: c"]. Released on the official soundtrack. Performed by The International Chamber Ensemble Darmstadt. Conducted by Bruno Maderna. EMI / TCM Turner Classic Movies Music, 1996. CD. [7243 8 55322 2 1]. Unreleased on the 1968 original soundtrack.

______. *Lux Aeterna.* Released on the official soundtrack. Performed by the Stuttgart Schola Cantorum. Conducted by Clytus Gottwald. EMI / TCM Turner Classic Movies Music, 1996. CD. [7243 8 55322 2 1]. Longer version originally released on MGM Records, 1968. LP. [MGM CS 8078]

______. *Requiem for Soprano, Mezzo-Soprano, Two Mixed Choirs, and Orchestra* ["Jupiter and Beyond: a"]. Released on the official soundtrack. Performed by The Bavarian Radio Orchestra. Conducted by Francis Travis. EMI / TCM Turner Classic Movies Music, 1996. CD. [7243 8 55322 2 1]. Originally released on MGM Records, 1968. LP. [MGM CS 8078]

Strauss, Johann Jr. *The Blue Danube* ["An Der Schönen Blauen Donau"]. Released on the official soundtrack. Performed by The Berlin Philharmonic Orchestra. Conducted by Herbert von Karajan. EMI / TCM Turner Classic Movies Music, 1996. CD. [7243 8 55322 2 1]. Originally released on MGM Records, 1968. LP. [MGM CS 8078]

Strauss, Richard. *Thus Spake Zarathustra* [Also Sprach Zarathustra], *Op. 30.* Released on the official soundtrack. Performed by The Vienna Philharmonic. Conducted by Herbert von Karajan. EMI / TCM Turner Classic Movies Music, 1996. CD. [7243 8 55322 2 1]. Originally released on MGM Records with Karl Böhm conducting the Berlin Philharmonic, 1968. LP. [MGM CS 8078]

Torch, Sidney. *Off Beat Moods Part 1.* Released on the soundtrack compilation *Kubrick's Music: Selections From the Films of Stanley Kubrick.* Performed by Sidney Torch. Cherry Red Records, 2018. CD. [B07FTY88S3]. Originally released on the album *Virtuosi Moderne—Off Beat Moods Part 1 & 2* by Sidney Torch. Chappell, 1960. Vinyl 12." [C683]

A Clockwork Orange (UK / USA 1971)

Beethoven, Ludwig van. *Symphony No. 5 in C-Minor, Op. 67* (Four-note opening motif). Performed by doorbell. Unreleased on soundtrack.

______. *Symphony No. 9 in D-Minor, Op. 125, Second Movement* (Abridged). Released on the official soundtrack. A Deutsche Grammophon Recording. Warner Bros. Records, 1990. CD. [2573-2]. Originally released on Warner Bros. Records, 1971. LP. [K 46127]

______. *Symphony No. 9 in D-Minor, Op. 125, Fourth Movement* (Abridged). Released on the official soundtrack. A Deutsche Grammophon Recording. Warner Bros. Records, 1990. CD. [2573-2]. Originally released on Warner Bros. Records, 1971. LP. [K 46127]

Bonar, Horatio. *I Was A Wondering Sheep.* Performed by convicts in the prison chapel. Unreleased on soundtrack.

Carlos, Walter. *March from A Clockwork Orange.* Based on *Symphony No. 9 in D-Minor, Op. 125, Fourth Movement* (Abridged) by Ludwig van Beethoven. Released on the official soundtrack. Arranged and performed by Walter Carlos. Articulations by Rachel Elkind. Warner Bros. Records, 1990. CD. [2573-2]. Originally released on Warner Bros. Records, 1971. LP. [K 46127]. Also released on the separate album *Walter Carlos' Clockwork Orange* by Walter Carlos. CBS Records, 1972. LP. [S 73059]

______. *Suicide Scherzo.* Based on *Symphony No. 9 in D-Minor, Op. 125, Second Movement* (Abridged) by Ludwig van Beethoven. Released on the official soundtrack. Arranged and performed by Walter Carlos. Warner Bros. Records, 1990. CD. [2573-2]. Originally released on Warner Bros. Records, 1971. LP. [K 46127]. Also released on the separate album *Walter Carlos' Clockwork Orange* by Walter Carlos. CBS Records, 1972. LP. [S 73059]

______. *Timesteps* (Excerpt). Released on the official soundtrack. Performed by Walter Carlos. Warner Bros. Records, 1990. CD. [2573–2]. Originally released on Warner Bros. Records, 1971. LP. [K 46127]. Full-length version released on the separate album *Walter Carlos' Clockwork Orange* by Walter Carlos. CBS Records, 1972. LP. [S 73059].

______. *William Tell Overture* (Abridged). Based on *William Tell Overture* [Guglielmo Tell Ouverture] by Gioacchino Rossini. Released on the official soundtrack. Performed by Walter Carlos. Warner Bros. Records, 1990. CD. [2573–2]. Originally released on Warner Bros. Records, 1971. LP. [K 46127]. Also released on the separate album *Walter Carlos' Clockwork Orange* by Walter Carlos. CBS Records, 1972. LP. [S 73059]

Carlos, Walter, and Rachel Elkind. *Theme from A Clockwork Orange ("Beethoviana").* Released on the official soundtrack. Performed by Walter Carlos. Warner Bros. Records, 1990. CD. [2573–2]. Originally released on Warner Bros. Records, 1971. LP. [K 46127]. Also released on the separate album *Walter Carlos' Clockwork Orange* by Walter Carlos. CBS Records, 1972. LP. [S 73059]

______. *Title Music From A Clockwork Orange.* Based on Henry Purcell's *March from Music for the Funeral of Queen Mary.* Released on the official soundtrack. Performed by Walter Carlos. Warner Bros. Records, 1990. CD. [2573–2]. Originally released on Warner Bros. Records, 1971. LP. [K 46127]. Also released on the separate album *Walter Carlos' Clockwork Orange* by Walter Carlos. CBS Records, 1972. LP. [S 73059]

Eigen, Erika. *I Want to Marry a Lighthouse Keeper* ["Lighthouse Keeper"]. Released on the official soundtrack. Performed by Erika Eigen. Warner Bros. Records, 1990. CD. [2573–2]. Originally released on the album *Sound of Sunforest* by Sunforest. Deram, 1969. LP. [SDN 7]

Elgar, Edward. *Pomp and Circumstance Op. 39, March No. 1.* Released on the official soundtrack. Warner Bros. Records, 1990. CD. [2573–2]. Originally released on Warner Bros. Records, 1971. LP. [K 46127]

______. *Pomp and Circumstance Op. 39, March No. 4* (Abridged). Released on the official soundtrack. Warner Bros. Records, 1990. CD. [2573–2]. Originally released on Warner Bros. Records, 1971. LP. [K 46127]

Freed, Arthur, and Nacio Herb Brown. *Singin' in the Rain.* Released on the official soundtrack. Performed by Gene Kelly and the MGM Studio Orchestra. Warner Bros. Records, 1990. CD. [2573–2]. Originally released on the soundtrack album *Singin' in the Rain* by the MGM Studio Orchestra. MGM Records, 1965. LP. [MS-599]

______. *Singin' in the Rain.* Performed by Malcolm McDowell (Alex). Unreleased on soundtrack.

Rossini, Gioacchino. *The Thieving Magpie* ["La Gazza Ladra"] (Abridged). Released on the official soundtrack. A Deutsche Grammophon Recording. Warner Bros. Records, 1990. CD [2573–2]. Originally released on Warner Bros. Records, 1972. LP. [K46127]

______. *William Tell Overture* ["Guglielmo Tell Ouverture"] (Abridged). Released on the official soundtrack. A Deutsche Grammophon Recording. Warner Bros. Records, 1990. CD. [2573–2]. Originally released on Warner Bros. Records, 1972. LP. [K46127]

Rimsky-Korsakov, Nikolai. *Scheherazade, Op. 35, First Movement: The Sea And Sinbad's Ship.* Released on the soundtrack compilation *Kubrick's Music: Selections From the Films of Stanley Kubrick.* Performed by the Chicago Symphony Orchestra. Conducted by Fritz Reiner. Cherry Red Records, 2018. CD. [B07FTY88S3].

Tucker, Terry. *Overture to the Sun.* Released on the official soundtrack. Warner Bros. Records, 1990. CD. [2573–2]. Originally released on the album *Sound of Sunforest* by Sunforest. Deram, 1969. LP. [SDN 7]

Yorkston, James. *Molly Malone* ["Cockles and Mussels"]. Performed by Paul Farrell (Tramp). Unreleased on soundtrack.

Barry Lyndon (UK / USA 1975)

Bach, Johann Sebastian. *Concerto for Two Harpsichords and Orchestra in C-Minor, BWV 1060, Adagio.* Released on the official soundtrack. An Archiv Produktion Recording. Performed by Karl Richter and Hedwig Bilgram, Harpsichords, and the Munich Bach-Orchestra. Warner Bros. Records, 1995. CD. [7599–25984–2]. Originally released on Warner Bros. Records, 1975. LP. [BS 2903]

Händel, Georg Friedrich. *Suite for Keyboard (Suite de piece), Vol.2, No.4 in D-Minor, HWV 437, Fourth movement: Sarabande* ["Main Title" / "Duel" / "End-Title"]. Released on the official soundtrack. Performed by the National Philharmonic Orchestra. Arranged and conducted by Leonard Rosenman. Warner Bros. Records, 1995. CD. [7599-25984-2]. Originally released on Warner Bros. Records, 1975. LP. [BS 2903]

LeClair, Jean-Marie. *Sonata VIII à Trois* ["Le Rondeau de Paris"]. Performed by Lady Lyndon (Marisa Berenson), Young Bullingdon (Dominic Savage) and Reverend Runt (Murray Melvin). Unreleased on soundtrack.

Mozart, Wolfgang Amadeus. *March from Idomeneo, KV. 366*. Released on the official soundtrack. An EMI Recording. Warner Bros. Records, 1995. CD. [7599-25984-2]. Originally released on Warner Bros. Records, 1975. LP. [BS 2903]

Ó'Riada, Sean. *Tin Whistles*. Released on the official soundtrack. Performed by Paddy Moloney and Sean Potts. Warner Bros. Records, 1995. CD. [7599-25984-2]. Originally released on Warner Bros. Records, 1975. LP. [BS 2903]

______. *Women of Ireland*. Released on the official soundtrack. Performed by The Chieftains. Warner Bros. Records, 1995. CD. [7599-25984-2]. Originally released on Warner Bros. Records, 1975. LP. [BS 2903]

Paisiello, Giovanni. *The Barber of Seville* ["Il Barbiere di Siviglia"], *Act I: Saper Bramate*. Orchestral version without vocals. Released on the official soundtrack. Performed by the National Philharmonic Orchestra (without vocals). Conducted by Leonard Rosenman. Warner Bros. Records, 1995. CD. [7599-25984-2]. Originally released on Warner Bros. Records, 1975. LP. [BS 2903]

______. *The Barber of Seville* ["Il Barbiere di Siviglia"], *Act 1: Saper Bramate*. Orchestral version with vocals by Unkown Artist. Released on the soundtrack compilation *Kubrick's Music: Selections From the Films of Stanley Kubrick*. Performed by the Collegium Musicum Italicum & I Virtuosi di Roma. Cherry Red Records, 2018. CD. [B07FTY88S3].

Traditional. *British Grenadiers*. Released on the official soundtrack. Performed by Fives and Drums. Warner Bros. Records, 1995. CD. [7599-25984-2]. Originally released on Warner Bros. Records, 1975. LP. [BS 2903]

______. *Hohenfriedberger March* ["Der Hohenfriedberger"]. Released on the official soundtrack. Prussian Military March Music. Assumed to be written by Frederick the Great. CD. [7599-25984-2]. Originally released on Warner Bros. Records, 1975. LP. [BS 2903]

______. *Lilliburlero*. Released on the official soundtrack. Arranged and conducted by Leslie Pearson. Warner Bros. Records, 1995. CD. [7599-25984-2]. Originally released on Warner Bros. Records, 1975. LP. [BS 2903]

______. *Lilliburlero*. Released on the official soundtrack. Performed by Fifes and Drums. Warner Bros. Records, 1995. CD. [7599-25984-2]. Originally released on Warner Bros. Records, 1975. LP. [BS 2903]

______. *Piper's Maggot Jig*. Released on the official soundtrack. Performed by The Chieftains. Warner Bros. Records, 1995. CD. [7599-25984-2]. Originally released on Warner Bros. Records, 1975. LP. [BS 2903]

______. *The Sea-Maiden*. Released on the official soundtrack. Performed by The Chieftains. Warner Bros. Records, 1995. CD. [7599-25984-2]. Originally released on Warner Bros. Records, 1975. LP. [BS 2903]

Schubert, Franz. *Impromptu No. 1 in C-Minor, D. 899/1, Op. 90/1* (First five measures). Released on the soundtrack compilation *Kubrick's Music: Selections From the Films of Stanley Kubrick*. Performed on the piano by Artur Schnabel. Cherry Red Records, 2018. CD. [B07FTY88S3].

______. *German Dance No. 1 in C-Major, D. 90*. Released on the official soundtrack. Performed by the National Philharmonic Orchestra. Conducted by Leonard Rosenman. Warner Bros. Records, 1995. CD. [7599-25984-2]. Originally released on Warner Bros. Records, 1975. LP. [BS 2903]

______. *Piano Trio No. 2 in E-Flat, D. 929, Op. 100, Second Movement* (Film adaptation). Released on the official soundtrack. Performed by Anthony Goldstone (Piano), Ralph Holmes (Violin), and Moray Welsh (Cello). Warner Bros. Records, 1995. CD. [7599-25984-2]. Originally released on Warner Bros. Records, 1975. LP. [BS 2903]

Vivaldi, Antonio. *Cello Concerto in E-Minor, RV 409, Third Movement*. Released on the official soundtrack. A Deutsche Grammophon Recording. Performed by Pierre Fournier (Cello) and Festival Strings Lucerne. Conducted by Rudolf Baumgartner. Warner Bros. Records, 1995. CD. [7599-25984-2]. Originally released on Warner Bros. Records, 1975. LP. [BS 2903]

The Shining (UK / USA 1980)

Bartók, Béla. *Music for Strings, Percussion and Celesta, Third Movement*. Released on the soundtrack compilation *Kubrick's Music: Selections From the Films of Stanley Kubrick*. A Deutsche Grammophon Recording. Performed by Berlin Philharmonic Orchestra. Conducted by Herbert von Karajan. Cherry Red Records, 2018. CD. [B07FTY88S3]. Originally released on Warner Bros. Records, 1980. LP. [HS 3449]

Campbell, Jimmy, Reginald Connelly, and Harry M. Woods. *Midnight, the Stars and You*. Released on the soundtrack compilation *Kubrick's Music: Selections From the Films of Stanley Kubrick*. Performed by Ray Noble and His Orchestra with Al Bowlly (Vocals). Cherry Red Records, 2018. CD. [B07FTY88S3]. Originally released on Victor, 1934. Shellac, 10." [24700]

Carlos, Wendy, and Rachel Elkind. *Heartbeat*. Released on the soundtrack compilation *Rediscovering Lost Scores—Volume One* by Wendy Carlos. East Side Digital, 2005. CD. [ESD 81752].

______. *Main Title "The Shining"* ["Dies Irae"]. Based on *Symphonie Fantastique, Dream of a Witches' Sabbath* by Hector Berlioz. Released on the soundtrack compilation *Dr. Strangelove: Music from the Films of Stanley Kubrick*. Performed by Mark Ayres. Silva America, 1999. CD. [SSD 1097]. Originally released on Warner Bros. Records, 1980. LP. [HS 3449]

______. *Rocky Mountains*. Released on the official soundtrack. Warner Bros. Records, 1980. LP. [HS 3449]. Carlos' own version was later released on the compilation *Rediscovering Lost Scores—Volume One*. East Side Digital, 2005. CD. [ESD 81752].

Clarkson, Geoffrey, Harry Clarkson, and Peter Van Steeden. *Home*. Released on the official soundtrack. Performed by Henry Hall and The Gleneagles Hotel Band with Maurice Elwin (Vocals). Warner Bros. Records, 1980. LP. [HS 3449]. Later released on the soundtrack compilation *Kubrick's Music: Selections From the Films of Stanley Kubrick*. Cherry Red Records, 2018. CD. [B07FTY88S3]. Originally released on Decca, 1932. [DDV-5001]

Webster, Paul Francis, and John Jacob Loeb. *Masquerade*. Released on the soundtrack compilation *Kubrick's Music: Selections From the Films of Stanley Kubrick*. Performed by Jack Hylton and His Orchestra. Cherry Red Records, 2018. CD. [B07FTY88S3]. Originally released on Decca, 1932. Shellac, 10." [F 3161]

Ligeti, György. *Lontano*. Released on the official soundtrack. Performed by Sinfonie Orchester des Südwestfunks. Conducted by Ernest Bour. Warner Bros. Records, 1980. LP. [HS 3449]

Noble, Ray. *It's All Forgotten Now*. Released on the soundtrack compilation *Kubrick's Music: Selections From the Films of Stanley Kubrick*. Performed by Ray Noble and His Orchestra with Al Bowlly (Vocals). Cherry Red Records, 2018. CD. [B07FTY88S3]. Originally released on Decca, 1934. Shellac, 10." [F. 5121]

Penderecki, Krzysztof. *The Awakening of Jacob*. Released on the official soundtrack. Performed by the Polish Radio National Symphony Orchestra. Conducted by Krzysztof Penderecki. Warner Bros. Records, 1980. LP. [HS 3449]

______. *De Natura Sonoris No. 1*. Unreleased on soundtrack.

______. *De Natura Sonoris No. 2*. Released on the official soundtrack. Performed by the Polish Radio National Symphony Orchestra. Conducted by Krzysztof Penderecki. Warner Bros. Records, 1980. LP. [HS 3449].

______. *Kanon for String Orchestra and Tape*. Unreleased on soundtrack.

______. *Polymorphia*. Unreleased on soundtrack.

______. *Utrenja II: The Resurrection of Christ, First Movement: The Gospel* ["Ewangelia"]. Released on the official soundtrack as "Utrenja (Excerpt)." Performed by the Symphony Orchestra of the National Philharmonic Warsaw. Conducted by Andrzej Markowski. Warner Bros. Records, 1980. LP. [HS 3449]

______. *Utrenja II: The Resurrection of Christ, Fifth Movement: Passover Canon, Song 8* ["Kanon Paschy, Pieśń 8"]. Unreleased on soundtrack.

FULL METAL JACKET (UK / USA 1987)

Barry, Jeff, Ellie Greenwich, and Phil Spector. *Chapel of Love.* Released on the official soundtrack. Performed by The Dixie Cups. Warner Bros. Records, 1987. CD. [9 25613-2]. Originally released on *Chapel of Love* by The Dixie Cups. Red Bird, 1964. LP. [RB 20-100].

Dodd, Jimmie. *Mickey Mouse Club March.* Performed by the Marines. Unreleased on soundtrack. Theme song for The Mickey Mouse Club TV program (1955–1959).

Frazier, Al, Carl White, Turner Wilson Jr., and John Harris. *Surfin' Bird.* Released on the official soundtrack. Performed by The Trashmen. Warner Bros. Records, 1987. CD. [9 25613-2]. Originally released on Garrett Records, 1965. 7." [GA-4002]

Hall, Tom T. *Hello Vietnam.* Released on the official soundtrack. Performed by Johnny Wright. Warner Bros. Records, 1987. CD. [9 25613-2]. Originally released on Decca, 1965. 7." [31821]

Hazlewood, Lee. *These Boots Are Made for Walking.* Released on the official soundtrack. Performed by Nancy Sinatra. Warner Bros. Records, 1987. CD. [9 25613-2]. Originally released on Reprise Records, 1965. 7." [0432]

Hill, Mildred Jane, and Patty Smith Hill. *Happy Birthday to You.* Performed by the Marines. Unreleased on soundtrack.

Jagger, Mick, and Keith Richards. *Paint It, Black.* Performed by The Rolling Stones. Unreleased on soundtrack. Originally released as a single on Decca, 1966. Vinyl, 7." [F.12395]. Opening track of the album *Aftermath* by The Rolling Stones. Decca, 1966. LP. [SKL 4786]

Kenner, Chris. *I Like It Like That.* Released on the official soundtrack. Performed by Chris Kenner. Warner Bros. Records, 1987. CD. [9 25613-2]. Originally released on Instant Records, 1961. 7." [VR-3229].

Kubrick, Vivian. *Attack.* Released on the official soundtrack. Performed and programmed by Abigail Mead [Vivian Kubrick]. Warner Bros. Records, 1987. CD. [9 25613-2].

______. *Leonard.* Released on the official soundtrack. Performed and programmed by Abigail Mead [Vivian Kubrick]. Warner Bros. Records, 1987. CD. [9 25613-2].

______. *Parris Island.* Released on the official soundtrack. Performed and programmed by Abigail Mead [Vivian Kubrick]. Warner Bros. Records, 1987. CD. [9 25613-2].

______. *Ruins.* Released on the official soundtrack. Performed and programmed by Abigail Mead [Vivian Kubrick]. Warner Bros. Records, 1987. CD. [9 25613-2].

______. *Sniper.* Released on the official soundtrack. Performed and programmed by Abigail Mead [Vivian Kubrick]. Warner Bros. Records, 1987. CD. [9 25613-2].

. *Time Suspended.* Released on the official soundtrack. Performed and programmed by Abigail Mead [Vivian Kubrick]. Warner Bros. Records, 1987. CD. [9 25613-2].

______. *Transition.* Released on the official soundtrack. Performed and programmed by Abigail Mead [Vivian Kubrick]. Warner Bros. Records, 1987. CD. [9 25613-2].

Offenbach, Jacques, Hector Crémieux, and Etienne Trefeu. *The Marines' Hymn.* Based on *Geneviève de Brabant, The Gendarmes' Duet* by Jacques Offenbach. Released on the official soundtrack. Performed by The Goldman Band. Warner Bros. Records, 1987. CD. [9 25613-2].

Samudio, Domingo. *Wooly Bully.* Released on the official soundtrack. Performed by Sam the Sham and The Pharaohs. Warner Bros. Records, 1987. CD. [9 25613-2]. Originally released on MGM Records, 1965. 7." [K13322].

EYES WIDE SHUT (UK / USA 1999)

Ellington, Duke, and Paul Francis Webster. *I Got It Bad (And That Ain't Good).* Released on the official soundtrack. Performed by The Oscar Peterson Trio. Reprise Records, 1999. CD. [9362-47450-2]. Originally released on the album *Oscar Peterson Plays Duke Ellington* by Oscar Peterson. Mercury, 1953. LP. [MGC-606]

Georges Garvarentz, and Charles Aznavour. *Old Fashioned Way.* Performed by The Victor Silvester Orchestra. Unreleased on soundtrack.

Heyman, Edward, and Victor Young. *When I Fall in Love*. Released on the official soundtrack. Performed by The Victor Silvester Orchestra. Reprise Records, 1999. CD. [9362-47450-2].

Isaak, Chris. *Baby Did a Bad Bad Thing*. Released on the official soundtrack. Performed by Chris Isaak. Reprise Records, 1999. CD. [9362-47450-2]. Originally released on the album *Live from Bimbos 365 Club In San Francisco* by Chris Isaak. Reprise Records, 1995. CD. [ISAAK 1]

Kahn, Gus, and Isham Jones. *It Had to Be You*. Performed by Tommy Sanderson and The Sandman. Unreleased on soundtrack.

Kaempfert, Bert, Charles Singleton, and Eddie Snyder. *Strangers In The Night*. Released on the official soundtrack. Performed by Peter Hughes Orchestra. Reprise Records, 1999. CD. [9362-47450-2].

Lee, Phil, Fraser Snell, and Les Cirkel. *Trio at Madame Jo-Jo's*. Performed by Phil Lee (Guitar), Fraser Snell (Acoustic Double Bass) and Les Cirkel (Drums). Unreleased on soundtrack.

Levant, Oscar, and Edward Heyman. *Blame It on My Youth*. Released on the official soundtrack. Performed by Brad Mehldau. Reprise Records, 1999. CD. [9362-47450-2].

Ligeti, György. *Musica Ricercata, II (Mesto, rigido e cerimoniale)*. Released on the official soundtrack. Performed by Dominic Harlan (Piano). Reprise Records, 1999. CD. [9362-47450-2].

Liszt, Franz. *Grey Clouds* ["Nuages Gris"]. Released on the official soundtrack. Performed by Dominic Harlan (Piano). Reprise Records, 1999. CD. [9362-47450-2].

McHugh, Jimmy, and Dorothy Fields. *I'm in the Mood for Love*. Performed by The Victor Silvester Orchestra. Unreleased on soundtrack.

Mozart, Wolfgang Amadeus. *Requiem, K626, Rex Tremendae*. Performed by Rais Chamber Chamber Chorus and Berlin Radio Symphony Orchestra. Released on the soundtrack compilation *Kubrick's Music: Selections From the Films of Stanley Kubrick*. Performed by the New York Philharmonic. Conducted by Bruno Walter. Cherry Red Records, 2018. CD. [B07FTY88S3].

Page, Benjamin, and Christopher Kiler. *I Want A Boy For Christmas*. Performed by The Del Vetts. Unreleased on soundtrack. Originally released on End, 1961. Vinyl, 7." [E-1106]

Pierpont, James. *Jingle Bells*. Performed in Toy Store. Unreleased on soundtrack.

Pook, Jocelyn. *The Dream*. Released on the official soundtrack. Performed by Jocelyn Pook. Conducted by Harvey Brough. Reprise Records, 1999. CD. [9362-47450-2].

______. *Masked Ball*. Released on the official soundtrack. Performed by Jocelyn Pook. Reprise Records, 1999. CD. [9362-47450-2]. Originally released on the album *Flood* by Jocelyn Pook. Virgin, 1999. [CDVE 944]

______. *Naval Officer*. Released on the official soundtrack. Performed by Jocelyn Pook and Electra Strings. Conducted by Harvey Brough. Reprise Records, 1999. CD. [9362-47450-2].

Pook, Jocelyn, and Harvey Brough. *Migrations*. Released on the official soundtrack. Performed by Jocelyn Pook and the Jocelyn Pook Ensemble with Manickam Yogeswaran, Kelsey Michael and Harvey Brough. Reprise Records, 1999. CD. [9362-47450-2]. Originally released on the album *Deluge* by Jocelyn Pook. Virgin, 1997. [CDVE 933]. Also released on the album *Flood* by Jocelyn Pook. Virgin, 1999. [CDVE 944]

Shanklin, Wayne. *Chanson D'Amour*. Performed by The Victor Silvester Orchestra. Unreleased on soundtrack.

Shapiro, Ted, Jimmy Campbell, and Reginald Connelly. *If I Had You*. Performed by Roy Gerson. Unreleased on soundtrack.

Shostakovich, Dmitri. *Jazz Suite, Waltz No. 2*. Released on the official soundtrack. Performed by the Royal Concertgebouw Orchestra. Conducted by Riccardo Chailly. Reprise Records, 1999. CD. [9362-47450-2]. Originally released on *The Jazz Album*. Decca, 1992. [433 702–2]

Sieczynski, Rudolph. *Wien, du Stadt meiner Träume* [Vienna, City Of My Dreams], *Op. 1*. Unreleased on soundtrack.

Warren, Harry, and Al Dubin. *I Only Have Eyes for You*. Released on the soundtrack compilation *Kubrick's Music: Selections From the Films of Stanley Kubrick*. Performed by The Victor Silvester Orchestra. Cherry Red Records, 2018. CD. [B07FTY88S3].

Bibliography

Abrams, Nathan. *Stanley Kubrick: New York Jewish Intellectual*. New Jersey: Rutgers University Press, 2018.

Appelt, Christian. "The Craft of Seeing." In *Stanley Kubrick Catalogue*, 255–256. Frankfurt am Main: Deutsches Filmmuseum, 2004.

Arnheim, Rudolf. *Art and Visual Perception: A Psychology of the Creative Eye*. 1954. Berkeley: University of California Press, 1974.

______. *Film as Art*. Berkeley: University of California Press, 1957.

______. "Perceptual Dynamics in Musical Expression," *The Musical Quarterly* 70, no. 3 (1984): 295–309.

______. "A Plea for Visual Thinking," *Critical Inquiry* 6, no. 3 (1980): 489–497.

______. *The Power of the Center*. Berkeley: University of California Press, 1988.

______. *Visual Thinking*. 1969. Berkeley: University of California Press, 1997.

Baker, Nancy Kovaleff, Max Halle Paddison, and Roger Scruton. "Expression." In *The New Grove Dictionary of Music and Musicians*, edited by Stanley Sadie, 463–472. London: Grove, 2002.

Bálint, Katalin, Moniek M. Kuijpers, and Miruna M. Doicaru. "The Effect of Suspense Structure on Felt Suspense and Narrative Absorption in Literature and Film." In *Narrative Absorption*, edited by Frank Hakemulder, Moniek M. Kuijpers, Ed S. Tan, Katalin Bálint, and Miruna M. Doicaru, 97–118. Amsterdam: John Benjamins, 2017.

Bálint, Katalin, and Ed S. Tan. "'It Feels Like There are Hooks Inside My Chest': The Construction of Narrative Absorption Experiences Using Image Schemata." *Projections: The Journal for Movies and Mind* 9, no. 2 (2015): 63–88.

Barcelona, Antonio, ed. *Metaphor and Metonymy at the Crossroads: A Cognitive Perspective*. Berlin: Mouton de Gruyter, 2003.

Barham, Jeremy. "Incorporating Monsters: Music as Context, Character and Construction in Kubrick's *The Shining*." In *Terror Tracks: Music and Sound in Horror Cinema*, edited by Philip Hayward, 137–170. London: Equinox Press, 2009.

Barrett, Lisa Feldman. "The Future of Psychology: Connecting Mind to Brain." *Perspectives on Psychological Science* 4, no. 4: 326–339.

______. *How Emotions are Made: The Secret Life of the Brain*. New York: Houghton Mifflin Harcourt, 2017.

Barrett, Lisa Feldman, Batja Mesquita, Kevin N. Ochsner, and James J. Gross. "The Experience of Emotion." *Annual Review of Psychology* 58 (2007): 373–403.

Barsalou, Lawrence. "Grounded Cognition." *Annual Review of Psychology* 59 (2008): 617–645.

______. "Perceptual Symbol Systems." *Behavioral and Brain Sciences* 22 (1999): 577–609.

Baxter, John. *Stanley Kubrick: A Biography*. New York: Carroll & Graf Publishers, 1997.

Benson, Michael. *Space Odyssey: Stanley Kubrick, Arthur C. Clarke, and the Making of a Masterpiece*. New York: Simon & Schuster, 2018.

Bettetini, Gianfranco. *The Language and Technique of the Film*. The Hague: Mouton, 1973.

Blair, Rhonda. *The Actor, Image, and Action: Acting and Cognitive Neuroscience*. London: Routledge, 2007.

Blair, Rhonda, and Amy Cook, eds. *Theatre, Performance and Cognition: Languages, Bodies and Ecologies*. London: Bloomsbury, 2016.

Boggs, Joseph M. *The Art of Watching Films*. 3th ed. California: Mayfield Publishing Company, Mountain View, 1991.

Bordwell, David. "Contemporary Film Studies and the Vicissitudes of Grand Theory." In *Post-Theory: Reconstructing Film Studies*, edited by David Bordwell, and Noël Carroll, 3–36. Madison: University of Wisconsin Press, 1996.

______. "Historical Poetics of Cinema." In *The Cinematic Text: Methods and Approaches*, edited by Robert Barton, 369–398. New York: AMS Press, 1989.

______. *Making Meaning: Inference and Rhetoric in the Interpretation of Cinema*. London: Harvard University Press, 1989.

______. *Narration in the Fiction Film*. Madison: University of Wisconsin Press, 1985.

Bordwell, David, Janet Staiger, and Kristin Thompson. *The Classical Hollywood Cinema*. New York: Routledge, 1985.

Bordwell, David, and Kristin Thompson. *Film Art: An Introduction*. 7th ed. New York: McGraw-Hill, 2004.

Boroditsky, Lera. "Metaphoric Structuring: Understanding Time Through Spatial Metaphors." *Cognition* 75, no. 1 (2000): 1–28.

Branigan, Edward. "Formal Permutations of the Point-of-View Shot." *Screen* 16, no. 3 (1975): 54–64.

______. *Narrative Comprehension and Film*. New York: Routledge, 1992.

______. *Projecting a Camera: Language-Games in Film Theory*. New York: Routledge, 2006.

Bransford, John D., J. Richard Barclay, and Jeffery J. Franks. "Sentence Memory: A Constructive Versus Interpretive Approach." *Cognitive Psychology* 3, no. 2 (1972): 193–209.

Broderick, Mick, ed. *The Kubrick Legacy*. New York: Routledge, 2019.

Brower, Candace. "A Cognitive Theory of Musical Meaning." *Journal of Music Theory* 44, no. 2 (2000): 323–379.

Buckland, Warren. *The Cognitive Semiotics of Film*. Cambridge: Cambridge University Press, 2000.

______. "Film Semiotics." In *A Companion to Film Theory*, edited by Toby Miller, and Robert Stam, 84–104. Oxford: Blackwell Publishing, 1999.

Burch, Noël. *Theory of Film Practice*. Translated by Helen R. Lane. New York: Praeger, 1973. Reprinted by Princeton: Princeton University Press, 1981.

Burgess, Anthony. *You've Had Your Time: Being the Second Part of the Confessions of Anthony Burgess*. London: Vintage, 2002.

Burt, George. *The Art of Film Music*. Boston: Northeastern University Press, 1994.

Cahill, Tim. "The *Rolling Stone* Interview: Stanley Kubrick." In *Stanley Kubrick Interviews*, edited by Gene D. Phillips, 189–203. Jackson: University Press of Mississippi, 2001.

Caracciolo, Marco. "Bones in Outer Space: Narrative and the Cosmos in *2001: A Space Odyssey* and Its Remediations." *Image [&] Narrative* 16, no. 3 (2015): 73–89.

Carnicke, Sharon Marie. "Screen Performance and Director's Visions." In *More Than a Method*, edited by Cynthia Baron, Diane Carson, and Frank P. Tomasulo, 42–67. Detroit: Wayne State University Press, 2004.

Carroll, John M. *Toward a Structural Psychology of Cinema*. New York: Mouton, 1980.

Carroll, Noël. "Art Interpretation: The 2010 Richard Wollheim Memorial Lecture." *British Journal of Aesthetics* 51, no. 2 (2011): 117–135.

______. "The Paradox of Suspense." In *Suspense: Conceptualizations, Theoretical Analyses, and Empirical Explorations*, edited by Peter Vorderer, Hans J. Wulff, and Mike Friedrichsen, 71–91. New York: Routledge, 1996.

______. "The Paradox of Suspense." In *Beyond Aesthetics*, edited by Noël Carroll, 254–270. New York: Cambridge University Press, 2001.

______. *The Philosophy of Motion Pictures*. Malden: Blackwell Publishing, 2007.

______. "Prospects for Film Theory: A Personal Assessment." In *Post-Theory: Reconstructing Film Studies*, edited by David Bordwell, and Noël Carroll, 37–68. Madison: University of Wisconsin Press, 1996.

______. "Towards a Theory of Film Suspense." In *Theorizing the Moving Image*, edited by Noël Carroll, 94–117. New York: Cambridge University Press, 1996.

Chandler, Daniel. *Semiotics: The Basics*. 2nd ed. New York: Routledge, 2007.

Chateau, Dominique. "Towards a Generative Model of Film Discourse." In *The Film Spectator: From Sign to Mind*, edited by Warren Buckland, 35–44. Amsterdam: Amsterdam University Press, 1995.

Chattah, Juan. "Film Music as Embodiment." In *Embodied Cognition and Cinema*, edited by Maarten Coëgnarts and Peter Kravanja, 81–112. Leuven: Leuven University Press, 2015.

Choi, Jinhee. "Leaving It Up to the Imagination: POV Shots and Imagining from the Inside." *The Journal of Aesthetics and Art Criticism* 63, no. 1 (2005): 17–25.

Chomsky, Noam. *Syntactic Structures*. The Hague: Mouton, 1957.

Ciment, Michel. *Kubrick: The Definitive Edition*. Translated by Gilbert Adair. New York: Faber and Faber, 2001. Originally published as *Kubrick* (Paris: Calmann-Lévy, 1980)

Clare, Ysabel. "Stanislavsky's System as an Enactive Guide to Embodied Cognition?" *Connection Science* 29, no. 1 (2017): 43–63.

Coëgnarts, Maarten. "Cinema and the Embodied Mind: Metaphor and Simulation in Understanding Meaning in Films." *Palgrave Communications* 3 (2017): 1–15.

______. "Stanley Kubrick and the Art of Embodied Meaning-Making in Film." *Cinergie: il Cinema e le altre Arti* 12 (2017), 53–71.

Coëgnarts, Maarten, and Miklós Kiss. "'Look Out Behind You!' Grounding Suspense in the Slasher Film." *New Review of Film and Television Studies* 15, no. 3 (2017): 348–374.

Coëgnarts, Maarten, and Peter Kravanja, eds. *Embodied Cognition and Cinema*. Leuven: Leuven University Press, 2015.

______. "Embodied Visual Meaning: Image Schemas in Film." *Projections: The Journal for Movies and Mind* 6, no. 2 (2012): 84–101.

______. "Perceiving Emotional Causality in Film: A Conceptual and Formal Analysis. *New Review of Film and Television Studies* 14, no.4 (2016), 440–466.

______. "With the Past in Front of the Character: Evidence for Spatial-Temporal Metaphors in Cinema." *Metaphor and Symbol* 30, no. 3 (2015): 218–239.

Coëgnarts, Maarten, Miklós Kiss, Peter Kravanja, and Steven Willemsen. "Seeing Yourself in the Future: The Role of Situational (Dis) continuity and Conceptual Metaphor in the Understanding of Complex Cases of Character Perception." *Projections: The Journal for Movies and Mind* 10, no. 1 (2016): 114–138.

Cohen, Annabel J. "Music as a Source of Emotion in Film." In *Music and Emotion: Theory and Research*, edited by Patrick N. Juslin, and John A. Sloboda, 249–272. Oxford: Oxford University Press, 2001.

______. "Perspectives from Cognitive Psychology." In *Music and Cinema*, edited by James Buhler, Caryl Flinn, and David Neumeyer, 360–377. Hanover and London: Wesleyan University Press, 2000.

Colin, Michel. "The Grande Syntagmatique Revisited." In *The Film Spectator: From Sign to Mind*, edited by Warren Buckland, 45–86. Amsterdam: Amsterdam University Press, 1995.

Correa-Beningfield, Gitte Kristiansen, Ignasi Navarro-Ferrando, and Claude Vandeloise. "Image Schemas vs. Complex Primitives in Cross-Cultural Spatial Cognition." In *From Perception to Meaning: Image Schemas in Cognitive Linguistics*, edited by Beate Hampe, 343–368. Chicago: University of Chicago Press, 2005.

Cox, Arnie. "The Metaphorical Logic of Musical Motion and Space." PhD diss., University of Oregon, 1999.

Currie, Gregory. *Image and Mind: Film, Philosophy, and Cognitive Science*. Cambridge: Cambridge University Press 1995.

D'Aloia, Adriano, and Ruggero Eugeni, eds. *Neurofilmology. Audiovisual Studies and the Challenge of Neuroscience*." Special issue, *Cinéma & Cie* 14, no. 22/23 (2014): 9–26.

Darwin, Charles. *The Expression of the Emotions in Man and Animals*. 1872. New York: Oxford University Press, 1998.

Davidson, Donald. "Mental Events." In *Essays on Actions and Events*, edited by Donald Davidson, 207–224. New York: Oxford University Press, 2002.

______. "Truth and Meaning." *Synthese* 17, no. 1 (1967): 304–323.

Dewell, Robert. "Dynamic patterns of CONTAINMENT." In *From Perception to Meaning: Image Schemas in Cognitive Linguistics*, edited by Beate Hampe, 369–394. Chicago: University of Chicago Press, 2005.

Dirven, René. "Emotions as Cause and the Cause of Emotions." In *The Language of Emotions*, edited by Susanne Niemeier and René Dirven, 55–86. Amsterdam: John Benjamins, 1997.

Dirven, René, and Ralf Pörings, eds. *Metaphor and Metonymy in Comparison and Contrast* (Cognitive Linguistic Research 20). Berlin/New York: Mouton de Gruyter, 2002.

Doicaru, Miruna. "Gripped by Movies: From Story-World to Artifact Absorption." PhD diss., University of Amsterdam, 2016.

Eco, Umberto. "Articulations of the Cinematic Code." *Cinematics* 1, no. 1 (1970): 590–605.

______. "Introduction to a Semiotics of Iconic Signs." *Versus* 2, no. 1 (1972): 1–15.

Eder, Jens. "Understanding Characters." *Projections: The Journal for Movies and Mind* 4, no. 1 (2010): 16–40.

Eisenstein, Sergei. *The Film Sense*. Edited and translated by Jay Leyda. New York: Meridian Books, 1957.

Ekman, Paul, and Wallace V. Friesen. *Unmasking the Face: A Guide to Recognizing Emotions from Facial Clues*. Los Altos: Malor Books, 2003.

Ekman, Paul, Wallace V. Friesen, and Sonia Ancoli. "Facial Signs of Emotional Experience." *Journal of Personality and Social Psychology* 39, no. 6 (1980): 1125–1134.

El Refaie, Elisabeth. "Reconsidering 'Image Metaphor' in the Light of Perceptual Simulation Theory." *Metaphor and Symbol* 30, no.1 (2005): 63–76.

Evans, Vyvyan. *The Structure of Time*. Amsterdam: John Benjamins, 2003.

Evans, Vyvyan, and Melanie Green. *Cognitive Linguistics: An Introduction*. Edinburgh: Edinburgh University Press, 2006.

Fahlenbrach, Kathrin. "Emotions in Sound: Audiovisual Metaphors in the Sound Design of Narrative Films." *Projections: The Journal for Movies and Mind* 2, no. 2 (2008): 85–103.

______, ed. *Embodied Metaphors in Film, Television, and Video Games: Cognitive Approaches*. London/New York: Routledge, 2016.

Falsetto, Mario. *A Narrative and Stylistic Analysis*. London: Praeger Publishers, 2001.

Fenwick, James, ed. *Understanding Kubrick's 2001: A Space Odyssey: Representation and Interpretation*. Bristol: Intellect, 2018.

Fenwick, James, I.Q. Hunter, and Elisa Pezzotta, eds. "Stanley Kubrick: A Retrospective." Special issue, *Cinergie: Il cinema e le alter arti*, no. 12 (2017).

Fodor, Jerry. *The Language of Thought*. New York: Thomas Y. Crowell Co., 1975.

Forceville, Charles. "Non-verbal and Multimodal Metaphor in a Cognitivist Framework: Agendas for Research." In *Multimodal Metaphor*, edited by Charles Forceville, and Eduardo Urios-Aparisi, 19–42. Berlin: Mouton de Gruyter, 2009.

Forceville, Charles, and Marloes Jeulink. "The Flesh and Blood of Embodied Understanding: The Source-Path-Goal Schema in Animation Film." *Pragmatics & Cognition* 19, no. 1 (2011): 37–59.

Frank, Mark G. "Facial expressions." In *International Encyclopedia of the Social and Behavioral Sciences*, edited by Nancy Eisenberg, 5230–5234. Oxford: Elsevier, 2004.

Gallese, Vittorio. "Mirror Neurons, Embodied Simulation and the Neural Basis of Social Identification." *Psychoanalytic Dialogues* 19, no. 5 (2009): 519–536.

______. "The Roots of Empathy: The Shared Manifold Hypothesis and the Neural Basis of Intersubjectivity." *Psychopathology* 36, no. 4 (2003): 171–180.

______. "The 'Shared Manifold' Hypothesis: From Mirror Neurons to Empathy." *Journal of Consciousness Studies* 8, no. 5–7 (2001): 33–50.

Gallese, Vittorio, Luciano Fadiga, Leonardo Fogassi, and Giacomo Rizzolatti. "Action Recognition in the Premotor Cortex." *Brain* 119, no. 2 (1996): 593–609;

Gallese Vittorio, and Michele Guerra. "Embodying Movies: Embodied Simulation and Film Studies." *Cinema: Journal of Philosophy and the Moving Image* 3 (2012): 183–210.

Gallese, Vittorio, and Corrado Sinigaglia. "What Is So Special About Embodied Simulation?" *Trends in Cognitive Sciences* 15, no. 11 (2011): 512–519.

Gaut, Berys. "Film Authorship and Collaboration." In *Film Theory and Philosophy*, edited by Richard Allen, and Murray Smith, 149–172. Oxford: Oxford University Press, 1997.

______. *A Philosophy of Cinematic Art*. Cambridge: Cambridge University Press, 2010.

Gelman, Susan A., and Cristine H. Legare. "Concepts and Folk Theories." *Annual Review of Anthropology* 40 (2011): 379–398.

Gelmis, Joseph. "The Film Director as Superstar: Stanley Kubrick." In *Stanley Kubrick Interviews*, edited by Gene D. Phillips, 80–104. Jackson: University Press of Mississippi, 2001.

Gengaro, Christine Lee. *Listening to Stanley Kubrick: The Music in His Films*. London: Rowman & Littlefield, 2012.

Gentner, Dedre. "Spatial Metaphors in Temporal Reasoning." In *Spatial Schemas and Abstract Thought*, edited by Merideth Gattis, 203–222. Cambridge: Cambridge University Press, 2001.

Gentner, Dedre, Mutsumi Imai, and Lera Boroditsky. "As Time Goes By: Evidence for Two Systems in Processing Space > Time Metaphors." *Language and Cognitive Processes* 17, no. 5 (2002): 537–565.

Gerrig, Richard J. *Experiencing Narrative Worlds: On the Psychological Activities of Reading*. New Haven: Yale University Press, 1993.

______. "Is There a PARADOX of Suspense? A Reply to Yanal." *The British Journal of Aesthetics* 37, no. 2 (1997): 168–174.

Gibbs, Raymond W. Jr. *Embodiment and Cognitive Science*. New York: Cambridge University Press, 2005.

Gibbs, Raymond W. Jr, and Herbert L. Colston. "Image Schema: The Cognitive Psychological Reality of Image Schemas and Their Transformations." In *Cognitive Linguistics: Basic Readings*, edited by Dirk Geeraerts, 239–268. Berlin: Mouton de Gruyter.

Gibbs, Raymond W. Jr., and Marcus Perlman. "The Contested Impact of Cognitive Linguistic Research on Psycholinguistic Theories of Metaphor Understanding." In *Cognitive Linguistics: Current Applications and Future Perspectives*, edited by Gitte Kristiansen, Michel Achard, René Dirven, and F. Ruiz de Mendoza Ibañez, 211–228. Berlin: Mouton de Gruyter, 2006.

Gleason, Daniel W. "The Visual Experience of Image Metaphor: Cognitive Insights into Imagist Figures." *Poetics Today* 30, no. 3 (2009): 423–470.

Goffman, Erving. *The Presentation of Self in Everyday Life*. Doubleday: Allen Lane The Penguin Press, 1959.

Goossens, Louis. "Metaptonymy: The Interaction of Metaphor and Metonymy in Expressions for Linguistic Action." *Cognitive Linguistics* 1, no. 3 (1990): 323–340.

Gorchakov, Nikolai M. *Stanislavsky Directs*. Translated by Miriam Goldina. New York: Funk & Wagnalls Company, 1954.

Greene, Andy. "Stephen King: The Rolling Stone Interview." *Rolling Stone*, October 31, 2014. Accessed November 16, 2018. https://www.rollingstone.com/culture/culture-features/stephen-king-the-rolling-stone-interview-191529/.

Grice, Herbert Paul. "The Causal Theory of Perception." In *Studies in the Way of Words*, edited by Herbert Paul Grice, 224–247. Cambridge: Harvard University Press, 1989.

______. "Meaning." *The Philosophical Review* 66, no. 3 (1957): 377–388.

Grodal, Torben. *Embodied Visions: Evolution, Emotion, Culture, and Film*. New York: Oxford University Press, 2009.

______. "The PECMA flow: A General Model of Visual Aesthetics." *Film Studies* 8, no. 1 (2006): 1–11.

Hakemulder, Frank, Moniek M. Kuijpers, Ed S. Tan, Katalin Bálint, and Miruna M. Doicaru, ed. *Narrative Absorption*. Amsterdam: John Benjamins, 2017.

Hampe, Beate, ed. *From Perception to Meaning: Image Schemas in Cognitive Linguistics*. Berlin: Mouton de Gruyter, 2005.

Hanich, Julian. "Reflecting on Reflections: Cinema's Complex Mirror Shots." In *Indefinite Visions: Cinema and the Attractions of Uncertainty*, ed. Martine Beugnet, Allan Cameron and Arild Fetveit, 131–156. Edinburgh: Edinburgh University Press, 2017.

Harlan, Jan, dir. *Stanley Kubrick: A Life in Pictures*. 2001; Burbank, CA: Warner Bros. Pictures, 2007. DVD Disc.

Hasson, Uri, Ohad Landesman, Barbara Knappmeyer, Ignacio Vallines, Nava Rubin, and David J. Heeger. "Neurocinematics: The Neuroscience of Film." *Projections: The Journal for Movies and Mind* 2, no. 1 (2008): 1–26.

Heider, Karl G. *Landscapes of Emotion*. Cambridge: Cambridge University Press, 1991.

Heimann, Katrin S., Maria Alessandra Umiltà, Michele Guerra, and Vittorio Gallese. "Moving Mirrors: A High Density EEG Study Investigating the Effects of Camera Movements on Motor Cortex Activation During Action Observation." *Journal of Cognitive Neuroscience* 26, no. 9 (2014): 2087–2101.

Heimann, Katrin S., Sebo Uithol, Marta Calbi, Maria Alessandra Umiltà, Michele Guerra, and Vittorio Gallese. "'Cuts in action': A High-Density EEG Study Investigating the Neural Correlates of Different Editing Techniques in Film." *Cognitive Science* 41 (2017): 1555–1588.

Heimann, Katrin S., Sebo Uithol, Marta Calbi, Maria Alessandra Umiltà, Michele Guerra, Joerg Fingerhut, and Vittorio Gallese. "Embodying the Camera: An EEG Study on the Effect of Camera Movements on Film Spectators' Sensorimotor Cortexactivation." *PLoSONE* 14, no. 3 (2019): e0211026.

Higgins, Scott. "Deft Trajectories For the Eye." In *Arnheim for Film and Media Studies*, edited by Scott Higgins, 107–126. New York: Routledge, 2011.

Hunt, Bill. "Vintage Bits Interview: Leon Vitali Talks Stanley Kubrick on DVD." *The Digital Bits*, January 03, 2019. http://thedigitalbits.com/featured/interviews/leon-vitali-talks-kubrick-on-dvd#

Hunter, I.Q., ed. "Kubrick and Adaptation." Special issue, *Adaptation* 8, no. 3 (December 2015).

Hyman, John. "The Evidence of Our Senses." In *Strawson and Kant*, edited by Hans-Johann Glock, 235–253. Oxford: Oxford University Press, 2003.

Hyslop, Alec. "Other Minds." In *The Stanford Encyclopedia of Philosophy*. Stanford University. Article published October 6, 2005; last modified Jan 14, 2014. https://plato.stanford.edu/entries/other-minds/

Iten, Corinne. *Linguistic Meaning, Truth Conditions, and Relevance: The Case of Concessives*. New York: Palgrave MacMillan, 2005.

Jenkins, Greg. *Stanley Kubrick and the Art of Adaptation: Three Novels, Three Films*. London: McFarland, 1997.

Johnson, Diane. "Writing *The Shining*." In *Depth of Field: Stanley Kubrick, Film, and the Uses of History*, edited by Geoffrey Cocks, James Diedrick, and Glenn Perusek, 55–61. Madison: The University of Wisconsin Press, 2006.

Johnson, Mark. *The Aesthetics of Meaning and Thought: The Bodily Roots of Philosophy, Science, Morality, and Art*. Chicago: University of Chicago Press, 2018.

______. *The Body in the Mind: The Bodily Basis of Meaning, Imagination and Reason*. Chicago: University of Chicago Press, 1987.

______. *Embodied Mind, Meaning, and Reason: How Our Bodies Give Rise to Understanding*. Chicago: University of Chicago Press, 2017.

______. "Identity, Bodily Meaning, and Art." In *Art and Identity: Essays on the Aesthetic Creation of Mind*, edited by Tone Roald and Johannes Lang, 15–38. Amsterdam: Rodopi, 2013.

______. *The Meaning of the Body: Aesthetics of Human Understanding*. Chicago: University of Chicago Press, 2007.

______. "The Philosophical Significance of Image Schemas." In *From Perception to Meaning: Image Schemas in Cognitive Linguistics*, edited by Beate Hampe, 15–33. Chicago: University of Chicago Press, 2005.

Johnson, Mark, and Steve Larson. "'Something in the Way She Moves'—Metaphors of Musical Motion." *Metaphor and Symbol* 18, no. 2 (2003): 63–84.

Johnson-Laird, Philip N. *Mental Models: Towards a Cognitive Science of Language, Inference, and Consciousness.* Cambridge: Harvard University Press, 1983.

Jonides, John. "Further Towards a Model of the Mind's Eye's Movement." *Bulletin of the Psychonomic Society* 21, no. 4 (1983): 247–50.

Kaiser, Susanne, and Thomas Wehrle. "Facial Expressions as Indicator of Appraisal Processes." In *Appraisal Processes in Emotion*, edited by Klaus R. Scherer, Angela Schorr, and Tom Johnstone, 285–300. Oxford: Oxford University Press, 2001.

Kappelhoff, Hermann, and Cornelia Müller. "Embodied Meaning Construction: Multimodal Metaphor and Expressive Movement in Speech, Gesture, and Feature Film." *Metaphor and the Social World* 1, no. 2 (2011): 121–153

Kemp, Rick. *Embodied Acting: What Neuroscience Tells Us About Performance.* London: Routledge, 2012.

Kim, Jaegwon. "Causation, Nomic Subsumption, and the Concept of Event." *The Journal of Philosophy* 70 (1973): 217–236.

______. *Philosophy of Mind.* Cambridge: Westview Press, 2006.

Kohler, Christian G., Travis Turner, Neal M. Stolar, Warren B. Bilker, Colleen M. Brensinger, Raquel E. Gur, and Ruben C. Gur. "Differences in Facial Expressions of Four Universal Emotions." *Psychiatry Research* 128, no. 3 (2004): 235–244.

Kolker, Robert P. *A Cinema of Loneliness.* 4th ed. Oxford: Oxford University Press, 2011.

______. *The Extraordinary Image: Orson Welles, Alfred Hitchcock, Stanley Kubrick, and the Reimagining of Cinema.* New Brunswick: Rutgers University Press, 2017.

Kövecses, Zoltán. *Metaphor and Emotion: Language, Culture, and Body in Human Feeling.* Cambridge: Cambridge University Press, 2000.

______. *Metaphor: A Practical Introduction.* Oxford: Oxford University Press, 2010.

Kövecses, Zoltán, and Günter Radden. "Metonymy: Developing a Cognitive Linguistic View." *Cognitive Linguistics* 9, no. 1 (1998): 37–77.

Kreider, Tim. "Introducing Sociology." In *Depth of Field: Stanley Kubrick, Film, and the Uses of History*, edited by Geoffrey Cocks, James Diedreck and James Pruseck (Madison: The University of Wisconsin Press, 2006), 280–297.

Kuberski, Philip. *Kubrick's Total Cinema: Philosophical Themes and Formal Qualities.* London: Bloomsbury, 2012.

Kubrick, Stanley. "Words and Movies." *Sight and Sound* 30, no. 1 (1960): 14.

Kubrick, Stanley, and Frederic Raphael, *Eyes Wide Shut: A Screenplay.* London: Penguin Books, 1999.

Kubrick, Vivian, dir. *The Making of The Shining.* 1980; Burbank, CA: Warner Bros. Pictures, 2007. Blu-ray Disc, 1080p.

Lakoff, George. "Image Metaphors." *Metaphor and Symbolic Activity* 2, no. 3 (1987): 219–222.

______. "Reflections on Metaphor and Grammar." In *Essays in Semantics and Pragmatics: In Honor of Charles J. Fillmore*, edited by Masayoshi Shibatani, and Sandra A. Thompson, 133–144. Amsterdam: John Benjamins Publishing, 1995.

______. *Women, Fire and Dangerous Things: What Categories Reveal About the Mind.* Chicago: University of Chicago Press, 1987.

Lakoff, George, and Mark Johnson. *Metaphors We Live By.* Chicago: University of Chicago Press, 1980.

______. *Philosophy in the Flesh: The Embodied Mind and its Challenge to Western Thought.* New York: Basic Books, 1999.

______. "Why Cognitive Linguistics Requires Embodied Realism," *Cognitive Linguistics* 13, no. 3 (2002): 245–263

Lakoff, George, and Mark Turner. *More Than Cool Reason: A Field Guide to Poetic Metaphor.* Chicago: University of Chicago Press, 1989.

Langacker, Ronald. *Foundations of Cognitive Grammar.* Vol. 1. Stanford: Stanford University Press, 1987.

Larson, Steve. "Musical Forces and Melodic Patterns." *Theory and Practice* 22 (1997): 55–72.

______. *Musical Forces: Motion, Metaphor, and Meaning in Music.* Bloomington: Indiana University Press, 2012.

Leman, Marc. *Embodied Music Cognition and Mediation Technology.* Cambridge: MIT Press, 2007.

Lightman, Herb. "Photographing Stanley Kubrick's *Barry Lyndon.*" *American Cinematographer* 57, no. 3 (1976): 269–275.

Lindsay, Vachel. *The Art of the Moving Picture.* New York: Macmillan, 1915.

Livingston, Paisley. *Cinema, Philosophy, Bergman: On Film as Philosophy.* Oxford: Oxford University Press, 2009.

______. "Cinematic Authorship." In *Film Theory and Philosophy*, edited by Richard Allen, and Murray Smith, 132–148. Oxford: Oxford University Press, 1997.

Ljujić, Tatjana, Peter Krämer, and Richard Daniels, eds. *Stanley Kubrick: New Perspectives*. London: Black Dog Publishing, 2015.

LoBrutto, Vincent. *Stanley Kubrick: A Biography*. New York: Donald I. Fine Books, 1997.

Lockhead, Judy. "The Metaphor of Musical Motion: Is There an Alternative?" *Theory and Practice* 14–5 (1988–89): 83–103.

Loughlin, Gerard. *Alien Sex: The Body and Desire in Cinema and Theology*. Malden/Oxford: Blackwell Publishing, 2004.

Lovisato, Marco. "(Do Not) Overlook. *Room 237* and the Dismemberment of *The Shining*. *Cinergie: il Cinema e le altre Arti* 12 (2017), 127–137.

Luckhurst, Roger. *The Shining*. London: British Film Institute, 2013.

McCabe, John. *Bartók Orchestral Music*. London: British Broadcoasting Corporation, 1974.

Mckee, Eric. "The Topic of the Sacred Hymn in Beethoven's Instrumental Music." *College Music Symposium* 47 (2007): 23–52.

McQuiston, Kate. *We'll Meet Again: Musical Design in the Films of Stanley Kubrick*. New York: Oxford University Press, 2013.

Mag Uidhir, Christy. "The Paradox of Suspense Realism." *The Journal of Aesthetics and Art Criticism* 69, no. 2 (2011): 161–171.

Magliano, Joseph P., Jason Miller, and Rolf A. Zwaan. "Indexing Space and Time in Film Understanding." *Applied Cognitive Psychology* 15, no. 5 (2001): 533–545.

Mather, Philippe. *Stanley Kubrick at Look Magazine: Authorship and Genre in Photojournalism and Film*. Bristol: Intellect, 2013.

Meskin, Aaron. "Authorship." In *The Routledge Companion to Philosophy and Film*, edited by Paisley Livingston, and Carl Plantinga, 12–28. New York: Routledge, 2009.

Metz, Christian. *Film Language: A Semiotics of the Cinema*. Translated by Michael Taylor. New York: Oxford University Press, 1974.

______. *Language and Cinema*. Translated by Donna Jean Umiker-Sebeok. The Hague: Mouton, 1974.

Michotte, Albert. *La perception de la causalité*. Louvain: Institut Supérieur de Philosophien, 1946.

Mullen, Elizabeth. "Do you Speak Kubrick?: Orchestrating Transgression and Mastering Malaise in *The Shining*." *Image [&] Narrative* 10, no. 2 (2009): 94–108.

Nabokov, Vladimir. Foreword to *Lolita: A Screenplay*, by Vladimir Nabokov, xii-xiii. New York: McGraw-Hill, 1974.

Nagel, Thomas. *The View from Nowhere*. Oxford: Oxford University Press, 1986.

Nannicelli, Ted, and Paul Taberham, eds. *Cognitive Media Theory*. London: Routledge, 2014.

Narayanan, Srini. "Embodiment in Language Understanding: Sensory-Motor Representations For Metaphoric Reasoning About Event Descriptions." PhD diss., University of California, 1997.

Nolan, Amy. "Seeing is Digesting: Labyrinths of Historical Ruin in Stanley Kubrick's *The Shining*." *Cultural Critique* 77 (2011): 180–204.

Nordern, Eric. "Playboy Interview: Stanley Kubrick." In *Stanley Kubrick Interviews*, edited by Gene D. Phillips, 47–74. Jackson: University Press of Mississippi, 2001.

Núñez, Rafael, and Eve Sweetser. "With the Future Behind Them: Convergent Evidence from Aymara Language and Gesture in the Crosslinguistic Comparison of Spatial Construals of Time." *Cognitive Science* 30, no. 3 (2006): 401–450.

Ortiz, Maria J. "Primary Metaphors and Monomodal Visual Metaphors." *Journal of Pragmatics* 43, no. 6 (2011): 1568–1580

Ortony, Andrew, Gerald L. Clore, and Allan Collins. *The Cognitive Structure of Emotions*. New York: Cambridge University Press, 1988.

Palmer, Alan. *Fictional Minds*. Lincoln: University of Nebraska Press, 2004.

Pears, David Francis. "The Causal Conditions of Perception." *Synthese* 33, no. 2 (1976): 25–40.

Pecher, Diane, Inge Boot, and Saskia Van Dantzig. "Abstract Concepts: Sensory-Motor Grounding, Metaphors, and Beyond." In *Psychology of Learning and Motivation*, edited by Brian Ross, 217–248. Burlington: Academic Press, 2011.

Persson, Per. *Understanding Cinema: A Psychological Theory of Moving Imagery*. Cambridge: Cambridge University Press, 2003.

Peters, Jan. M. *Pictorial Signs and the Language of Film*. Amsterdam: Rodopi, 1981.

Pezzotta, Elisa. *Stanley Kubrick: Adapting the Sublime*. Jackson: University Press of Mississippi, 2013.

Philips, Gene D., ed. *Stanley Kubrick: Interviews*. Jackson: University Press of Mississippi, 2001.

Phillips, Gene D., and Rodney Hill. *The Encyclopaedia of Stanley Kubrick*. New York: Checkmark, 2002.

Plantinga, Carl. "Cognitive Film Theory: An Insider's Appraisal." *Cinémas* 12, no. 2 (2002): 15–37.

Prince, Stephen. "The Discourse of Pictures: Iconicity and Film Studies." *Film Quarterly* 47, no. 1 (1993): 16–28.

______. "Psychoanalytical Film Theory and the Problem of the Missing Spectator." In *Post-Theory: Reconstructing Film Studies*, edited by David Bordwell and Noël Carroll, 71–86. Madison: The University of Wisconsin Press, 1996.

Pryluck, Calvin. "The Film Metaphor Metaphor: The Use of Language-Based Models in Film Study." *Literature/Film Quarterly* 3, no. 2 (1975): 117–123.

Pudovkin, V.I. Introduction to the German Edition of *Film Technique and Film Acting*, by V.I Pudovkin, xiii-xvii. Translated by Ivor Montagu. London: Vision Press Limited, 1954.

Radden, Günter. "The Conceptualisation of Emotional Causality by Means of Prepositional Phrases." In *Speaking of Emotions: Conceptualisation and Expression*, edited by Angeliki Athanasiadou and Elzbieta Tabakowska, 273–294. Berlin: Mouton de Gruyter, 1998.

______. "Motion Metaphorized: The Case of *Coming* and *Going*." In *Cognitive Linguistics in the Redwoods: The Expansion of a New Paradigm in Linguistics*, edited by Eugene H. Casad, 423–458. Berlin: Mouton de Gruyter, 1996.

Radden, Günter, and Zoltán Kövecses. "Towards a Theory of Metonymy." In *Metonymy in Language and Thought*, edited by Klaus-Uwe Panther and Günter Radden, 17–59. Amsterdam: John Benjamins, 1999.

Ramachandran, Vilaymur S., and William Hirstein. "The Science of Art: A Neurological Theory of Aesthetic Experience." *Journal of Consciousness Studies* 6, no. 6–7 (1999): 15–51.

Randel, Don Michael, ed. *The Harvard Dictionary of Music*. 4th ed. Cambridge/London: The Belknap Press of Harvard University Press, 1986.

Rapf, Maurice. "A Talk With Stanley Kubrick About 2001." In *Stanley Kubrick Interviews*, edited by Gene D. Phillips, 75–79. Jackson: University Press of Mississippi, 2001.

Raphael, Frederic. *Eyes Wide Open: A Memoir of Stanley Kubrick*. New York: Ballantine, 1999.

Reddy, Michael. "The Conduit Metaphor. A Case of Frame Conflict in Our Language About Language." In *Metaphor and Thought*, edited by Andrew Ortony, 164–201. Cambridge: Cambridge University Press, 1993.

Rizzolatti, Giacomo, Luciano Fadiga, Vittorio Gallese, and Luciano Fogassi. "Premotor Cortex and the Recognition of Motor Actions." *Cognitive Brain Research* 3, no. 2 (1996): 131–141.

Robb, David, and John Heil. "Mental Causation." In *Stanford Encyclopedia of Philosophy*. Stanford University, 1997–. Article published December 18, 2003; last modified Jan 14, 2013. https://plato.stanford.edu/entries/mental-causation/

Ruiz de Mendoza Ibánez, Francisco José. "Metaphor, Metonymy and Conceptual Interaction." *Atlantis. Journal of the Spanish Association for Anglo-American Studies* 19, no. 1 (1997): 281–295.

Saslaw, Janna. "Forces, Containers, and Paths: The Role of Body-Derived Image Schemas in the Conceptualization of Music." *Journal of Music Theory* 40, no. 2 (1996): 217–243.

Scherer, Klaus R. "What Does Facial Expression Express?" In *International Review of Studies on Emotion*, edited by Kenneth T. Strongman, 139–165. Chichester: Wiley, 1992.

Scholl, Brian J., and Patrice D. Tremoulet. "Perceptual Causality and Animacy." *Trends in Cognitive Sciences* 4, no. 8 (2000): 299–309.

Schultheis, Bernd. "Expanses of Possibilities: Stanley Kubrick's Soundtracks in Notes." In *Stanley Kubrick Catalogue*, 266–279. Frankfurt am Main: Deutsches Filmmuseum, 2004.

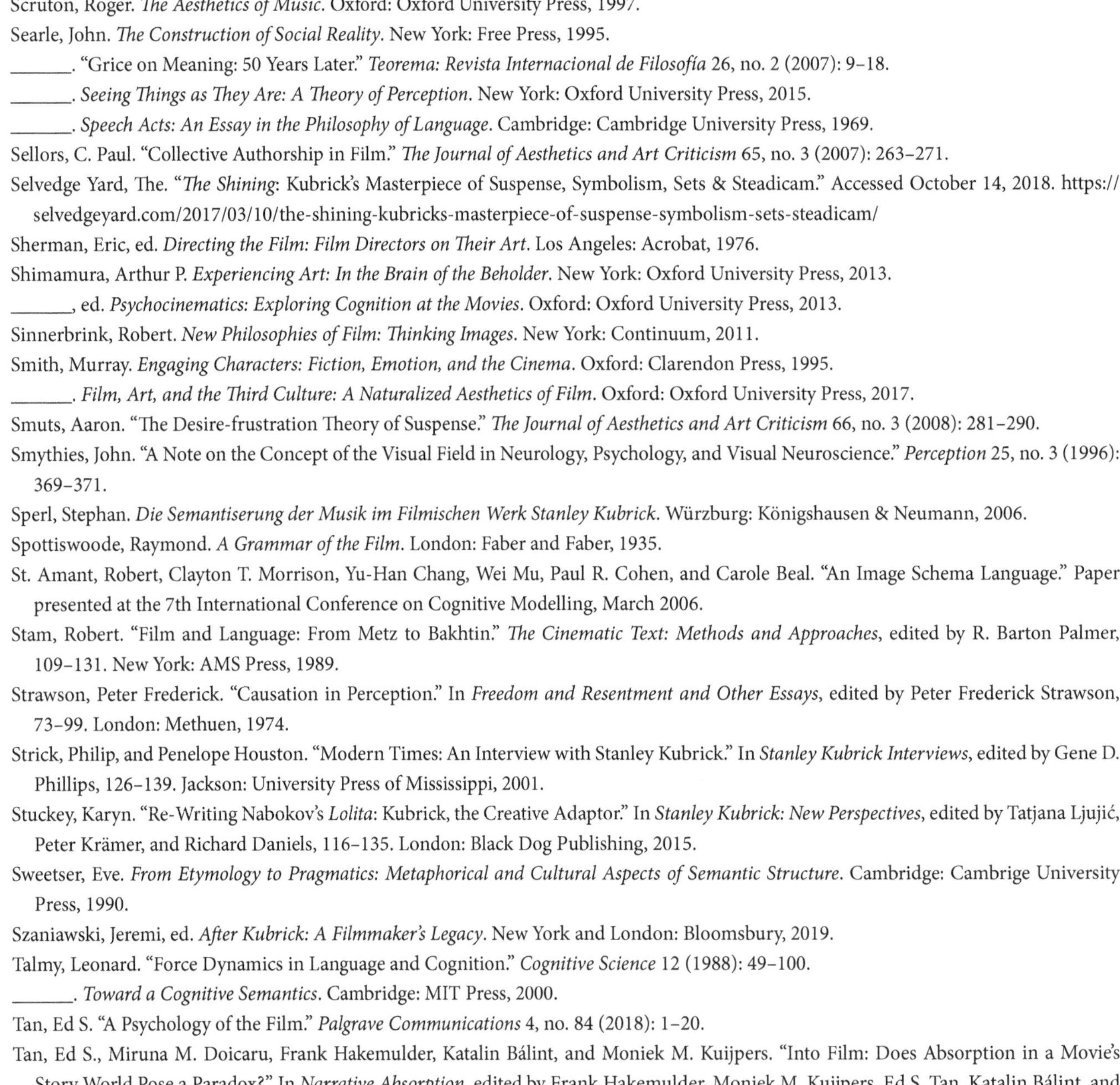

Scruton, Roger. *The Aesthetics of Music*. Oxford: Oxford University Press, 1997.

Searle, John. *The Construction of Social Reality*. New York: Free Press, 1995.

______. "Grice on Meaning: 50 Years Later." *Teorema: Revista Internacional de Filosofía* 26, no. 2 (2007): 9–18.

______. *Seeing Things as They Are: A Theory of Perception*. New York: Oxford University Press, 2015.

______. *Speech Acts: An Essay in the Philosophy of Language*. Cambridge: Cambridge University Press, 1969.

Sellors, C. Paul. "Collective Authorship in Film." *The Journal of Aesthetics and Art Criticism* 65, no. 3 (2007): 263–271.

Selvedge Yard, The. "*The Shining*: Kubrick's Masterpiece of Suspense, Symbolism, Sets & Steadicam." Accessed October 14, 2018. https://selvedgeyard.com/2017/03/10/the-shining-kubricks-masterpiece-of-suspense-symbolism-sets-steadicam/

Sherman, Eric, ed. *Directing the Film: Film Directors on Their Art*. Los Angeles: Acrobat, 1976.

Shimamura, Arthur P. *Experiencing Art: In the Brain of the Beholder*. New York: Oxford University Press, 2013.

______, ed. *Psychocinematics: Exploring Cognition at the Movies*. Oxford: Oxford University Press, 2013.

Sinnerbrink, Robert. *New Philosophies of Film: Thinking Images*. New York: Continuum, 2011.

Smith, Murray. *Engaging Characters: Fiction, Emotion, and the Cinema*. Oxford: Clarendon Press, 1995.

______. *Film, Art, and the Third Culture: A Naturalized Aesthetics of Film*. Oxford: Oxford University Press, 2017.

Smuts, Aaron. "The Desire-frustration Theory of Suspense." *The Journal of Aesthetics and Art Criticism* 66, no. 3 (2008): 281–290.

Smythies, John. "A Note on the Concept of the Visual Field in Neurology, Psychology, and Visual Neuroscience." *Perception* 25, no. 3 (1996): 369–371.

Sperl, Stephan. *Die Semantiserung der Musik im Filmischen Werk Stanley Kubrick*. Würzburg: Königshausen & Neumann, 2006.

Spottiswoode, Raymond. *A Grammar of the Film*. London: Faber and Faber, 1935.

St. Amant, Robert, Clayton T. Morrison, Yu-Han Chang, Wei Mu, Paul R. Cohen, and Carole Beal. "An Image Schema Language." Paper presented at the 7th International Conference on Cognitive Modelling, March 2006.

Stam, Robert. "Film and Language: From Metz to Bakhtin." *The Cinematic Text: Methods and Approaches*, edited by R. Barton Palmer, 109–131. New York: AMS Press, 1989.

Strawson, Peter Frederick. "Causation in Perception." In *Freedom and Resentment and Other Essays*, edited by Peter Frederick Strawson, 73–99. London: Methuen, 1974.

Strick, Philip, and Penelope Houston. "Modern Times: An Interview with Stanley Kubrick." In *Stanley Kubrick Interviews*, edited by Gene D. Phillips, 126–139. Jackson: University Press of Mississippi, 2001.

Stuckey, Karyn. "Re-Writing Nabokov's *Lolita*: Kubrick, the Creative Adaptor." In *Stanley Kubrick: New Perspectives*, edited by Tatjana Ljujić, Peter Krämer, and Richard Daniels, 116–135. London: Black Dog Publishing, 2015.

Sweetser, Eve. *From Etymology to Pragmatics: Metaphorical and Cultural Aspects of Semantic Structure*. Cambridge: Cambrige University Press, 1990.

Szaniawski, Jeremi, ed. *After Kubrick: A Filmmaker's Legacy*. New York and London: Bloomsbury, 2019.

Talmy, Leonard. "Force Dynamics in Language and Cognition." *Cognitive Science* 12 (1988): 49–100.

______. *Toward a Cognitive Semantics*. Cambridge: MIT Press, 2000.

Tan, Ed S. "A Psychology of the Film." *Palgrave Communications* 4, no. 84 (2018): 1–20.

Tan, Ed S., Miruna M. Doicaru, Frank Hakemulder, Katalin Bálint, and Moniek M. Kuijpers. "Into Film: Does Absorption in a Movie's Story World Pose a Paradox?" In *Narrative Absorption*, edited by Frank Hakemulder, Moniek M. Kuijpers, Ed S. Tan, Katalin Bálint, and Miruna M. Doicaru, 97–118. Amsterdam: John Benjamins, 2017.

Taylor, Aaron. "Blind Spots and Mind Games: Performance, Motivation, and Emotion in the Films of Stanley Kubrick." *The Velvet Light Trap* 77 (2016): 5–27.

Turner, Mark, ed. *The Artful Mind*. New York: Oxford University Press, 2006.

Vaage, Margrethe Bruun. "Fiction Film and the Varieties of Empathic Engagement." *Midwest Studies in Philosophy* 34, no. 1 (2010): 158–179.

Van Dijk, Teun A., and Walter Kintsch. *Strategies in Discourse Comprehension*. New York: Academic Press, 1983.

Velasco, Olga Isabel Díez. "Metaphor, Metonymy, and Image-Schemas: An Analysis of Conceptual Interaction Patterns." *Journal of English Studies* 3 (2001): 47–63.

Walker, Alexander. *Stanley Kubrick Directs*. New York: Harcourt Brace Jovanovich, 1972.

Walton, Kendall L. *Mimesis as Make-believe: On the Foundations of the Representational Arts*. Cambridge: Harvard University Press, 1990.

______. "What Is Abstract About the Art of Music?" *The Journal of Aesthetics and Art Criticism* 46, no. 3 (1988): 351–364

Welsh, James. "A Kubrick Tribute: Adapting to Cinema." *Literature/Film Quarterly* 29, no. 4 (2001): 252–255.

Williamson, John. *Strauss: Also Sprach Zarathustra*. Cambridge: Cambridge University Press, 1993.

Wilson, Deirdre, and Dan Sperber. *Meaning and Relevance*. Cambridge: Cambridge University Press, 2012.

Wilson, George. "Interpretation." In *The Routledge Companion to Philosophy and Film*, edited by Paisley Livingston, and Carl Plantinga, 162–172. New York: Routledge, 2009.

Wilson, Margaret. "Six Views of Embodied Cognition." *Psychonomic Bulletin & Review* 9, no. 4 (2002): 625–636.

Wimsatt, William K., and Monroe C. Beardsley. "The Intentional Fallacy." *The Sewanee Review* 54, no. 3 (1946): 468–488.

Winter, Bodo. "Horror Movies and the Cognitive Ecology of Primary Metaphors." *Metaphor and Symbol* 29, no. 3 (2014): 151–170

Wittgenstein, Ludwig. *Philosophical Investigations*, 4th ed. Translated by G.E.M. Anscombe, P.M.S. Hacker, and Joachim Schulte. Oxford: Blackwell, 1953. Reprinted by Malden: Wiley-Blackwell, 2009.

Wölfflin, Heinrich. "Ueber das Rechts und Links im Bilde." In *Gedanken zur Kunstgeschichte: Gedrucktes und Ungedrucktes*, edited by Heinrich Wölfflin, 82–96. Basel, 1941.

Yamanashi, Masa-aki. "Metaphorical Modes of Perception and Scanning." In *Tropical Truth(s): The Epistemology of Metaphor and Other Tropes*, edited by Armin Burkhardt and Brigitte Nerlich, 157–175. Berlin: Walter De Gruyter, 2010.

Yanal, Robert J. "The Paradox of Suspense." *The British Journal of Aesthetics* 36 no. 2 (1996): 146–158.

Young, Colin. "The Hollywood War of Independence." In *Stanley Kubrick Interviews*, edited by Gene D. Phillips, 3–8. Jackson: University Press of Mississippi, 2001

Yu, Ning. "Chinese Metaphors of Thinking." *Cognitive Linguistics* 14, no. 2/3 (2003): 141–165.

______. "The Eyes For Sight and Mind." *Journal of Pragmatics* 36, no. 4 (2004): 663–686.

Zbikowski, Lawrence M. "Metaphor and Music." In *The Cambridge Handbook of Metaphor and Thought*, edited by Raymond W. Gibbs, 502–524. Cambridge: Cambridge University Press, 2008.

Zwaan, Rolf A. "Situation Models, Mental Simulations, and Abstract Concepts in Discourse Comprehension." *Psychonomic Bulletin & Review* 23, no. 4 (2016): 1028–1034.

Zwaan, Rolf A., Mark C. Langston, and Arthur C. Graesser. "The Construction of Situation Models in Narrative Comprehension: An Event-Indexing Model." *Psychological Science* 6, no. 5 (1995): 292–297.

Zwaan, Rolf A., Joseph P. Magliano, and Arthur C. Graesser. "Dimensions of Situation-Model Construction in Narrative Comprehension." *Journal of Experimental Psychology: Learning, Memory, and Cognition* 21, no. 2 (1995): 386–397.

Zwaan, Rolf A., and Gabriel A. Radvansky. "Situation Models in Language Comprehension and Memory." *Psychological Bulletin* 123, no. 2 (1998): 162–185.

Index

www.ingramcontent.com/pod-product-compliance
Lightning Source LLC
LaVergne TN
LVHW081250100826
845148LV00009B/1188

* 9 7 8 1 6 4 4 6 9 1 1 2 0 *